JAPAN

INVESTMENT AND BUSINESS GUIDE

VOLUME 1

STRATEGIC AND PRACTICAL INFORMATION

International Business Publications, USA
Washington DC, USA - Japan

JAPAN

INVESTMENT AND BUSINESS GUIDE

VOLUME 1 STRATEGIC AND PRACTICAL INFORMATION

UPDATED ANNUALLY

We express our sincere appreciation to all government agencies and international organizations which provided information and other materials for this guide

Cover Design: International Business Publications, USA

2016 Updated Reprint International Business Publications, USA
ISBN 1-5775-1869-1

For customer service and information, please contact:

in the USA: **International Business Publications, USA**
P.O.Box 15343, Washington, DC 20003
Phone: (202) 546-2103, Fax: (202) 546-3275.
E-mail: rusric@erols.com

Printed in the USA

JAPAN

INVESTMENT AND BUSINESS GUIDE

VOLUME 1

STRATEGIC AND PRACTICAL INFORMATION

TABLE OF CONTENTS

STRATEGIC AND DEVELOPMENT PROFILES

STRATEGIC PROFILE

Capital	Tokyo 35°41′N 139°46′E35.683°N 139.767°E
Official languages	None
Recognised regional languages	• Aynu itak • Ryukyuan languages • Eastern Japanese • Western Japanese • several other Japanese dialects
National language	Japanese
Ethnic groups (2011)	• 98.5% Japanese • 0.5% Korean • 0.4% Chinese • 0.6% other
Demonym	Japanese
Government	Unitary parliamentary constitutional monarchy
- Emperor	Akihito
- Prime Minister	Shinzō Abe
- Deputy Prime Minister	Tarō Asō
Legislature	National Diet
- Upper house	House of Councillors
- Lower house	House of Representatives
	Formation
- National Foundation Day	February 11, 660 BC
- Meiji Constitution	November 29, 1890
- Current constitution	May 3, 1947
- San Francisco Peace Treaty	April 28, 1952
	Area
- Total	377,944 km^2 (62nd) 145,925 sq mi
- Water (%)	0.8
	Population
- estimate	126,659,683 (10th)
- 2010 census	128,056,026
- Density	337.1/km^2 (36th) 873.1/sq mi
GDP (PPP)	2014 estimate
- Total	$4.835 trillion (4th)
- Per capita	$38,053 (22nd)
GDP (nominal)	2014 estimate
- Total	$4.846 trillion (3rd)
- Per capita	$38,142 (25th)
Gini (2008)	37.6 medium · 76th
HDI	▼0.890 very high · 17th
Currency	Yen (¥) / En 円(JPY)

Time zone	JST (UTC+9)
- Summer (DST)	not observed (UTC+9)
Date format	• yyyy-mm-dd • yyyy年m月d日 • Era yy年m月d日 (AD−1988)
Drives on the	left
Calling code	+81
ISO 3166 code	JP
Internet TLD	.jp

Japan is an island nation in East Asia. Located in the Pacific Ocean, it lies to the east of the Sea of Japan, China, North Korea, South Korea and Russia, stretching from the Sea of Okhotsk in the north to the East China Sea and Taiwan in the south. The characters that make up Japan's name mean "sun-origin", which is why Japan is often referred to as the "Land of the Rising Sun".

Japan is a stratovolcanic archipelago of 6,852 islands. The four largest islands are Honshu, Hokkaido, Kyushu, and Shikoku, which together comprise about ninety-seven percent of Japan's land area. Due to its location in the Pacific Ring of Fire, Japan is substantially prone to earthquakes and tsunami, having the highest natural disaster risk in the developed world. Japan has the world's tenth-largest population, with over 126 million people. Honshū's Greater Tokyo Area, which includes the *de facto* capital of Tokyo and several surrounding prefectures, is the largest metropolitan area in the world, with over 30 million residents.

Archaeological research indicates that people lived in Japan as early as the Upper Paleolithic period. The first written mention of Japan is in Chinese history texts from the 1st century AD. Influence from other nations followed by long periods of isolation has characterized Japan's history. From the 12th century until 1868, Japan was ruled by successive feudal military shoguns in the name of the Emperor. Japan entered into a long period of isolation in the early 17th century, which was only ended in 1853 when a United States fleet pressured Japan to open to the West. Nearly two decades of internal conflict and insurrection followed before the Meiji Emperor was restored as head of state in 1868 and the Empire of Japan was proclaimed, with the Emperor as a divine symbol of the nation. In the late 19th and early 20th centuries, victories in the First Sino-Japanese War, the Russo-Japanese War and World War I allowed Japan to expand its empire during a period of increasing militarism. The Second Sino-Japanese War of 1937 expanded into part of World War II in 1941, which came to an end in 1945 following the atomic bombings of Hiroshima and Nagasaki. Since adopting its revised constitution in 1947, Japan has maintained a unitary constitutional monarchy with an emperor and an elected legislature called the Diet.

Japan is a member of the UN, the G7, the G8, the G20. A major economic great power, Japan is a developed country and has the world's third-largest economy by nominal GDP and the world's fourth-largest economy by purchasing power parity. It is also the world's fourth-largest exporter and fourth-largest importer. Although Japan has officially renounced its right to declare war, it maintains a modern military with the world's eighth largest military budget, used for self-defense and peacekeeping roles. Japan ranks high in metrics of prosperity such as the Human Development Index, with Japanese women enjoying the highest life expectancy of any country in the world and the infant mortality rate being the third lowest globally

GEOGRAPHY

Location: Eastern Asia, island chain between the North Pacific Ocean and the Sea of Japan, east of the Korean Peninsula

Geographic coordinates: 36 00 N, 138 00 E

Map references: Asia

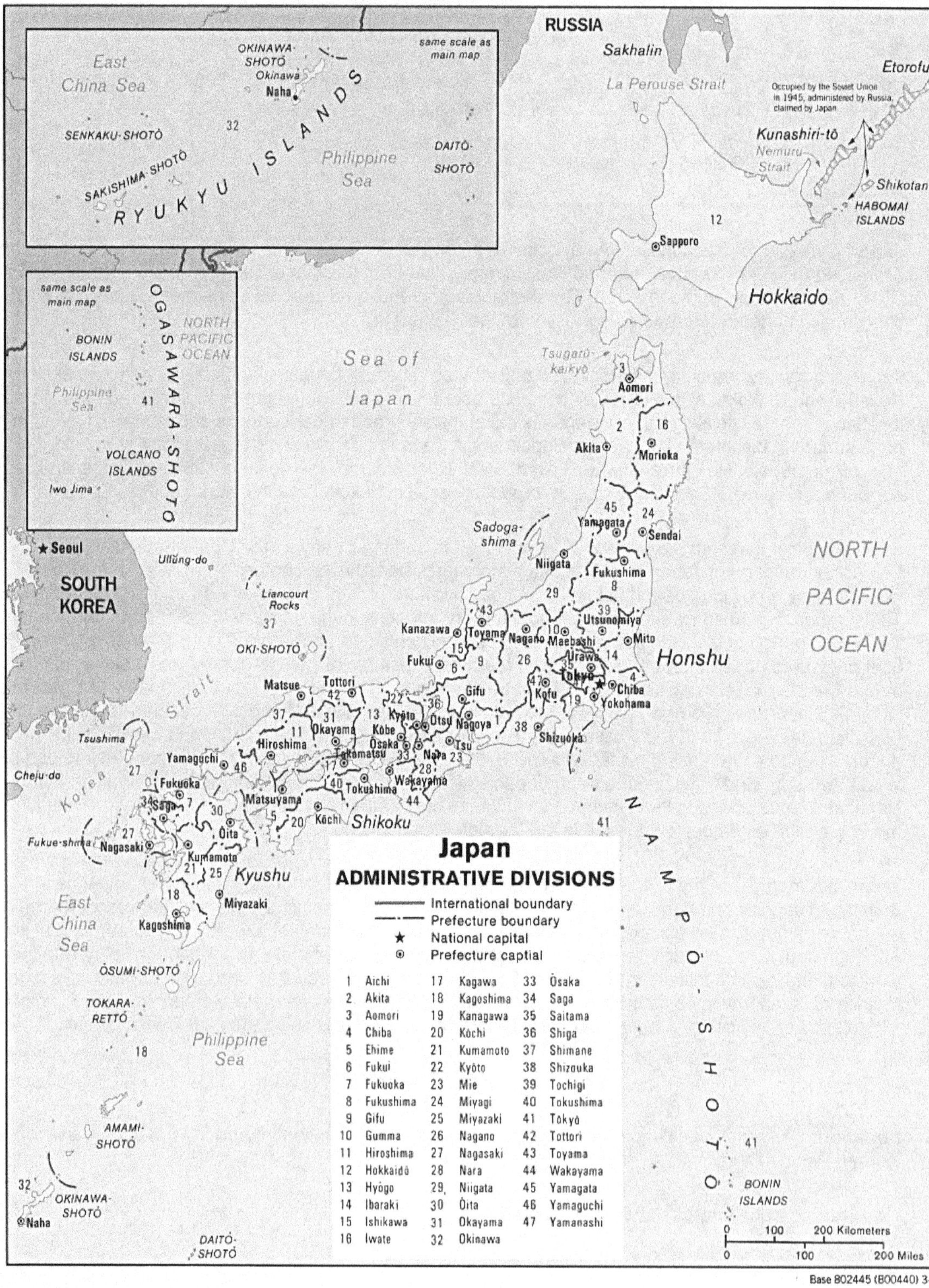
Japan
ADMINISTRATIVE DIVISIONS
International boundary
Prefecture boundary
National capital
Prefecture captial
1 Aichi
2 Akita
3 Aomori
4 Chiba
5 Ehime
6 Fukui
7 Fukuoka
8 Fukushima
9 Gifu
10 Gumma
11 Hiroshima
12 Hokkaidō
13 Hyōgo
14 Ibaraki
15 Ishikawa
16 Iwate
17 Kagawa
18 Kagoshima
19 Kanagawa
20 Kōchi
21 Kumamoto
22 Kyōto
23 Mie
24 Miyagi
25 Miyazaki
26 Nagano
27 Nagasaki
28 Nara
29 Niigata
30 Ōita
31 Okayama
32 Okinawa
33 Ōsaka
34 Saga
35 Saitama
36 Shiga
37 Shimane
38 Shizouka
39 Tochigi
40 Tokushima
41 Tōkyō
42 Tottori
43 Toyama
44 Wakayama
45 Yamagata
46 Yamaguchi
47 Yamanashi
RUSSIA
Sakhalin
La Perouse Strait
Etorofu-tō
Occupied by the Soviet Union in 1945, administered by Russia, claimed by Japan.
Kunashiri-tō
Nemuru Strait
Shikotan-tō
HABOMAI ISLANDS
Sapporo
Hokkaido
East China Sea
OKINAWA-SHOTŌ
Okinawa
Naha
SENKAKU-SHOTŌ
SAKISHIMA-SHOTŌ
RYUKYU ISLANDS
Philippine Sea
DAITŌ-SHOTŌ
same scale as main map
BONIN ISLANDS
OGASAWARA-SHOTO
NORTH PACIFIC OCEAN
VOLCANO ISLANDS
Iwo Jima
Sea of Japan
Tsugaru-kaikyō
Aomori
Akita
Morioka
Yamagata
Sendai
Sadoga-shima
Niigata
Fukushima
Seoul
SOUTH KOREA
Ullŭng-do
Liancourt Rocks
OKI-SHOTŌ
Kanazawa
Toyama
Nagano
Maebashi
Utsunomiya
Mito
Fukui
Urawa
Tokyo
Chiba
Yokohama
Kofu
Gifu
Nagoya
Shizuoka
Honshu
Matsue
Tottori
Kyoto
Otsu
Tsu
Nara
Okayama
Kobe
Osaka
Hiroshima
Takamatsu
Wakayama
Tokushima
Yamaguchi
Fukuoka
Saga
Matsuyama
Kōchi
Shikoku
Tsushima
Korea Strait
Cheju-do
Fukue-shima
Nagasaki
Ōita
Kumamoto
Kyushu
Miyazaki
Kagoshima
ŌSUMI-SHOTŌ
TOKARA-RETTŌ
AMAMI-SHOTŌ
NAMPŌ-SHOTŌ
200 Kilometers
200 Miles
Base 802445 (B00440) 3-96

Area:
total: 377,835 sq km
land: 374,744 sq km
water: 3,091 sq km
note: includes Bonin Islands (Ogasawara-gunto) , Daito-shoto, Minami-jima, Okino-tori-shima, Ryukyu Islands (Nansei-shoto) , and Volcano Islands (Kazan-retto)

Area - comparative: slightly smaller than California

Land boundaries: 0 km

Coastline: 29,751 km

Maritime claims:
exclusive economic zone: 200 nm
territorial sea: 12 nm; between 3 nm and 12 nm in the international straits - La Perouse or Soya, Tsugaru, Osumi, and Eastern and Western Channels of the Korea or Tsushima Strait

Climate: varies from tropical in south to cool temperate in north

Terrain: mostly rugged and mountainous

Elevation extremes:
lowest point: Hachiro-gata -4 m *highest point:* Fujiyama 3,776 m

Natural resources: negligible mineral resources, fish

Land use:
arable land: 11% *permanent crops:* 1%
permanent pastures: 2% *forests and woodland:* 67% *other:* 19%

Irrigated land: 27,820 sq km (1993 est.)
Natural hazards: many dormant and some active volcanoes; about 1,500 seismic occurrences (mostly tremors) every year; tsunamis

Environment - current issues: air pollution from power plant emissions results in acid rain; acidification of lakes and reservoirs degrading water quality and threatening aquatic life; Japan is one of the largest consumers of fish and tropical timber, contributing to the depletion of these resources in Asia and elsewhere

Environment - international agreements:
party to: Antarctic-Environmental Protocol, Antarctic Treaty, Biodiversity, Climate Change, Desertification, Endangered Species, Environmental Modification, Hazardous Wastes, Law of the Sea, Marine Dumping, Nuclear Test Ban, Ozone Layer Protection, Ship Pollution, Tropical Timber 83, Tropical Timber 94, Wetlands, Whaling
signed, but not ratified: Climate Change-Kyoto Protocol

Geography - note: strategic location in northeast Asia.

PEOPLE

Population: 126,549,976

Age structure:
0-14 years: 15% (male 9,575,637; female 9,105,713)
15-64 years: 68% (male 43,363,054; female 42,980,253)
65 years and over: 17% (male 9,024,015; female 12,501,304)

Population growth rate: 0.18%
Birth rate: 9.96 births/1,000 population
Death rate: 8.15 deaths/1,000 population
Net migration rate: 0 migrant(s) /1,000 population

Sex ratio:
at birth: 1.05 male(s) /female
under 15 years: 1.05 male(s) /female
15-64 years: 1.01 male(s) /female
65 years and over: 0.72 male(s) /female
total population: 0.96 male(s) /female

Infant mortality rate: 3.91 deaths/1,000 live births

Life expectancy at birth:
total population: 80.7 years
male: 77.51 years
female: 84.05 years

Total fertility rate: 1.41 children born/woman
Nationality:
noun: Japanese (singular and plural)
adjective: Japanese
Ethnic groups: Japanese 99.4%, other 0.6% (mostly Korean)
Religions: observe both Shinto and Buddhist 84%, other 16% (including Christian 0.7%)
Languages: Japanese

Literacy:
definition: age 15 and over can read and write
total population: 99%
male: NA%
female: NA%

GOVERNMENT

Country name:
conventional long form: none
conventional short form: Japan
local long form: Nihon-koku/Nippon-koku
local short form: Nihon/Nippon

Government type:
a parliamentary government with a constitutional monarchy

Capital:
name: Tokyo

geographic coordinates: 35 41 N, 139 45 E
time difference: UTC+9 (14 hours ahead of Washington, DC, during Standard Time)

Administrative divisions:
47 prefectures; Aichi, Akita, Aomori, Chiba, Ehime, Fukui, Fukuoka, Fukushima, Gifu, Gunma, Hiroshima, Hokkaido, Hyogo, Ibaraki, Ishikawa, Iwate, Kagawa, Kagoshima, Kanagawa, Kochi, Kumamoto, Kyoto, Mie, Miyagi, Miyazaki, Nagano, Nagasaki, Nara, Niigata, Oita, Okayama, Okinawa, Osaka, Saga, Saitama, Shiga, Shimane, Shizuoka, Tochigi, Tokushima, Tokyo, Tottori, Toyama, Wakayama, Yamagata, Yamaguchi, Yamanashi

Independence:
3 May 1947 (current constitution adopted as amendment to Meiji Constitution); notable earlier dates: 660 B.C. (traditional date of the founding of the nation by Emperor JIMMU); 29 November 1890 (Meiji Constitution provides for constitutional monarchy)

National holiday:
Birthday of Emperor AKIHITO, 23 December (1933)

Constitution:
previous 1890; latest approved 6 October 1946, adopted 3 November 1946, effective 3 May 1947 (2013)

Legal system:
civil law system based on German model; system also reflects Anglo-American influence and Japanese traditions; judicial review of legislative acts in the Supreme Court

International law organization participation:
accepts compulsory ICJ jurisdiction with reservations; accepts ICCt jurisdiction

Suffrage:
20 years of age; universal

Executive branch:
chief of state: Emperor AKIHITO (since 7 January 1989)
head of government: Prime Minister Shinzo ABE (since 26 December 2012); Deputy Prime Minister Taro ASO (since 26 December 2012)
cabinet: Cabinet is appointed by the prime minister
(For more information visit the World Leaders website **)**
elections: Diet, the bicameral legislature, designates the prime minister; constitution requires that the prime minister commands parliamentary majority; following legislative elections, the leader of majority party or leader of majority coalition in House of Representatives usually becomes prime minister; the monarchy is hereditary

Legislative branch:
bicameral Diet or Kokkai consists of the House of Councillors or Sangi-in (242 seats - members elected for fixed six-year terms; 146 members in multi-seat constituencies and 96 by proportional representation) half elected every three years; and the House of Representatives or Shugi-in (480 seats - members elected for maximum four-year terms; 300 in single-seat constituencies; 180 members by proportional representation in 11 regional blocs); the prime minister has the right to dissolve the House of Representatives

at any time with the concurrence of the cabinet
elections: House of Councillors - last held on 21 July 2013 (next to be held in July 2016); House of Representatives - last held on 16 December 2012 (next to be held by 15 December 2016)
election results: House of Councillors - percent of vote by party - NA; seats by party - LPD 115, DPJ 59, New Komeito 20, Your Party 18, JCP 11, JRP 9, SDP 3, others 4, independents 3
House of Representatives - percent of vote by party (by proportional representation) - LDP 31.6%, DPJ 16.6%, JRP 22.2%, New Komeito 12.2%, Your Party 7.7%, JCP 4.4%, TRP 3.9%, others 1.4%; seats by party LDP 294, DPJ 57, JRP 54, New Komeito 31, Your Party 18, TPJ 9, JCP 8, others 4, independents 5

Judicial branch:
highest court(s): Supreme Court or Saiko saibansho (consists of the chief justice and 14 associate justices)
note - the Supreme Court has jurisdiction in constitutional issues
judge selection and term of office: Supreme Court chief justice designated by the Cabinet and appointed by the monarch; associate justices appointed by the Cabinet and confirmed by the monarch; all justices are reviewed in a popular referendum at the first general election of the House of Representatives following each judge's appointment and every 10 years afterward
subordinate courts: 8 High Courts (Koto-saiban-sho), each with a Family Court (Katei-saiban-sho); 50 District Courts (Chiho saibansho), with 203 additional branches; 438 Summary Courts (Kani saibansho)

Political parties and leaders:
Democratic Party of Japan or DPJ [Banri KAIEDA]
Japan Communist Party or JCP [Kazuo SHII]
Japan Restoration Party or JRP [Shintaro ISHIHARA]
Liberal Democratic Party or LDP [Shinzo ABE]
New Komeito or NK [Natsuo YAMAGUCHI]
People's Life Party or PF [Ichiro OZAWA]
Social Democratic Party or SDP [Tadatomo YOSHIDA]
Tomorrow Party of Japan or TPJ [Tomoko ABE]
Your Party or YP [Yoshimi WATANABE]

Political pressure groups and leaders:
other: business groups; trade unions

International organization participation:
ADB, AfDB (nonregional member), APEC, ARF, ASEAN (dialogue partner), Australia Group, BIS, CD, CE (observer), CERN (observer), CICA (observer), CP, EAS, EBRD, EITI (implementing country), FAO, FATF, G-20, G-5, G-7, G-8, G-10, IADB, IAEA, IBRD, ICAO, ICC (national committees), ICRM, IDA, IEA, IFAD, IFC, IFRCS, IGAD (partners), IHO, ILO, IMF, IMO, IMSO, Interpol, IOC, IOM, IPU, ISO, ITSO, ITU, ITUC (NGOs), LAIA (observer), MIGA, NEA, NSG, OAS (observer), OECD, OPCW, OSCE (partner), Pacific Alliance (observer), Paris Club, PCA, PIF (partner), SAARC (observer), SELEC (observer), SICA (observer), UN, UNCTAD, UNDOF, UNESCO, UNHCR, UNIDO, UNMISS, UNRWA, UNWTO, UPU, WCO, WFTU (NGOs), WHO, WIPO, WMO, WTO, ZC

Diplomatic representation in the US:
chief of mission: Ambassador Kenichiro SASAE (since 19 November 2012)
chancery: 2520 Massachusetts Avenue NW, Washington, DC 20008
telephone: (202) 238-6700
FAX: (202) 328-2187

consulate(s) general: Atlanta, Boston, Chicago, Denver, Detroit, Agana (Guam), Honolulu, Houston, Los Angeles, Miami, Nashville (TN), New York, Portland (OR), San Francisco, Seattle
consulate(s): Anchorage (AK), Saipan (Northern Mariana Islands)

Diplomatic representation from the US:
chief of mission: Ambassador Caroline Bouvier KENNEDY (since 19 November 2013)
embassy: 1-10-5 Akasaka, Minato-ku, Tokyo 107-8420
mailing address: Unit 9800, Box 300, APO AP 96303-0300
telephone: [81] (03) 3224-5000
FAX: [81] (03) 3505-1862
consulate(s) general: Naha (Okinawa), Osaka-Kobe, Sapporo
consulate(s): Fukuoka, Nagoya

Flag description:
white with a large red disk (representing the sun without rays) in the center

National symbol(s):
red sun disc; chrysanthemum

National anthem:
name: "Kimigayo" (The Emperor"s Reign)

ECONOMY

Economy - overview:
In the years following World War II, government-industry cooperation, a strong work ethic, mastery of high technology, and a comparatively small defense allocation (1% of GDP) helped Japan develop a technologically advanced economy. Two notable characteristics of the post-war economy were the close interlocking structures of manufacturers, suppliers, and distributors, known as keiretsu, and the guarantee of lifetime employment for a substantial portion of the urban labor force. Both features are now eroding under the dual pressures of global competition and domestic demographic change. Japan's industrial sector is heavily dependent on imported raw materials and fuels.

A small agricultural sector is highly subsidized and protected, with crop yields among the highest in the world. While self-sufficient in rice production, Japan imports about 60% of its food on a caloric basis. For three decades, overall real economic growth had been spectacular - a 10% average in the 1960s, a 5% average in the 1970s, and a 4% average in the 1980s. Growth slowed markedly in the 1990s, averaging just 1.7%, largely because of the after effects of inefficient investment and an asset price bubble in the late 1980s that required a protracted period of time for firms to reduce excess debt, capital, and labor. Modest economic growth continued after 2000, but the economy has fallen into recession three times since 2008.

A sharp downturn in business investment and global demand for Japan's exports in late 2008 pushed Japan into recession. Government stimulus spending helped the economy recover in late 2009 and 2010, but the economy contracted again in 2011 as the massive 9.0 magnitude earthquake and the ensuing tsunami in March disrupted manufacturing. The economy has largely recovered in the two years since the disaster, but reconstruction in the Tohoku region has been uneven.

Prime Minister Shinzo ABE has declared the economy his government's top priority; he has overturned his predecessor's plan to permanently close nuclear power plants and is pursuing an economic revitalization agenda of fiscal stimulus, monetary easing, and structural reform. Japan joined the Trans Pacific Partnership negotiations in 2013, a pact that would open Japan's economy to increased foreign competition and create new export opportunities for Japanese businesses. Measured on a purchasing power parity (PPP) basis that adjusts for price differences, Japan in 2013 stood as the fourth-largest economy in the world after second-place China, which surpassed Japan in 2001, and third-place India, which edged out Japan in 2012.

The new government will continue a longstanding debate on restructuring the economy and reining in Japan's huge government debt, which is exceeding 230% of GDP. To help raise government revenue and reduce public debt, Japan decided in 2013 to gradually increase the consumption tax to a total of 10% by the year 2015. Japan is making progress on ending deflation due to a weaker yen and higher energy costs, but reliance on exports to drive growth and an aging, shrinking population pose other major long-term challenges for the economy.

GDP (purchasing power parity):
$4.729 trillion
country comparison to the world: 5
$4.638 trillion (2012 est.)
$4.549 trillion (2011 est.)
note:data are in 2013 US dollars

GDP (official exchange rate):
$5.007 trillion

GDP - real growth rate:
2%
country comparison to the world: 142
2% (2012 est.)
-0.6% (2011 est.)

GDP - per capita (PPP):
$37,100
country comparison to the world: 36
$36,300 (2012 est.)
$35,600 (2011 est.)
note:data are in 2013 US dollars

Gross national saving:
22.1% of GDP
country comparison to the world: 69
21.6% of GDP (2012 est.)
22% of GDP (2011 est.)

GDP - composition, by end use:
household consumption: 61%
government consumption: 20.7%
investment in fixed capital: 21.6%
investment in inventories: -0.6%
exports of goods and services: 15.8%
imports of goods and services: -18.4%

GDP - composition, by sector of origin:
agriculture: 1.1%
industry: 25.6%
services: 73.2%

Agriculture - products:
rice, sugar beets, vegetables, fruit; pork, poultry, dairy products, eggs; fish

Industries:
among world's largest and most technologically advanced producers of motor vehicles, electronic equipment, machine tools, steel and nonferrous metals, ships, chemicals, textiles, processed foods

Industrial production growth rate:
1%
country comparison to the world: 145

Labor force:
65.62 million
country comparison to the world: 9

Labor force - by occupation:
agriculture: 3.9%
industry: 26.2%
services: 69.8% (2010 est.)

Unemployment rate:
4.1%
country comparison to the world: 34
4.4% (2012 est.)

Population below poverty line:
16% (2010)

Household income or consumption by percentage share:
lowest 10%: 1.9%
highest 10%: 27.5% (2008)

Distribution of family income - Gini index:
37.6 (2008)
country comparison to the world: 76
24.9 (1993)

Budget:
revenues: $1.739 trillion
expenditures: $2.149 trillion

Taxes and other revenues:

34.7% of GDP
country comparison to the world: 69

Budget surplus (+) or deficit (-):
-8.2% of GDP
country comparison to the world: 198

Public debt:
226.1% of GDP
country comparison to the world: 1
219.1% of GDP (2012 est.)

Fiscal year:
1 April - 31 March

Inflation rate (consumer prices):
0.2%
country comparison to the world: 13
0% (2012 est.)

Central bank discount rate:
0.1% (31 December 2012)
country comparison to the world: 139
0.3% (31 December 2009)

Commercial bank prime lending rate:
1.5% (31 December 2013 est.)
country comparison to the world: 175
1.48% (31 December 2012 est.)

Stock of narrow money:
$5.604 trillion (31 December 2013 est.)
country comparison to the world: 2
$6.176 trillion (31 December 2012 est.)

Stock of broad money:
$13.12 trillion (31 December 2011 est.)
country comparison to the world: 2
$13.41 trillion (31 December 2010 est.)

Stock of domestic credit:
$12.39 trillion (31 December 2013 est.)
country comparison to the world: 3
$13.72 trillion (31 December 2012 est.)

Market value of publicly traded shares:
$3.681 trillion (31 December 2012 est.)
country comparison to the world: 3
$3.541 trillion (31 December 2011)
$NA (31 December 2010 est.)

Current account balance:
$56.6 billion
country comparison to the world: 10
$60.8 billion (2012 est.)

Exports:
$697 billion
country comparison to the world: 6
$776.6 billion (2012 est.)

Exports - commodities:
motor vehicles 13.6%; semiconductors 6.2%; iron and steel products 5.5%; auto parts 4.6%; plastic materials 3.5%; power generating machinery 3.5%

Exports - partners:
China 18.1%, US 17.8%, South Korea 7.7%, Thailand 5.5%, Hong Kong 5.1% (2012)

Imports:
$766.6 billion
country comparison to the world: 6
$830.1 billion (2012 est.)

Imports - commodities:
petroleum 15.5%; liquid natural gas 5.7%; clothing 3.9%; semiconductors 3.5%; coal 3.5%; audio and visual apparatus 2.7% (2011 est.)

Imports - partners:
China 21.3%, US 8.8%, Australia 6.4%, Saudi Arabia 6.2%, UAE 5%, South Korea 4.6%, Qatar 4% (2012)

Reserves of foreign exchange and gold:
$1.268 trillion (31 December 2012 est.)
country comparison to the world: 2
$1.296 trillion (31 December 2011 est.)

Debt - external:
$3.017 trillion (31 December 2012 est.)
country comparison to the world: 6
$3.115 trillion (31 December 2011)

Stock of direct foreign investment - at home:
$231.2 billion (31 December 2013 est.)
country comparison to the world: 25
$222.2 billion (31 December 2012 est.)

Stock of direct foreign investment - abroad:
$1.179 trillion (31 December 2013 est.)
country comparison to the world: 8
$1.054 trillion (31 December 2012 est.)

Exchange rates:
yen (JPY) per US dollar -
97.44
79.79 (2012 est.)
87.78 (2010 est.)
93.57 (2009)
103.58 (2008)

ENERGY

Electricity - production:
936.2 billion kWh (
country comparison to the world: 5

Electricity - consumption:
859.7 billion kWh (
country comparison to the world: 5

Electricity - exports:
0 kWh (2012 est.)
country comparison to the world: 152

Electricity - imports:
0 kWh
country comparison to the world: 159

Electricity - installed generating capacity:
287 million kW
country comparison to the world: 4

Electricity - from fossil fuels:
63.5% of total installed capacity (
country comparison to the world: 127

Electricity - from nuclear fuels:
17.1% of total installed capacity
country comparison to the world: 13

Electricity - from hydroelectric plants:
7.8% of total installed capacity (
country comparison to the world: 118

Electricity - from other renewable sources:
2.8% of total installed capacity
country comparison to the world: 65

Crude oil - production:

135,500 bbl/day
country comparison to the world: 46

Crude oil - exports:
0 bbl/day (2010 est.)
country comparison to the world: 132

Crude oil - imports:
3.472 million bbl/day
country comparison to the world: 3

Crude oil - proved reserves:
44.12 million bbl
country comparison to the world: 79

Refined petroleum products - production:
3.862 million bbl/day
country comparison to the world: 6

Refined petroleum products - consumption:
4.464 million bbl/day
country comparison to the world: 4

Refined petroleum products - exports:
349,900 bbl/day
country comparison to the world: 19

Refined petroleum products - imports:
1.311 million bbl/day
country comparison to the world: 5

Natural gas - production:
3.273 billion cu m
country comparison to the world: 56

Natural gas - consumption:
112.6 billion cu m
country comparison to the world: 6

Natural gas - exports:
0 cu m
country comparison to the world: 123

Natural gas - imports:
122.2 billion cu m
country comparison to the world: 2

Natural gas - proved reserves:
20.9 billion cu m
country comparison to the world: 77

Carbon dioxide emissions from consumption of energy:
1.181 billion Mt

COMMUNICATIONS

Telephones - main lines in use:
64.273 million (

country comparison to the world: 3

Telephones - mobile cellular:
138.363 million
country comparison to the world: 7

Telephone system:
general assessment: excellent domestic and international service
domestic: high level of modern technology and excellent service of every kind
international: country code - 81; numerous submarine cables provide links throughout Asia, Australia, the Middle East, Europe, and US; satellite earth stations - 7 Intelsat (Pacific and Indian Oceans), 1 Intersputnik (Indian Ocean region), 2 Inmarsat (Pacific and Indian Ocean regions), and 8 SkyPerfect JSAT

Broadcast media:
a mixture of public and commercial broadcast TV and radio stations; 6 national terrestrial TV networks including 1 public broadcaster; the large number of radio and TV stations available provide a wide range of choices; satellite and cable services provide access to international channels

Internet country code:
.jp

Internet hosts:
64.453 million
country comparison to the world: 2

Internet users:
99.182 million
country comparison to the world: 3

TRANSPORTATION

Airports:
175
country comparison to the world: 33

Airports - with paved runways:
total: 142
over 3,047 m: 6
2,438 to 3,047 m: 45
1,524 to 2,437 m: 38
914 to 1,523 m: 28
under 914 m: 25 (2013)

Airports - with unpaved runways:
total: 33
914 to 1,523 m: 5
under 914 m:
28

Heliports:
16

Pipelines:
gas 4,456 km; oil 174 km; oil/gas/water 104 km

Railways:
total: 27,182 km
country comparison to the world: 11
standard gauge: 4,251 km 1.435-m gauge (4,251 km electrified)
dual gauge: 486 km 1.435-1.067-m gauge (486 km electrified)
narrow gauge: 96 km 1.372-m gauge (96 km electrified); 22,301 km 1.067-m gauge (15,222 km electrified); 48 km 0.762-m gauge (48 km electrified)

Roadways:
total: 1,210,251 km
country comparison to the world: 6
paved: 973,234 km (includes 7,803 km of expressways)
unpaved: 237,017 km

Waterways:
1,770 km (seagoing vessels use inland seas) (2010)
country comparison to the world: 45

Merchant marine:
total: 684
country comparison to the world: 16
by type: bulk carrier 168, cargo 34, carrier 3, chemical tanker 29, container 2, liquefied gas 58, passenger 11, passenger/cargo 117, petroleum tanker 152, refrigerated cargo 4, roll on/roll off 52, vehicle carrier 54
registered in other countries: 3,122 (Bahamas 88, Bermuda 2, Burma 1, Cambodia 1, Cayman Islands 23, China 2, Cyprus 16, Honduras 4, Hong Kong 79, Indonesia 8, Isle of Man 19, Liberia 110, Luxembourg 3, Malaysia 2, Malta 5, Marshall Islands 59, Mongolia 2, Netherlands 1, Panama 2372, Philippines 77, Portugal 9, Saint Kitts and Nevis 2, Saint Vincent and the Grenadines 3, Sierra Leone 4, Singapore 164, South Korea 14, Tanzania 1, UK 5, Vanuatu 39, unknown 7) (2010)

Ports and terminals:
major seaport(s): Chiba, Kawasaki, Kobe, Mizushima, Moji, Nagoya, Osaka, Tokyo, Tomakomai, Yokohama
container port(s) (TEUs): Kobe (2,725,304), Nagoya (2,471,821), Osaka (2,172,797), Tokyo (4,416,119), Yokohama (2,992,517)

MILITARY

Military branches:
Japanese Ministry of Defense (MOD): Ground Self-Defense Force (Rikujou Jieitai, GSDF); Maritime Self-Defense Force (Kaijou Jieitai, MSDF); Air Self-Defense Force (Koukuu Jieitai, ASDF)

Military service age and obligation:
18 years of age for voluntary military service; no conscription; mandatory retirement at age 53 for senior enlisted personnel and at 62 years for senior service officers

Manpower available for military service:
males age 16-49: 27,301,443
females age 16-49: 26,307,003

Manpower fit for military service:
males age 16-49: 22,390,431
females age 16-49: 21,540,322

Manpower reaching militarily significant age annually:
male: 623,365
female: 591,253

Military expenditures:
0.99% of GDP
country comparison to the world: 103
1.01% of GDP (2011)
0.99% of GDP (2010)

TRANSNATIONAL ISSUES

Disputes - international:
the sovereignty dispute over the islands of Etorofu, Kunashiri, and Shikotan, and the Habomai group, known in Japan as the "Northern Territories" and in Russia as the "Southern Kuril Islands," occupied by the Soviet Union in 1945, now administered by Russia and claimed by Japan, remains the primary sticking point to signing a peace treaty formally ending World War II hostilities; Japan and South Korea claim Liancourt Rocks (Take-shima/Tok-do) occupied by South Korea since 1954; China and Taiwan dispute both Japan's claims to the uninhabited islands of the Senkaku-shoto (Diaoyu Tai) and Japan's unilaterally declared exclusive economic zone in the East China Sea, the site of intensive hydrocarbon prospecting

Refugees and internally displaced persons:
stateless persons: 1,100 (2012)

IMPORTANT INFORMATION FOR UNDERSTANDING JAPAN[1]

Official Name: Japan

PROFILE

OFFICIAL NAME: Japan

Geography
Area: 377,864 sq. km. (145,902 sq. mi.) ; slightly smaller than California.
Cities: *Capital*--Tokyo. *Other cities*--Yokohama, Osaka, Nagoya, Sapporo, Kobe, Kyoto, Fukuoka.
Terrain: Rugged, mountainous islands.
Climate: Varies from subtropical to temperate.

People
Nationality: *Noun and adjective*--Japanese.
Population: 127.5 million.
Population growth rate (est.) : -0.02%.
Ethnic groups: Japanese; Korean (0.6%) .
Religions: Shinto and Buddhist; Christian (about 0.7%) .
Language: Japanese.
Education: *Literacy*--99%.
Health: *Infant mortality rate*--3.3/1,000. *Life expectancy*--males 77 yrs., females 84 yrs.
Work force (67 million, 2003) : *services*--42%; *trade, manufacturing, mining, and construction*--46%; *agriculture, forestry, fisheries*--5%; *government*--3%.

Government
Type: Constitutional monarchy with a parliamentary government.
Constitution: May 3, 1947.
Branches: *Executive*--prime minister (head of government) . *Legislative*--bicameral Diet (House of Representatives and House of Councillors) . *Judicial*--civil law system based on the model of Roman law.
Administrative subdivisions: 47 prefectures.
Political parties: Liberal Democratic Party (LDP) , Democratic Party of Japan (DPJ) , New Clean Government Party (Komeito) , Japan Communist Party (JCP) , Social Democratic Party (SDP) .
Suffrage: Universal at 20.

GEOGRAPHY

Japan, a country of islands, extends along the eastern or Pacific coast of Asia. The four main islands, running from north to south, are Hokkaido, Honshu (or the mainland) , Shikoku, and Kyushu. Okinawa Island is about 380 miles southwest of Kyushu. About 3,000 smaller islands are included in the archipelago. In total land area, Japan is slightly smaller than California. About 73% of the country is mountainous, with a chain running through each of the main islands. Japan's highest mountain is the world famous Mt. Fuji (12,385 feet) . Since so little flat area exists, many hills and mountainsides are cultivated all the way to the summits. As Japan is situated in a volcanic zone along the Pacific depth, frequent low intensity earth tremors and occasional volcanic activity are felt throughout the islands. Destructive earthquakes occur several times a century. Hot springs are numerous and have been developed as resorts.

Temperature extremes are less pronounced than in the United States, but the climate varies considerably. Sapporo, on the northernmost main island, has warm summers and long, cold winters with heavy snowfall. Tokyo, Nagoya, Kyoto, Osaka, and Kobe, in central and western parts of the largest island of Honshu, experience relatively mild winters with little or no snowfall and hot, humid summers. Fukuoka, on the island of Kyushu, has a climate similar to that of Washington, DC, with mild winters and short summers. Okinawa is subtropical.

[1] US State Department Profile

PEOPLE

Japan's population, currently some 128 million, has experienced a phenomenal growth rate during the past 100 years as a result of scientific, industrial, and sociological changes, but this has recently slowed because of falling birth rates. In 2005, Japan's population declined for the first time, two years earlier than predicted. High sanitary and health standards produce a life expectancy exceeding that of the United States.

Japan is an urban society with only about 4% of the labor force engaged in agriculture. Many farmers supplement their income with part-time jobs in nearby towns and cities. About 80 million of the urban population is heavily concentrated on the Pacific shore of Honshu and in northern Kyushu. Major population centers include: Metropolitan Tokyo with approximately 14 million; Yokohama with 3.3 million; Osaka with 2.6 million; Nagoya with 2.1 million; Sapporo with 1.6 million; Kyoto with 1.5 million; Kobe with 1.4 million; and Kitakyushu, Kawasaki, and Fukuoka with 1.2 million each. Japan faces the same problems that confront urban industrialized societies throughout the world: overcrowded cities, congested roads, air pollution, and rising juvenile delinquency.

Shintoism and Buddhism are Japan's two principal religions. Shintoism is founded on myths and legends emanating from the early animistic worship of natural phenomena. Since it was unconcerned with problems of afterlife which dominate Buddhist thought, and since Buddhism easily accommodated itself to local faiths, the two religions comfortably coexisted, and Shinto shrines and Buddhist temples often became administratively linked. Today many Japanese are adherents of both faiths. From the 16th to the 19th century Shintoism flourished.

Adopted by the leaders of the Meiji restoration, Shintoism received state support and was cultivated as a spur to patriotic and nationalistic feelings. Following World War II, state support was discontinued, and the emperor disavowed divinity. Today Shintoism plays a more peripheral role in the life of the Japanese people. The numerous shrines are visited regularly by a few believers and, if they are historically famous or known for natural beauty, by many sightseers. Many marriages are held in the shrines, and children are brought there after birth and on certain anniversary dates; special shrine days are celebrated for certain occasions, and numerous festivals are held throughout the year. Many homes have "god shelves" where offerings can be made to Shinto deities.

Buddhism first came to Japan in the 6th century and for the next 10 centuries exerted profound influence on its intellectual, artistic, social, and political life. Most funerals are conducted by Buddhist priests, and many Japanese visit family graves and Buddhist temples to pay respects to ancestors.

Confucianism arrived with the first great wave of Chinese influence into Japan between the 6th and 9th centuries. Overshadowed by Buddhism, it survived as an organized philosophy into the late 19th century and remains today as an important influence on Japanese thought and values.

Christianity, first introduced into Japan in 1549, was virtually stamped out by the government a century later; it was reintroduced in the late 1800s and has spread slowly. Today it has 1.4 million adherents, including a relatively high percentage of important figures in education and public affairs.

Beyond the three traditional religions, many Japanese today are turning to a great variety of popular religious movements normally lumped together under the name "new religions." These religions draw on the concept of Shinto, Buddhism, and folk superstition and have developed in part to meet the social needs of elements of the population. The officially recognized new religions number in the hundreds, and total membership is reportedly in the tens of millions.

HISTORY

Japanese legend maintains that Japan was founded in 600 BC by the Emperor Jimmu, a direct descendant of the sun goddess and ancestor of the present ruling imperial family. About AD 405, the Japanese court officially adopted the Chinese writing system. Together with the introduction of Buddhism in the sixth century, these two events revolutionized Japanese culture and marked the beginning of a long period of Chinese cultural influence. From the establishment of the first fixed capital at Nara in 710 until 1867, the emperors of the Yamato dynasty were the nominal rulers, but actual power was usually held by powerful court nobles, regents, or "shoguns" (military governors) .

Contact With the West

The first recorded contact with the West occurred about 1542, when a Portuguese ship, blown off its course to China, landed in Japan. During the next century, traders from Portugal, the Netherlands, England, and Spain arrived, as did Jesuit, Dominican, and Franciscan missionaries. During the early part of the 17th century, Japan's shogunate suspected that the traders and missionaries were actually forerunners of a military conquest by European powers. This caused the shogunate to place foreigners under progressively tighter restrictions. Ultimately, Japan forced all foreigners to leave and barred all relations with the outside world except for severely restricted commercial contacts with Dutch and Chinese merchants at Nagasaki. This isolation lasted for 200 years, until Commodore Matthew Perry of the U.S. Navy negotiated the opening of Japan to the West with the Convention of Kanagawa in 1854.

Within several years, renewed contact with the West profoundly altered Japanese society. The shogunate resigned, and the emperor was restored to power. The "Meiji restoration" of 1868 initiated many reforms. The feudal system was abolished, and numerous Western institutions were adopted, including a Western legal and educational system and constitutional government along parliamentary lines.

In 1898, the last of the "unequal treaties" with Western powers was removed, signaling Japan's new status among the nations of the world. In a few decades, by creating modern social, educational, economic, military, and industrial systems, the Emperor Meiji's "controlled revolution" had transformed a feudal and isolated state into a world power.

Wars With China and Russia

Japanese leaders of the late 19th century regarded the Korean Peninsula as a potential threat to Japan. It was over Korea that Japan became involved in war with the Chinese Empire in 1894-95 and with Russia in 1904-05. The war with China established Japan's domination of Korea, while also giving it the Pescadores Islands and Formosa (now Taiwan) . After Japan defeated Russia in 1905, the resulting Treaty of Portsmouth awarded Japan certain rights in Manchuria and in southern Sakhalin, which Russia had received in 1875 in exchange for the Kurile Islands. Both wars gave Japan a free hand in Korea, which it formally annexed in 1910.

World War I to 1952

World War I permitted Japan, which fought on the side of the victorious Allies, to expand its influence in Asia and its territorial holdings in the Pacific. The postwar era brought Japan unprecedented prosperity. Japan went to the peace conference at Versailles in 1919 as one of the great military and industrial powers of the world and received official recognition as one of the "Big Five" of the new international order. It joined the League of Nations and received a mandate over Pacific islands north of the Equator formerly held by Germany.

During the 1920s, Japan progressed toward a democratic system of government. However, parliamentary government was not rooted deeply enough to withstand the economic and political pressures of the 1930s, during which military leaders became increasingly influential.

Japan invaded Manchuria in 1931 and set up the puppet state of Manchukuo. In 1933, Japan resigned from the League of Nations. The Japanese invasion of China in 1937 followed Japan's signing of the "anti-Comintern pact" with Nazi Germany the previous year and was part of a chain of developments culminating in the Japanese attack on the United States at Pearl Harbor, Hawaii, on December 7, 1941.

After years of war, resulting in the loss of 3 million Japanese lives and the atomic bombings of Hiroshima and Nagasaki, Japan signed an instrument of surrender on the U.S.S. *Missouri* in Tokyo Harbor on September 2, 1945. As a result of World War II, Japan lost all of its overseas possessions and retained only the home islands. Manchukuo was dissolved, and Manchuria was returned to China; Japan renounced all claims to Formosa; Korea was occupied and divided by the U.S. and the U.S.S.R.; southern Sakhalin and the Kuriles were occupied by the U.S.S.R.; and the U.S. became the sole administering authority of the Ryukyu, Bonin, and Volcano Islands. The 1972 reversion of Okinawa completed the U.S. return of control of these islands to Japan.

After the war, Japan was placed under international control of the Allies through the Supreme Commander, Gen. Douglas MacArthur. U.S. objectives were to ensure that Japan would become a peaceful nation and to establish democratic self-government supported by the freely expressed will of the people. Political, economic, and social reforms were introduced, such as a freely elected Japanese Diet (legislature) and universal adult suffrage. The country's constitution took effect on May 3, 1947. The United States and 45 other Allied nations signed the Treaty of Peace with Japan in September 1951. The U.S. Senate ratified the treaty in March 1952, and under the terms of the treaty, Japan regained full sovereignty on April 28, 1952.

GOVERNMENT AND POLITICAL CONDITIONS

Japan is a constitutional monarchy with a parliamentary government. There is universal adult suffrage with a secret ballot for all elective offices. Sovereignty, previously embodied in the emperor, is vested in the Japanese people, and the Emperor is defined as the symbol of the state.

Japan's Government is a parliamentary democracy, with a House of Representatives and a House of Councillors. Executive power is vested in a cabinet composed of a prime minister and ministers of state, all of whom must be civilians. The prime minister must be a member of the Diet and is designated by his colleagues. The prime minister has the power to appoint and remove ministers, a majority of whom must be Diet members. The judiciary is independent.

The five major political parties represented in the National Diet are the Liberal Democratic Party (LDP) , the Democratic Party of Japan (DPJ) , the New Clean Government Party (Komeito) , the Japan Communist Party (JCP) , and the Social Democratic Party (SDP) .

Japan's judicial system, drawn from customary law, civil law, and Anglo-American common law, consists of several levels of courts, with the Supreme Court as the final judicial authority. The Japanese constitution includes a bill of rights similar to the U.S. Bill of Rights, and the Supreme Court has the right of judicial review. Japanese courts do not use a jury system, and there are no administrative courts or claims courts. Because of the judicial system's basis, court decisions are made in accordance with legal statutes. Only Supreme Court decisions have any direct effect on later interpretation of the law.

Japan does not have a federal system, and its 47 prefectures are not sovereign entities in the sense that U.S. states are. Most depend on the central government for subsidies. Governors of prefectures, mayors of municipalities, and prefectural and municipal assembly members are popularly elected to 4-year terms.

Recent Political Developments

The post-World War II years saw tremendous economic growth in Japan, with the political system dominated by the Liberal Democratic Party (LDP) . That total domination lasted until the Diet Lower House elections on July 18, 1993, in which the LDP failed for the first time to win a majority. The LDP returned to power in 1994.

Shinzo Abe was elected Prime Minister in a Diet vote in September 2006. Abe is the first Prime Minister to be born after World War II and the youngest Prime Minister since the war. Abe comes from one of Japan's political families. His grandfather, Nobusuke Kishi, was elected Prime Minister in 1957 and his father, Shintaro Abe, was a former foreign minister. Abe took over his father's parliamentary seat after his death in 1993 and gained national popularity for his firm stance against North Korea for its abductions of Japanese citizens. Despite a reputation as a conservative nationalist, Shinzo Abe has taken positive steps to improve relations with South Korea and China. He visited Beijing and Seoul during his first trip overseas as Prime Minister.

Principal Government Officials

Office	Incumbent
Prime Minister	Shinzō Abe
Deputy Prime Minister Minister for Finance	Tarō Asō

Minister of State for Financial Services Minister of State for Overcoming Deflation	
Minister for Internal Affairs and Communications	Sanae Takaichi
Minister for Justice	Midori Matsushima
Minister for Foreign Affairs	Fumio Kishida
Minister for Education, Culture, Sports, Science and Technology Minister of State for Education Rebuilding Minister of State for the Tokyo Olympic and Paralympic Games	Hakubun Shimomura
Minister for Health, Labour and Welfare	Yasuhisa Shiozaki
Minister for Agriculture, Forestry and Fisheries	Koya Nishikawa
Minister for Economy, Trade and Industry Minister of State for Industrial Competitiveness Minister of State for the Response to the Economic Impact caused by the Nuclear Accident Minister of State for the Nuclear Damage Compensation and Decommissioning Facilitation Corporation	Yūko Obuchi
Minister for Land, Infrastructure, Transport and Tourism Minister of State for Water Cycle Policy	Akihiro Ota
Minister for the Environment Minister of State for Nuclear Emergency Preparedness	Yoshio Mochizuki
Minister for Defence Minister of State for Security Legislation	Akinori Eto
Chief Cabinet Secretary Minister of State for Alleviating the Burden of the Bases in Okinawa	Yoshihide Suga
Minister of State for Reconstruction Minister of State for Comprehensive Policy Coordination for Revival from the Nuclear Accident at Fukushima	Wataru Takeshita
Chairperson of the National Public Safety Commission Minister of State for the Abduction Issue Minister of State for Ocean Policy and Territorial Issues Minister of State for Building National Resilience Minister of State for Disaster Management	Eriko Yamatani
Minister of State for Okinawa and Northern Territories Affairs Minister of State for Science and Technology Policy Minister of State for Space Policy Minister of State for Information Technology Policy Minister of State for the Challenge Again Initiative Minister of State for the Cool Japan Strategy	Shunichi Yamaguchi
Minister of State for Promoting Women's Active Participation Minister of State for Administrative Reform Minister of State for Civil Service Reform Minister of State for Consumer Affairs and Food Safety Minister of State for Regulatory Reform Minister of State for Measures for Declining Birthrate Minister of State for Gender Equality	Haruko Arimura
Minister of State for Economic Revitalization Minister of State for Total Reform of Social Security and Tax Minister of State for Economic and Fiscal Policy	Akira Amari
Minister of State for Overcoming Population Decline and Vitalizing Local Economy Minister of State for National Strategic Special Zones	Shigeru Ishiba

Japan maintains an embassy in the United States at 2520 Massachusetts Avenue NW, Washington, DC 20008 (tel: 202-238-6700; fax: 202-328-2187) .

ECONOMY

Rank	3rd (nominal) / 4th (PPP)
Currency	Japanese yen (JPY)
Fiscal year	1 April – 31 March
Trade organisations	APEC, WTO, OECD, G-20, G8 and others
	Statistics
GDP	¥536,122,300,000,000 (Q2 2014 est.) (real) $5.96 trillion (est.) (nominal; 3rd) $4.704 trillion(est.) (PPP; 4th)
GDP growth	-1,7% (H1 2014)
GDP per capita	$46,736 (est.) (nominal; 14th) $35,855 (est.) (PPP; 23rd)
GDP by sector	agriculture: 1.2%, industry: 27.5%, services: 71.4%
Inflation (CPI)	3.2%
Population below poverty line	16%
Gini coefficient	38.1
Labour force	65.93 million
Labour force by occupation	agriculture: 3.9%, industry: 26.2%, services: 69.8%
Unemployment	4.6%
Main industries	motor vehicles, electronic equipment, machine tools, steel and nonferrous metals, ships, chemicals, textiles, processed foods
Ease-of-doing-business rank	24th
	External
Exports	$697 billion
Export goods	motor vehicles 13.6%; semiconductors 6.2%; iron and steel products 5.5%; auto parts 4.6%; plastic materials 3.5%; power generating machinery 3.5%
Main export partners	China 18.1% United States 17.8% South Korea 7.7% Thailand 5.5% Hong Kong 5.1%
Imports	$766.6 billion
Import goods	petroleum 15.5%; liquid natural gas 5.7%; clothing 3.9%; semiconductors 3.5%; coal 3.5%; audio and visual apparatus 2.7%
Main import partners	China 21.3% United States 8.8% Australia 6.4% Saudi Arabia 6.2% United Arab Emirates 5.0% South Korea 4.6% Qatar 4.0%
FDI stock	$161.4 billion
Gross external debt	$2.719 trillion
	Public finances
Public debt	$13.64 trillion / 229.77% of GDP
Revenues	$1.1trillion
Expenses	$1.157trillion
Economic aid	$9.7 billion ODA
Credit rating	Standard & Poor's: AA- (Domestic) AA- (Foreign) AAA (T&C Assessment) Outlook: Stable Moody's: Aa2 Outlook: Positive Fitch: A- Outlook: Positive
Foreign reserves	US$1.154 trillion

The **economy of Japan** is the third largest in the world by nominal GDP, the fourth largest by purchasing power parity and is the world's second largest developed economy. According to the International Monetary Fund, the country's per capita GDP (PPP) was at $35,855 or the 22nd highest in 2012. Japan is a member of Group of Eight. The Japanese economy is forecasted by the Quarterly Tankan survey of business sentiment conducted by the Bank of Japan.

Japan is the world's third largest automobile manufacturing country, has the largest electronics goods industry, and is often ranked among the world's most innovative countries leading several measures of global patent filings. Facing increasing competition from China and South Korea, manufacturing in Japan today now focuses primarily on high-tech and precision goods, such as optical instruments, hybrid vehicles, and robotics. Beside the Kantō region, the Kansai region is one of the leading industrial clusters and the manufacturing center for the Japanese economy.

Japan is the world's largest creditor nation, generally running an annual trade surplus and having a considerable net international investment surplus. As of 2010, Japan possesses 13.7% of the world's private financial assets (the second largest in the world) at an estimated $14.6 trillion. As of 2013, 62 of the Fortune Global 500 companies are based in Japan

Japan's industrialized, free market economy is the second-largest in the world. Its economy is highly efficient and competitive in areas linked to international trade, but productivity is far lower in protected areas such as agriculture, distribution, and services. After achieving one of the highest economic growth rates in the world from the 1960s through the 1980s, the Japanese economy slowed dramatically in the early 1990s, when the "bubble economy" collapsed, marked by plummeting stock and real estate prices.

Japan's reservoir of industrial leadership and technicians, well-educated and industrious work force, high savings and investment rates, and intensive promotion of industrial development and foreign trade have produced a mature industrial economy. Japan has few natural resources, and trade helps it earn the foreign exchange needed to purchase raw materials for its economy.

Japan's long-term economic prospects are considered good, and it has largely recovered from its worst period of economic stagnation since World War II. Real GDP in Japan grew at an average of roughly 1% yearly in the 1990s, compared to growth in the 1980s of about 4% per year. The Japanese economy is now in its longest postwar expansion after more than a decade of stagnation. Real growth in 2005 was 2.7% and is expected to reach 2.8% in 2006.

Agriculture, Energy, and Minerals
Only 15% of Japan's land is arable. The agricultural economy is highly subsidized and protected. With per hectare crop yields among the highest in the world, Japan maintains an overall agricultural self-sufficiency rate of about 40% on fewer than 5.6 million cultivated hectares (14 million acres) . Japan normally produces a slight surplus of rice but imports large quantities of wheat, corn, sorghum, and soybeans, primarily from the United States. Japan is the largest market for U.S. agricultural exports.

Given its heavy dependence on imported energy, Japan has aimed to diversify its sources. Since the oil shocks of the 1970s, Japan has reduced dependence on petroleum as a source of energy from more than 75% in 1973 to about 57% at present. Other important energy sources are coal, liquefied natural gas, nuclear power, and hydropower.

Deposits of gold, magnesium, and silver meet current industrial demands, but Japan is dependent on foreign sources for many of the minerals essential to modern industry. Iron ore, coke, copper, and bauxite must be imported, as must many forest products.

Labor
Japan's labor force consists of some 67 million workers, 40% of whom are women. Labor union membership is about 12 million.

FOREIGN RELATIONS

Japan is the world's second-largest economy and a major economic power both in Asia and globally. Japan has diplomatic relations with nearly all independent nations and has been an active member of the United Nations since 1956. Japanese foreign policy has aimed to promote peace and prosperity for the Japanese people by working closely with the West and supporting the United Nations.

In recent years, the Japanese public has shown a substantially greater awareness of security issues and increasing support for the Self Defense Forces. This is in part due to the Self Defense Forces' success in disaster relief, including the 2004 Indian Ocean tsunami, and its participation in peacekeeping operations in Cambodia in the early 1990s and reconstruction/stabilization efforts in Iraq in 2003-2008. However, there are still significant political and psychological constraints on strengthening Japan's security profile. Although a military role for Japan in international affairs is highly constrained by its constitution and government policy, Japanese cooperation with the United States through the 1960 U.S.-Japan Security Treaty has been important to the peace and stability of East Asia. In recent years, there have been domestic discussions about possible reinterpretation or revision of Article 9 of the Japanese constitution. All postwar Japanese governments have relied on a close relationship with the United States as the foundation of their foreign policy and have depended on the Mutual Security Treaty for strategic protection.

While maintaining its relationship with the United States, Japan has diversified and expanded its ties with other nations. Good relations with its neighbors continue to be of vital interest. After the signing of a peace and friendship treaty with China in 1978, ties between the two countries developed rapidly. Japan extended significant economic assistance to the Chinese in various modernization projects and supported Chinese membership in the World Trade Organization (WTO) . In recent years, however, Chinese exploitation of gas fields in the East China Sea has raised Japanese concerns given disagreement over the demarcation of their maritime boundary. A long-running boundary dispute involving the Chinese and Taiwanese over the Senkaku (Diaoyu Tai) Islands also continues. Chinese President Hu Jintao's May 2008 visit to Tokyo, the first such visit in 10 years, helped improve relations with China. Japan maintains economic and cultural but not diplomatic relations with Taiwan, with which a strong bilateral trade relationship thrives.

A surprise visit by Prime Minister Koizumi to Pyongyang, North Korea on September 17, 2002, resulted in renewed discussions on contentious bilateral issues--especially that of abductions to North Korea of Japanese citizens--and Japan's agreement to resume normalization talks in the near future. In October 2002, five abductees returned to Japan, but soon after negotiations reached a stalemate over the fate of abductees' families in North Korea. Japan's economic and commercial ties with North Korea plummeted following Kim Jong-il's 2002 admission that D.P.R.K. agents abducted Japanese citizens. Japan strongly supported the United States in its efforts to encourage Pyongyang to abide by the nuclear Non-Proliferation Treaty and its agreements with the International Atomic Energy Agency (IAEA) . In 2006, Japan responded to North Korea's July missile launches and October nuclear test by imposing sanctions and working with the United Nations Security Council. The U.S., Japan, and South Korea closely coordinate and consult trilaterally on policy toward North Korea, and Japan participates in the Six-Party Talks to end North Korea's nuclear arms ambitions. Japan and North Korea reached an agreement in August 2008 in which Pyongyang promised to reinvestigate abduction cases. However, the D.P.R.K. has failed to implement the agreement. Continued North Korean missile tests and bellicose language is viewed with serious concern in Japan.

In recent years, Japan and the Republic of Korea have stepped up high-level diplomatic activity and coordination. However, historical differences, including territorial disputes involving the Liancourt Rocks, complicate Japan's political relations with South Korea despite growing economic and cultural ties.

Japan's relations with Russia are hampered by the two sides' inability to resolve their territorial dispute over the islands that make up the Northern Territories (Southern Kuriles) seized by the U.S.S.R. at the end of World War II. The stalemate over territorial issues has prevented conclusion of a peace treaty formally ending the war between Japan and Russia. The United States recognizes Japanese sovereignty over the islands. Russian Coast Guard boats sometimes seize Japanese fishing vessels operating in waters surrounding the disputed area. In August 2006, a Russian patrol shot at a Japanese fishing vessel, claiming the vessel was in Russian waters, killing one crewmember and taking three seamen into custody. In October 2007, Russia raised objections to U.S.-Japan cooperation on missile defense, and in February 2008, Tokyo protested the incursion into Japanese airspace of a Russian bomber. Then-Prime Minister Aso and Russian President Medvedev held inconclusive discussions on the issue during a March 2009 meeting. During his initial meeting with Medvedev in September 2009, Prime Minister Hatoyama said he wanted to resolve the issue and sign a peace treaty. Despite the lack of progress in resolving the Northern Territories and other disputes, however, Japan and Russia continue to develop other aspects of the overall relationship, including two large, multi-billion dollar oil-natural gas consortium projects on Sakhalin Island.

Japan has pursued a more active foreign policy in recent years, recognizing the responsibility that accompanies its economic strength, and has expanded ties with the Middle East, which provides most of its oil. In 2006, Japan's Ground Self Defense Force completed a successful two-year mission in Iraq, and the Diet extended the Anti-Terrorism Special Measures Law which allowed for Japan's Maritime Self Defense Force refueling activities in support of Operation Enduring Freedom in the Indian Ocean. The Air Self-Defense Force's (ASDF) airlift support mission in Iraq formally ended in December 2008.

Japan increasingly is active in Africa and Latin America--recently concluding negotiations with Mexico and Chile on an Economic Partnership Agreement (EPA) and undertaking negotiations with Peru--and has extended significant support to development projects in both regions. Japan's economic engagement with its neighbors is increasing, as evidenced by the conclusion of EPAs with Singapore, the Philippines, Thailand, Malaysia, Indonesia, and Vietnam.

As host of the G8 Summit in July 2008, Japan focused on four themes: environment and climate change, development and Africa, the world economy, and political issues including non-proliferation. Since 2007 successive Japanese prime ministers have announced their support for initiatives to address greenhouse gas emissions and to mitigate the impact of energy consumption on climate. In September 2009, Prime Minister Hatoyama strengthened the Japanese Government's commitment to this effort by pledging to reduce Japan's greenhouse gas emissions by 25% by 2020 from 1990 levels.

U.S.-JAPAN RELATIONS

The U.S.-Japan alliance is the cornerstone of U.S. security interests in Asia and is fundamental to regional stability and prosperity. Despite the changes in the post-Cold War strategic landscape, the U.S.-Japan alliance continues to be based on shared vital interests and values. These include stability in the Asia-Pacific region, the preservation and promotion of political and economic freedoms, support for human rights and democratic institutions, and securing of prosperity for the people of both countries and the international community as a whole.

Japan provides bases and financial and material support to U.S. forward-deployed forces, which are essential for maintaining stability in the region. Under the U.S.-Japan Treaty of Mutual Cooperation and Security, Japan hosts a carrier battle group, the III Marine Expeditionary Force, the 5th Air Force, and elements of the Army's I Corps. The United States currently maintains approximately 50,000 troops in Japan, about half of whom are stationed in Okinawa.

Over the past decade the alliance has been strengthened through revised Defense Guidelines, which expand Japan's noncombatant role in a regional contingency, the renewal of our agreement on Host Nation Support of U.S. forces stationed in Japan, and an ongoing process called the Defense Policy Review Initiative (DPRI) . The DPRI redefines roles, missions, and capabilities of alliance forces and outlines key realignment and transformation initiatives, including reducing the number of troops stationed in Okinawa, enhancing interoperability and communication between our respective commands, and broadening our cooperation in the area of ballistic missile defense. In February 2009 Secretary of State Clinton and then-Foreign Minister Nakasone signed the Guam International Agreement (GIA) in Tokyo. The GIA commits both nations to completing the transfer of approximately 8,000 U.S. Marines from bases in Okinawa to new facilities in Guam built with the assistance of Japan.

Implementation of these agreements will strengthen our capabilities and make our alliance more sustainable. After the tragic events of September 11, 2001, Japan has participated significantly in counterterrorism efforts by providing major logistical support for U.S. and coalition forces in the Indian Ocean.

Because of the two countries' combined economic and technological impact on the world, the U.S.-Japan relationship has become global in scope. The United States and Japan cooperate on a broad range of global issues, including development assistance, combating communicable disease such as the spread of HIV/AIDS and avian influenza, and protecting the environment and natural resources. Both countries also collaborate in science and technology in such areas as mapping the human genome, research on aging, and international space exploration. As one of Asia's most successful democracies and its largest economy, Japan contributes irreplaceable political, financial, and moral support to U.S.-Japan diplomatic efforts. The United States consults closely with Japan and the Republic of Korea on policy regarding North Korea. The United States works closely with Japan and Australia under the auspices of the Trilateral Strategic Dialogue and the Security and Defense Cooperation Forum to exchange views and increase coordination on global and regional initiatives. In Southeast Asia, U.S.-Japan cooperation is vital for stability and for political and economic reform. Outside Asia, Japanese political and financial support has substantially strengthened the U.S. position on a variety of global geopolitical problems, including the Gulf, Middle East peace efforts, and the Balkans. Japan, currently a member of the United Nations Security Council for the 2009-2010 term, is an indispensable partner in the UN and the second-largest contributor to the UN budget. Japan broadly supports the United States on nonproliferation and nuclear issues.

Economic Relations
U.S. economic policy toward Japan is aimed at increasing access to Japan's markets and two-way investment, stimulating domestic demand-led economic growth, promoting economic restructuring, improving the climate for U.S. investors, and raising the standard of living in both the United States and Japan. The U.S.-Japan bilateral economic relationship--based on enormous flows of trade, investment, and finance--is strong, mature, and increasingly interdependent. Further, it is firmly rooted in the shared interest and responsibility of the United States and Japan to promote global growth, open markets, and a vital world trading system. In addition to bilateral economic ties, the U.S. and Japan cooperate closely in multilateral fora such as the WTO, the G20, the Organization for Economic Cooperation and Development, the World Bank, and the International Monetary Fund, and regionally in the Asia-Pacific Economic Cooperation forum (APEC) . Japan will host APEC in 2010, followed by the United States in 2011, allowing for increased coordination between the two governments.

Japan is a major market for many U.S. products, including chemicals, pharmaceuticals, films and music, commercial aircraft, nonferrous metals, plastics, and medical and scientific supplies. Japan also is the third-largest foreign market for U.S. agricultural products, with total agricultural exports valued at $13.2 billion in 2008, an almost 30% increase over the $10.2 billion in agricultural exports recorded by the U.S. Department of Agriculture in 2007. Revenues from Japanese tourism to the United States reached nearly $14.6 billion in 2008.

Trade between the United States and Japan remained strong in 2008. U.S. exports to Japan reached $66.6 billion in 2008, up from $62.7 billion in 2007. U.S. imports from Japan totaled $139.2 billion in 2008 ($145.5 billion in 2007) .

U.S. foreign direct investment in Japan reached $101.6 billion in 2008, up from $91.8 billion in 2006, according to data compiled by the U.S. Department of Commerce's Bureau of Economic Analysis. New U.S. investment was especially significant in financial services, Internet services, and software, generating new export opportunities for U.S. firms and employment for U.S. workers.

Principal U.S. Embassy Officials
Ambassador--Caroline Bouvier Kennedy

Ambassador Kennedy assumed duty as Ambassador Extraordinary and Plenipotentiary to Japan following the presentation of her credentials to His Imperial Majesty the Emperor on Nov. 19, 2013 .

Deputy Chief of Mission--James Zumwalt
Political Minister-Counselor--Robert Luke
Economic Minister-Counselor--Marc Wall
Consul General--Raymond Baca
Commercial Minister--John Peters
Public Affairs--Ronald Post
Defense Attaché--Capt. James White, USN

The street address and the international mailing address of the U.S. Embassy in Japan is 10-5 Akasaka 1-chome, Minato-ku, Tokyo (107) ; tel. 81-3-3224-5000; fax 81-3-3505-1862. The APO mailing address is American Embassy Tokyo, Unit 45004, Box 258, APO AP 96337-5004. U.S. Consulates General are in Osaka, Sapporo, and Naha, and Consulates are in Fukuoka and Nagoya. The American Chamber of Commerce in Japan is at 7th floor, Fukide No. 2 Bldg., 1-21 Toranomon 4-chome, Minato-ku, Tokyo (105) . Additional information is available on the U.S. Embassy's Internet home page: http://tokyo.usembassy.gov.

TRAVEL AND BUSINESS INFORMATION

The U.S. Department of State's Consular Information Program provides Consular Information Sheets, Travel Warnings, and Public Announcements.

Consular Information Sheets exist for all countries and include information on entry requirements, currency regulations, health conditions, areas of instability, crime and security, political disturbances, and the addresses of the U.S. posts in the country.

Travel Warnings are issued when the State Department recommends that Americans avoid travel to a certain country. **Public Announcements** are issued as a means to disseminate information quickly about terrorist threats and other relatively short-term conditions overseas that pose significant risks to the security of American travelers. Free copies of this information are available by calling the Bureau of Consular Affairs at 202-647-5225 or via the fax-on-demand system: 202-647-3000. Consular Information Sheets and Travel Warnings also are available on the Consular Affairs Internet home page: http://travel.state.gov. Consular Affairs Tips for Travelers publication series, which contain information on obtaining passports and planning a safe trip abroad, are available on the Internet and hard copies can be purchased from the Superintendent of Documents, U.S. Government Printing Office, telephone: 202-512-1800; fax 202-512-2250.

Emergency information concerning Americans traveling abroad may be obtained from the Office of Overseas Citizens Services at (202) 647-5225. For after-hours emergencies, Sundays and holidays, call 202-647-4000.

The National Passport Information Center (NPIC) is the U.S. Department of State's single, centralized public contact center for U.S. passport information. Telephone: 1-877-4USA-PPT (1-877-487-2778) . Customer service representatives and operators for TDD/TTY are available Monday-Friday, 8:00 a.m. to 8:00 p.m., Eastern Time, excluding federal holidays.

Travelers can check the latest health information with the U.S. Centers for Disease Control and Prevention in Atlanta, Georgia. A hotline at 877-FYI-TRIP (877-394-8747) and a web site at http://www.cdc.gov/travel/index.htm give the most recent health advisories, immunization recommendations or requirements, and advice on food and drinking water safety for regions and countries. A booklet entitled Health Information for International Travel (HHS publication number CDC-95-8280) is available from the U.S. Government Printing Office, Washington, DC 20402, tel. (202) 512-1800.

Information on travel conditions, visa requirements, currency and customs regulations, legal holidays, and other items of interest to travelers also may be obtained before your departure from a country's embassy and/or consulates in the U.S. (for this country, see "Principal Government Officials" listing in this publication) .

U.S. citizens who are long-term visitors or traveling in dangerous areas are encouraged to register their travel via the State Department's travel registration web site at https://travelregistration.state.gov or at the Consular section of the U.S. embassy upon arrival in a country by filling out a short form and sending in a copy of their passports. This may help family members contact you in case of an emergency.

PRACTICAL INFORMATION FOR BUSINESS AND INVESTMENTS[2]

DOING BUSINESS IN JAPAN

As the world's fourth-largest buyer of American products, Japan is a market that American companies should not overlook, but approach with a thoughtful strategy. Japan is a technology powerhouse, a "proving ground" for consumer requirements, and stands in the vanguard with respect to the sweeping changes recently seen in developed market demographics. Most U.S. state economic development agencies are also well aware of the important foreign direct investment coming into their communities from Japan. While the reasons U.S. firms engage with Japan are diverse, savvy firms recognize that underestimating the strategic of the Japanese market may disadvantage them not only in Japan, but in the United States and third-country markets as well.

MARKET OVERVIEW

• Japan is back in the business news headlines in 2013, owing in part to a rising stock market, a sharply lower yen, and stirrings of domestic demand for both personal consumption and capital investment. The new economic policy linked to these developments is known as "Abenomics"-- a three pronged strategy of bold monetary loosening, fiscal stimulus centered on infrastructure spending, and growth-oriented structural reform. While the implications and ultimate success of this strategy in reigniting growth in Japan are far from certain, it has drawn considerable attention from U.S. businesses.

• In April 2013 the U.S. and Japanese governments agreed on a package of actions and agreements that pave the way for the Obama Administration to support Japan's participation in the Trans-Pacific Partnership (TPP). With Japan's participation in the TPP, its members would account for nearly 40 percent of World GDP. Moreover, the liberalization expected to be required of TPP member countries may play an important role in promoting the domestic economic reforms likely to be called for under "Abenomics."

• While Japan has made significant steps toward economic healing following the tragic combined earthquake, tsunami, and nuclear incident of March 2011, there are lasting changes noticeable on various levels, including idled nuclear power plants.

• Japan remains the world's third-largest economy, after the United States and China, with a GDP of roughly $5.8 trillion. Japan is the fourth-largest export market for U.S. goods and services, and our fourth-largest trading partner overall. In 2012 the U.S. exported $70 billion in goods to Japan. The United States runs a persistent trade deficit with Japan in merchandise, and a surplus in services.

• Japan is the second-largest foreign investor in the United States, with more than $257 billion invested.

• During 2012 the Japanese yen was stable against the dollar. However, the yen weakened appreciably in the first half of 2013. Even so, U.S. products remain competitive in Japan.

• Japan's large government debt, which totals over 200 percent of GDP, persistent deflation, and an aging and shrinking population are major challenges confronting the economy.

[2] US Governmetn MAterials. Commercial Guide on Japan

• In 2012, the top exporters to Japan were China, the United States, Australia, Saudi Arabia, the UAE, South Korea, and Indonesia. The top importers from Japan were China, the United Sates, South Korea, Taiwan, and Hong Kong.

• The U.S.-Japan alliance is a cornerstone of U.S. security interests in Asia and is fundamental to regional stability and prosperity. The United States-Japan alliance continues to be based on shared vital interests and values. These include stability in the Asia-Pacific region, the preservation and promotion of political and economic freedoms, support for human rights and democratic institutions, and securing of prosperity for the people of both countries and the international community as a whole. Japan is one of the world's most prosperous and stable democracies.

MARKET CHALLENGES

The degree of difficulty in penetrating the Japanese market depends on the product or service involved. Key variables include the degree of local or third-country competition, the number of regulatory hurdles to be overcome, and cultural factors such as language (both spoken and written), service and quality expectations, and business practices.

Generally, tariffs on most imported goods into Japan are low. However, cultural, regulatory, or other non-tariff barriers continue to exist that can make market entry difficult. These can include Japanese import license requirements, restricted or prohibited imports, temporary entry of goods, certifications, standards, labeling requirements, etc. For more details, see Chapter 5, Trade Regulations, Customs and Standards of this Guide.

MARKET OPPORTUNITIES

The Japanese market offers numerous opportunities for U.S. companies in a wide variety of sectors. Best prospects for U.S. exporters in the Japanese market include the following sectors:

Aerospace
Agricultural products and services including high-value food and beverage
Biotechnology
Cloud Computing
Cosmetics & Toiletries
Education & Corporate Training
Electronic Components
Healthcare IT
Medical Equipment
Pharmaceuticals
Renewable Energy
Safety & Security
Environmental Remediation & Engineering Services
Telecommunications Equipment
Travel & Tourism

MARKET ENTRY STRATEGY

U.S. companies wishing to enter the Japanese market should consider hiring a reputable, well-connected agent or distributor, and cultivating business contacts through frequent personal visits. Japan's business culture attaches a high degree of importance to personal relationships, and these take time to establish and nurture. Patience and repeated follow-up are typically required to clinch a deal. The nature and pace of deal-making in Japan are quite different from those in the United States. U.S. business executives are advised to retain a professional interpreter, as many Japanese executives and decision-makers do not speak English, or prefer to speak Japanese. For more details, please refer to Chapter 8, Business Travel, of this Guide.

Please note that throughout this report the following dollar / yen exchange rates were used:
2009 93.68

2010 87.78
2011 79.70
2012 79.82
2013 79.82*
2014 79.82*
2016 - 113.83

*GOJ new easy-money fiscal policies have had a considerable effect thus far this year—102.58 as of 5/20/13-- and may continue to have a weakening effect on the yen.

POLITICAL AND ECONOMIC ENVIRONMENT

GOVERNMENT ROLE IN THE ECONOMY

Traditionally, the bureaucracy played a leading role in the Japanese economy. Members of the National Diet, from whose ranks come most of Japan's Cabinet ministers, have small staffs and rely on bureaucrats for policy initiatives and the drafting of legislation. In addition, the ministries have exercised power directly through the issuance of required licenses, permits and approvals that tightly regulate business activity. For much of the post-war period, ministries also issued informal (but in practice, virtually compulsory) directives called "administrative guidance" to the industries they regulated, further controlling business activity. The reach of the bureaucracy also extended through a dense web of close relations with leading business organizations. In addition to the reliance of Japanese elected officials on campaign contributions from business, major industry associations and quasi-governmental regulatory bodies also provided lucrative post-government employment called *amakudari* (literally "descent from heaven") for senior bureaucrats as well as lower-level bureaucrats who regulate their industries. However, in 2007, the Diet approved legislation that established restrictions on the types of post-retirement jobs former senior government officials can accept and centralized authority for finding such employment in the National Personnel Agency. The central government is continuing efforts to address problems relating to the system of post-government employment.

The role of government institutions in the economy has been changing over the past decade as the central government pursues a long-term program of administrative reform, deregulation, and decentralization. In 2001, the bureaucracy was reorganized from 22 ministries and agencies to 13. The Cabinet Office was also established to coordinate policies and to provide staff support for Japan's leaders separate from the individual ministries. At the same time, the number of Diet members posted to senior positions in the ministries was increased from an average of two to five, with the aim of strengthening the control of elected officials over the bureaucracy. Through such measures and other administrative reforms, the bureaucracy's influence over the economy has diminished, but by no means has it been eliminated completely. The Government of Japan (GOJ) continues to play a significant role in promoting certain favored industries, and GOJ policy and regulatory practices in many cases still favor the interests of domestic producers.

While Japan's economic structure and business culture are somewhat different from those of the United States, U.S. companies can and do successfully adapt. The American Chamber of Commerce in Japan (ACCJ) is one of the largest overseas chambers in the world. Its members come from more than 1,000 companies

representing over 40 countries, and its more than 60 committees, sub-committees, and task forces are highly visible advocates for U.S. business interests. U.S. Embassy officers and staff liaise with these committees and work closely with the ACCJ on market access, deregulation, competition, trade, and investment issues. Some regulatory barriers still exist, and when a company cannot solve such problems by itself or through its legal advisers in Japan, the U.S. Government stands ready to help.

INFRASTRUCTURE

Japan has a fully developed physical infrastructure of roads, highways, railroads, subways, airports, harbors, warehouses, and telecommunications for distribution of all types of goods and services. As is the U.S. and elsewhere, the need for replacement or upgrading of aged infrastructure has been brought to the fore by recent high-profile infrastructure accidents. Moreover, the recently returned Liberal Democratic Party under Prime Minister Abe has signaled that renewed infrastructure spending will be a focus of its fiscal stimulus. Road tolls, however, are expensive. Although the government has periodically implemented initiatives to reduce certain tolls, as of April 2013, a large truck will pay over the equivalent of $300 in tolls each way between Tokyo and Osaka (about 315 miles). Tolls for a small passenger car on the same trip amount to about $120. Japan's airport fees push airline ticket costs up to be among the most expensive in the world. Japan's port practices and import processing are generally efficient.

AGRICULTURAL PRODUCTS MARKET

The importance of food in the Japanese culture is reflected by size of its food and agricultural market, recently valued at approximately $821 billion (2011), and Japan is the largest food importer in the world. At 23 percent of disposable income, per capita spending (for households of two or more people) on food in Japan is higher than anywhere else on earth. This high per capita food spending is a function of higher food prices, but it is also a reflection of the fact that Japanese consumers are willing to pay a premium for quality and convenience. Given the wide variety of foods produced in the United States, the internationalization of food in Japan has given the United States an important advantage in the Japanese food market. Until recently Japan had a relatively uniform food market, with rice, vegetables, fish, eggs, and soy products making up the traditional Japanese diet. As Japan became more affluent, and more Japanese were exposed to diverse food products from around the world, there has been a major trend toward diet diversification. One hallmark of this market is the Japanese consumers' obsession with quality. Japanese tend to value the taste of food over the quantity of food. However, this has changed slightly and many Japanese consumers are seeking value. Still, Japanese consumers are highly brand-conscious, cognizant of the seasonality of certain foods. Japanese are increasingly health-conscious, and given their aging society, are leading the world in demand for functional foods. They also consider a food product's aesthetic appearance, on the shelf, in the package, and on the table to be important and indicative of quality and healthfulness of the product.

Japan is the 4th largest destination for U.S. agricultural products, and is the number one destination for consumer ready food products. U.S. wheat, rice, corn, soybeans, pork, beef, processed fruits and vegetables, citrus, wine, cherries, and processed snack foods make up the largest sectors. In 2012, about 10 percent of all U.S. agricultural, forestry and fishery product exports, valued at $14.9 billion were destined for Japan, of which $6.3 billion were consumer ready foods. The combination of improved market access, declining domestic production, and investments in cultivating the brand awareness of American agricultural products, have helped to make Japan one of the United States' top overseas export markets. Given competition from third countries, and the changes in consumer spending resulting from nearly 20 years of stagnant economic growth, Japan is a competitive environment for U.S. food companies. However, long-term prospects for American food and agricultural exporters in Japan are excellent for the following reasons: (1) growing consumer demand for value plays to U.S. strengths (U.S. foods typically cost less than local products); (2) Japanese agriculture continues to decline, leading to increased dependence on imports for stable food supplies; (3) continued Westernization of the Japanese diet away from fish and rice toward meats, dairy products and other American staples; and (4) American agricultural products enjoy a reputation for being safer than foods from competing markets.

Though domestic protection is still strong, market access has improved over the years via persistent negotiations in the WTO by the United and others, leading Japan to eliminate some of the agricultural market access barriers for which it was once famous. Where earlier quotas and outright bans restricted the market for U.S. beef, citrus, fruit juice, cherries, and ice cream, all of these markets have now, to some degree been opened. For example, on February 1, 2013, Japan expanded access for U.S. beef by revising its import regulations, including raising the cut-off age for beef importation from cattle from 20 months to 30 months. U.S. beef and beef product exports to Japan reached nearly $1.03 billion in FY2012, the United States' second largest export market, accounting for 19 percent of U.S. trade. However, access issues still hamper greater farm trade due to high tariffs on processed food products, restrictive plant quarantine measures on fruits and vegetables, trade-limiting quotas and complicated labeling practices. In addition, a stringent system for regulation of agrochemical residues including strict inspection of imported foods and a time –consuming approval process for biotechnology products also hinder trade in agricultural products. For additional information about U.S. agricultural, food, forestry and fishery product exports to Japan, please see the Global Agricultural Information Network (GAIN) reports of the U.S. Department of Agriculture's (USDA) Foreign Agriculture Service at:

http://gain.fas.usda.gov/Lists/Advanced%20Search/AllItems.aspx .

LEADING ECONOMIC REGIONS

Tokyo

Japan's capital city, Tokyo (population 13 million), forms the core of an urban area that, along with the suburban prefectures of Kanagawa, Saitama, and Chiba, boasts a total population of over 35 million, roughly equivalent to the New York and Los Angeles metropolitan areas combined. It is Japan's undisputed center of government, business, higher education, information, media, fashion, and culture. The entire geographical region centered on the capital – often referred to as the "Kantō" region – accounts for about one-third of Japan's total GDP.

Most major Japanese companies, trade associations, and foreign companies have their headquarters or major branches in Tokyo. Consumers in the capital are more likely to come into contact with foreign products, foods, and fashions than elsewhere in Japan, and consumer trends often originate in Tokyo. For U.S. firms, the major advantages of establishing a presence in Tokyo, despite the high cost of residential and office space, are the city's concentration of major companies and high-income consumers, proximity to the powerful central government regulatory agencies, and location at the hub of Japan's highly centralized transportation networks, including its two busiest airports: New Tokyo International Airport in Narita, Chiba Prefecture (often called "Tokyo Narita"), and Tokyo International Airport (commonly known as "Tokyo Haneda"), just south of central Tokyo. In addition, major urban renewal schemes completed or underway in metropolitan Tokyo have contributed to lower land and business costs in recent years. Attractive areas for U.S. exporters in the greater Tokyo area are environmental technologies, biotechnology, information and telecommunications technologies, medical equipment and welfare services, and the lifestyle market.

Northern Japan (Hokkaido/Tohoku)

Northern Japan consists of Hokkaido and the six prefectures of northern Honshu that are called Tohoku (Aomori, Akita, Miyagi, Iwate, Fukushima, and Yamagata). Together they comprise roughly one third of the Japan's landmass and one ninth of its population. Hokkaido has a population of approximately 5.5 million and Tohoku has a population of approximately 9.2 million (as of 2011). The Gross Regional Product (GRP) for Hokkaido is approximately $184 billion and for Tohoku is approximately $333 billion (JPY100 to the dollar). Hokkaido, located roughly 500 miles north of Tokyo, is Japan's northernmost island.

These prefectures comprise Japan's agricultural heartland, with large-scale dairy production and diverse farming in Hokkaido, and highly prized rice growing in Akita and Miyagi Prefectures in Tohoku. Hokkaido's agricultural output was about $9.9 billion and accounted for 12% of national agricultural output in 2010. According to Ministry of Agriculture, Forestry and Fisheries' statistics (2011), Hokkaido is the number one producer of wheat (67%), potatoes (78.9%), soybeans (27.1%), red beans (90%), kidney beans (94.6%), buckwheat (35.6%), sugar beets (100%), onions (53.7%) and fresh milk (51.9%) in Japan. Despite agriculture's importance, only 7.2 percent of Hokkaido's 2.51 million labor force is working in Primary Industries. 80% of Hokkaido's workforce is in the Tertiary Sector. According to a 2012 Hokkaido Prefectural Government Economic Indicators report on the prefecture's industrial structure, Hokkaido's manufacturing sector accounts for 8.1 percent of the workforce, which is half of the national average, and the construction sector accounts for 8.9 percent of the workforce, which is 1.4 percent larger than the national average. These figures illustrate Hokkaido's economic dependence on public works.

Tohoku on the other hand has succeeded in clustering manufacturing plants in sectors such as auto assembly, auto parts, electronic components, devices, circuits, and ICT equipment. Manufacturing accounted for 16.3 percent of regional output in 2009, with farming at 2.7 percent and construction at 5.7 percent (source: Tohoku Economy 2012 document issued by Tohoku METI).

The Great East Japan Earthquake and Tsunami Disaster, which occurred on March 11, 2011, inflicted considerable damage on Tohoku's manufacturing capability, Pacific fisheries and some of its most productive farmland. Cities and towns on the Pacific Coast of Aomori, Iwate, Miyagi, and Fukushima Prefectures were severely damaged by the tsunami waves which followed the massive earthquake. Much of the inland manufacturing had recovered by mid-2012, but small and medium size suppliers who lost contracts to competitors in other parts of Japan after the disaster have struggled to resume operations. Fisheries and coastal farms hit by the tsunami face more significant challenges and, by some estimates, could take years to regain pre-disaster production levels.

Fukushima Prefecture, which hosts two large nuclear plants with a total of ten reactors, still faces tremendous nuclear-related problems resulting from the March 11, 2011 disaster. These include radioactive substance decontamination, reactor decommissioning, and harmful rumors about the prefecture's agricultural produce. Technologies that could help resolve these issues would be highly prized in the area.

The Government of Japan's (GOJ) Reconstruction Design Council has estimated that post-disaster reconstruction in Tohoku will cost up to 20 trillion yen ($200 billion). Most of the major reconstruction projects will occur during the next 10 years, and annual public works spending is estimated at 2 trillion yen ($20 billion), a fourfold increase over pre-disaster expenditures for public works. Shortages of labor and concrete for reconstruction projects are constraining the pace of reconstruction efforts. The shortage of technical personnel such as civil engineers, in addition to the shortage of regular construction workers, has inflated construction sector wages not only in Tohoku but also in other regions of Japan.

Uncertainty over the future of nuclear power following the March 11 earthquake and the Fukushima nuclear reactor incident is stimulating interest in new energy technologies in Northern Japan. Many of the tsunami-devastated coastal communities seek to develop renewable energy projects as part of their reconstruction plans. The largest of these cities is Ishinomaki (population 149,000), which is working with a consortium of private companies and NGOs on a "smart city" project.

Private sector renewable energy development is more active in Hokkaido, which ranks first among all the prefectures of Japan for the number and scale of mega-solar projects (75 such facilities on 466 hectares of land). A wide range of Japanese energy and non-energy sector companies have entered the solar power market in Hokkaido. These include construction companies, agricultural entities, and Softbank, one of Japan's major telecommunications companies. Softbank is operating test sites in Hokkaido and has plans to build one of Japan's largest mega-solar plants in Tomakomai City. This plant would produce 100,000 kilowatts of electricity, enough to meet the annual demand of 20,000 households, starting as early as 2014. Public sector renewable energy projects include vegetable cultivation using biomass fuel and geothermal energy; fertilizer manufacturing and energy generation using livestock waste; and the development of small-scale hydraulic power systems in agricultural irrigation ditches.

Hokkaido and Tohoku both have significant geothermal resources, particularly within the boundaries of national parks that have been off-limits to commercial development in the past. Changes in regulations that permit development of these resources may create opportunities for firms with expertise in horizontal drilling.

Northern Japan's well-developed infrastructure, highly skilled workers, and relatively low real estate costs and wages, combined with municipal and regional government investment incentives, have prompted many foreign companies to view Hokkaido and Tohoku as attractive destinations for investment. Especially with regard to reconstruction efforts in the Tohoku region, new energy technologies, home building materials, biotechnology, marine and agricultural inputs, pharmaceuticals and medical and homecare equipment are some of the more promising sectors.

Northern Japan has ample capacity for air passenger and cargo traffic. Tourism and related industries are an important source of growth, having largely recovered from the 2011 earthquake and tsunami disaster. Direct flights from Sapporo to Honolulu and Bangkok since late 2012, new service between Sendai and Honolulu from summer 2013, and an increasing number of flights by Japanese and international Low Cost Carriers (LCC) are boosting traffic at regional airports in Hokkaido and Tohoku. Further economic stimulus is expected in 2015, when Shinkansen bullet train service reaches Hakodate in southern Hokkaido, passing under the Tsugaru Strait via the Seikan Tunnel, the longest in the world.

In early 2012 the Japanese Government approved construction of the next and final leg of the Shinkansen, between Hakodate and Sapporo, with a target construction period of 24 years. The total investment for the Hokkaido leg is estimated at 1.67 trillion yen ($17 billion), with the Hokkaido Prefectural Government covering at least 290 billion yen ($3 billion). When completed, the Hokkaido Shinkansen will connect Tokyo with Sapporo in less than five hours one-way, making the "bullet train" a truly nationwide high-speed passenger rail network.

Kansai

The region of Western Japan known as Kansai lies in the western-central part of Japan's main island of Honshu. With a land area of 17,360 square miles, a population exceeding 24 million and an economy of $886 billion, Kansai is an essential segment of the Japanese market. The region is anchored by Osaka, a vast metropolitan area second only to Tokyo in scale, and includes the major cities of Kobe and Kyoto.

Kansai is an economic powerhouse in a wide range of sectors: electronics, food, pharmaceuticals, biotech, chemicals, textiles, energy and other vibrant industries. With its current GDP, Kansai by itself would rank as the world's 11th largest economy (between Korea and the Netherlands). The region leads Japan in the production of lithium-ion batteries, solar cells and medicinal drugs. Its SMEs also hold world market share in products as diverse as gear measuring machinery, nuts and bolts for nuclear power plants and barber chairs. Kansai is home to some of Japan's – and the world's – best known corporations, such as Sharp, Panasonic, Nintendo and Kyocera. Other Kansai-based companies offer products with a global reputation: Takeda's pharmaceuticals, Capcom's video games, Wacoal's lingerie and Mizuno's sporting goods.

In addition to this manufacturing might, Kansai has a rich history of leading research in the life sciences. Kansai's bioscience clusters are leading global contributors to advances in areas such as the human immune system, the fight against infectious diseases and cerebral and cardiovascular research. In addition, Kansai is home to the world's largest third-generation synchrotron radiation facility, known as "Spring 8," and one of the world's fastest supercomputer, known as "Kei."

Kansai's extensive infrastructure features railway networks of bullet trains that connect Osaka, Kobe, and Kyoto to all parts of the country, three major airports that link the region to multiple domestic and international destinations and a combined super port that serves as a hub for East Asia. In 2013, Grand Front Osaka, a major redevelopment project of businesses and residences, opened at Osaka's central railway station. Grand Front's centerpiece is Knowledge Capital, a group of R&D facilities designed to foster innovation and exchanges among tenant companies, startups and academic institutions. In 2014, Abeno Harukas, set to be Japan's tallest skyscraper, will open its complex of shopping, offices and hotel in downtown Osaka.

Kansai is attracting companies looking to establish a base in Asia. Japan's first low-cost international carrier, Peach Air, has based its operations at Kansai International Airport (KIX). In 2012, one U.S. leader in emissions controls also strategically opened its manufacturing plant adjacent to KIX in order to position itself to expand its Asia business from Japan. Amazon has built its logistic center for Asia in Sakai (in southern Osaka) and will open its second Japan office in Osaka in 2013. In 2014, FedEx will establish its North Pacific Regional hub at KIX to continue the trend.

Kansai, as the cultural and historical heart of Japan, is home to 5 UNESCO World Heritage sites. Six of the top seven prefectures, in terms of national treasures, are located in the region. Kansai is also known for its food, most notably Osaka's takoyaki (fried octopus balls), world renowned Kobe beef and the refined cuisine of Kyoto (considered to be the best in Japan). With its two professional teams, the Hanshin Tigers and the Orix Buffaloes, Kansai is a go-to destination in baseball-crazy Japan. In addition, the Tigers home of Koshien is the most famous ballpark in the country, given its long history of hosting Japan's nationwide high school baseball tournaments.

The people of Kansai are descended from Osaka's merchant culture. With their pragmatic, entrepreneurial and down-to-earth personalities, Kansai residents have a keen business sense, making them ideal business partners. Citizens of Kansai are also reputed to have Japan's best sense of humor – another useful trait.

The U.S. Commercial Service (CS) Osaka-Kobe provides a broad range of programs and services designed to help U.S. companies capitalize on opportunities in Kansai, particularly in the region's key industries of biotechnology, pharmaceuticals, medical devices, renewable energy, environmental technologies, educational services and tourism. In addition, from its base at the U.S. Consulate General in Osaka, CS

Osaka-Kobe has national responsibility for building products, sporting goods, apparel and textiles. Working closely with the Kansai chapter of the American Chamber of Commerce in Japan and the local chambers of commerce in Osaka, Kobe and Kyoto, CS Osaka-Kobe helps promote American exports of goods and services and tourism to the United States through promotional events, U.S. Pavilions, business counseling, partnership searches, matchmaking services, networking and advocacy. For more information about the opportunities in Kansai for U.S. firms, please visit our CS Japan website at www.buyusa.gov/japan/en

Central Japan (Chūbu)

The Chūbu region (lit., Central Japan) is Japan's third most populous region, located midway between the largest (Tokyo/Kantō) to the northeast and the second largest (Osaka/Kansai) to the southwest. The four prefectures of Aichi, Gifu, Mie and Shizuoka are home to 15.1 million people, and the region is known as Japan's industrial heartland leading its economy.

Central Japan's theme is "monozukuri," or "making things," and the region boasts large shares of Japan's manufacturing sectors. For example, Central Japan's share of transportation sector manufacturing is well over 50 percent as the region hosts the headquarters or main factories of world-class manufacturers in autos (Toyota, Honda, Mitsubishi, Suzuki and Yamaha), auto parts (Denso, Aisin), aerospace (Mitsubishi, Kawasaki and Fuji), composite materials (Toray), machine tools (Mazak, Okuma), power tools (Makita), ceramics (Noritake, NGK Insulators and NGK Spark Plug) and office automation (Brother). Additionally, thousands of supporting suppliers make this one of the top industrial accumulations in the world.

Thus, the region accounts for about 0.84 percent of the world economy, 12.8 percent of Japan's GDP, and nearly 30 percent of Japan's total exports to the United States. Aichi Prefecture (pop. 7.4 million) is the political, economic, and transportation center of the region and it has ranked number one in the shipment of manufactured goods every year since 1977. The U.S. Consulate Nagoya is located in the city of Nagoya (pop. 2.3 million), the prefectural capital.

The auto industry experienced unexpected and serious hardships in 2011. Supply chain disruption caused by the March 11 earthquake/tsunami and the floods in Thailand temporarily crippled production and deferred sales. The industry has been recovering steadily with the region's traditional resilience by restructuring its supply chain and accelerating development and production of "green cars" (low fuel consumption and emission vehicles).

About half of Japan's 1.3 trillion yen aerospace sector is based in the region, and Mitsubishi, Kawasaki, and Fuji produce 35 percent of the Boeing 787 Dreamliner. A dozen U.S. suppliers are partnering with the Mitsubishi to develop Japan's first jetliner, the 70-90 seat Mitsubishi Regional Jet which is expected to start test flights in 2013 or 2014.

In December 2011, the Japanese government designated the Greater Nagoya area as a Special Economic Zone for promoting the aerospace industry. The program includes a free trade zone, investment incentives, networking of suppliers, and the creation of a national composite material center in Aichi and Gifu prefectures. In April 2013, the GOJ expanded the initiative to include Mie prefecture and also to incorporate small to medium size enterprises as well as major corporations. 37 cities and 65 companies will participate in the program. The GOJ is likely to approve the expansion plan in September 2013. In October 2012, the region hosted Asia's largest aerospace trade show, "Japan Aerospace 2012" which featured a total of 665 aerospace-related firms and organizations from over 32 countries. Sixty U.S. firms exhibited the largest number outside of Japan. About one third of the firms were housed in the Foreign Commercial Service-supported pavilion, with five of them obtaining $3 million in sales and partnership agreements during the show.

Though none of its facilities were damaged during the March 11 earthquake/tsunami, Chubu Electric Power Company (CEPCO), Japan's third-largest utility and based in Chubu, was ordered by the Japanese Government (GOJ) to shut down its only nuclear plant as a precautionary measure and it has been constructing a tsunami defense wall and other related tsunami-defense facilities, even without clear GOJ guidelines. CEPCO plans to complete all of the protective measures by the spring of 2015. Even then it is uncertain whether or not the plant will be restarted due to anti-nuclear sentiment. The high costs of switching to alternative power sources threatens CEPCO's profitability and the utility is working diligently to introduce "renewable energy" use as well as to find ways to reduce costs, such as through aggressive global procurement for cost-competitive equipment and products and negotiations with American firms regarding the importation of shale gas.

A boost to Central Japan's economy should come as Central Japan Railway Company's (JR Tokai) Maglev (superconducting magnetic levitation) train efforts have progressed from the feasibility study stage to the project stage. Construction of the new "Linear New Line," which will connect Nagoya to Tokyo in 40 minutes at a maximum speed of 500 kilometers per hour (rather than current hour and 40 minutes via the "bullet train") is expected to start in FY 2014 with a budget of $50 billion (5 trillion yen). The target completion year is 2027.

Kyushu/Yamaguchi Region

The Kyushu/Yamaguchi region of southwestern Japan consists of seven prefectures on Kyushu Island (Fukuoka, Oita, Saga, Nagasaki, Kumamoto, Miyazaki, Kagoshima) and Yamaguchi Prefecture on the southern tip of Honshu, with a combined population of about 13 million. The region's $495 billion economy constitutes Japan's fourth largest economic center, representing about 8.8 percent of national GDP – comparable in size to Belgium. This region is traditionally known as Japan's gateway to Asia and enjoys extensive historical, cultural and trade ties with continental Asia, particularly South Korea, Taiwan and mainland China. The United States remains an important trading partner, but trade with Asia is predominant and Kyushu is becoming increasingly integrated into the East Asian regional economy.

Kyushu is often called "Silicon Island," "Car Island," "Food Island" and "Solar Island." The region accounts for 15 percent of Japan's total production of semiconductors and IC chips. American companies like Teradyne have facilities here. Northern Kyushu also boasts more than 14 percent of Japan's automobile output, up from 5 percent in 2000, with Toyota, Nissan and Daihatsu operating state-of-the-art final assembly facilities, and Honda has an advanced motorcycle plant in the region. Kyushu's agricultural sector produces 19 percent of Japan's agricultural output and ranks first in Japan in livestock output (about $7 billion in 2010), while the region accounts for about 25 percent of solar module production. The region also includes important industries such as steel manufacturing, ship-building and tourism. Japan's two space-launch facilities are located in Kagoshima Prefecture. A recent report shows that as of 2011, Kyushu has 247 offices of America-related companies (excluding hotels, airlines, retail outlets, insurance and food services) with almost half being pharmaceutical/medical firms, such as Baxter, Boston Scientific Japan and GE Healthcare Japan.

With a population of 1.4 million, Fukuoka City is the economic, educational and cultural center of Kyushu. While manufacturing is prevalent in Fukuoka Prefecture's surrounding areas, the city's economy is services-based, with many large retail outlets and regional headquarters offices for banking, insurance and real estate. The city enjoys an excellent transportation infrastructure, including Kyushu's principal international airport, with access to much of Asia and direct flights to Hawaii and Guam; ferry services to South Korea and China; and the new Kyushu Shinkansen bullet train line to Kagoshima. Fukuoka has over the past few years welcomed new American businesses to the Kyushu market such as Groupon Japan, Krispy Kreme Doughnuts, Delta Air Lines and Hawaiian Airlines.

The Political/Economic Section of the U.S. Consulate in Fukuoka has been actively assisting U.S. businesses and promoting their interests in the region for almost 50 years. The Consulate believes many sectors of the Kyushu/Yamaguchi economy offer promising opportunities. With its long history of openness to foreign influences, the Fukuoka area has an established reputation as a useful test market for new consumer products, services and retail concepts before they are expanded to wider areas of Japan. Major U.S. companies have established research and production facilities in electronics, computers and medical devices, and are also active in architecture, design and construction, energy, insurance and finance. A sector of growing interest is environmental products and services. Good export prospects exist in many other sectors, including building materials, medical equipment and health care products.

Okinawa

Okinawa – Japan's only subtropical region and its southernmost prefecture – comprises 160 islands stretching 623 miles from mainland Japan to Taiwan, but its 1.4 million people and $43-billion economy are concentrated on the largest island, also called Okinawa. Although Okinawa's market is relatively small by Japanese standards, there are significant opportunities for U.S. businesses, in part due to Okinawa's history as a U.S.-administered territory from 1945-1972 and the continued U.S. military presence in Okinawa. Okinawans are open to imported goods and are already familiar with many American products and American food culture. Okinawa's growing and well-educated workforce is the youngest in Japan and average wages are among the lowest in Japan. In addition, Okinawa offers a wide range of subsidies and tax incentives for investors and employers.

Because of Okinawa's unique circumstances, the central government provides an extra annual subsidy to promote economic development in the prefecture. In FY2013, this subsidy will total $3.77 billion, a 2.2 percent increase (in Japanese Yen) over FY2012, including a $2.02-billion lump-sum subsidy controlled exclusively by the local government. Officials plan to invest approximately $2.46 billion in public infrastructure in FY2013, including port upgrades, roads, and construction of the second runaway at Naha International Airport. The GOJ approved $160 million for the initial year of runway construction, and the total construction cost, including landfill, will be approximately $2.48 billion.

Tourism is Okinawa's major economic activity, and we project this approximately $4.7 billion industry will continue growing. In 2012, the total number of tourists visiting Okinawa increased 7.8 percent to 5.84 million due to new domestic airline routes launched by low-cost carriers, new foreign airline routes, and increased visits by cruise ships. The number of foreign tourists visiting Okinawa increased 34.5 percent to 380,000 million in 2012, but 93.5 percent of all tourists visiting Okinawa are mainland Japanese, which offers unique opportunities to introduce new products to Japan via Okinawa.

Although public sector spending and tourism dominate Okinawa's economy, government policy is encouraging diversification into information and communication technology (ICT), biotechnology, and air cargo. Since 1990, 263 ICT companies, some affiliated with American firms, have begun operating in Okinawa. By January 2012, these firms had created 23,741 employment opportunities, about three-quarters of which are in call centers. In addition, Okinawa Island has fewer large earthquakes than other Japanese regions, and has therefore become a popular location for business continuity and disaster recovery-related investment.

The Okinawa Institute of Science and Technology (OIST) Graduate University, a world-leading natural sciences graduate school with an annual operating budget of about $124 million, admitted its first 34 doctoral students in September 2012. OIST aims to contribute to the development of Okinawa by conducting ground-breaking research and attracting corporate research institutions and venture businesses to Okinawa, with the eventual goal of forming an intellectual and industrial cluster.

Okinawa's Naha International Airport is just two to four hours from major Asian cities such as Tokyo, Osaka, Seoul, Shanghai, Taipei, Hong Kong and Bangkok, and cargo operations at the airport go on 24 hours a day. In 2009, All Nippon Airways (ANA) took advantage of Okinawa's location in Asia to establish an international cargo hub. In 2012, Naha International Airport handled the 4th-largest amount of international air cargo in Japan after Narita, Kansai and Haneda. In FY2013, the local government approved $54.6 million to build a new logistics center in the Okinawa International Logistics Industry Zone located adjacent to the airport, and we expect this center will attract new industries to Okinawa.

Government policies are funneling new investment into renewable energy systems. The four year, "Okinawa Smart Energy Island Infrastructure Project," launched in FY2011 and concentrated in Miyakojima City and the northern part of the main island, will facilitate large-scale introduction of renewable energy sources, particularly photovoltaic solar and wind power. The 50kW ocean thermal energy conversion (OTEC) demonstration plant on the island of Kumejima will start operation in June 2013.

The U.S. Consulate General in Okinawa and the American Chamber of Commerce in Okinawa, which has over 140 members from the American and Okinawan business communities, welcome contact with American companies seeking to initiate or expand exports into this regional market. Both are well plugged into local business and public sector entities, and are working to discover commercial opportunities for U.S. firms in this dynamic regional market.

SELLING U.S. PRODUCTS AND SERVICES

USING AN AGENT OR DISTRIBUTOR

For some companies, establishing a direct presence in Japan is the best way to enter the Japanese market, but this can be an extremely expensive strategy. The use of agents or distributors is a more realistic first step for most small- or medium-sized U.S. firms, but this approach requires great care in the selection of the representative and the establishment of the terms of agreement.

U.S. firms are cautioned against trying to use contact lists for "cold calls" on prospective Japanese agents. Most Japanese business people prefer to do business with someone only when they have been properly introduced and have met face-to-face, and an introduction by a familiar "go-between" typically helps to dispel reluctance. Appropriate third parties for such introductions include other Japanese firms, U.S. companies that have successfully done business in Japan, banks, trade associations, chambers of commerce, the Japanese External Trade Organization (JETRO), U.S. state representative offices in Japan, the U.S. Department of Commerce and the U.S. Commercial Service in Japan (CS Japan).

Distributors in Japan usually cover a specific territory or industry. Importers are often appointed as sole agents for the entire country. In some cases granting exclusivity may be necessary to ensure a strong commitment by the Japanese agent towards expanding sales. However, under no circumstances should a U.S. company be pressured into granting exclusivity if there is doubt as to the ability or willingness of the Japanese agent to develop the entire market. Even if a U.S. company's ultimate goal is to offer an exclusive agency arrangement to its Japanese partner, the U.S. company may want to consider starting with any of the following good, first-step measures before moving

forward with a greater commitment: regional exclusivity, a limited term of representation, minimum sales thresholds, or qualitative indicators of sales efforts.

While the Japanese Fair Trade Commission has guidelines applicable to exclusive agency contracts, there are no statutory damages required upon termination of an agency. But given the close-knit nature of business circles and the traditional wariness towards foreign suppliers in Japan, replacing an agent or distributor could damage a U.S. firm's reputation – and even compromise its entire market strategy – if not handled sensitively. A U.S. company should at all costs avoid being viewed as lacking adequate commitment to its Japanese business relationships. Japanese agents may request "parting compensation" in the event the foreign exporter decides to dissolve a business relationship. Since this is a common practice in this market, U.S. companies should address this eventuality prior to executing a contract.

U.S. companies should be selective in choosing a Japanese business partner. Credit checks, a review of the Japanese company's industry standing and existing relations with Japanese competitors, and trust building are all part of the process. Many problems can be avoided by carrying out comprehensive due diligence.

Part of the difficulty in choosing a Japanese agent is assuring that the agent will devote sufficient attention to expanding the market share of the U.S. product. Distributors that target only limited, high-price niches, that are bound by strong ties to one particular industry group (*keiretsu*), that fail to compete directly with established Japanese products, or that are not prepared to pursue volume sales for the U.S. exporter should be avoided. U.S. firms should also be wary of distributors that handle competing lines or are subject to other potential conflicts of interest.

Another important factor that merits consideration is sales commissions paid to agents and distributors. Under an agency contract, the supplier normally invoices the agent for the same amount that the agent will sell to the customer ("back-to-back"). The supplier then pays a sales commission to the agent at the percentage provided for in the agency contract or agreement. Under a distributorship contract, the supplier sells the product to the distributor, who is then free to add to the purchase price whatever markup it chooses in determining the sales price to the customer. Commission rates vary according to the product and contract terms. Generally speaking, sales commissions range from ten to twenty percent for "spot" (one-time or irregular) transactions, and from five to ten percent for regular, ongoing business transactions. In the case of bulk materials (*e.g.,* iron ore or coal), however, commission rates are much lower, in the neighborhood of one to three percent. In the case of medical, laboratory, and scientific analytical instruments, commission rates typically are much higher, in the neighborhood of twenty percent or above.

Japan's business world is small and relatively concentrated, both politically and economically. Business relationships are formed, conducted, nurtured, and ended with an extraordinary degree of attention to appearances and decorum. Caution and diplomacy are therefore warranted if an overseas company wishes to sever its relationship with its existing Japanese agent or distributor.

Once an agent or distributor agreement is signed and the U.S. company's products gain a foothold in the Japanese market, the U.S. company may want to consider establishing a representative office in Japan (see below) to support the distributor's sales and marketing efforts and to facilitate communications with U.S. company headquarters. For businesses offering goods and/or services of a technical nature, a technical engineer is often best suited for this role because such a person generally understands product capabilities and end-user requirements. This is, of course, more of a long-term consideration, but one that U.S. companies may wish to consider when putting together their strategic mid- to long-term plan for Japan.

ESTABLISHING AN OFFICE

Before setting up an office in Japan, U.S. companies may wish to examine programs of Japan's Ministry of Economy, Trade & Industry (METI) for promoting foreign investment into Japan. Programs include loans available through the Japan Bank for International Cooperation and the Development Bank of Japan. Entry-level business support programs are provided by the Japan External Trade Organization (JETRO) as well as by some municipal and prefectural governments. Current information on investing in Japan, establishing an office, and other JETRO programs for foreign businesses can be found on JETRO's website at http://www.jetro.go.jp. Please also review Chapter 6, "Investment Climate," of this Country Commercial Guide.

Finding suitable local staff is also an important consideration for U.S. companies seeking to establish an office in Japan. There are a number of executive search firms in Japan that can help address this important issue. For a list of some of these firms, please visit the Business Service Providers section of the CS Japan website at http://export.gov/japan/bsp/index.asp, or the Membership Directory of the American Chamber of Commerce in Japan website at http://www.accj.or.jp .

FRANCHISING

Based on available data, the total number of franchise chains increased during fiscal year (FY) 2011 ended March 31, 2012 to 1,260 from 1,233 in FY2010, continuing a growth trend for two years in a row. The total number of stores and outlets were 238,838, up 2.0% or 4,692 stores from a year earlier. The total turnover amounted to ¥21.6 trillion, showing an increase of 1.1%, or ¥235.2 billion from FY2010, the second consecutive year of growth after reversing its course in FY2010. Approximately 41.7% of the total turnover at franchised outlets was from convenience stores (CVS), up from 39.6% in FY2010. Food service chains accounted for 17.4% compared to 18.1% in FY2010.

The overall franchise market in FY2011 felt the negative impacts of the March 11, 2011 earthquake and radioactive concerns over the crippled nuclear power plants. Many businesses, particularly the food service sector, were interrupted or forced to close in the directly affected regions. Even in the metropolitan areas, scheduled rolling blackouts gave a heavy blow to their business. Nonetheless, industry experts point out that CVS demonstrated resilience and grew both in terms of sales revenues and the number of stores. In the retail business, secondhand store models were on the rise, which include books, home appliances, games & home entertainment (equipment and software), CD & DVD, clothing, luxury brand products, sporting goods, toys, jewelry, and mobile phones. These trends are expected to continue in FY2012 and for the near future.

U.S. franchising has heavily influenced the development of Japan's franchise industry since the early 1970s. Although Japanese consumers are generally receptive to U.S. franchise concepts, products and services must be adjusted to local tastes and expectations to ensure success in Japan. U.S. franchising businesses have a number of ways to enter the Japanese market, such as establishing a wholly-owned subsidiary as a master franchisee with a flagship store(s), seeking a joint venture partner to develop the market in Japan, or entering into an agreement with a master franchisee.

Identifying the right business partner in Japan requires time and effort, and it can be difficult to find companies that are willing to invest in master franchise rights or to invest in business concepts that do not have a clear market or strong growth potential in Japan. Therefore, thorough market research and a long-term commitment are necessary for U.S. companies that are considering launching a franchise-based business in Japan.

DIRECT MARKETING

The scale of direct marketing in Japan, which includes mail order, telemarketing, direct response television, and Internet sales, is still modest by U.S. standards. However, sales were estimated at 5.09 trillion yen in 2011. Business-to-consumer (B2C) Internet shopping has grown rapidly, and according to a survey by the Japan Direct Marketing Association (JADMA), 67.3 percent of direct sales shoppers (15-79 years old) used the Internet to place their orders in 2011. (up by 12.8 point from 2010). The other popular methods to place orders were: via home phones (excluding mobile phones) at 36.5 percent of shoppers, and mail order, 27.4 percent.

The most popular way of gathering product information in 2011 was the Internet via computer (58.7 percent), followed by hardcopy catalogs (32.1 percent) and Internet via mobile devices (21.9 percent). Young people are particularly adept at gathering product information via mobile devices. 63.1 percent of young women aged 29 or younger report using mobile devices to get product information. Since 66 percent of Japanese smartphone owners are women in their 20's, this is a booming channel for marketing to this segment. Japanese direct marketers use websites optimized for both PC and mobiles to reach consumers. U.S. exporters wishing to sell products targeting young Japanese will need to optimize their platforms for mobile access.

Because of ongoing revisions to credit card and e-commerce laws that provide increased protection for consumers in Japan, including protection against identity theft, Japanese consumers have less hesitation than in the past to buy online. C.O.D. (cash on delivery), payments at convenience stores (where Japanese are able to pay various bills), and credit cards were the three major payment methods in 2011.

Shopping from hard copy or online foreign catalogs is referred to as “personal importing” in Japan. Personal importing surged in the mid-1990s due to the novelty of the concept, a very strong yen, and a growing appreciation of foreign consumer goods. Although providing adequate customer service and handling product returns challenged those firms that did not have in-country representation, many U.S. companies enjoyed an enormous expansion of orders from Japan.

There may be good opportunities for U.S. companies that can offer Japanese consumers high quality products with unique attributes. Products Japanese consumers currently order from abroad include apparel, accessories, books, magazines, toiletries, and cosmetics.

JOINT VENTURES/LICENSING

U.S. companies often consider joint ventures or licensing agreements when considering entering the Japanese market. For the latest information on regulations and procedures for establishing an operation in Japan, please visit the JETRO website at http://www.jetro.go.jp.

Although the vast majority of U.S. commercial exports to Japan do not require export licenses, the export of any form of technical data from the United States can be subject to U.S. export control laws. In such a case, a thorough review of the U.S. Department of Commerce's Export Administration Regulations (EAR) should precede the signing of any licensing agreement. To learn more about the EAR, please visit the following website:

Government Printing Office's EAR database:

http://www.access.gpo.gov/bis/ear/ear_data.html

SELLING TO THE GOVERNMENT

On January 1, 1996, Japan implemented the WTO Agreement on Government Procurement (GPA) in an effort to expand opportunities for foreign firms and increase international competition in government procurement in Japan. The Agreement extended coverage to include the procurement of services as well as procurement throughout Japan by what are referred to as "sub-central government entities." These entities include all prefectural (regional) governments in Japan, major cities and designated municipalities, and a host of other quasi-governmental agencies, corporations, companies and authorities.

Government procurement contracts covered by the Agreement must have a value not less than the thresholds (denominated in special drawing rights of the International Monetary Fund or "SDRs") specified by the Agreement, and include the procurement of products and services by purchase, lease, or rental by the agencies and organizations subject to the Agreement. Under revisions to the GPA, the present voluntary specified threshold for procurement by central government entities of 100,000 SDRs (except for construction and architectural, engineering and other technical services) will become obligatory in April 2013. For sub-central government entities, with the same exceptions noted above, Japan's voluntary threshold is 200,000 SDRs.

There are three types of government tendering procedures in Japan covered by the Agreement: 1) open tendering; 2) selective tendering; and 3) limited or single tendering.

Under an open tender, the procuring entity publishes an invitation for qualified suppliers to participate in the tendering process. Contracts are awarded to the bidder that offers the greatest advantage in terms of price. Selective tendering is done in cases when the number of potential suppliers is limited (due to the nature of the contract), or when open tendering is otherwise regarded as inappropriate. In this case, the procuring entity designates those companies it considers capable from a list of qualified suppliers and invites them to bid. Again, the contract is awarded to the bidder with the best offer in terms of tendered price and other required criteria. Limited or single tenders are used in a variety of cases where products or services cannot be obtained through open or selective procurement procedures, where there has been an absence of bids in response to a public notice, where it has been determined there is a need for protection of exclusive rights such as patents, or where the procurement is of extreme urgency.

Open tender and selective tender invitations are published in Japan's official (central) government procurement gazette or *Kanpō* – http://kanpou.npb.go.jp (Japanese only) – or in an equivalent regional-level or local publication. The procuring entity publishes the invitation to tender at least 50 days (40 days is required by the GPA) in advance of the closing date for receipt of bids. In order to increase access opportunities for foreign suppliers, as a voluntary measure, many procuring entities publish notices on the use of limited (closed) tenders at least 20 days in advance of the awarding of a contract. When the tender is announced on open bids, the type and quantity of products, time limits set for submission of bids, and names and contact data of the procuring entity are published within the announcement in English. Notices on selective tendering also outline the requirements necessary for firms to be designated for participation in the tender bidding process. Most companies find it useful to contact the procuring entity directly with any specific questions before a tender is submitted for consideration. Recent revisions to the GPA Agreement allow for modern procurement procedures such as electronic bidding.

Japan's Ministry of Foreign Affairs (MOFA) hosts a Government Procurement Seminar each spring where central government procuring entities explain their procurement plans for the fiscal year. Individual ministries sometimes follow this with their own seminars. Notice of these meetings can also be found in the *Kanpō* gazette.

U.S. suppliers can find information about Japanese government procurement on the Japan External Trade Organization (JETRO) website at (http://www.jetro.go.jp/en/matching/procurement), which includes an online database of government procurement notices and invitations published in the National Printing Bureau's

"Official Gazette." Users can search by publication date, product/service category as well as location. For additional information including suggestions for accessing the government procurement market in Japan please visit the MOFA website (http://www.mofa.go.jp/policy/economy/procurement), which maintains a detailed list of contact points for entities covered by the Agreement.

Potential suppliers must first be qualified by the procuring agency and registered on the tendering agency's permanent list of qualified suppliers. Each procuring entity in Japan specifies the qualifications required of any potential supplier participating in open or selective tenders. Procuring entities are allowed to review a company's capacity to implement a contract, including the scale of business and past business performance. In most cases, Japanese subsidiaries, agents, or distributors of a U.S. company can register on behalf of the firm. Documents required for qualification are set out in the public notice, but typically include: an application form, registration certificate, company history, financial statements, and tax payment certificate. The qualification is usually valid for one to two years.

Sealed bids must be submitted to the designated location by the closing date and time specified in the tender notice. Although a five percent guarantee fee is stipulated, payment is usually waived since those participating are normally pre-qualified. If there are tenders made by unqualified suppliers or in violation of the tender requirements, the procuring entity will rule them invalid and notify the unsuccessful bidder. The contract is normally awarded to the lowest qualified bid and bidders are informed of the result in writing by the procuring entity.

Pursuant to the 1996 GPA, Japan has established a mechanism to process complaints about procurements by entities other than sub-central government entities. The Office of Government Procurement Review (OGPR), within the Prime Minister's Office, implements the provisions of the WTO Agreement regarding bid challenge procedures. For procurement by central government entities the Government Procurement Review Board processes and considers complaints in accordance with the specific procedures set out by the OGPR. Prefectural governments and designated cities have established their respective procedures to process complaints regarding procurement subject to the Agreement. Complaints by qualified bidders may be filed with the Secretariat of the Board in the Office for Government Procurement Challenge System (CHANS). For additional information, please visit http://www5.cao.go.jp/access/english/chans_main_e.html .

Further information on recent developments regarding Japanese government procurement can be found in Japan's most recent submission to the WTO Trade Policy Review Mechanism: http://www.wto.org/english/tratop_e/tpr_e/tp311_e.htm

DEFENSE PROCUREMENT

For Japan's Fiscal Year 2013, which began in March 2013, the Japanese defense budget was the fifth largest in the world and second largest in Asia at US$58.6 billion.

Japanese defense expenditure is mainly driven by the threat from North Korea's long-range ballistic missiles and China's maritime expansion. The Japanese Ministry of Defense (MOD) spends most of its budget on salaries, operational expenses, training, and development. Capital expenditure represents the second largest share, and includes the procurement of military equipment, material and R&D expenses, aircraft acquisition and shipbuilding.

Over recent decades, Japanese defense expenditure as a percentage of GDP has accounted for 1%, and this is expected to remain stable for the coming five-year period. Japan's defense posture and procurement strategy is grounded in a pair of foundational documents, the "National Defense Program Guidelines (NDPG) for FY 2011 and Beyond" and the "Mid-Term Defense Program, FY2011-2015 (MTDP)". Both documents were last approved by Japan's Cabinet in December 2010 under leadership of the now-opposition Democratic Party of Japan (DPJ), and are undergoing a review by the new Abe Administration, the results of which should be promulgated in December 2013.

The FY 2012 supplementary budget approved by the Abe cabinet included spending on defense. MOD requested US$2.4 billion for telecommunications equipment, base renovations, and missile defense capabilities. The Japan Coast Guard, part of the Ministry of Land, Infrastructure, Transport, and Tourism, also requested funds for six additional patrol ships. Also, the MOD requested US$1.3 billion more in fiscal year 2013 than it did last year. The Policy Research Council of the governing Liberal Democratic Party (LDP) supported this request in a highly publicized statement on January 7, 2013. This represented the first increase in eleven years for MOD.

Foreign Military Sales (FMS) by U.S. companies to Japan are administered by the Defense Security Cooperation Agency (DSCA), which is part of the U.S. Department of Defense. The Mutual Defense Assistance Office (MDAO) at the U.S. Embassy in Tokyo is the in-country office for FMS. All transactions are initiated by a request from the Government of Japan for price and availability data for a specific item or service. Direct Commercial Sales (DCS) are handled by Japanese defense trading firms, distributors and agents.

The Equipment Procurement and Construction Office (EPCO) of the JMOD is charged with the central procurement of military equipment and services valued at over 1.5 million yen ($17,071 at 87.78 yen/USD) for such items as firearms, guided weapons, telecommunications instruments, ships, aircraft, vehicles, machinery, ammunitions, foods, fuel, textile, and other necessary materials. EPCO is also charged with overseeing implementation plans for construction work at Self-Defense Force (SDF) bases. Regional Defense Bureaus, also part of the JMOD, handle military items of 1.5 million yen or less and other local supplies.

As with any other government procurement, potential vendors to the JMOD and SDF are required to apply for and register with the EPCO. It is recommended that potential U.S. military equipment makers partner with Japanese trading firms, distributors or agents to conduct business with the Japanese military. A Japanese partner is also helpful with the local language and unique cultural and business practices.

The Japan Ministry of Defense (JMOD) http://www.mod.go.jp/e/index.html

Defense Security Cooperation Agency (DSCA) http://www.dsca.mil/

Equipment Procurement and Construction Office (EPCO) http://www.epco.mod.go.jp/en/

DISTRIBUTION AND SALES CHANNELS

Distribution channels in Japan have undergone much consolidation over the past two decades. Many of the traditional channels have been streamlined, yet complexities still exist. Paradoxically, in some sectors, cutting edge technologies have been applied to channels that nevertheless retain significant structural inefficiency and redundancy. Channels vary significantly between consumer goods and industrial products. For detailed information on distribution channels for specific products and sectors, it is best to contact the relevant Commercial Specialist at CS Japan. Contact information can be found on the CS Japan website at http://export.gov/japan.

International Courier Services for Food Samples

In 2010, three major international couriers began enforcing a policy of not accepting packages that contain foods requiring phytosanitary certificates. This policy could potentially affect the ability of U.S. exporters to ship product samples to Japan. The reason for this policy shift is that these couriers are now refusing to handle any items involving animal or plant quarantine (including dried fruit and nuts) for express/overnight service since one parcel containing items subject to quarantine regulations can delay a whole container containing hundreds of parcels for about two hours until the package with the phytosanitary certificate is cleared. The carriers have decided that they cannot afford the delay in their express service but it should be noted that the carrier's policies only affect express/overnight shipments. These couriers will still accept packages that require phytosanitary certificate as regular air freight services that may take an extra few days to be delivered. For more information please see the following report afford the delay in their express service but it should be noted that the carrier's policies only affect express/overnight shipments. These couriers will still accept packages that require phytosanitary certificate as regular air freight services that may take an extra few days to be delivered. For more information please see the following report afford the delay in their express service but it should be noted that the carrier's policies only affect express/overnight shipments.

These couriers will still accept packages that require phytosanitary certificate as regular air freight services that may take an extra few days to be delivered. For more information please see the following report

SELLING FACTORS/TECHNIQUES

As in the United States, sustained personal contact with customers is usually essential for successful market entry and expansion in Japan. Having a visiting U.S. company representative accompany the firm's Japanese agent or distributor on visits to existing or potential customers strengthens the potential for sales. Such joint sales calls demonstrate commitment to clients and provide unparalleled opportunities to obtain market feedback.

Learning how to negotiate and maintain relationships with Japanese face-to-face can significantly increase a U.S. company's chances for success in the market. Japanese language skills and familiarity with the nation's culture and etiquette can be invaluable. Be prepared to attend after-hours social events: these informal gatherings go a long way towards establishing mutual trust and understanding between new partners. It has been said that many business deals in Japan are made "after five," though this does not mitigate the important roles that price, quality and after-sales service play in making an export sale.

Initial contact between Japanese firms is usually formal and made at the executive level, with more detailed negotiations often delegated to the working level. Typically, the point of an initial meeting is to allow the parties to become acquainted, to establish the interest of the calling party, and to allow both sides an opportunity to size each other up. Don't expect too much from a first visit – sometimes the actual business subject may be overtaken by more mundane topics. A series of meetings with a large number of Japanese company representatives is common, as part of the "sizing up" process. Business negotiations may proceed slowly, as the Japanese side might prefer to avoid an agreement rather than risk being criticized later for making a mistake.

While many Japanese business executives speak some English, a skilled and well-briefed interpreter is essential to prevent communication problems. A good interpreter is worth the expense. Firms that choose to skimp on or forego this expense not only significantly increase their chances for miscommunication, but also risk sending a message that they lack commitment to their Japanese counterpart and to the Japanese market. Though there are some U.S. firms that do business in Japan without a signed contract, the use of written contracts between U.S. and Japanese firms is an accepted practice. Contracts satisfy tax, customs, and other legal requirements. Japanese companies prefer shorter and more general contracts as opposed to lengthy, detailed documents spelling out every right and obligation in detail. Personal contact and relationships are important in Japan, and a contract should be viewed as just one element of a broader effort to create a mutual understanding of obligations and expectations.

ELECTRONIC COMMERCE

A website is a must for any business looking to break into the market in Japan. There are some key elements that should be incorporated into your website to gain familiarity and trust among potential Japanese buyers. Details in the "About Us" section of your website are especially important since this is a main information source that potential Japanese buyers will review. An "About Us" page for a U.S. website usually contains the company's mission statement, description of the company's business, management bios and contact information. In Japan, however, an "About Us" page includes more details such as a section called "Corporate Profile" in which corporate information such as the official company name, date of establishment, capital stock, revenue, board member names, number of employees, business partners, industry associations, banking, and the period of accounting are included. This additional information is not a requirement in Japan but many companies, including small businesses, disclose this information to help build trust and legitimacy with potential customers.

According to statistics published in August 2012

(http://www.meti.go.jp/policy/it_policy/statistics/outlook/ie_outlook.htm) by the Japanese Ministry of Economy, Trade and Industry (METI), the market size of business-to-business (B2B) electronic commerce in Japan in 2011 was ¥258 trillion ($3.2 trillion), and the market size of the business-to-consumer (B2C) electronic commerce market in the same period was ¥8.5 trillion ($106.7 billion). For cross-border e-commerce, METI estimates U.S. exports to Japan via e-commerce to be ¥47.1 billion ($591 Million) in 2011.

There are few open B2B sites for foreign exporters in Japan, with most Japanese B2B sites focusing on domestic business transactions. Japan's international B2B site is: http://www.export-japan.com/ . On the other hand, B2C ecommerce sites are flourishing, and include Amazon Japan, Yahoo! Japan, and Japan's largest e-commerce site, Rakuten. The growth of online entertainment sites is also notable in Japan, especially in the mobile arena. Japan's major providers of online games are:

GREE: http://developer.gree.co.jp/en/

DeNA: http://dena.jp/intl/

U.S. firms interested in ecommerce might consider listing on the Japan External Trade Organization (JETRO)'s business matchmaking database known as TTPP (http://www.jetro.go.jp/ttppoas/howto/index.html#). Registration is free and may be done in English.

TRADE PROMOTION AND ADVERTISING

Unless a U.S. company is setting up operations directly in Japan, the company's agent or distributor in Japan will likely execute the advertising and marketing effort. It is quite expensive to advertise in Japan. Because of this, local firms often look for some type of cooperation from their overseas suppliers. Willingness to support this effort sends a strong signal of commitment to the Japanese market.

Not all companies can afford to place advertisements in Japan's major national daily newspapers or commercials on Japanese television. Regional and local newspapers and television stations, and daily sports newspapers are less expensive and might make sense for a product with strong potential in a specific region or demographic segment. A more affordable option for small- to medium-size or new-to-market U.S. companies might be advertising in some of Japan's roughly 4,500 weekly or monthly magazines

These publications often represent a cost-effective means to reach a specific target consumer – whether gourmet or gardener, cyclist or camper. For industrial and commercial products, Japan's many industrial daily, weekly or monthly newspapers and trade journals might offer the best advertising options.

Japan's railways, as the primary transportation option for commuters in major cities, carry hundreds of millions of passengers every year. Therefore, transit advertising should not be overlooked. Transit advertisements can be found inside commuter rail cars, buses, and in stations. Advertisements inside trains and buses include hanging flyers, framed posters, stickers, and flat-panel video.

Internet advertising and email newsletters (generally called "mail magazines" or "*merumaga*") have become popular in Japan. American companies considering using such methods in Japan should be aware of Japan's Law on Regulation of Transmission of Specified Electronic Mail: unlike the "opt out" system in the United States in which the sender must stop sending to recipients who choose not to receive future emails, Japanese law requires use of an "opt in" system in which email can only be sent to people who have agreed in advance to receive it.

Japan's media primarily arrange advertising placements by working with advertising agencies, and typically do not deal directly with advertisers themselves. Generally, mood or image advertising achieves the best results. Hard-sell, combative advertising is considered to be in bad taste and is usually counterproductive, but comparative advertising is becoming more accepted in an increasingly competitive and tight economy.

U.S. exporters can benefit from Japan's extensive trade event circuit: not only in Tokyo and Osaka, but also in the huge regional economies and industrial centers where many of Japan's international conferences, seminars, and trade shows take place. U.S. Department of Commerce-certified trade shows and trade missions, as well as events sponsored by U.S. states and industrial organizations, are an excellent means of gaining exposure in the Japanese market. For a listing of U.S. Department of Commerce supported events in Japan, please visit our website: http://export.gov/japan/tradeevents/index.asp

PRICING

Tough economic times have made price an increasingly important consideration for Japanese consumers. Traditionally, many people made their buying decisions based on a product's attributes, quality, and brand name and they were willing to pay more for superior quality, reputation, or reliability. However, Japanese consumers are now more price-conscious and notions such as bargains and value have become mainstream. If an imported product can be purchased more inexpensively than a domestic product, consumers will be interested. This has proven to many Japanese that U.S. products can be affordable and offer quality that equals or even exceeds that of Japanese goods.

The strength of the yen, streamlining of distribution channels, and Japanese economic reforms have recently helped open doors for U.S. products by improving their price competitiveness. However, landed cost is only one part of a total pricing scheme and should not be the only consideration for U.S. firms interested in exporting to Japan.

Distribution markups often cause imports to price at levels far higher than comparable domestic products. For instance, shipping costs between the port of Osaka and Tokyo have been shown to be much higher than shipping costs from the U.S. West Coast to Osaka. A good example is imported U.S. apparel products, where street prices are often three to four times FOB.

Japanese manufacturers traditionally set prices at each level of the distribution chain and enforce compliance using complicated rebate systems. Such price maintenance has recently come under pressure from consumers who are demanding lower prices, and from manufacturers who themselves find the rebate system burdensome. As distribution practices have undergone reform, costs have come down and distributors have gained additional flexibility in selecting and purchasing items.

Distribution of imported goods has also traditionally followed a multi-layered system, with established lines of product flow and pricing structures that vary according to the types of services provided by the importer or wholesaler (e.g., inventory, advertisement costs, packaging costs, financing, acceptance of unsold/returned goods, etc.). As with the distribution of Japanese manufactured goods, increased price sensitivity among Japanese consumers has led to more and more middlemen either being forced to cut their markups or eliminated from the distribution chain altogether.

Some Japanese retailers now import products directly in order to offer lower retail prices. However, U.S. suppliers should understand that retailers usually import smaller quantities, and other importers and wholesalers usually are uninterested in representing products that are imported directly by retailers.

Finally, U.S. exporters should also consider yen/dollar fluctuations in their product pricing and sales strategies. Starting in early 2013 and continuing through midyear, the yen has fallen significantly against the dollar, limiting the price competitiveness of U.S. goods.

SALES SERVICE/CUSTOMER SUPPORT

High-quality, highly-responsive product service and customer support throughout the sales cycle are crucially important in Japan. This begins with establishing a close working relationship with, and long-term commitment to, a U.S. exporter's potential Japanese partners. Every effort should be made to answer technical questions in detail, to ensure that delivery dates are met, and to maintain absolute clarity regarding all issues from initial order through shipment and delivery. Problems most often arise from misunderstandings, lack of communication, language difficulties, and differing business practices.

The arrival times and condition of shipments are critical. Shipments should arrive on time, they should be well packed, and they must not be damaged upon arrival. Customs documentation should be complete and accurate; if it is not, the entry of the merchandise could be delayed or, in certain cases, the merchandise might be returned to the sender. Japanese buyers are highly concerned with the quality of packing and poor packaging may lead to market entry problems. Missed deadlines and the arrival of goods damaged through poor packaging and shipping practices are interpreted as a "message" from, and about, the supplier.

PROTECTING YOUR INTELLECTUAL PROPERTY

Japan generally provides strong IPR protection and enforcement. Any U.S. company doing business in Japan should have an intellectual property plan and register their intellectual property prior to entering the market. The Japanese registration of patents and trademarks is on a first-in-time, first-in-right basis as opposed to the U.S. first-to-invent system which means that U.S. companies need to be especially diligent in protecting their intellectual property. The U.S. Government works with the Government of Japan to improve the intellectual property environment, however, rights holders should take the basic steps to secure and enforce their intellectual property in a timely manner.

Protecting Your Intellectual Property in Japan:

Several general principles are important for effective management of intellectual property ("IP") rights in Japan. First, it is important to have an overall strategy to protect your IP. Second, IP is protected differently in Japan than in the U.S. Third; rights must be registered and enforced in Japan, under local laws. Your U.S. trademark and patent registrations will not protect you in Japan. There is no such thing as an "international copyright" that will automatically protect an author's writings throughout the entire world. Protection against unauthorized use in a particular country depends, basically, on the national laws of that country. However, most countries do offer copyright protection to foreign works under certain conditions, and these conditions have been greatly simplified by international copyright treaties and conventions.

Registration of patents and trademarks is on a first-in-time, first-in-right basis, so you should consider applying for trademark and patent protection even before selling your products or services in the Japan market. It is vital that companies understand that intellectual property is primarily a private right and that the U.S. government generally cannot enforce rights for private individuals in Japan. It is the responsibility of the rights' holders to register, protect, and enforce their rights where relevant, retaining their own counsel and advisors. Companies may wish to seek advice from local attorneys or IP consultants who are experts in Japan law. The U.S. Commercial Service can provide a list of local lawyers upon request: http://japan.usembassy.gov/e/acs/tacs-7113.html .

While the U.S. Government stands ready to assist, there is little we can do if the rights holders have not taken these fundamental steps necessary to securing and enforcing their IP in a timely fashion. Moreover, in many countries, rights holders who delay enforcing their rights on a mistaken belief that the USG can provide a political resolution to a legal problem may find that their rights have been eroded or abrogated due to legal doctrines such as statutes of limitations, laches, estoppel, or unreasonable delay in prosecuting a law suit. In no instance should U.S. Government advice be seen as a substitute for the obligation of a rights holder to promptly pursue its case.

It is always advisable to conduct due diligence on potential partners. Negotiate from the position of your partner and give your partner clear incentives to honor the contract. A good partner is an important ally in protecting IP rights. Consider carefully, however, whether to permit your partner to register your IP rights on your behalf. Doing so may create a risk that your partner will list itself as the IP owner and fail to transfer the rights should the partnership end. Keep an eye on your cost structure and reduce the margins (and the incentive) of would-be bad actors. Projects and sales in Japan require constant attention. Work with legal counsel familiar with Japan laws to create a solid contract that includes non-compete clauses, and confidentiality/non-disclosure provisions. It is also recommended that small and medium-size companies understand the importance of working together with trade associations and organizations to support efforts to protect IP and stop counterfeiting. There are a number of these organizations, both Japan or U.S.-based. These include:

- The U.S. Chamber of Commerce and the local American Chamber of Commerce in Japan (ACCJ)
- National Association of Manufacturers (NAM)

- International Intellectual Property Alliance (IIPA)

- International Trademark Association (INTA)

- The Coalition Against Counterfeiting and Piracy

- International Anti-Counterfeiting Coalition (IACC)

- Pharmaceutical Research and Manufacturers of America (PhRMA)

- Biotechnology Industry Organization (BIO)

IP RESOURCES

A wealth of information on protecting IP is freely available to U.S. rights holders. Some excellent resources for companies regarding intellectual property include the following:

- For information about patent, trademark, or copyright issues -- including enforcement issues in the U.S. and other countries -- call the STOP! Hotline: **1-866-999-HALT** or register at www.StopFakes.gov .

- For more information about registering trademarks and patents (both in the U.S. as well as in foreign countries), contact the U.S. Patent and Trademark Office (USPTO) at: **1-800-786-9199**.

- For more information about registering for copyright protection in the U.S., contact the U.S. Copyright Office at: **1-877-476-0778** (toll free) or **1-202-707-5959**.

- For more information about how to evaluate, protect, and enforce intellectual property rights and how these rights may be important for businesses, a free online training program is available at www.StopFakes.gov .

- For U.S. small and medium-size companies, the Department of Commerce offers a "SME IP Advisory Program" available through the American Bar Association that provides one hour of free IP legal advice for companies with concerns in Brazil, China, Egypt, India and Russia. For details and to register, visit: Brazil, China, Egypt, India and Russia. For details and to register, visit: Brazil, China, Egypt, India and Russia. For details and to register, visit:

- For information on obtaining and enforcing intellectual property rights and market-specific IP Toolkits visit: www.StopFakes.gov . This site is linked to the USPTO website for registering trademarks and patents (both in the U.S. as well as in foreign countries), the U.S. Customs & Border Protection website to record registered trademarks and copyrighted works (to assist customs in blocking imports of IP-infringing products) and allows you to register for Webinars on protecting IP.

DUE DILIGENCE

A U.S. company resident in Japan is not legally required to use a Japanese attorney for filings, registrations, contracts or other legal documents, which can be prepared by in-house staff, but retaining a competent Japanese attorney *(bengoshi),* patent practitioner *(benrishi),* or other legal professional is a practical necessity. A U.S. company not resident in Japan should also retain competent Japanese counsel. Projects and sales in Japan require constant attention. Legal counsel familiar with Japan laws may assist with creating solid contracts that include non-compete clauses and confidentiality/non-disclosure provisions, among others.

Japanese companies may be affected by downsizing and bankruptcies. Importers, wholesalers and distributors can find it difficult to obtain trade financing in the present environment. Banks in Japan have become less inclined to provide credit to small- and medium-sized enterprises of all types. Larger companies, especially those with excessive debt, may also experience problems obtaining financing.

The U.S. Embassy in Tokyo encounters trade dispute cases of all kinds. It has become more common for small- and medium-sized Japanese trading companies to run into payment problems. For information about structuring payment options, see *How Do I Get Paid (Methods of Payment)* under Chapter 7, Trade and Project Financing.

As a result of these concerns, U.S. companies are advised to establish due diligence procedures and check the *bona fides* of their Japanese agents, distributors and/or customers. To assist with this need, the U.S. Commercial Service in Japan provides the International Company Profile (ICP) service designed to help U.S. companies evaluate potential business partners. For information on the ICP and other services available from the Commercial Service in Japan, please visit our website: http://export.gov/japan/ (Please note that the ICP is not intended to be a substitute for a comprehensive due diligence review to meet obligations under the Foreign Corrupt Practices Act of 1977.)

LOCAL PROFESSIONAL SERVICES

CS Japan's website features lists of business service providers in different fields who may be of assistance to U.S. firms doing business with Japan. Although these lists are not comprehensive, and inclusion does not in any sense constitute an endorsement or recommendation by the U.S. Commercial Service or the U.S. Government, they are a useful starting point for firms that need professional services in Japan. Please visit the Business Service Providers section of our website at: Business Service Providers section of our website at: Business Service Providers section of our website at:

WEB RESOURCES

As mentioned above:

www.StopFakes.gov

http://www.abanet.org/intlaw/intlproj/iprprogram_consultation.html

Information on investing in Japan, establishing an office, and other programs for foreign businesses:

Japan External Trade Organization (JETRO)

http://www.jetro.go.jp/en/invest/setting_up

Information on business service providers in Japan:

U.S. Commercial Service, U.S. Embassy, Tokyo

http://export.gov/japan/bsp/index.asp

Foreign Agricultural Service (FAS), U.S. Embassy, Tokyo

http://www.usdajapan.org

FAS Trade Lead System

U.S. Embassy, American Citizen Services

http://tokyo.usembassy.gov/e/tacs-main.html

Information on Japanese government procurement:

Japan External Trade Organization (JETRO)

http://www.jetro.go.jp/en/matching/procurement

Office for Government Procurement Challenge System (CHANS)

Cabinet Office

http://www5.cao.go.jp/access/english/chans_main_e.html

Japan's Submission to WTO Trade Policy Review Mechanism
http://www.wto.org/english/tratop_e/tpr_e/tp311_e.htm

B-to-B e-commerce marketplaces:

Trade Tie-up Promotion Program by Japan External Trade Organization

http://www.jetro.go.jp/ttppoas/

Connect with the Commercial Service in Japan:

https://twitter.com/BuyUSAJapan

LEADING SECTORS FOR U.S. EXPORT AND INVESTMENT

Aircraft and related parts, equipment and services

This is a best prospect industry sector for this country. Includes a market overview and trade data.

Last Published: *2/28/2016*

	2013	2014	2015 (estimated)	2016 (estimated)
Total Market Size	15,717	16,512	17,337	18,204
Total Local Production	13,576	14,734	15,471	16,244
Total Exports	9,980	10,450	10,973	11,521
Total Imports	12,121	12,228	12,839	13,481
Imports from the U.S.	8,350	8,294	8,709	9,144
Exchange Rate: ¥/$1	97.60	105.74	105.74	105.74

Notes: 2015 and 2016 estimates are based on projections provided by the Society of Japanese Aerospace Companies (SJAC). SJAC forecasted a 5% annual increase for the next 5-6 years. Japanese firms participate in various programs with Boeing and Airbus who have many backorders.

Japan continues to offer a lucrative market for imported aircraft, aircraft parts, and engines. U.S. firms have an overwhelming presence in the market due to long-standing relationships, some spanning over 50 years, with domestic manufacturers and trading firms. U.S. firms are presented with opportunities in the market as the Japanese industry undertakes international projects, develops transport and patrol aircraft for defense, and develops small jets and small jet engines for civil aviation.

In the civil aircraft market, Japanese manufacturers such as Mitsubishi Heavy Industries, Kawasaki Heavy Industries (KHI), and Fuji Heavy Industries, supply about 35% of the content for the Boeing's 787. It was announced in April 2014 that Japan will supply about 20% of the content for the Boeing 777X. The Japanese firms are starting to invest and expand their facilities in order to meet this new demand.

Mitsubishi Heavy Industries established Mitsubishi Aircraft Corporation (MAC) in April 2008 to undertake the design, type certification, procurement, sales and marketing and customer support for the Mitsubishi Regional Jet (MRJ). MAC announced in October 2007 that it selected Pratt & Whitney to supply Geared Turbofan engines for the aircraft. This next-generation engine will make the planes 20-30% more efficient and about 15% cheaper to operate than conventional regional jets. Other U.S. manufacturers such as Parker Aerospace (hydraulic systems), Hamilton Sundstrand Corporation (electrical power system), and Rockwell Collins (flight control system) are also suppliers for the MRJ. As of April 2015, MAC plans to conduct the MRJ's first flight in the second half of 2015.

In the defense sector, Japan adopted new principles and guidelines on arms exports, the first major overhaul in nearly half a century of its arms embargo policy. Japan will now allow arms exports only if they serve the purpose of contributing to international cooperation and its security interests. The development of the P-1, the next maritime patrol aircraft, and the C-2, the next transport aircraft, began in 2001 with the intent of replacing the P-3C and C-1, and now both models shift to mass production together. KHI is selected as prime contractor for two aircrafts, both being developed in parallel.

Sub-Sector Best Prospects

Commercial aircraft and aircraft engines, helicopters, aircraft parts and supplies, avionics.

Opportunities

Japan Aerospace International Exhibition
Location: Tokyo
Dates: October 12-15, 2016
English language website: http://www.japanaerospace.jp/eng/Index
Description: Japan's only air show held every four years, Japan Aerospace 2012 was held in Nagoya, Japan, with 655 companies from 33 countries including 69 U.S. firms. The U.S. Commercial Service Japan provided on-site counseling to the U.S. Pavilion exhibitors at the previous show.

Web Resources

Japan Civil Aviation Bureau (Ministry of Land, Infrastructure, Transport and Tourism)
Web: http://www.mlit.go.jp/en/koku/inddex.html
Society of Japanese Aerospace Companies (SJAC)
Web: http://www.sjac.or.jp/en_index.html
Japan Business Aviation Association (JBAA)
Web: http://www.jbaa.org/english/index_e.html

CS Japan Contact:
Ms. Sayoko Koto, Commercial Specialist
Sayoko.Koto@trade.gov

ANALYTICAL SCIENTIFIC INSTRUMENTS

Analytical Scientific Instruments

	2012	2013	2014
Total Market Size	3,397.9	3,073.3	2,913.4
Total Local Production	5,195.6	4,131.9	4,424.4
Total Exports	3,168.9	2,500.1	2,763.2
Total Imports	1,371.2	1,441.5	1252.2
Imports from the U.S.	382.1	407.0	342.1
Exchange Rate: ¥/$1	83.01	101.52	110.1

Unit: $ millions
Analytical and scientific instruments play vital roles in a wide range of applications in Japan's manufacturing and service industries, including R&D, production, inspection, and monitoring

processes.

According to the Japan Analytical Instruments Manufacturers' Association (JAIMA), the annual production of some 200 member firms in fiscal year 2014 amounted to ¥487.1 billion. Over the past several years imported analytical instruments have accounted for over 40% of the total market.

Many American analytical instruments manufacturers have had success in the Japanese market. American analytical instrument makers have steadily expanded their share of the total market from 11.2% in 2012, to 13.2% in 2013, and up to 13.4% in 2014.

While many American firms with a long history in the market have established their own sales offices in Japan, new-to-market American firms are advised to consider partnering with local agents or distributors with industry knowledge and sales networks to market their products to end-users in Japan.

Sub-Sector Best Prospects

Analytical instruments for advanced diagnostic: genetic analysis, protein marker searching, metabolic marker searching, and cell research.

Bioresearch: genomics, proteomics and metabolomics.

Preventive healthcare products to serve patients with more tailor-made treatments.

Environmental and food safety: advanced instruments, reagents, software and other products.

Opportunities

Event: JASIS 2015
Date: September 2–4, 2015
Venue: Makuhari Messe, Chiba, Japan
Web: http://www.jasis.jp/2014/en/topics/info-of-2015.html

JASIS is a major annual industry event which is comprised of exhibits, seminars and conferences and is comparable to the U.S. PITTCON in areas of scientific and laboratory instruments for government, academia and industry users.

In 2014, JASIS 2014 registered about 23,794 visitors, ranking it second in attendance in JASIS history. Visitors included:

- 50.6% were users of analytical and scientific instruments
- 12.3% were analytical instrument distributors
- 17.2% were analytical instrument manufacturers

These visitors were from a wide variety of industry sectors including:

- Electronics, electric, machinery: 17.2%
- Trading, commerce: 12.9%;
- Technical service: 8.2%
- Education 7.2%
- Chemical products 6.8%

- Government, pharmaceuticals, reagents, cosmetics, food industry, steel and metals, automotive, construction, transportation, rubber, plastics, petrochemicals, etc.

Event: Measurement and Control Show 2015 Tokyo
Date: December 2-4, 2015
Venue: Tokyo Big Sight, Tokyo, Japan
Web: http://jemima.or.jp/tokyo/en/#exhibit

Event: INTERPHEX Japan 2015
Date: July 1–3, 2015
Venue: Tokyo Big Sight, Tokyo, Japan
Web: http://www.interphex.jp/en/

Event: nano tech 2016 (International Nanotechnology Exhibition & Conference)
Date: January 27-29, 2016
Venue: Tokyo Big Sight, Tokyo, Japan
Web: http://www.nanotechexpo.jp/index.html

Web Resources

JAIMA, Japan Analytical Instruments Manufacturers' Association
www.jaima.or.jp/en/

CS Japan Contact:
Ms. Akiko Sugiura, Commercial Assistant
Akiko.Sugiura@trade.gov

CLOUD COMPUTING

Cloud Computing Market Size Unit: USD million

	2012	2013	2014 (estimate)	2015 (forecast)
Total Market Size	1,083	1,350	1,804	2,100
Exchange Rate: ¥/$1	100	100	100	100

Data Sources: Ministry of Internal Affairs and Communications and IDC Japan

According to analyst reports, the Japanese Cloud Computing market is expected to have a compound annual growth rate (CAGR) of 9.7% from 2013-2018. Such strong growth is forecasted due in large part to the under-utilization of cloud computing by Japanese companies currently. In a survey of both large and small medium sized enterprises (SMEs), the Ministry of Internal Affairs and Communications (MIC) compared the rate of cloud usage by U.S. and Japanese companies. The 2012 survey found that 70.6% of U.S. companies were utilizing cloud computing in some form while only 42.4% of Japanese companies had adopted the cloud into their business processes. A more recent 2013 survey found that the larger the firm, the more likely it was to have adopted cloud computing. For instance, 58.2% of Japanese companies with a capital base of $50 million reported using the cloud in some way. This rate, however, is still considerably lower than the 74.2% rate of cloud usage reported by large U.S. companies. Japanese companies in the financial sector, including insurance companies, were the highest cloud users while companies in the transportation sector were amongst the lowest. Japanese companies named a wide variety of reasons for their reluctance to adopt cloud computing. The most common reason cited was the lack of necessity (42.8%), followed by security concerns (37.4%), the high cost associated with the service (22.9%), general lack of understanding (21.9%) and concerns about risk to existing networks (15.7%).

Since 2010, MIC has spear headed a government wide effort to encourage early adoption of cloud computing particularly in the fields of medical care, education, and agriculture. The government is also keen on increasing cloud computing usage by SMEs in an effort to increase efficiencies and help spur more economic growth. While these efforts are notable, the announcement in early 2014 by Sony Corporation to transition to cloud gaming for its PlayStation 4 appears to have given cloud computing a boost in the Japanese market. According to Strategy Analytics, the Boston-based market research firm, with the advent of cloud gaming, Sony and other gaming companies may increase their user base five-fold from 30 million to 150 million players worldwide.

In early 2015, NTT East, a subsidiary of the telecommunication giant, NTT Communications, announced plans to partner with a video game developer to begin testing supercomputer cloud gaming on NTT's high-speed optical fiber network and distribution system. In fact all the major Japanese telecommunications companies in addition to NTT Communications, including KDDI Corporation and Softbank Telecom Corporation, have been aggressively making inroads into the cloud computing market in recent months. Presently, the key players in the Japanese cloud computing market include such well known U.S. vendors as Amazon Web Services Inc., Cisco Systems, Google, HP, IBM, Microsoft, Oracle and Salesforce.com, as well as established Japanese IT firms including Fujitsu and Hitachi Data Systems.

Sub-Sector Best Prospects
Cloud services, Mobile, Big Data and Analytics, Social Technology

Opportunities

Japan IT Week is the largest IT tradeshow in Japan geared toward the IT solutions providers and IT system managers
Date: May 11-13, 2016
Venue: Tokyo Big Sight
http://www.japan-it.jp/en/

Cloud Days
Venue & Dates: Tokyo Prince Tower on March 12-13, 2016
Venue & Dates: Osaka Grant Front on March 17-18, 2016
http://expo.nikkeibp.co.jp/itevents/

IT Pro Expo
Date: September 30 to October 2, 2015
Venue: Tokyo Big Sight
http://expo.nikkeibp.co.jp/itpexpo/2015/english/

Web Resources

Japan Electronics and Information Technology Industry Association (JEITA)
http://www.jeita.or.jp/english/

Ministry of Internal Affairs and Communications (MIC)
http://www.soumu.go.jp/english/index.html

IDC Japan (a market research firm)
http://www.idcjapan.co.jp/

CS Japan Contact:
Ms. Rika Saito, Senior Commercial Specialist
Rika.Saito@trade.gov

HEALTHCARE IT

Market size ($ million):

Year	2011	2012	2013	2014 (estimate)	2015 (estimate)
Total	5,281	5,076	4,800	4,870	5,360
Electronic Health Record	1,622	1,560	1,573	1,600	n/a
Ordering Systems	696	625	575	477	n/a
Medical Imaging Systems	540	530	449	414	n/a
Regional Cooperation Systems	44	59	78	83	n/a
Exchange Rate (¥/$1)	¥79.70	¥79.82	¥97.60	¥105.74	¥105.74

Source: Japanese Association of Healthcare Information Systems Industries (JAHIS)

Japan ranked in the top position among 80 countries according to ITA's country case studies on healthcare IT metrics. For one such metric, Japan has the third highest GDP level globally (behind only the United States and China); a large Health IT market size (exceeding $1 billion); the oldest-skewing population distribution; a high concentration of population clustered in urban areas; a tech-friendly society; and very good Health IT infrastructure. All of these factors indicate that Health IT already has a good foundation in Japan, with the potential for more growth.

Japanese government will implement the "Social Security and Tax Number System" (or "My Number System") in January 2016 to improve social infrastructure and governmental administrative efficiency. The system's utilization in the healthcare area is limited to administrative procedures for health insurance. According to surveys, most companies are not ready to support the system, and expanding areas of utilizing the My Number System will continue to be discussed to include healthcare information. Also, development of a special new number system for medical information for healthcare institutions has also been considered by the Ministry of Health, Labour, and Welfare (MHLW).

Japanese government expects that the adoption of information technology in the medical care and home nursing care fields will increase, and regional medical cooperation will expand by sharing information between these two fields. However, security and privacy protection concerns still exist in utilizing of database and healthcare big data including the linkage of medical information numbers and the My Number System. Demands for wearable devices and technologies would enhance business opportunities in the areas of chronic diseases and prevention in addition to the sports fitness-related market.

In 2014 the market size of healthcare IT systems in Japan totaled $4.8 billion, which is approximately a 15.6% increase from the previous year in Japanese yen based amounts. In order to effectively utilize health information as big data, the adoption of electronic medical records is a major priority in Japan. According to an industry source, the adoption rate for electronic medical records and ordering systems among hospitals in 2013 was 27.1% and 32.4% respectively.

61.5% of the hospitals with more than 400 beds implemented electronic medical records and 75.5% of them have ordering systems. Due to rapid demographic changes and hospital shortages, demand for home nursing care in regional cooperation is expected to grow.

Sub-Sector Best Prospects

With the implementation of the My Number System and increasing attention to the regional medical cooperation, areas with new business opportunities include security/privacy, big data, and cloud computing, where the U.S. technologies are believed to be advanced and more experienced in the healthcare.

In the niche market for large pharmaceutical industry, the MHLW will require drug makers to submit electronic data in Clinical Data Interchange Standards Consortium (CDISC) standard format from October 2016. As the CDISC standards are already used in the United States, the Japanese market will need information and seek introduction of U.S. advanced solutions that will be welcomed by contract research organizations (CROs) as well as pharmaceutical companies.

Opportunities

Event: The International Modern Hospital Show 2015 (IMHS2014)
Date: July 15-17, 2015
Venue: Tokyo Big Sight
Web: http://noma-hs.jp/hs/2015/en/

Event: CEATEC Japan 2015
Date: October 7-10, 2015
Venue: Makuhari Messe
Web: http://www.ceatec.com/en/application/

Event: HOSPEX Japan 2015
Date: November 25-27, 2015
Venue: Tokyo Big Sight
Web: http://www.jma.or.jp/hospex/en/index.html

Event: MedTech Japan
Date: April 20-22, 2016
Venue: Tokyo Big Sight
Web: http://www.medtecjapan.com/en

Web Resources

American Chamber of Commerce Japan (ACCJ) http://www.accj.or.jp/
Japanese Association of Healthcare Information Systems Industries (JAHIS) http://www.jahis.jp/english/
Japan Medical Imaging and Radiological Systems Industries Association (JIRA) http://www.jira-net.or.jp/e/index.htm
HL-7 Japan http://www.hl7.jp/english/index.html
DICOM http://dicom.nema.org/
Integrating the Health Enterprise Japan (IHE-J) http://www.ihe-j.org/en/
Clinical Data Interchange Standards Consortium (CDISC) http://cdisc.org/

CS Japan Contact:
Ms. Yasue Morimoto, Commercial Specialist
Yasue.Morimoto@trade.gov

MEDICAL EQUIPMENT

Unit: $ thousands

	2013	2014 (estimated)	2015 (estimated)	2016 (estimated)
Total Market Size	33,616	27,202	27,568	27,934
Total Local Production	23,938	19,036	19,373	19,716
Total Exports	6,665	5,217	5,426	5,643
Total Imports	16,342	13,383	13,620	13,861
Imports from the U.S.	7,681	6.025	7,355	7,485
Exchange Rate: $ 1	97.60	105.74	105.74	105.74

Figures for 2014, 2015 and 2016 are unofficial CS Japan estimates and reflect yen depreciation from 97.6 to 113.00 to the dollar.

Japan's market for medical devices and materials continues to be among the world's largest. According to the latest official figures from the Ministry of Health, Labour and Welfare (MHLW) Annual Pharmaceutical Production Statistics, the Japanese market for medical devices and materials in 2013 was approximately $33.6 billion (up 3.2 % from 2012 in yen terms). Japan's total imports of U.S. medical devices were approximately $7.7 billion in 2013. In the near term, the market is expected to increase due to Japan's aging population and continued demands for advanced medical technologies. The market remains heavily dependent on imports, especially sophisticated medical technologies. U.S. exports to Japan have a 23 % total market share according to the official figures. However for advanced devices and diagnostics, the total market share of U.S.-origin medical devices in Japan would be significantly higher than suggested by official statistics, approaching 60 % for advanced medical technologies.

Prime Minister Shinzo Abe's economic revitalization and growth strategy, introduced in June 2013, calls for promotion of the pharmaceutical and medical device industries. The Japanese government has made progress in several areas, including the reduction of lengthy approval periods for medical devices as well as Diet passage in November 2013 of amendments to the Pharmaceutical Affairs Law (PAL). The PAL was amended and renamed the Pharmaceutical and Medical Devices Law (PMDL) on November 25, 2014. The PMDL will enable further improvements to the regulatory review process, including the establishment of a device-specific regulatory framework. Notable changes under the PMDL include expanding the scope of products eligible for third-party certification; allowing quality inspections to be conducted for product groupings as opposed to individual products; simplifying the manufacturer accreditation process; and making stand alone software a Class II device.

While the regulatory environment is expected to continue improving and the market for U.S. medical equipment in Japan remains strong, there remains strong financial pressure for the Government of Japan (GOJ) to contain healthcare spending in the country due to the rapid aging of Japan's population, especially when the GOJ is aiming to achieve a primary surplus by JFY2020. In the short term, the postponing of scheduled tax hikes from 8% in October 2015 to 10% in April 2017 has created a more challenging financial environment as it generated additional revenues to fund healthcare expenditure, and also raised concerns with price revisions happening for three years in succession from 2016-2018. Should potential price revisions under the proposed 2017 consumption tax raise take place, and the scheduled biennial price revisions occur in even-numbered fiscal years (2016 and 2018), this will lead to de facto annual revisions. Both U.S. and Japanese pharmaceutical industries are concerned that these changes could be used by advocates as ammunition to push for their proposal for annual revisions to continue from 2019. In addition, as national health expenditures are expected to further increase in the coming years, the GOJ will continue to take measures to contain overall healthcare costs including reducing medical device reimbursement rates.

Sub-Sector Best Prospects

Given Japan's aging population and the increasing number of patients with chronic and life-style diseases, medical devices that alleviate pain, complement lost functions, and improve the quality of life should show steady growth in demand. Also, the market for in-home care devices, technologies, and health IT related products is expected to grow as the number of people in out-patient care increases. Due to stronger consumer health concerns, other promising growth areas include self-care and preventive care medical devices and products.

Opportunities

Event: The International Modern Hospital Show 2015
Date: July 15 - 17, 2015
Venue: Tokyo Big Sight
Web: http://noma-hs.jp/hs/2015/en/

Event: HOSPEX Japan 2015
Date: November 25 - 27, 2015
Venue: Tokyo Big Sight
Web: http://www.jma.or.jp/hospex/en/index.html

Event: Medical Japan 2016
Date: February 24 – 26, 2016
Venue: Intex Osaka
Web: http://www.interphex-osaka.jp/en/

Event: MEDTECH Japan 2016
Date: April 20 - 22, 2016
Venue: Tokyo Big Sight
Web: http://www.medtecjapan.com/en

Web Resources

Ministry of Health, Labour and Welfare (MHLW) www.mhlw.go.jp
Pharmaceutical and Medical Device Agency (PMDA) www.pmda.go.jp
Advanced Medical Technology Association (AdvaMed) www.advamed.org
The American Medical Devices and Diagnostics Manufacturers' Association (AMDD) amdd.jp/en/index.html
Japan Federation of Medical Device Associations (JFMDA) www.jfmda.gr.jp

CS Japan Contact:
Mr. Hiroyuki Hanawa, Senior Commercial Specialist
Hiroyuki.Hanawa@trade.gov

PHARMACEUTICAL

Unit: $ thousands

	2013	2014 (estimated)	2015 (estimated)	2016 (estimated)
Total Market Size	123,639	90,371	93,657	98,339
Total Local Production	86,608	61,624	63,473	66,646

Total Exports	1,629	1,325	1,391	1,460
Total Imports	38,660	30,071	31,575	33,154
Imports from the U.S.	7,281	6,029	6,330	6,647
Exchange Rate: $ 1	97.60	105.74	105.74	105.74

Japan continues to be one of the largest pharmaceuticals market in the world despite the more challenging business landscape due to demographics. According to the latest official figures from the Ministry of Health, Labour and Welfare (MHLW) Annual Pharmaceutical Production Statistics, the Japanese market for prescription and nonprescription pharmaceuticals in 2013 totaled $123 billion (up 1.9 % from 2012 in yen terms). More than 90 % of the total market consists of prescription pharmaceuticals. Imports of foreign pharmaceuticals accounted for approximately 31% of the total Japanese market in 2013. Japan's total imports of U.S. pharmaceuticals totaled $7.3 billion in 2013, a 6% market share. However, the total market share of U.S.-origin pharmaceuticals in Japan would be significantly higher than suggested by official statistics (approaching 20%) if local production by U.S. firms and compounds licensed to Japanese manufacturers were included. In the near term, the size of the market is expected to increase due to continued demands for drugs from Japan's aging population and the rising number of chronic and long-term diseases. The market growth is also supported by innovative medicines due to Japan's improved regulatory environment and a new premium price system that minimizes downward price revisions on new drugs, which was the system implemented in the 2010 price revision.

In 2014, there were some positive developments to support growth of the pharmaceutical industry in Japan. Review times were reduced as a result of a series of measures taken by the Government of Japan (GOJ) to reduce the drug lag. The Pharmaceuticals and Medical Devices Agency (PMDA) continues to speed up the overall review time. Under the JFY2015 plan, for example, the PMDA aims to shed the overall review time to 12 months for at least 70% of new drugs (regular products) filed for approval, up from the 60% targeted in FY2014. On the pricing front, in the 2014 price revision, the GOJ decided, for the second time in a row, to continue the new premium system trial for an additional two years starting from April 1, 2014. The impact of the new premium system has been significant for pharmaceutical firms. According to a U.S. pharmaceutical industry association representative, it has led foreign pharmaceutical companies to bring their pipelines to Japan more quickly; and the number of drugs developed in Japan has increased significantly and is expected to increase further in coming years. Both Japanese and foreign pharmaceutical industries will continue calling for making the new premium system a regular part of the National Health Insurance (NHI) system in the planned 2016 price revision as they believe that the system is working as expected and will lead to elimination of the drug lag in the long-term. Other positive developments included a decision to establish the Japan Agency for Medical Research and Development (AMED) in April 2015, known as a Japanese version of the translational sciences office of the US National Institutes of Health (NIH). Japan will also introduce what is called the "sakigake designation system," which is designed to expedite the review of innovative drugs developed in Japan earlier than the rest of the world by granting a series of privileges, such as prioritized consultations and priority review status.

Contrary to certain positive developments, there remains strong financial pressure for the GOJ to contain healthcare spending in the country due to the rapid aging of Japan's population, especially when the GOJ is aiming to achieve a primary surplus by JFY2020. In the short term, the postponing of a scheduled tax hike, from 8% to 10%, from October 2015 to April 2017, has created a more challenging financial environment as it generated additional revenues to fund healthcare expenditure, and also raised concerns with price revisions happening for three years in succession from 2016-2018. Should potential price revisions under the proposed 2017 consumption tax raise take place, and the scheduled biennial price revisions occur in even-numbered fiscal years (2016 and 2018), this will lead to de facto annual revisions. Both U.S. and

Japanese pharmaceutical industries are concerned that these changes could be used by advocates as ammunition to push for their proposal for annual revisions to continue from 2019.

Sub-Sector Best Prospects

The market for regenerative medicine is expected to expand due to the revised Pharmaceutical Affairs Law (PAL). In November 2014, the PAL was amended and renamed to the Pharmaceutical and Medical Devices Law (PMDL). The PMDL will enable further improvements to the regulatory review process, including the establishment of a new product category for regenerative medicine products. The rapid approval system on regenerative medical products was introduced with the enforcement of the law, which raised Japan to the forefront of regenerative medicine.

Generics will also have good potential in the Japanese market as the GOJ continues to regard the promotion of generics as a key solution for reducing soaring healthcare costs. According to the Japan Society of Generic Medicines (JSGM), the usage rate of generics (volume-based) was at 58.1% as of August 2014 and is expected to reach 80% by the end of FY 2020.

Opportunities

Event: INTERPHEX JAPAN
Date: July 1 -3, 2015
Venue: Tokyo Big Sight
Web: www.interphex.jp/en/Home/

Event: BioJapan 2015
Date: October 14 - 16, 2015
Venue: Pacifico Yokohama
Web: http://www.ics-expo.jp/biojapan/index.html

Event: Medical Japan 2016
Date: February 24 – 26, 2016
Venue: Intex Osaka
Web: http://www.interphex-osaka.jp/en/

Event: CPhI Japan 2016
Date: April 20 – 22, 2016
Venue: Tokyo Big Sight
Web: http://www.cphi.com/japan/home/

Web Resources

Ministry of Health, Labor and Welfare (MHLW)	www.mhlw.go.jp
Pharmaceutical and Medical Device Agency (PMDA)	www.pmda.go.jp
Pharmaceutical Research and Manufacturers of America	www.phrma-jp.org
The Japan Pharmaceutical Manufacturers Association	www.jpma.or.jp
The Federation of Japan Pharmaceutical Wholesalers Association (JPWA)	http://www.jpwa.or.jp
Pharmaceutical and Medical Device Regulatory Science Society of Japan (PMRJ)	http://www.pmrj.jp
The Pharmaceutical Society of Japan (PSJ)	http://www.pharm.or.jp
Japan Generic Medicines Association (JGA)	http://www.jga.gr.jp

CS Japan Contact:
Mr. Hiroyuki Hanawa, Senior Commercial Specialist
Hiroyuki.Hanawa@trade.gov

RENEWABLE ENERGY

Installed Generation Capacity of 2015 (at the end of January, 2015)*
unit: Megawatt

	Before FIT	After FIT			
	Accumulated Capacity	Installed Capacity			Certified Capacity
	up to end of Jun. 2012	Jul. 2012 - Mar. 2013	Apr. 2013 - Mar. 2014	Apr. 2014 - Jan. 2015	Jul. 2012 - Jan. 2015
Solar (residential)	4,700	969	1,307	675	3,519
Solar (non-resid.)	900	704	5,735	6,868	68,102
Wind	2,600	63	47	146	1,566
Hydroelectric	9,600	2	4	38	378
Biomass	2,300	30	92	29	1,492
Geothermal	500	1	0	3	15
Total	20,600	1,769	7,185	7,759	75,073 (1,557,385 cases)
		16,713 (924,107 cases)			

*April 18, 2015 issued by Ministry of Economy, Infrastructure, and Transportation (METI)

Feed-in Tariff (FIT)

Category			FIT (per kWh, excl. tax) FY 2014 (4/1/2014 - 3/31/2015)	FY 2015 (4/1/2015 - 3/31/2016)	Purchase Period
Solar	< 10kW	generators are not required	¥37	¥33	10 years
		generators are required		¥35	
	≧ 10kW		¥32	¥29 (4/1-6/30/2015)	20 years
				¥27 (from 7/1/2015)	
Wind	offshore wind power		¥36	¥36	20 years
	< 20kW	land-based wind power	¥55	¥55	
	≧ 20kW	land-based wind power	¥22	¥22	
Small-Medium Hydropower	< 200kW	utilizing existing head race channels	¥25	¥25	20 years
		installing fully new facilities	¥34	¥34	
	≧ 200kW < 1,000kW	utilizing existing head race channels	¥21	¥21	
		installing fully new facilities	¥29	¥29	
	≧ 1,000kW < 30,000kW	utilizing existing head race channels	¥14	¥14	
		installing fully new facilities	¥24	¥24	
Geothermal	< 15,000kW		¥40	¥40	15 years
	≧ 15,000kW		¥26	¥26	
Biomass	Wood (timber from forest thinning)	< 2,000kW	¥32	¥40	20 years
		≧ 2,000kW		¥32	
	Wood (general)		¥24	¥24	
	Wood (waste materials of buildings)		¥13	¥13	
	Waste materials		¥17	¥17	
	Methane fermentation		¥39	¥39	

We expect Japan's future energy strategy will see a substantial reduction in the use of nuclear power and a massive deployment of renewable energy.

Japan had supported modest renewable energy development since 2005, and moved quickly after the 2011 earthquake and tsunami. The Government of Japan (GOJ) introduced a Feed-in-Tariff (FIT) in July 2012, to boost electric power generated by renewable sources. In the year following the introduction of the FIT, Japan approved 23.6 GW of new renewable energy capacity, and as of January 2015, 16.7 GW of that approved is online.

Renewable energy still only accounts for 10.8% of electricity generation including hydro-power generation, and 2.52% excluding hydro-power generation in 2013. In April 2014, Japan's cabinet approved the country's first Basic Energy Plan since the Fukushima disaster. In it, the Government calls for Japan to surpass its previous target of 13.5% power generation from renewable sources by 2020 and 20% by 2030.

Currently, the electric power generated from renewable energy is mainly bought and sold by Japanese electric utilities through the FIT (Feed-in Tariff). However, another renewable energy market has newly been being formed: Some new power producers and suppliers have emerged to procure and provide electricity as a business through a liberalized retail market (currently, liberalized electricity is limited to high-pressure electricity that satisfies the demands of 50kw or more). The renewable energy market in 2014, reached a value of $1.38 billion, based on the sales of high-pressure electricity. According to Yano Research Institute Ltd., with the annual average growth rate of renewable energy from 2013 to 2020 projected to be 36.6%, the market is expected to grow to approximately $1.4 billion in 2015 and to reach to $11.35 billion by 2020.

Note: Renewable energy here is defined as electricity produced from solar (both residential and non-residential), wind, small-medium hydro, biomass, and geothermal.

Sub-Sector Best Prospects

Solar PV

The introduction of a feed-in-tariff (FIT) has attracted significant in the Japanese renewable energy market, particularly in the solar sector where demand for products outpaces Japan's domestic production capacity because solar installations have short lead times and are not subject to long environmental impact assessment studies. The both of installed and certified capacities of solar power account for more than 95% of total capacities of installed and certified renewable energy. Residentialsolar power used to account for 80% of the total solar power generated, but industrial solar power now accounts for 65% of total solar power generated in Japan. As seen in the above table, the total capacity of non-residential solar power capacity is recorded 14.2GW as of January 2015.
Despite an almost 10% reduction of the FIT, the rate is still relatively attractive to investors and developers. However, solar development will be slower compared with last two years. Yano ResearchInstitute Ltd. predicts that the total solar market size reached its peak in 2014, and industrial solar willgradually decrease toward 2020 as large mega projects are constructed. Residential solar on the otherhand, is expected to continue to grow during the same time period.

Wind Power Generation

Japan's wind resources are concentrated in the northern part of Japan (Hokkaido and Tohoku) and the southern part of Kyushu. Wind power is a major portion of renewable generation in the U.S. and Europe, but it is underrepresented in Japan.

Japan Wind Power Association (JWPA) calculates the cumulative installed capacity of wind power generation in Japan as of the end of December 2014 as 2,788 MW with 1,971 units at 418 sites.

The old initial subsidies system had been terminated in Japanese fiscal year 2010, and the new FIT system was introduced in July 2012. The Ministry of Economy, Trade and Industry (METI) had offered ¥22/kWh (excluding tax) for large-scale (more than 20kW) wind power. However, currently METI offers¥ 36/kWh (excluding tax) for offshore wind power.

For the past three years, wind power installation was very slow mainly due to an environment assessment process which generally takes four to seven years. It seems to take a further 2-7 years for the current certified projects to start operation.

METI is also addressing the lack of well-developed transmission grid lines in the areas with windresources. METI is developing a new financial scheme for utilities and developers to share the burden of expanding the grid to accommodate wind power generation.

Geothermal Power Generation
Japan has the world's third largest geothermal reserves, estimated approximately 23GW (behindIndonesia 30GW and the U.S. 28GW). Due to permitting and land use issues, most of the best geothermal spots are near national parks or hot-spring areas, only 537MW has been developed.

METI has been looking at ways to ease regulations governing access to geothermal resources, andpartial deregulation has recently been adopted to generate a positive example of new geothermal power station development.

Biomass Power Generation
Before the FIT law was implemented, biomass power generation had been the second largest renewable power source in terms of electricity sold to the power utilities.

METI added a new category "Wood (timber from forest thinning), under 2MW" FIT in 2015 and underthe FIT, biomass fuels are now grouped into six categories: wood (timber from forest thinning) under 2,000 kW, wood (timber from forest thinning) and more 2,000kW, wood (general), wood (waste materials of buildings, waste materials, and methane fermentation.

Since the introduction of the FIT, five to ten MW of biomass projects have been developed and most of the large projects are completed. In the years ahead, small-medium sized biomass projects are expected to grow by utilizing the newly added FIT for wood (timber from forest thinning), which is currently is the highest rate in the biomass categories at ¥ 40/kWh.

Opportunities

World Smart Energy Week 2015
Date: March 2 – 4, 2016
Venue: Tokyo Big Sight, Tokyo Organizer: Reed Exhibition Japan Ltd. URL: http://www.wsew.jp/en/

PV Japan 2015
Date: July 29 – 31, 2015
Venue: Tokyo Big Sight, Tokyo
Organizer:
Japan Photovoltaic Energy Association (JPEA) URL: www.jpea.gr.jp/pvj2015/englis

h/

Web Resources
Agency for Natural Resources and Energy
http://www.enecho.meti.go.jp/en/

Ministry of Economy, Trade and Industry
http://www.meti.go.jp/english

New Energy and Industrial Technology Development Organization
http://www.nedo.go.jp/english

Japan Photovoltaic Energy Association
http://jpea.gr.jp/en/greeting/index.html

Japan Wind Power Association
http://jwpa.jp/index_e.html

CS Japan Contact:
Ms. Minae Suzuki, Commercial Specialist
Minae.Suzuki@trade.gov

SAFETY AND SECURITY

Unit: USD thousands

	2012	2013	2014 (estimated)	2015 (estimated)
Total Market Size	7,230,020	5,962,100	5,948,770	6,018,440
Total Local Production	7,822,882	6,677,552	6,662,622	6,740,653
Total Exports*	1,315,864	1,311,662	1,308,729	1,324,057
Total Imports*	723,002	596,210	594,877	601,844
Imports from the U.S.*	n/a	n/a	n/a	n/a
Exchange Rate: 1 USD	79.82	97.60	97.60	97.60

Data Source:

Total Market Size: Japan Security Systems Association and Fuji Keizai
*figures are unofficial CS Japan estimates

According to the Fuji Keizai Research Company, Japan's security systems industry, including equipment and services, is projected to have steady growth for the next several years. Amongst the strongest growth sector is in cybersecurity where the market research firm, IDC, predicts the market will grow to more than $425 billion by 2018.

With the planned 2020 Tokyo Olympic Games, investment in new technologies for security equipment and disaster prevention management will be a driving force for the physical security market. In particular the recent hostage taking of two Japanese citizens by ISIS in early 2015 combined with a suspected drone intrusion at the Prime Minister's official residence has heightened the Japanese Government's urgency for upgrading anti-terrorism measures. U.S. security-related products for thegovernment procurement and anti-terrorism market enjoy a favorable position in the Japanese market, as U.S. technological leadership in this arena is highly recognized.

The mid-term outlook for the IP (Internet Protocol) -based surveillance systems market is expected togrow due to increasing demand for replacement and upgrade of existing systems. The development ofvarious IP-based systems along with cloud computing has had a significant impact on the physical security market. There are various potential business opportunities in IP-based security systems andequipment which employ more sophisticated digital technologies.

In light of the experiences of the 2011 disaster in Japan, many Japanese companies had to review andmodify their existing Business Continuity Planning (BCP) to cope with possible risks. The demands forBCP solutions including consulting service and disaster prevention solutions are expected to sustaingrowth. Cloud-based disaster recovery services have become a popular way to protect important company data and there are great potential business opportunities in this area. Due to growing awareness about natural disaster prevention measures, the market demand for business continuity and disaster management-related solutions will steadily grow over the next few years. According to the Japanese research company Yano Research, the BCP/disaster prevention solution market will grow 2.5% from ¥187.6 billion in 2011 to ¥223.4 billion in 2018.

Cybersecurity

Specific to cybersecurity is the growing governmental apparatus around this concern and the accompanying increased funding for the prevention of cybercrimes. The National Information Security Center (NISC) was established to coordinate the various governmental agencies and entities involved in cybercrime prevention. The four key agencies include: 1) the National Police Agency (NPA); 2) the Ministry of Internal Affairs and Communications (MIC); 3) the Ministry of Economy, Trade and Industry (METI); and 4) the Ministry of Defense (MOD) which houses a newly created Cyber Defense Force. Each agency has been allotted roughly ¥2-3 billion per annum to develop detection and response systems and to train personnel. The lion's share of the funds of about ¥20 billion per annum is dedicated to defense purposes. Since 2012, these agencies have spent upwards of ¥118.6 billion on cybersecurity related expenditures with 2014 representing a two fold increase from previous years as a result of extensive infrastructure build-out and upgrades. During 2015, these agencies are projected to spend an estimated ¥32.6 billion on cybersecurity. In addition, the Japanese Government recently announced plans to spend ¥2-3 billion per annum to enhance cyber defense technology for the 2020 Tokyo Olympic Games.

It is worth noting that these public sector expenditures are in addition to the private sector as companies and financial institutions are pressed to significantly increase their investments in the latest and most effective technology to combat cyberattacks. According to Bloomberg news, cyberattacks against Japanese firms have more than doubled since 2010 to one every 30 seconds. Such high profile attacks on prominent members of corporate Japan, including Sony, Mitsubishi Heavy Industries, and Yahoo Japan, have only added to the heightened sense of urgency amongst the Japanese business community. As a result of the reported short fall of some 80,000 information security engineers, Japan must heavily rely upon imported technology and expertise for which U.S. firms have a distinct edge due to the close security and bilateral relationship along with U.S. firms' recognized expertise in this area.

Sub-Sector Best Prospects

Steady demand is expected in the Japanese airport security market, since Japanese airports are highlyreceptive to new security technologies and must comply with International Civil Aviation Organization standards.

Next generation surveillance technologies, including video analytics applications and smart cameras, present potential growth opportunities also.

In addition, security products and services tailored specially for terrorist attacks present potential opportunities in the following areas:

- Monitoring & warning system – night vision device, Through-wall radar, Thermo-graphic camera, Ocean surveillance system, Illegal intrusion monitoring system, Autonomous underwater vehicle
- Detector – Explosive detector, Drug detector, Chemical detector, Biological agent detector, Radiation detector, and Gas detector
- Special Equipment – Holographic sight, Virus dissemination inhibitor, Chemical protective clothing, Ballistic shield/bulletproof vest, and Remotely operated vehicle
- ICT – Real time enhanced video, 3D scanner, Biometrics system, Virtual Training system, Cyber intelligence solutions, Unmanned aerial vehicle system

Finally, as mentioned earlier, products and services related to cybersecurity including but not limited to the following areas:

- Identify and Access Management
- Content Security
- Data Loss Prevention
- Datacenter Security
- Next Generation Firewall
- Unified Threat Management
- VPN & Web Security

Opportunities

Risk Control in Tokyo (RISCON) - Safety and Security Trade Expo Special Equipment Exhibition &Conference for Anti-Terrorism (SEECAT)
Dates: October 14-16, 2015
Venue: Tokyo Big Sight – West Hall
http://www.kikikanri.biz/english/index.html http://www.seecat.biz/english/

Security Show is Japan's comprehensive safety and security industry show. Exhibits include video surveillance systems, access control systems, information security systems and many security related products.
Dates: March 8-11, 2016
Venue: Tokyo Big Sight
http://www.shopbiz.jp/en/ss/

Office Security Expo (OSEC) is mainly focused on human resource recruitment and personnel for the security industry.
Dates: July 7-19, 2015
Venue: Tokyo Big Sight http://www.osec.jp/

Web Resources

Safety and Security Resources
Cabinet Office Disaster Management http://www.cao.go.jp/en/disaster.html National Poli ceAgency http://www.npa.go.jp/english/index.html
Fire
& DisasterManagement Agency http://www.fdma.go.jp/en/

Japan Fire Equipment Inspection Institute http://www.jfeii.or.jp/en/index.html
ASIS International, Japan Chapter http://www.asis-japan.org/
Japan Security Systems Association http://www.ssaj.or.jp/index.html

Cybersecurity Resources
CIPPS: Center for Int'l Public Policy Studies http://cipps.org/english/
NICT: Nat'l Inst. of Info and Communication Tech http://www.nict.go.jp/en/
NISC: Nat'l Information Security Center http://www.nisc.go.jp/en/

CS Japan Contact:
Mr. Koji Sudo, Senior Commercial Specialist (for Safety and Security)
Koji.Sudo@trade.gov

Ms. Rika Saito. Senior Commercial Specialist (for Cybersecurity)
Rika.Saito@trade.gov

SEMICONDUCTORS

Unit: USD millions

	2013	2014	2015 (estimates)	2016 (forecasts)
Total Market Size	40,553	52,212	57,238	52,681
Total Local Production	48,497	56,998	60,706	62,528
Total Exports	32,192	33,285	33,821	41,110
Total Imports	24,248	28,499	30,353	31,264
Imports from the U.S.	7,274	8,550	9,106	9,379
Exchange Rate: 1 USD	97.60	97.60	97.60	97.60

Data Sources: Japan Electronics Information & Technology Industries Association (JEITA), Distributors Association of Semiconductors & Components of Japan (DAFS)
Benchmarked to 2013 with exchange rate of 97.6

2013-2014 appears to have been a watershed year for the Japanese electronics industry. For the first time since 2011, domestic production of electronic and digital devices posted positive growth (3%) after several years of contraction due to increased offshore production in the wake of the March 2011 earthquake and tsunami. According to a recent report by the Japan Electronics and Information Technologies Industries Association (JEITA), domestic semiconductor production led the growth with exports of semiconductors rising to second place, in terms of export value, after the export of automobiles. This trend is mirrored on the global stage where global semiconductor production also experienced strong growth driven by increased demand for memory intensive devices such as smartphones and tablets as well as the increased computerization of automobiles. Industry analysts all forecast continued strong growth in semiconductor production both domestically and globally for 2015 through 2016, barring any unexpected changes to macroeconomic factors.

The past several years have witnessed restructuring and further consolidation of the Japanese semiconductor industry. Renesas, the merger of NEC Electronic with the former Hitachi and Mitsubishi spin-off, benefited from an injection of new capital from both private and government sources in 2013. Similarly the former Elpida chipmaker was acquired by Micron which has allowed that firm to significantly expand its market share in select memory sectors. More recently strategic partnerships such as those between Toshiba and SanDisk or Fujitsu and ON

Semiconductor are expected to lead to increased production in Japan.

According to analyst estimates the anticipated utilization rate at foundries would suggest that capital expenditures in equipment upgrades to be strong in 2015-2016. Indeed, the Semiconductor Equipment Association of Japan (SEAJ) released its first quarter 2015 figures in June 2015 and reports that among the major semiconductor producing countries, Japan experienced one of highest increases in semiconductor equipment billings at $1.3 billion for the first three months of 2015 or a 31% year on year quarterly increase. Since most integrated device manufacturers (IDMs) or foundries do not manufacturer their own equipment, demand for front and back end processing equipment presents strong export opportunities for U.S. suppliers. JEITA estimates that Japan is expected to spend between $7-9 billion in capital expenditure over the course of the next two years, representing a 25% increase in the Japanese equipment market.

Sub-Sector Best Prospects

Front-end fab equipment including RTP (rapid thermal processing), CMP (chemical mechanical planarization), photoresist processing, etch, lithography, and process controls.

Back-end equipment including packaging and assembly equipment and automated testing equipment.

Opportunities

SEMICON Japan 2015 – Certified by U.S. Commercial Service
December 16-18, 2015
Tokyo Big Sight, Tokyo
http://www.semiconjapan.org/en/

CEATEC Japan – Certified by U.S. Commercial Service
October 7-10, 2015
http://www.jesa.or.jp/en/exhibition/ceatec/

International Broadcast Equipment Exhibition 2015 (Inter BEE 2015) – Certification pending
November 18-20, 2015
Chiba City
http://www.inter-bee.com/en/about/outline/

Web Resources

Semiconductor Equipment and Materials International (SEMI)
www.semi.org

SEMICON Japan
http://www.semiconjapan.org/en/

Distributors Association of Semiconductors & Components of Japan (DAFS)
http://www.dafs.or.jp/index_e.html

Japan Electronics Information & Technology Industries Association (JEITA)
http://www.jeita.or.jp/english/

CS Japan Contact:
Ms. Rika Saito, Senior Commercial Specialist
Rika.Saito@trade.gov

SMART GRID

Unit: $ thousands

	2013	2014	2015 (estimated)	2016 (estimated)
Total Market Size	5,787,037	6,944,444	8,333,333	9,583,333
Exchange Rate: $ 1	120	120	120	120

Total Market Size = (Total Local Production + Total Imports) – (Total Exports)
Data Sources: Marketing Data Bank

There is no concise and universal definition of a smart grid. Many countries have prioritized the need for smart grid development but the various components and technology can differ widely. In Japan, the general view is that a smart grid applies various technologies to the nationwide electricity supply system to maximize its efficiency, quality, and reliability.

Japanese city planners see that this concept is achieved by not only combining the management of traditional centralized power sources and transmission power network systems, but also by fully utilizing the information and communication technology (ICT). An information system would then integrate information derived from decentralized power sources (such as photovoltaic solar), and also would integrate and utilize real-time information from the customers themselves. Analyzing the information would allow for precise understanding of needs and usage, further permitting the reduction by a large degree the superfluous generation that typically takes place to meet peaks and uneven demand.

Since 2009, the Government of Japan (GOJ) has been working eagerly on research and development of smart grids through various demonstration projects. It is now safe to say developments of component technologies (or element technologies) have been completed.

In the recent past, the biggest challenge for Japan's smart grids was how to integrate intermittent power from renewable sources. A surge in electricity generated from photovoltaic solar or wind-power flowing into a traditional grid system created an expensive problem for utilities.

However, the Great East Japan Earthquake in March 2011 changed the view of the benefits of smart grid technology. Currently, cities are building smart grids to balance centralized and distributed power sources. Moreover, they see that a smart grid means increasing reliability and customer satisfaction.

Japan is now undergoing historical transformations of their electric power supply system. The triple disaster in 2011 has created many opportunities for U.S. technology and services as Japan seeks to close the power generation gap and reduce dependency on imported fossil fuels.

Japan can no longer rely on nuclear power that used to supply 30% of the nation's power demand. At the same time, renewable energy will still maintain a high growth rate into the foreseeable future, but it cannot cover the gap that the nuclear power occupied. In view of the current circumstances, Japanese electric power companies look to smart grid systems to establish a stable electricity supply system.

Sub-Sector Best Prospects
The U.S. Embassy Commercial Section sees that Japan is seeking the following component elements for Smart Grids:

1. Monitoring and Controlling Systems for Transmission Networks and Distribution Networks
2. Management systems of Distributed Power Sources (Photovoltaic Solar and Wind Power Generation)
3. Smart Meters
4. Smart Storage
   (Storage Batteries, Thermal Storage Equipment, Electric Vehicles, Air Compression Storage Facilities, Heat Pumps)
5. Demand Response
6. Smart Asset Management

U.S. Smart Grid companies wishing to enter the Japanese market, should provide products, services and technologies in at least one of the above six categories.

Opportunities
Commercial Service Japan annually holds a one-on-one business matchmaking event between U.S. firms and Japan's electric power companies. The event is called the New Orleans Association (NOA) Conference, which is held in May. At the Conference, CS Japan provides an opportunity for representatives of U.S. suppliers of non-fuel products (and their Japanese agents) to sit down in individual meetings with procurement managers from Japan's 12 Japanese electric power companies (10 major utilities and 2 wholesalers), all in one place. This is the only event in Japan where U.S. firms can meet all Japanese electric power companies.

The last Conference, the 30th NOA Conference was held successfully on May 21, 2015. As for the date of the 2016 event, contact Takahiko Suzuki at takahiko.suzuki@trade.gov

Web Resources
Agency for Natural Resources and Energy (ANRE), Ministry of Economy, Trade and Industry (METI), Government of Japan (GOJ)
http://www.enecho.meti.go.jp/en/

CS Japan Contact:
Mr. Takahiko Suzuki, Senior Commercial Specialist
takahiko.suzuki@trade.gov

TRADE REGULATIONS, CUSTOMS AND STANDARDS

IMPORT TARIFFS

On average, the applied tariff rate in Japan is one of the lowest in the world. In fiscal year (April-March) 2012, the simple average applied MFN (most favored nation) tariff rate was 6.3 percent, up slightly from 5.8 percent in FY2010, reflecting a change in nomenclature, and an increase in the average *ad valorem* equivalents (AVEs) of non-*ad valorem* duties. While import duties on many agricultural items continue to remain high, tariffs in many major sectors, such as autos and auto parts, aircraft, marine vessels, software, computers, industrial machinery and works of fine art are zero. However, certain products including leather, rubber, footwear and travel goods, textiles and clothing, certain processed foods and some manufactured goods have relatively high tariff rates. While Japan's import tariffs are generally low overall, the nation's average agricultural import tariff of 22.2 percent (2012) is among the world's highest for industrialized countries. By comparison, the average agricultural import tariff is 5.2 percent (2012) in the U.S. and 13.5 percent (2012) in the European Community.

The Customs and Tariff Bureau of Japan's Ministry of Finance administers tariffs. As a member of the Harmonized System Convention, Japan shares the same trade classification system as the United States (limited to six-digit code). Japan's tariff schedule has five columns of applicable rates: general, WTO, preferential (GSP), Economic Partnership Agreement (EPA) and temporary. Goods from the United States are charged WTO rates unless a lesser "temporary" rate exists. Japan assesses tariff duties on the CIF value at *ad valorem* or specific rates, and in a few cases, charges a combination of both. Japan's preferential system of tariffs grants lower or duty-free rates to products imported from developing countries. Japan's harmonized tariff schedule is available through the website of Japan Customs: http://www.customs.go.jp/english/index.htm .

A simplified tariff system for low-value imported freight valued at less than ¥100,000, such as small packages for personal imports, simplifies determination of tariff rates. This system also eliminates the extra time necessary to classify the product and its precise value, and thereby minimizes customs brokers' handling charges. Importers can choose

either the normal rate or the simple tariff, which could be higher or lower depending on the product.

Japan grants preferential treatment to products from certain developing and least developed countries under its Generalized System of Preference (GSP) scheme. Under the GSP, preferential tariff treatment is offered to 137 developing countries and 14 territories, including 49 least developed countries (LDCs). The simple average GSP tariff rate is 5.3 percent whereas the rate for LDCs is 0.5 percent. The main beneficiaries of Japan's GSP scheme are China, Thailand, Indonesia, the Philippines and Viet Nam. The GSP scheme excludes many agricultural products and some industrial products. Japan also grants preferential access to imports from Singapore, Mexico, Malaysia, Chile, Thailand, Indonesia, Brunei, the Philippines, Switzerland and Viet Nam under bilateral free-trade agreements.

Japan Customs can provide advance rulings on tariff classification and duty rates. A summary of Japan's customs procedures, including the customs valuation system, import procedures, temporary admission procedures, refunds and duty drawback payments, as well as relevant customs forms can be found on the Japan Customs website noted above. (See also the section below on *Customs Regulations and Contact Information* in this chapter.)

TRADE BARRIERS

While tariffs are generally low, Japan does have non-tariff barriers that impede or delay the importation of foreign products into Japan. Although competition, U.S. and other foreign government pressure, as well as other factors have lessened the impact of these impediments, U.S. companies may still encounter non-tariff barriers such as the following:

- standards unique to Japan (formal, informal, *de facto,* or otherwise);
- a requirement in some sectors or projects for companies to demonstrate prior experience in Japan, effectively shutting out new entrants in the market;
- official regulations that favor domestically-produced products and discriminate against foreign products;
- licensing powers in the hands of industry associations with limited membership, strong market influence, and the ability to control information and operate without oversight:
- cross stock holding and interconnection of business interests among Japanese companies that disadvantage suppliers outside the traditional business group;
- cartels (both formal and informal) and,
- the cultural importance of personal relationships in Japan and the reluctance to break or modify business relationships.

The tools available to overcome these non-tariff barriers depend on the industry, the product or service's competitiveness, and the creativity and determination of the firm's management. The U.S. Department of Commerce's Trade Compliance Center (TCC) helps U.S. exporters and investors overcome foreign trade barriers and works to ensure that foreign countries comply with their trade agreement obligations to the United States. U.S. exporters experiencing non-tariff barriers or other unfair trade practices in foreign markets can report such problems online at http://tcc.export.gov .

For additional information on Japan-specific trade barriers see the National Trade Estimates Report available on the United States Trade Representative Website: http://www.ustr.gov/about-us/press-office/reports-and-publications .

IMPORT REQUIREMENTS AND DOCUMENTATION

Any person wishing to import goods must declare them to the Director-General of Customs and obtain an import permit after necessary examination of the goods concerned. The formalities start with the lodging of an import declaration and end with issuance of an import permit after the necessary examination and payment of Customs duty and excise tax. For additional information see the section below on *Customs Regulations and Contact Information* in this chapter.

Certain items may require a Japanese import license. These include hazardous materials, animals, plants, perishables, and in some cases articles of high value. Import quota items also require an import license, usually valid for four months from the date of issuance. Other necessary documents for U.S. Exporters may include an Import Declaration Form (Customs Form C-5020) and a certificate of origin if the goods are entitled to favorable duty treatment determined by preferential or WTO rates. In practice, shipments from the United States are routinely assessed using WTO or “temporary” rates without a certificate of origin. Any additional documents necessary as proof of compliance with relevant Japanese laws, standards, and regulations at the time of import may also apply.

Correct packing, marking, and labeling are critical to smooth customs clearance in Japan. Straw packing materials are prohibited. Documents required for customs clearance in Japan include standard shipping documents such as a commercial invoice, packing list, and an original and signed bill of lading, or, if shipped by air, an air waybill. Air shipments of values greater than ¥100,000 must also include a commercial invoice. The commercial invoice should be as descriptive as possible for each item in the shipment. The packing list should include the exact contents and measurement of each container, including the gross and net weights of each package. The Japanese Measurement Law requires that all weights and measures on a packing list be reflected in Metric System values.

Japan's Ministry of Finance maintains a website at http://www.customs.go.jp/english/

that describes import and customs clearance procedures, and provides contact information and other detailed information in English.

Japan prohibits the importation of certain items including narcotics, firearms, explosives, counterfeit currency, pornography, and products that violate intellectual property laws. For additional information see the section below on For additional information see the section below on For additional information see the section below on

When planning to import goods into Japan, you may wish to consult with your international shipper for specific details regarding your shipment since your international shipper should be up-to-date on Japanese import requirements.

U.S. EXPORT CONTROLS

As an active member of the Wassenaar Arrangement as well as all international export control regimes, Japan has the benefit of the least restrictive treatment under U.S. export control law. In response to the threat from global terrorism, the Japanese government administers its own export control legislation (Foreign Exchange and Foreign Trade Act, Export Trade Control Order, and Foreign Exchange Order) and implements "catch-all" controls to prevent Japanese firms from exporting goods and technologies that could be related to the development of weapons of mass destruction. Japan has been conducting outreach activities in Asian countries including Japan to maintain a strict export control system. At the same time, however, Japanese firms are engaged in business activities with countries against which the United States currently has embargoes. As such, U.S. exporters are encouraged to conduct thorough research and background checks pertaining to any potential sale of controlled or sensitive items, in particular for transactions that may involve possible transshipment or re-export through Japan.

For the latest in U.S. export and re-export control regulations, contact the Department of Commerce Bureau of Industry and Security (BIS) at http://www.bis.doc.gov.

For the latest in defense trade controls information, contact the Department of State Directorate of Defense Trade Controls at http://www.pmddtc.state.gov.

For current U.S. embargo information, contact the Department of Treasury Office of Foreign Assets Control at http://www.treasury.gov/resource-center/sanctions/Pages/default.aspx .

TEMPORARY ENTRY

Japan is a member of the International Convention to Facilitate the Importation of Commercial Samples and Advertising Materials under the ATA Carnet System. Use of a *carnet* allows goods such as commercial and exhibition samples, professional equipment, musical instruments, and television cameras to be carried or sent temporarily into a foreign country without paying duties or posting bonds. A *carnet* should be arranged in advance by contacting a local office of the United States Council for International Business (http://www.uscib.org) or its New York office by phone (212-354-4480) or by e-mail (info@uscib.org).

Advertising materials, including brochures, films, and photographs, may enter Japan duty free. Articles intended for display - but not for sale - at trade fairs and similar events are also permitted to enter duty free but only when the fair or event is held at a bonded exhibition site. After the event, these bonded articles must be re-exported or stored at a bonded facility. A commercial invoice for these goods should be marked "no commercial value, customs purposes only" and "these goods are for exhibition and are to be returned after conclusion of the exhibition." It is also important to identify the trade show or exhibition site, including exhibition booth number (if known), on shipping documents.

LABELING AND MARKING REQUIREMENTS

Japanese law requires labels for products in several categories. Generally, labeling for most imported products is not required at the customs clearance stage, but at the point of sale. Consequently, it is common for a Japanese importer to affix a label to an imported product after it has cleared customs. While importers do not have to affix a label to fresh foods such as grapefruit or oranges, the retailer is required to display country of origin near the product. To ensure that a given product meets all applicable requirements and is properly labeled, it is important for the U.S. exporter to work with a Japanese agent or importer.

JAS law requires that place of origin be displayed for all fresh food products. If the products are sold individually, in-store signs must display both the name and place of origin of the products. Although this information is required to be displayed for both domestic and imported products, processed food products produced in Japan are not required to show the country of origin labeling. However, all imported processed foods and beverages are required to bear country of origin labeling. The definition of country of origin by CODEX is "When a food undergoes processing in a second country which changes its nature, the country in which the processing is performed shall be considered to the country of origin for the purposes of labeling". For example, the country of origin for coffee beans imported into and roasted in the United States is the United States. However, the country of origin of the coffee beans themselves should also be noted. This is not a legal requirement but a commercial requirement. If labels indicating origin are later determined to be false or misleading, the labels must be removed or corrected. False or misleading labels which display the names of countries, regions or flags other than the country of origin, and/or names of manufacturers or designers outside the country of origin are not permissible.

Food and agricultural products are subject to a number of complex labeling regulations in Japan. Previously, the Ministry of Agriculture, Forestry and Fisheries (MAFF) administered quality labeling standards and the Ministry of Health, Labor and Welfare (MHLW) administered separate voluntary and mandatory standards such as nutritional labeling and food additive/allergen labeling for processed foods and beverages. However, in September 2009, responsibility for all labeling issues, including food labeling, was officially transferred from MAFF, MHLW, and other ministries, and then consolidated under the new Consumer Affairs Agency.

For more information on labeling and marking requirements, please see the following web-based resources:

Consumer Affairs Agency: http://www.caa.go.jp/en/index.html

Japan External Trade Organization (JETRO) Guide to Japanese Household Goods Quality Labeling Law: http://www.jetro.go.jp/en/reports/regulations/

U.S. Foreign Agriculture Service 2009 GAIN Report on the creation of the Consumer Affairs Agency: http://tinyurl.com/ydwqsch

U.S. Foreign Agriculture Service GAIN Report on the proposed new food labeling law: http://goo.gl/NQZYu

U.S. Foreign Agriculture Service GAIN Report on Food and Agriculture Import Regulations and Standards (FAIRS) – Japan:

http://goo.gl/wLyDE

PROHIBITED AND RESTRICTED IMPORTS

Japan strictly prohibits entry of narcotics and related utensils, firearms, firearm parts and ammunition, explosives and gunpowder, precursor materials for chemical weapons, germs which are likely to be used for bio-terrorism, counterfeit goods or imitation coins or currency, obscene materials, or goods that violate intellectual property rights. Other restricted items include but are not limited to certain agricultural and meat products, endangered species and products such as ivory, animal parts and fur where trade is banned by international treaty. For more information on prohibited goods, see Japan Customs: http://www.customs.go.jp/english/summary/prohibit.htm .

In addition, Japan imposes restrictions on the sale or use of certain products including those related to health such as medical products, pharmaceuticals, agricultural products and chemicals. For these products, Japanese Customs reviews and evaluates the product for import suitability before shipment to Japan. The use of certain chemicals and other additives in foods and cosmetics is severely regulated and follows a "positive list" approach.

Regarding importation of products for personal use, Japan restricts entry of:

- more than one months' supply of medicines that are toxicants, dangerous or prescription drugs;
- more than two months' supply of medicines that are non-prescription drugs or quasi-drugs; or
- more than 24 units (normal size) of similar cosmetic products.

Please note that body (hand) soaps, shampoos, toothpastes, hair dye and other toiletries fall under the category of quasi-drugs or cosmetics.

Veterinary drugs are subject to import restrictions in accordance with Japan's Pharmaceutical Affairs Law.

For more information on prohibited and restricted imports visit the FAQ section on the Japan Customs web site: http://www.customs.go.jp/english/index.htm .

CUSTOMS REGULATIONS AND CONTACT INFORMATION

Any person wishing to import goods must declare them to the Director-General of Customs and obtain an import permit after necessary examination of the goods concerned. The formalities start with the lodging of an import declaration and end with issuance of an import permit after the necessary examination and payment of Customs duty and excise tax.

Nearly all customs difficulties result from first time applications. Japanese customs officials are generally helpful when it comes to explaining procedures and regulations to overcome these issues. It may be necessary to employ an import agent or customs broker to help facilitate customs entry. See Chapter 3, Using and Agent or Distributor for more information.

The typical time between arrival of goods and the granting of import permission was between two and three days for sea cargo and about a day for air cargo (including time required under the "immediate import permission system upon arrival"). Under the "immediate import permission system upon arrival", import permission may be granted as soon as cargo entry is confirmed. To be eligible for this system, importers must file a preliminary declaration online (through the Nippon Automated Cargo Clearance System (NACCS). Customs examines the documents and a material submitted before cargo entry, and provides the results of the examination. For more information on the NACCS see: http://www.naccs.jp/e/index.html

All importers must file a declaration with Japan Customs. For most goods, the declaration must be made after the goods have been taken into a bonded customs (*hozei*) area or other designated place; items requiring approval by the Director-General of Customs can be declared before they are taken to the *hozei* area. The declaration must include details of the quantity and value of the goods to be imported as well as an invoice, a packing list, freight account, insurance certificate, and certificate of origin (for, inter alia, preferential tariff rates), where applicable. Additional documentation may be required, for example, for goods requiring an import license or health certificate. Once the documentation is verified by Customs, an import permit is issued.

Imports are valued according to their c.i.f. (cost, insurance + freight) value, which is taken to be the transaction value of the imports. Customs duty can be paid through a multi-payment network system, which connects teller institutions (government authorities) with financial institutions. No fee is charged by the government for the use of this system; however, the financial institutions involved may collect variable fees. The system is managed by the Japan Multi-payment Network Management Organization (JAMMO), a non-profit organization established by major financial institutions in Japan. Only institutions that participate in the organization may use the system. Written advance rulings are issued at the written request of importers and other parties concerned. These rulings can be published on the Customs website with the applicants' consent. For more information on Japan's AEO program see: http://www.customs.go.jp/english/aeo/index.htm

Complaints against Japan Customs' decisions may be made to the Director-General of Customs within two months of the decision. Further appeals may be lodged with the Minister of Finance within one month of the decision by the Director-General of Customs.

CONTACT INFORMATION

Japan Customs http://www.customs.go.jp/english/index.htm

Japans Customs' procedures http://www.customs.go.jp/english/procedures/index_pf.htm Customs Counselors System in Japan, Tokyo Headquarters http://www.customs.go.jp/zeikan/seido/telephone_e.htm

Japan Tariff Association http://www.kanzei.or.jp/english

TRADE AND EXPORT STANDARDS

Many domestic and imported products alike are subject to product testing and cannot be sold in Japan without certification of compliance with prescribed standards. Knowledge of, and adherence to, these standards and their testing procedures can be the key to accessing the market.

Product requirements in Japan fall into two categories: technical regulations (or mandatory standards) and non-mandatory voluntary standards. Compliance with regulations and standards is also governed by a certification system in which inspection results determine whether or not approval (certification/quality mark) is granted.

Approval is generally required before a product can be sold in the market or even displayed at a trade show; unapproved medical equipment may be displayed at a trade show if accompanied by a sign indicating that the product is not yet approved for sale. To affix a mandatory quality mark or a voluntary quality mark requires prior product type approval and possibly factory inspections for quality control assessment. Regulated products must bear the appropriate mandatory mark when shipped to Japan in order to clear Japanese Customs. Regulations may apply not only to the product itself, but also to packaging, marking or labeling requirements, testing, transportation and storage, and installation. Compliance with "voluntary" standards and obtaining "voluntary" marks of approval can greatly enhance a product's sales potential and help win Japanese consumer acceptance.

There are two ongoing trends in Japan regarding standards. One is a move toward standards reform and the other towards harmonizing Japanese standards with prevailing international standards. While reform is underway, there are numerous laws containing Japan-specific mandatory standards most of which have not been translated into English. Therefore, it is important that a Japanese agent or partner be fully aware of the wide variety of standards in effect that could impact the sale of the imported product.

The Japan External Trade Organization website contains numerous documents on Japan's standards and regulations, including import procedures, quarantine periods, technical requirements, etc. The website also details relevant laws, ordinances and amendments concerning import standards and regulations. For more information see: http://www.jetro.go.jp/en/reports/regulations/

PRODUCT LIABILITY INSURANCE

Japanese business entities are subject to various laws and product safety standards, which vary depending upon the industry or product segment. Japanese importers and distributers of foreign products, in general, cover product liability risk through the product liability clause in their own liability insurance. The covered items and exemptions may vary from underwriter to underwriter and among industry segments. Whether the U.S. exporter will be required to buy product liability insurance to cover worldwide or specific overseas markets for their exports will be subject to negotiation with the firm's Japanese business partner and the advice of legal counsel.

STANDARDS ORGANIZATIONS

The Japan Industrial Standards Committee (JISC) plays a central role in standards activities in Japan (http://www.jisc.go.jp/eng). Its mission consists of four elements: 1) establishment and maintenance of Japan Industrial Standards (JIS); 2) administration of accreditation and certification; 3) participation in international standards activities; and 4) development of measurement standards and technical infrastructure for standardization. JISC publishes plans each month for the preparation of new and revised JIS drafts on its website at http://www.jisc.go.jp/eng/jis-act/drafts-preparation.html .

Existing JIS standards are reviewed and revised every five years. Once a new or revised draft JIS standard has been prepared, JISC posts these draft standards for a sixty-day public comment period. The JISC website also provides information regarding how foreign entities may participate in the JIS drafting process. A list of newly published JIS standards can be found on the website of the Japan Standards Association: http://www.jsa.or.jp/default_english.asp .

NIST NOTIFY U.S. SERVICE

Member countries of the World Trade Organization (WTO) are required under the Agreement on Technical Barriers to Trade (TBT Agreement) to report to the WTO all proposed technical regulations that could affect trade with other Member countries. **Notify U.S.** is a free, web-based e-mail subscription service that offers an opportunity to review and comment on proposed foreign technical regulations that can affect your access to international markets. Register online at Internet URL: http://www.nist.gov/notifyus/

CONFORMITY ASSESSMENT

Please see the *Product Certification* section below.

PRODUCT CERTIFICATION

Under the JIS mark scheme, product certification bodies accredited by the Ministry of Economy, Trade and Industry (METI) conduct a series of tests to verify compliance of products with JIS and audit the quality management system of facilities at which the products are manufactured. Any products manufactured at a factory that successfully passes such an audit will be authorized to affix the JIS mark. Additional information on this process can be found on the JISC website: http://www.jisc.go.jp/eng/jis-mark/newjis-eng.html .

ACCREDITATION

The Japan Accreditation System for Product Certification Bodies of JIS Mark (JASC) is an accreditation program defined by the Japanese Industrial Standards (JIS) Law, and operated by the JASC office in the Ministry of Economy, Trade and Industry (METI). JASC accredits product certification bodies in the private sector and allows these bodies to certify companies so that the companies may place the JIS Mark on their products. A list of Japanese and foreign organizations accredited by JASC as "JIS mark" certification bodies is available on the JISC website at http://www.jisc.go.jp/eng/jis-mark/acc-insp-body.html . This list provides contact information as well as the JIS fields of certification for these testing organizations.

The two major non-governmental accreditation bodies in Japan are the Incorporated Administrative Agency (IAJapan – within the quasi-governmental National Institute of Technology and Evaluation) and the Japan Accreditation Board for Conformity Assessment (JAB). IAJapan operates several accreditation programs including the Japan National Laboratory Accreditation System (JNLA) and the Japan Calibration Service System (JCSS). IAJapan's website (http://www.nite.go.jp/asse/iajapan/en/index.html) provides lists of laboratories accredited under its programs and laboratories accredited by JAB can be found at http://www.jab.or.jp/english/index.html .

A limited number of testing laboratories in the U.S., not listed on the websites noted above, have also been designated by various Japanese government agencies to test and approve U.S. products for compliance with Japanese mandatory certification standards and laws. Products not covered by these arrangements must be tested and approved by Japanese testing labs before these products can be sold in Japan.

For conformity assessment bodies recognized by Japan for electrical appliances see: http://www.meti.go.jp/english/policy/denan/procedure/07.htm

For other information on third-party conformity assessment for electrical products see: http://www.meti.go.jp/english/policy/denan/procedure/index.htm

PUBLICATION OF TECHNICAL REGULATIONS

Each Japanese ministry posts draft regulations for public comment on their respective websites. These draft regulations can also be found in a consolidated list, available in Japanese, on the e-Gov web portal: http://search.e-gov.go.jp/servlet/Public . The website was designed to help facilitate public participation in Japan's regulatory process by improving the public's ability to find, view, and comment on regulatory actions.

It should be noted that although U.S. entities may submit comments on draft regulations, the amount of time given for submissions varies widely and all comments must be submitted in Japanese. To assist U.S. entities that wish to participate in the Japanese regulatory process, Commercial Service staff at the U.S. Embassy in Tokyo prepares a weekly summary translation in English of public comment announcements by Japanese government agencies. For information on how to obtain this summary translation please contact the Commercial Section by email at: Tokyo.Office.Box@trade.gov

Finalized technical regulations and standards are published in Japan's national gazette known as the *Kanpō* (http://kanpou.npb.go.jp , Japanese only).

LABELING AND MARKING

The "voluntary" Japan Industrial Standards (JIS) mark, administered by the Ministry of Economy, Trade and Industry (METI), applies to nearly 600 different industrial products and consists of over 10,259 standards (as of March, 2011). Adherence to JIS is also an important determinant for companies competing on bids in the Japanese government procurement process. Products that comply with these standards will be given preferential treatment in procurement decisions under Japan's Industrial Standardization Law. JIS covers industrial and mineral products with the exception of: 1) medicines; 2) agricultural chemicals; 3) chemical fertilizers; 4) silk yarn; and 5) foodstuffs, agricultural and forest products designated under the Law Concerning Standardization and Proper Labeling of Agricultural and Forestry Products.

The Japan Agricultural Standards (JAS) is another "voluntary" but widely used product standard system administered by the Ministry of Agriculture, Forestry and Fisheries (MAFF). The Council for Agricultural and Forestry Standards, a JAS Council consisting of consumers, manufacturers, commercial users, and academic experts, establishes JAS's standards. Existing JAS Standards are reviewed every five years by each JAS Council. As of March, 2011 (the latest available information), there were 214 JAS standards covering 66 products. JAS is comprised of five different category standards including general and specific, which are product-based standards. The other three categories are based on the manufacturing or distribution process, one example being organic production standards. The general category applies to beverages, processed foods, forest products, agricultural commodities, livestock products, oils and fats, products of the fishing industry, and processed goods made from agricultural, forestry, and fishing industry raw materials. Specific JAS apply to aged ham, aged sausage and aged bacon.

JAS certification is a complicated process requiring approval by a Registered (Overseas) Certified Body (ROCB). At this time there are only three approved ROCB for forest products and two for organic products located in the U.S. More information on the JAS labeling system can be found at the following Ministry of Agriculture, Forestry and Fisheries (MAFF) website: on the JAS labeling system can be found at the following Ministry of Agriculture, Forestry and Fisheries (MAFF) website: on the JAS labeling system can be found at the following Ministry of Agriculture, Forestry and Fisheries (MAFF) website:

All producers and distributors are required to ensure that their labels are in compliance with "Quality Labeling" standards. Cross-Category Quality Labeling Standards such as the "Quality Labeling Standards for Processed Foods, Fresh Foods and Genetically Modified Foods" were established in 1999. These standards are available in English at: http://www.maff.go.jp/e/jas/labeling/index.html . As of January, 2011 (the latest available information), there were 56 individual quality labeling standards under the JAS law.

In September 2009, responsibility for all labeling issues in Japan, including food labeling, was officially transferred to the new Consumer Affairs Agency. More information on product labeling can be found on Japan's Consumer Affairs Agency website: http://www.caa.go.jp/en/index.html .

Other quality labeling standards are available (in Japanese only) at:

http://www.maff.go.jp/j/jas/hyoji/kijun_itiran.html .

As noted above, Japanese laws requiring product certification and labeling are numerous. A good reference for additional information on these requirements is JETRO's *Handbooks for Industrial and Consumer Product Import Regulations* available at: http://www.jetro.go.jp/en/reports/regulations/ .This website also includes specifications, standards and testing methods for foodstuffs, implements, containers and packaging, toys and detergents.

For additional information see the section above on *Labeling and Marking Requirements* in this chapter.

CONTACTS

Japan Industrial Standards Committee:
Contact: Secretariat Office
Tel: (81-3) 3501-9473
E-mail: jisc@meti.go.jp
Website: http://www.jisc.go.jp/eng/index.html
Japan Standards Association:
Contact: Secretariat Office
Tel: (81-3) 3583-0462
E-mail: please use the enquiry form at https://www.jsa.or.jp/eng/form_mail_e.asp
Website: http://www.jsa.or.jp/default_english.asp
Japan External Trade Organization (JETRO) on Standards and Regulations:
http://www.jetro.go.jp/en/reports/regulations
National Metrology Institute of Japan:
http://www.nmij.jp/english/
Building Center of Japan:
http://www.bcj.or.jp/en
Telecommunication Technology Committee:
http://www.ttc.or.jp/e/index.html
Japan Cable Television Engineering Association: http://www.catv.or.jp/jctea/english/index.html
Association of Radio Industries and Businesses:
http://www.arib.or.jp/english/index.html
Conformity Assessment Bodies:
Japan Accreditation Board for Conformity Assessment (JAB):
Contact: Customer Service, General Affairs Dept.
Fax: (81-3) 5475-2780
E-mail: please use the enquiry form at http://www.jsa.or.jp/aboutus/query.asp
Website: http://www.jab.or.jp/english/index.html
International Accreditation Japan:
Contact: Quality Manager
Tel: (81-3) 3481-1946
Fax: (81-3) 3481-1937
E-mail: iajapan-qm@nite.go.jp
Website: http://www.iajapan.nite.go.jp/iajapan/en/index.html

Foreign Registered Conformity Assessment Bodies in Japan:
http://www.meti.go.jp/english/policy/denan/procedure/07.htm

Japan Accreditation System for Product Certification Bodies: http://www.jisc.go.jp/eng/index.html

Japan National Institute of Technology and Evaluation: http://www.nite.go.jp/index-e.html

Specified Measurement Laboratory Accreditation Scheme: http://www.iajapan.nite.go.jp/mlap/en/top.html

Japan National Laboratory Accreditation System: http://www.iajapan.nite.go.jp/jnla/en/index.html

Japan Calibration Service System: http://www.iajapan.nite.go.jp/jcss/en/index.html

Accreditation System of National Institute of Technology and Evaluation:
http://www.iajapan.nite.go.jp/asnite/en/index.html

Third-party Conformity Assessment for Electrical Products in Japan:
http://www.meti.go.jp/english/policy/denan/procedure/index.htm

Japanese Draft Standards, Regulations and Public Comment: http://search.e-gov.go.jp/servlet/Public

Japan's National Gazette (*Kanpō):* http://kanpou.npb.go.jp (Japanese only)

For Japanese technical regulations notified to the WTO, sign up for the U.S. National Institute of Standards and Technology (NIST) "Notify U.S." service at: http://www.nist.gov/notifyus

TRADE AGREEMENTS

As of May 2013, Japan had entered into economic partnership agreements (EPAs) with 12 countries: Brunei, Chile, Indonesia, Malaysia, Mexico, Singapore, Switzerland, Thailand, the Philippines, Vietnam, India and Peru. In addition to bilateral agreements, Japan and the Association of Southeast Asian Nations (ASEAN) have also entered into an agreement on a Comprehensive Economic Partnership. EPAs are currently being negotiated with the Republic of Korea, Australia, the Gulf Cooperation Council, Columbia, Mongolia, Canada, and the European Union.

Japan has also committed to joining the Trans-Pacific Partnership multilateral free trade agreement. Additional information on Japan's trade agreements can be found on the Ministry of Foreign Affairs website at: http://www.mofa.go.jp/policy/economy/fta/index.html

For information on sector-specific agreements between the United States and Japan visit the Department of Commerce Market Access and Compliance Japan website: http://www.mac.doc.gov/japan/sector-specific/sector-specific.htm

Japan is a full member of the World Trade Organization (WTO). For more information on Japan and the WTO visit: http://www.wto.org/english/thewto_e/countries_e/japan_e.htm

WEB RESOURCES

Agriculture changes to requirements (e.g. MRL changes), as well as annual commodity reports:
http://gain.fas.usda.gov/Lists/Advanced%20Search/AllItems.aspx

Information on trading in agricultural products with Japan:

FAIRS Narrative report: http://goo.gl/wLyDE

FAIRS Certification report: http://goo.gl/Neued

Japanese import clearance and customs procedures:

Japanese Ministry of Finance/Japan Customs http://www.customs.go.jp/english/

Customs Counselors System in Japan http://www.customs.go.jp/zeikan/seido/telephone_e.htm

Japan Tariff Association http://www.kanzei.or.jp/english

U.S. export control procedures:

U.S. Department of Commerce

Bureau of Industry and Security (BIS) http://www.bis.doc.gov

(for defense-related articles)

U.S. Department of State

Office of Defense Trade Controls http://www.pmddtc.state.gov

(for current U.S. embargo information)

U.S. Department of the Treasury

Office of Foreign Assets Control http://www.treas.gov/offices/enforcement/ofac

Obtaining a temporary-entry *camet:*

United States Council for International Business

Local Offices — http://www.uscib.org http://www.atacarnet.com

Standards (key organizations; see also "Standards Contacts" above):

Japan Industrial Standards Committee (JISC) http://www.jisc.go.jp/eng/index.html

International Accreditation Japan (IAJapan) http://www.nite.go.jp/asse/iajapan/en/index.html

Japan Accreditation Board for Conformity Assessment (JAB) http://www.jab.or.jp/english/index.html

Public comment on Japanese government regulations:

Japan National Gazette (*Kanpō*) http://kanpou.npb.go.jp (Japanese only)

Japanese Import Standards and Regulations:

Japan External Trade Organization (JETRO) http://www.jetro.go.jp/en/market/regulations/index.html
https://twitter.com/BuyUSAJapan

INVESTMENT CLIMATE

OPENNESS TO, AND RESTRICTIONS UPON, FOREIGN INVESTMENT

Japan is the world's third largest economy, the United States' fourth largest trading partner, and an important destination for U.S. foreign direct investment (FDI). The Government of Japan explicitly promotes inward FDI and has established formal programs to attract it. The Japanese government's commitment to implement policies to improve the climate for foreign investment, however, has been uneven. Japan's stock of FDI, as a percentage of gross domestic product (GDP), stood at 3.9% at the end of 2011, compared with 28.7% on average for all Organization for Economic Cooperation and Development (OECD) member countries. While the FDI stock has risen substantially since the 1990's, Japan still has the lowest ratio of FDI as a proportion of GDP of any OECD member.

In terms of trends, outbound investment continued moving upwards during 2012 as Japanese companies' large cash holdings combined with low global equity values and the strong yen supported their active merger and acquisition (M&A) activity abroad. Meanwhile, investment activity inside Japan showed a modest increase in numbers of M&A transactions during 2012, ending a five-year downward trend. Final 2011 statistics for FDI in Japan show a net outflow of about $1.7 billion for the year, and provisional figures for the nine months through September 2012 indicated an outflow of $0.4 billion. Notwithstanding the imbalance between inward and outward FDI, and the increase in M&A activity by Japanese firms overseas, Japan's outward FDI as a percentage of GDP also remains among the lowest of major OECD members.

Japan has largely recovered from the economic shocks caused by the March 2011 Tohoku earthquake and tsunami, and gross domestic product has returned to its pre-quake levels. Japan continues to face challenges of low growth, deflation, and an aging population and shrinking workforce. While the strong yen posed challenges for Japan's export sector in 2012, some exports – particularly automobiles – still performed well. At the same time, the strong yen cushioned the cost of increased fuel imports resulting from reduced reliance on nuclear power generation in the wake of the March 2011 disasters. Japan's unemployment rate of 4.6% is low compared to many other developed economies, but is relatively high by domestic standards as the rate has historically ranged between 3.0% and 3.5%. As of 2012, the International Monetary Fund estimates Japan's public debt at about 235% of GDP – the highest percentage among advanced economies. The national Diet voted in 2012 to raise the consumption tax from 5% to 10% in stages by 2015 to help reduce the fiscal imbalance.

Economic issues featured prominently in the Diet Lower House election of December 2012, in which the Liberal Democratic Party (LDP) returned to power after three years of government led by the Democratic Party of Japan (DPJ). The LDP claimed 294 of the 480 Lower House seats. LDP President Shinzo Abe became Prime Minister on December 26; Abe had previously served as Prime Minister from 2006-2007. The new Abe Government has set economic recovery and revitalization as key goals and has proposed a large supplementary budget, with half earmarked for public works projects, to stimulate the economy. The Government is also expected to prod the Bank of Japan to ease monetary policy in order to tackle deflation, and will aim to stimulate growth through science and technology research and innovation.

The Ministry of Economy Trade and Industry (METI) and the quasi-governmental Japan External Trade Organization (JETRO) are the lead agencies responsible for assisting foreign firms wishing to invest in Japan. Many prefectural and city governments also have active programs to attract foreign investors, but they lack many of the financial tools U.S. states use to attract investment.

Risks associated with investment in many other countries, such as expropriation and nationalization, are not of concern in Japan. The Japanese Government does not impose export balancing requirements or other trade-related FDI measures on firms seeking to invest in Japan.

Japan ranked 17th on Transparency International's Corruption Perceptions Index in 2012, with a score of 74. The World Bank ranked Japan number 24 on its Ease of Doing Business 2013 report, covering the period June 2011 through May 2012. The 2012 Index of Economic Freedom compiled by the Heritage Foundation ranked Japan number 22, with a score of 71.6, or "mostly free." In each instance, Japan's ranking was slightly lower than the previous year.

Measure	Index/Ranking	Year
TI Corruption Perceptions Index	17	2012
Heritage Economic Freedom	22	2012
World Bank Doing Business	24	2013

In addition to business considerations relevant to investing in a mature economy with an aging population, foreign investors seeking a presence in the Japanese market, or to acquire a Japanese firm through corporate takeover, face a number of challenges, many of which relate more to prevailing practices comprising the business environment rather than to government regulations. The most notable are:

- An insular and consensual business culture that is resistant to hostile mergers and acquisitions (M&A) and prefers to do business, especially M&A transactions, with familiar corporate partners;

- A lack of independent directors on most company boards;

• Cross-shareholding networks among listed corporations in which shares are held for non-economic reasons, resulting in a minimal float of available common stock relative to total capital;

• Exclusive supplier networks and alliances between business groups that can restrict competition from foreign firms and domestic newcomers;

• Cultural and linguistic challenges; and

• Labor practices that tend to inhibit labor mobility.

The U.S. and Japanese governments have discussed these issues bilaterally under several different initiatives. In recent years, economic policy dialogues serving as the principal fora for discussing issues relating to the investment environment were the U.S.-Japan Economic Harmonization Initiative; the U.S.-Japan Dialogue to Promote Innovation, Entrepreneurship and Job Creation; and the U.S.-Japan Policy Cooperation Dialogue on the Internet Economy.

Legal Reform Facilitates M&A Activity

In recent years, reforms in the financial, communications, and distribution sectors have encouraged foreign investment in these industries. The 2005 Companies Act, an amended bankruptcy law, and the 2007 Financial Instruments and Exchange Act helped increase the attractiveness of Japan as a destination for FDI. The most significant legislative change was the substantial revision of Japan's corporate-related law. The changes enacted in 2005 significantly expanded the types of corporate structures available in Japan as well as the variety of M&A transactions available for corporate consolidation and restructuring.

The 2007 Financial Instruments and Exchange Act (amended in 2008) established a flexible regulatory system for financial markets and applied a uniform set of rules for similar financial instruments. At the same time, the law allows brokers and financial advisors to treat investors differently, depending on whether they are deemed "professional" investors (assumed to be capable of more sophisticated investment strategies and requiring less protection and disclosure) or "general," i.e., retail investors. Brokerage firms must provide the latter with detailed disclosure of risks related to different types of financial products at the time of offering.

The structural reforms, revisions to Japan's legal code, and pro-active Japanese government policies to welcome FDI and promote corporate restructuring of the past decade have increased foreign investment in Japan through M&A activity. The numbers have generally tracked the performance of the broader economy, declining as Japan's economy struggled after 2008 but rebounding somewhat between January and November 2012, with the 1,652 transactions in that period representing a 10.5% increase over the corresponding period of 2011, according to estimates by RECOF, a Tokyo-based M&A consultancy. The majority of these mergers were domestic transactions, but transactions involving foreign counterparts have also increased. The number of takeover bids (TOB) in Japan exceeded 100 for the first time in 2007 but has since dropped to more modest levels, amounting to 42 between January and October 2012 according to RECOF. The total value of M&A deals involving Japanese companies between January and November 2012 was 10.4 trillion yen, up 5.5% from the previous year. Japanese M&A directed at overseas companies amounted to 6.86 trillion yen during this period, accounting for 66% of total M&A and up 16.8% from 2011, according to RECOF.

Limited Sector-specific Investment Restrictions Remain

Japan has gradually eliminated most formal restrictions governing FDI. One important restriction remaining in law limits foreign ownership in Japan's former land-line monopoly telephone operator, Nippon Telegraph and Telephone (NTT), to 33%. Japan's Radio Law and separate Broadcasting Law also limit foreign investment in broadcasters to 20%, or 33% for broadcasters categorized as facility-supplying. Foreign ownership of Japanese companies invested in terrestrial broadcasters will be counted against these limits. These limits do not apply to communication satellite facility owners, program suppliers or cable television operators.

Though the Ministry of Land, Infrastructure, Transport and Tourism (MLIT) was expected to begin new discussions in 2012 on the possibility of further privatization of Tokyo's Narita International Airport, the discussions have not progressed. The GOJ had also planned to establish an "Action Plan of Airport Management Reform" by the summer of 2012, based on the proposals in the MLIT Airport Administration Study Group report completed in July 2011, but none was made. The GOJ submitted a bill to the Diet in March 2012 that would allow private firms to manage 27 airports that are currently managed by the GOJ, including larger airports like Sendai and Hiroshima, but the bill was not acted on and did not carry over to the new Diet session in January 2013.

Laws and Regulations Governing Investment

The Foreign Exchange and Foreign Trade Act governs investment in sectors deemed to have national sovereignty or national security implications. In most cases, foreign investors need only report transactions to the Ministry of Finance, and to the ministry having jurisdiction over that business sector, through the Bank of Japan within 15 days of acquiring more than 10% of the shares in a publicly listed company or any shares of a closely held company. However, if a foreign investor wants to acquire over 10% of the shares of a listed company in certain designated sectors, it must provide prior notification (and thus obtain specific approval) of the intended transaction to the Ministry of Finance and the ministry that regulates the specific industry. Designated sectors include agriculture, aerospace, forestry, petroleum, electric/gas/water utilities, telecommunications, and leather manufacturing. Amendments to the prior notification and reporting requirements under the law, effective in 2009, reduced the administrative burden on foreign investors so as to facilitate inward investment.

Several sections of the Japanese Anti-Monopoly Act (AMA) are relevant to FDI. Chapter Four of the AMA includes extensive anti-trust provisions pertaining to international

contract notification (article 6), shareholdings (articles 10, 11 and 14), interlocking corporate directorates (article 13), mergers (article 15), and acquisitions (article 16). The stated purpose of these provisions is to restrict shareholding, management, joint venture, and M&A activities that may constitute unreasonable restraints on competition or involve unfair trade practices. The Japanese Government has emphasized these provisions are not intended to discriminate against foreign companies or discourage FDI.

Amendments to the AMA, effective January 1, 2010, improved the climate for M&A by clarifying the pre-merger review process and significantly raising the thresholds for pre-merger reporting to antitrust authorities. The amendments make share acquisitions subject to the same pre-merger notification rules as mergers and asset acquisitions. The thresholds for notification rose to apply when the domestic sales amount of any one of the parties exceeds 20 billion yen and the domestic sales amount of another one of the parties exceeds five billion yen. The 20 billion yen threshold can be applied for either the acquirer or the target company, and likewise the five billion yen threshold. Also these can apply in the case where more than two companies are involved in the merger. The amendments also expanded the scope of exemptions from notification.

Limitations on Facility Development and Availability of Investment Real Estate

Aiming to increase the liquidity of Japanese real estate markets, the government in recent years has progressively lowered capital gains, registration, and license taxes on real estate. It also reduced inheritance and gift taxes to promote intergenerational transfer of land and other real assets. Japan's real estate sector experienced a painful contraction following the credit crunch of 2008 as prices declined. The real estate market, particularly for premium properties, has rebounded after the Bank of Japan (BOJ) began buying real estate investment trust (REIT) shares in 2010. As of December 2012, BOJ has 110 billion yen of REIT shares on its books, a very small portion of BOJ's total assets but up substantially from just 2.2 billion yen in 2010. The small number of large real estate deals between unrelated parties, however, continues to impede recovery of the real estate market. Additionally, U.S. investors have reported isolated instances of criminal elements interfering with real estate transactions in Japan, particularly those involving distressed assets.

Japan continues restricting development of retail and commercial facilities in some areas to prevent excessive concentration of development in the environs of Tokyo, Osaka, and Nagoya, and to preserve agricultural land. Conversely, many prefectural governments outside the largest urban areas make property available for development in public industrial parks. Japan's zoning laws give local officials and residents considerable discretion to screen almost all aspects of a proposed building. In some areas, these factors have hindered real estate development projects and led to construction delays and higher building costs; in particular in cases where proposed new retail development would affect existing businesses.

Japanese law permits marketing of REITs and mutual funds that invest in property rights, although the REIT market in Japan remains relatively small. As of December 2012, there are 40 REITs listed on the Tokyo Stock Exchange (TSE). The TSE's REIT Office Index has rebounded from the all-time low it reached in December 2011, and as of December 2012 was at its highest point since January 2011.

Corporate Tax Treatment

Local branches of foreign firms are generally taxed only on corporate income derived within Japan, whereas domestic Japanese corporations are taxed on their worldwide income. Calculations of taxable income and allowable deductions, and payments of the consumption tax (sales tax) for foreign investors are otherwise the same as those for domestic companies. Corporate tax rules classify corporations as either foreign or domestic depending on the location of their "registered office," which may be the same as – or a proxy for – the place of incorporation.

The current U.S.-Japan bilateral tax treaty allows Japan to tax the business profits of a U.S. resident only to the extent those profits are attributable to a "permanent establishment" in Japan. It also provides measures to mitigate double taxation. This "permanent establishment" provision combined with Japan's currently high 40 percent corporate tax rate serves to encourage foreign and investment funds to keep their trading and investment operations off-shore.

Cross-border dividends on listed stock in Japan are not subject to Japanese withholding tax if the parent company owns 50 percent or more of the foreign subsidiary. Interest on financial transactions payable to a nonresident and royalties paid to a foreign licensor are no longer subject to source country withholding tax. A special tax measure allows designated inward investors to carry over certain losses for tax purposes for ten years rather than for the normal five years. The government implemented an exemption for foreign investors from paying taxes on interest income (previously 15 percent) on corporate bonds, fiscal loan and investment program bonds and those issued by the Japan Finance Organization for Municipalities in June 2010.

The option of consolidated taxation is available to corporations. The purpose of these rules is to facilitate investment and corporate restructuring, because losses usually expected from a new venture or recently acquired subsidiary can be charged against the profits of the parent firm or holding company.

In June 2011, the U.S. Department of the Treasury announced that it planned to begin formal negotiation of amendments to the existing bilateral income tax treaty with Japan in order to bring the existing tax treaty into closer conformity with the current tax treaty policies of the United States and Japan.

Investment Promotion and Incentives

Since 2001, the Japanese Government has made increased inward FDI an explicit policy goal, but policies and programs to achieve this goal have changed over time. Most recently, in November 2011 the GOJ established a “Conference on Promoting Japan as an Asian Industrial Center and Direct Investment into Japan,” a task force chaired by the Parliamentary Secretary of the Cabinet Office and composed of officials from relevant government ministries. It subsequently released a “Program for Promoting Japan as an Asian Business Center and Direct Investment into Japan” with the aim of boosting investment profitability, utilizing a special zone system, and improving support structures for investment. The Conference set a target in June 2012 to double Japan's FDI stock up to 35 trillion yen by 2020, and this target was incorporated into the Comprehensive Strategy for the Rebirth of Japan, which was endorsed by the Cabinet on July 31, 2012.

JETRO operates six Invest Japan Business Support Centers in major urban areas to provide investment-related information and "one-stop" support services to foreign companies interested in investing in Japan. (Detailed information is available at http://www.jetro.go.jp/en/invest .) Most national level ministries also have information desks to help guide potential investors in navigating Japanese Government administrative procedures.

Many city or regional governments work to attract foreign capital through outreach to prospective foreign investors, business start-up support services, and limited financial incentives. JETRO supports local government investment promotion efforts. Detailed information on local and regional FDI promotion programs is available in English on the JETRO website (www.jetro.org).

Post-Disaster Reconstruction Policy and Special Zone Legislation

The Diet has allocated 18.9 trillion yen to date for reconstruction of the Tohoku region that was devastated by the March 11, 2011 earthquake and tsunami. The appropriations cover the five years from FY2011 to FY2015 (designated as the "concentrated reconstruction period"). The total combines funds allocated in the three supplementary budgets passed in FY2011 and the FY2012 budget, and includes major portions for rebuilding infrastructure along with various grant programs, some to be administered by local governments. As of December 6, 2012, approximately 420 billion yen in grants had been made to 26 towns and villages to promote collective housing relocation, and approximately 396 billion yen to 53 towns and villages for public housing developments. There are calls for additional reconstruction money in the FY2013 budget.

Under GOJ guidelines, participation in Tohoku reconstruction should be open to foreign contractors and investors. Japan's new Reconstruction Agency, established in February 2012, has hosted numerous briefings in conjunction with other agencies for foreign private companies and the diplomatic corps in Japan to promote private foreign direct investment and explain investment incentive measures in the disaster-hit areas. The Reconstruction Agency maintains a website on the reconstruction status at http://www.reconstruction.go.jp/english/, and is available at invest.tohoku@cas.go.jp to answer questions and consult with the private sector, including foreign companies, interested in investing in the disaster-hit regions.

Local governments in the Tohoku region play a central role in formulating reconstruction plans and implementing nationally-approved measures. The special economic zones legislation of 2011 includes 222 municipalities in the 11 prefectures of the affected region. Local municipalities may choose from a given menu of regulatory, tax relief, and other measures from which to craft special economic zones specific to their needs. As of December 14, 2012, 30 reconstruction promotion plans that feature special zones have been approved. The list of approved plans, and details on each, are available on the Reconstruction Agency website. While local governments are responsible for creating their own recovery plans, central government officials are providing technical assistance in drafting plans, exchanging information, and coordinating joint projects. On April 1, 2012, Corporate Coordination Promotion Offices were set up in the Reconstruction Agency's headquarters as well as in the Tohoku Bureaus.

Another key aspect of the special measures is the possibility to rezone agricultural, residential, and industrial areas to fit local plans. Each locality has decided or will

determine the aspects of its own special zone, so tax incentives and relaxed zoning may vary from locality to locality. Companies wishing to participate in Tohoku reconstruction should be aware of these circumstances, and may wish to seek a Japanese partner to negotiate the various zones and search for opportunities through the diverse proposals presented by local governments.

While Tohoku reconstruction efforts present significant potential opportunities for investors, challenges remain. According to a report submitted to the Diet by the Reconstruction Agency in November 2011, public infrastructure recovery has largely progressed according to the project plan and time schedule. However, shortages of skilled labor and construction materials have hindered progress in housing relocation and reconstruction. As a result, many local municipalities have been unable to begin housing projects and their allocated budgets have not been used. The GOJ is working with local governments to address these problems.

CONVERSION AND TRANSFER POLICIES

Generally, all foreign exchange transactions to and from Japan -- including transfers of profits and dividends, interest, royalties and fees, repatriation of capital, and repayment of principal -- are freely permitted. Japan maintains an ex-post facto notification system for foreign exchange transactions that prohibits specified transactions, including certain foreign direct investments (e.g., from countries under international sanctions) or others that are listed in the appendix of the Foreign Exchange and Foreign Trade Act.

Japan is an active partner in combating terrorist financing. In coordination with other OECD members, Japan has strengthened due-diligence requirements for financial institutions, and has had a "Know Your Customer" law since 2002. Customers wishing to make cash transfers exceeding 100,000 yen must do so through bank clerks, not ATMs, and must present photo identification. However, Japan is still working to rectify deficiencies noted in the 2008 Financial Action Task Force (FATF) evaluation of Japan's anti-money-laundering and terrorist finance regime, particularly on customer due diligence, international cooperation, freezing terrorist assets, and criminalizing terrorist finance.

EXPROPRIATION AND COMPENSATION

In the post-war period, the Japanese Government has not expropriated any enterprises and the expropriation or nationalization of foreign investments in Japan is extremely unlikely. Historically, nationalizations of enterprises have been rare and have all involved Japanese firms: the 1998 nationalization of two large Japanese capital-deficient banks and the 2002 nationalization of two failed Japanese regional banks, as part of the government's efforts to clean up the banking system after its near collapse in 1998, and the 2010 nationalization of Japan Airlines as a part of a two-year corporate reorganization plan. The airline has since been re-privatized.

Most recently, in the wake of the March 2011 nuclear accident at the Fukushima Daiichi Nuclear Power Station, the Tokyo Electric Power Company (TEPCO) was placed under "temporary public control" when the government injected $12.5 billion through the Nuclear Damage Liability Facilitation Fund to procure a 50.1% stake in the company in

May 2012. Total government support for TEPCO and its compensation payments to victims and evacuees of the nuclear accident reached $37 billion in December 2012. The utility is scheduled to pay back the funds over time, but the plan is contingent on the uncertain restart of TEPCO's large nuclear plant on Japan's west coast.

DISPUTE SETTLEMENT

There have been no major bilateral investment disputes since 1990. There have been no cases of international binding arbitration of investment disputes between foreign investors and Japan's Government since 1952. Japan is a member of the 1958 New York Convention on the Recognition and Enforcement of Foreign Arbitration Awards. Nevertheless, Japan is considered an inhospitable forum for international commercial arbitration.

Legal Services

There are no legal restrictions on foreign investors' access to Japanese lawyers, and reforms in the legal services sector and the judicial system have increased the ability of foreign investors to obtain international legal advice related to their investments in Japan. Japan does, however, retain certain restrictions on the ability of foreign lawyers to provide international legal services in Japan in an efficient manner. Only individuals who have passed the Japanese Bar Examination and qualified as Japanese lawyers (bengoshi) may practice Japanese law. However, under Japan's Foreign Legal Practitioner system foreign qualified lawyers may establish Japanese/foreign joint legal enterprises (gaikokuho kyodo jigyo) and provide legal advice and integrated legal services on matters within the competence of its members. Foreign lawyers qualified under Japanese law (gaiben), may provide advice on international legal matters. Gaiben and bengoshi in joint enterprises can adopt a single law firm name of their choice and may determine the profit allocation among them freely and without restriction. However, foreign lawyers are unable to form professional corporations in the same manner as Japanese lawyers and are prohibited from opening branch offices in Japan. Gaiben may hire Japanese lawyers to work directly with them or in a joint legal enterprise or in a Foreign Japanese Joint Legal Office (gaikokuho-jimu-bengoshi jimusho) composed of multiple gaiben. In March 2012, the Cabinet endorsed the draft revisions of the Act on Special Measures concerning the Handling of Legal Services by Foreign Lawyers to allow gaiben to form professional corporations and branch offices, and the amendment bill was submitted to the Diet. However, it was dropped when the Diet was dissolved in late 2012 and it is unclear whether it will be taken up again in the new session.

Courts and Arbitration

Japan's civil courts enforce property and contractual rights and do not discriminate against foreign investors. Japanese courts, like those in other countries, operate rather slowly and experience has shown them sometimes ill-suited for litigation of investment and business disputes. Japanese courts lack powers to compel witnesses to testify or a party to comply with an injunction. Timely temporary restraining orders and preliminary injunctions are difficult to obtain. Filing fees are based on the amount of the claim, rather than a flat fee. Lawyers usually require large up-front payments from their clients before filing a lawsuit, with a modest contingency fee, if any, at the conclusion of litigation. Contingency fees familiar in the U.S. are relatively uncommon. A losing party can delay execution of a judgment by appealing. In appeals to higher level courts, additional witnesses and other evidence may be allowed.

Japan's Alternative Dispute Resolution (ADR) law provides a legal framework for arbitration, including international commercial arbitration. Foreign lawyers qualified under Japanese law can represent parties in ADR proceedings taking place in Japan in which one of the parties is foreign or foreign law is applicable, at least to the extent such representation is not inconsistent with Japanese law. The United States continues to urge Japan to promote alternative dispute resolution mechanisms by ensuring that gaiben and non-lawyer experts can act as neutrals in international arbitration or other international ADR proceedings in Japan, in whole or in part, regardless of the governing law or matter in dispute.

Courts have the power to encourage mediated settlements and there is a supervised mediation system. However, this process is often time-consuming and judges transfer frequently, so continuity is often lost. As a result, it is common for companies to settle cases out of court.

PERFORMANCE REQUIREMENTS AND INCENTIVES

Japan does not maintain performance requirements or requirements for local management participation or local control in joint ventures.

RIGHT TO PRIVATE OWNERSHIP AND ESTABLISHMENT

Foreign and domestic private enterprises have the right to establish and own business enterprises and engage in all forms of remunerative activity.

However, the 2005 Companies Act includes a provision -- Article 821 -- which creates uncertainty among foreign corporations that conduct their primary business in the Japanese market through a branch company. As written, Article 821 appears to prohibit branches of foreign corporations from engaging in transactions in Japan "on a continuous basis." The Japanese Diet subsequently issued a clarification of the legislative intent of Article 821 that makes clear the provision should not apply to the activities of legitimate entities. However, some legal uncertainty remains, particularly with respect to possible private litigation against directors and officers of affected firms. The U.S. Government has urged Japan to revoke Article 821 or more formally clarify its meaning. The Japanese Government has said it will ensure Article 821 will not adversely affect the operations of foreign companies duly registered in Japan and conducting business in a lawful manner.

PROTECTION OF PROPERTY RIGHTS

In general, Japan maintains a strong intellectual property rights (IPR) regime, but there are costs and procedures of which prospective investors should be aware. Companies doing business in Japan are encouraged to be clear about all rights and obligations with respect to IPR in any trading or licensing agreements. Explicit arrangements and clear understanding between parties will help to avert problems resulting from differences in culture, markets conditions, legal procedures, or business practices.

Registering Patents, Trademarks, Utility Models and Designs

The IPR rights holder must register patents and trademarks in order to ensure protection in Japan. Filing the necessary applications requires hiring a Japanese lawyer or patent practitioner (benrishi) registered in Japan to pursue the patent or trademark application. A U.S. patent or trademark attorney may provide informal advice, but is not able to perform some required functions.

While patent and trademark procedures in Japan have historically been costly and time-consuming, the GOJ has made strides to improve procedures in recent years. Specific complaints included the weaknesses of Japanese enforcement and legal redress; for example, judges are not adequately trained or that court procedures do not adequately protect business-confidential information required to file a case. In response, Japan's government has revised the law and continues to take steps to address these concerns and it is becoming easier and cheaper to obtain patent and trademark protection. Procedures have been simplified, fees cut, and an IPR court has been established. Courts have strengthened rules to protect sensitive information and the government has established criminal penalties for inappropriate use of sensitive information used in court or administrative proceedings.

Prompt filing of patent applications is very important. Printed publication of a description of the invention anywhere in the world, or knowledge or use of the invention in Japan, prior to the filing date of the Japanese application, could preclude the granting of a patent. Japan grants patents on a first-to-file basis. It accepts initial filings in English (to be followed by a Japanese translation), but companies should be careful as translation errors can have significant negative consequences. Unlike the United States, where examination of an application is automatic, in Japan an applicant must request examination of a patent application within three years of filing.

The Japanese Patent Office (JPO) publishes all patent applications 18 months after filing, and if it finds no impediment to granting a patent, publishes the revised application a second time before the patent is granted. The patent is valid for 20 years from the date of filing. Currently, the law allows parties to contest the terms of a patent after issuance (for up to six months), rather than prior to registration as was the previous practice.

Patent Prosecution Highway

The Patent Prosecution Highway (PPH) is a noteworthy development for U.S. firms seeking patent protection in Japan. In place since January 2008, the PPH allows filing of streamlined applications for inventions determined to be patentable in other participating countries and is expected to reduce the average processing time. The program, which is based on information sharing between national patent offices and standardized application and examination procedures, should reduce costs and encourage greater utilization of the patent system.

Trademarks, Utility Models, and Designs

Japan's Trademark Law protects trademarks and service marks and, like patent protection, requires registration by means of an application filed by a resident agent (lawyer or patent agent). As the process takes time, firms planning on doing business in Japan should file for trademark registration as early as practicable. Japan is a signatory of the Madrid Protocol. Trademarks registered at the WIPO Secretariat are protected among all member countries.

Japan's Utility Model Law allows registration of utility models (a form of minor patent) and provides a 10-year term of protection. Under a separate design law, effective April 2007, protection is available for designs for a 20-year term from the date of registration.

Semiconductor chip design layouts are protected for 10 years under a special law, if registered with the Japanese "Industrial Property Cooperation Center" -- a government-established public corporation.

Unfair Competition and Trade Secrets

The Unfair Competition Prevention Law provides for protecting trademarks prior to registration. The owner of the mark must demonstrate that the mark is well known in Japan and that consumers will be confused by the use of an identical or similar mark by an unauthorized user. The law also provides some protection for trade secrets, such as know-how, customer lists, sales manuals, and experimental data. Recent amendments to the law provide for injunctions against wrongful use, acquisition or disclosure of a trade secret by any person who knew, or should have known, the information in question was misappropriated. Criminal penalties were also strengthened. In May 2011, the GOJ enacted a partial amendment to the Unfair Competition Prevention Law that protects trade secrets from being disclosed during court trials and makes it illegal to sell items designed to circumvent technological protection measures, even if the device has other legal uses. Both of these changes address specific issues of concern with the previous law. The partial amendment came into enforcement on December 1, 2011.

Copyrights

In conformity with international agreement, Japan maintains a non-formality principle for copyright registration -- i.e., registration is not a pre-condition to the establishment of copyright protection. However, the Cultural Affairs Agency maintains a registry for such matters as date of first publication, date of creation of program works, and assignment of copyright. United States copyrights are recognized in Japan by international treaty.

TRANSPARENCY OF REGULATORY SYSTEM

The Japanese economy continues to suffer from over-regulation, which can restrain potential economic growth, raise the cost of doing business, restrict competition, and impede investment. It also increases the costs for Japanese businesses and consumers. Over-regulation underlies many market access and competitive problems faced by U.S. companies in Japan.

The United States has for several years called on Japan to make improvements in its regulatory system to support domestic reform efforts and ensure universal access to government information and the policymaking process.

The Japanese Government has taken steps to improve its public comment procedures, but these improvements are not uniform throughout the government. The United States continues to urge Japan to apply consistently high transparency standards, including by issuing new rules to ensure transparency and access for stakeholders in the rulemaking process; by allowing effective public input into the regulatory process; and by giving due consideration to comments received. The United States also has asked Japan to lengthen its public comment period and to require ministries and agencies to issue all new regulations or statements of policy in writing or provide applicable interpretations to interested stakeholders in plain language.

In the financial sector, the Financial Services Agency (FSA) has made efforts to expand the body of published written interpretations of Japan's financial laws, and has improved outreach to the private sector regarding these changes.

The United States has engaged in bilateral working-level discussions since 2002 in an effort to encourage the Japanese Government to promote deregulation, improve competition policy, and undertake administrative reforms that could contribute to sustainable economic growth, increase imports and foreign direct investment into Japan. The National Trade Estimate Report on Foreign Trade Barriers, issued by the Office of the U.S. Trade Representative (USTR), contains a description of Japan's regulatory regime as it affects foreign exporters and investors.

CAPITAL MARKETS AND PORTFOLIO INVESTMENT

Stock Exchanges

Japan maintains no formal restrictions on inward portfolio investment and foreign capital plays an important role in Japan's financial markets. However, many company managers and directors resist the actions of activist shareholders, especially foreign private equity funds, potentially limiting the attractiveness of Japan's equity market to large-scale foreign portfolio investment. Nevertheless, some firms have taken steps to facilitate the exercise of shareholder rights by foreign investors, including the use of electronic proxy voting. The Tokyo Stock Exchange (TSE) maintains an Electronic Voting Platform for Foreign and Institutional Investors in which more than 400 listed companies participate as of December 2012. All holdings of TSE-listed stocks are required to transfer paper stock certificates into electronic form.

The TSE has stepped up efforts to attract investors. Following receipt of a license from the FSA on May 29, 2009, the TSE launched Tokyo AIM, a new equity market for venture firms, in cooperation with the London Stock Exchange. However, in March 2012 AIM was integrated into TSE and rebranded as "Tokyo PRO Market." As of December 2012, only three companies were listed on the Tokyo PRO Market, out of 2,303 total listed on TSE.

Japan's stock exchanges face competitive pressures. In 2012, 56 firms delisted from the TSE. Other major stock exchanges in Asia -- including Taiwan, Hong Kong, Seoul, and Singapore – continue to seek stock listings by Japanese companies, and media reports indicate that some Japanese firms chose to conduct initial public offerings of shares offshore. In part to improve their competitiveness internationally, Japan's two biggest stock exchanges, Tokyo and Osaka, completed a merger on January 1, 2013. Cash equity trading will be consolidated on the Tokyo Exchange in July 2013, while derivatives trading is slated to be consolidated on the Osaka Exchange in January 2014.

Environment for Mergers and Acquisitions

Japan's aversion to M&A is receding gradually, accelerated by the unwinding of previously extensive corporate cross-shareholding networks between banks and corporations in the same business family, improved accounting standards, and government mandates that began in the late 1990s that require banks to divest cross-holdings above a set threshold. The majority of M&A over the past decade has been driven by the need to consolidate and restructure mature industries or in response to severe financial difficulties.

Friendly transfer of wholly-owned or majority-owned subsidiaries remains by far the more common form of M&A in Japan. Similarly, unlisted, owner-operated firms – which traditionally would only sell out as a last resort before bankruptcy – are becoming more amenable to acquisition, including by foreign investors. Nevertheless, there remains a strong preference among Japanese managers and directors for M&A that preserves the independence of the target company. If companies are forced to seek an acquirer, they are often most comfortable receiving an investment from or being acquired by a domestic firm with which they have a pre-existing business relationship.

After the Companies Act took full effect in 2007, expanding the types of M&A structure available in the Japanese market, many companies adopted defensive measures against hostile takeovers, though the prevalence of such measures has since declined. The most common of these are "advance warning systems" or "poison pill"-type rights distribution plans. While the financial crisis starting in 2008 reduced the threat of hostile takeovers by reducing available capital, the decline also flowed from intensified criticism of such measures from investors and growing recognition by management that takeover defense plans are not in the interests of either the firm or its shareholders. Nevertheless, a number of technical factors continue to limit greater entry into the Japanese market through M&A. These factors include a lack of independent directors, uncertainty regarding tax treatment of certain M&A structures, weak disclosure practices, and a relative shortage of M&A infrastructure in the form of specialists skilled in making matches and structuring M&A deals.

Company Law Revisions

The extensive revision of Japan's Company Law (Commercial Code) in 2005-06 significantly expanded the flexibility of corporate capital structures and increased the types of governance structures available to Japanese firms. The new law, which fully entered into force in May 2007 as the Companies Act, revised and combined Part II of the previous Commercial Code with existing laws governing limited liability companies (yugen gaisha) and audits. The law also introduced changes to facilitate start-ups and make corporate structures more flexible, including elimination of minimum capital requirements for joint-stock companies (kabushiki kaisha). It merged a number of different corporate structures and created a new structure (godo kaisha) modeled on the U.S.-style limited liability company. The Companies Act also allowed formation of corporate holding companies in Japan for the first time since World War II. This step has facilitated use of domestic stock swaps in corporate restructuring, through which one party becomes a wholly-owned subsidiary of the other. Japan's tax law now provides special tax treatment and deferral of taxes on such stock-swap transactions at the time of exchange and transfer.

Changes in Corporate Governance

Under the Companies Act and the Industrial Revitalization Law, publicly traded companies have the option of adopting a U.S.-style corporate governance system instead of the traditional Japanese statutory auditor (kansayaku) system of corporate governance. This system requires the appointment of executive officers and the establishment of a board committee system in which at least the audit, nomination, and compensation committees are composed of a majority of outside directors. Initially available only under the Industrial Revitalization Law and effectively limited to distressed companies, the Companies Act makes these options available to all listed companies. Unfortunately, very few listed Japanese companies have adopted the board committee system. Companies can also use the Internet or other electronic means to provide notices of annual general meetings or similar communication with shareholders. Where available, shareholders may exercise voting rights electronically and companies are permitted to make required disclosures of balance sheet and other financial information in an electronic format.

Reflecting growing concern within Japan that weaknesses in existing systems of corporate governance were a disincentive for foreign investors, the Japanese Government in the last few years has taken an increasingly strong stance towards corporate misconduct. In March 2012, the Financial Services Agency (FSA) implemented an amendment to corporate disclosure rules to require disclosure of information on the degree of independence of outside directors and outside company auditors, such as the relationship between the company and the current or previous employer of those outside directors/auditors. In addition, FSA launched a review of existing regulation and government supervision of Japan's asset management sector. The FSA has recently published draft amendments aimed at reducing the likelihood of cases like the AIJ Investment Advisors scandal, which involved fraudulent handling of pension fund assets by an investment management firm.

Broadly, the FSA's proposed amendments are aimed at introducing systems to help domestic trust banks and pension funds verify financial information provided by discretionary investment management companies, as well as increasing the volume of information which discretionary investment management companies are required to provide. In addition, the FSA proposes implementing heavier penalties for false statements made by discretionary investment management companies and introducing a more rigorous system of regulatory supervision and inspection. Following the proposals, the FSA has also imposed administrative punishments (including suspension of certain business operations) on three investment advisors who managed investments for the fund which AIJ is suspected of defrauding.

In 2010 the Ministry of Justice (MOJ) convened a Legislative Advisory Council having the authority to consider amendments to the Companies Act of 2005. The Company Act Sub-Committee did not specify a clear scope for its deliberations or signal a commitment to increasing the number of independent members on company boards at the outset. However, TEPCO's failure to take steps that would have prevented the March 2011 nuclear disaster, as well as high-profile Olympus and AIJ scandals that resulted from lax corporate governance sparked renewed interest in corporate governance reform in 2011.

In August 2012, MOJ published and submitted to the Justice Minister draft amendments to the Companies Act with an accompanying resolution that "there is the need to establish discipline in the rules and regulations of financial instruments exchanges to the effect that listed companies shall strive to secure at least one independent board member that is an outside director." Although MOJ did not recommend a change in the law to require listed company boards to have at least one outside director – due at least in part to opposition by Japanese business groups – the amendments would require those companies which do not have an outside director to disclose why it considers the appointment of an outside director as inappropriate. The amendments also create an alternative structure where companies may institute an audit and supervisory committee (kansa kantoku iinkai setchi geisha) whose members do not serve as directors. It is expected that the amendment bill will be submitted to the Diet in early 2013. While viewed as a positive step, the international business community has expressed concern that the amendments do not go far enough to strengthen corporate governance.

In 2009, the TSE implemented new restrictions on private placements to protect the interests of shareholders and published its Listing System Improvement Action Plan. The plan sets out steps to enhance corporate governance, improve disclosure, and improve the governance of group companies. At the end of 2009 the TSE released its revised Principles of Corporate Governance for Listed Companies, the first revision since their formulation in 2004, adding points to enhance corporate governance not only of the parent company, but of the corporate group as a whole; strengthen statutory auditors' functions; and identify suitable governance models. The TSE published a "TSE Listed Companies White Paper on Corporate Governance," and revised its requirements to handle earnings forecast disclosure in a "practical manner" in 2011. In March 2012, TSE relaxed rules for listed firms' earnings forecasts. Firms now have more flexibility to choose items to include, how to present items, and which periods to cover. The changes are intended to steer firms preparing disclosure in the direction of dialogue with investors, rather than "perfunctory conformation with rules," and came into effect with TSE financial statement filings for the fiscal year ending March 2012. In response to the MOJ Subcommittee's recommendations on corporate governance, TSE has requested that its listed companies make efforts to secure an independent outside director.

Cross-shareholdings and M&A

Potential foreign investors in Japan frequently point out that cross-shareholding between Japanese listed companies greatly complicates market-based M&A activity and reduces the potential impact of shareholder-based corporate governance. Such cross-shareholding practices allow senior management to put a priority on internal loyalties over shareholder returns and can lead to premature rejection of M&A bids. Traditionally, a company maintained a close relationship with a large-scale commercial bank, known as a "main bank," usually part of the same loose corporate grouping. In return for holding a bloc of the company's shares, the bank provided both regular financing and emergency support if the company ran into financial difficulties. This "main bank" system largely dissolved in the late 1990's as Japan's banking system came close to collapse.

Within a decade, however, some company boards began rebuilding cross-shareholding networks, this time with suppliers or nominal competitors rather than a commercial bank. While many boards saw such linkages as an effective means of defense against hostile takeovers, the sharp decline in Japanese stock prices in the autumn of 2008 highlighted the risks of this strategy. According to a March 2011 study by Nomura Holdings Inc., the cross-shareholding ratio (market value basis) in FY ended March 2011 was a record-low 11.1%, a 0.4% decline from the previous year.

Accounting and Disclosure

Implementation of so-called "Big Bang" reforms since 1998 has significantly improved Japan's accounting standards. Consolidated accounting has been mandatory since 1999 and "effective control and influence" standards have been introduced in place of conventional holding standards, expanding the range of subsidiary and affiliated companies included for the settlement of accounts. Consolidated disclosure of contingent liabilities, such as guarantees, is also mandatory. All marketable financial assets held for trading purposes, including cross-shareholdings and other long-term securities holdings, are recorded at market value.

Companies are required to disclose unfunded pension liabilities by valuing pension assets and liabilities at fair value. Fixed asset impairment accounting, in effect since 2005, requires firms to record losses if the recoverable value of property, plant, or equipment is significantly less than book value. The greater focus on consolidated results and mark-to-market accounting had a significant effect in encouraging the unwinding of cross-shareholdings and the "main bank" system. Corporate restructuring has taken place, in many cases with companies reducing pension under-funding and banks disposal of many low-yield assets.

In December 2009, the FSA issued an order allowing companies to submit their financial statements based on international accounting standards. This order prepares the legal groundwork for a complete switch to IFRS in the future, but a final decision has not been made on the mandatory introduction of International

Financial Reporting Standards (IFRS). In June 2011, the FSA announced it would delay its road map towards adoption of IFRS for publicly traded companies due to concerns over additional costs for Japanese companies struggling after the March 11 earthquake. The FSA's road map originally indicated it would be mandatory for Japanese companies to report under IFRS in 2015 or 2016. The FSA said instead there will be a transition period of five to seven years prior to mandatory adoption in order to allow companies sufficient time to prepare for the new reporting standard.

There has been greater disclosure of proxy voting during the past few years. The above-mentioned Financial System Council report issued in June 2009 urged the government to consider introducing legislation similar to the American ERISA law that would spell out the fiduciary duties of pension fund managers to exercise their proxy voting rights on behalf of pension beneficiaries. The report called upon the investment industry to establish rules or other means to require institutional fund managers and other large-scale investors who invest on behalf of retail investors to disclose how they exercise their proxy votes.

Taxation and M&A

Japan's standard tax rate for individual capital gains is 20%. However, under special policy measures intended to stimulate capital markets, Japan applied a special 10% capital gains tax rate on the proceeds of sales of listed stocks through 2011, and was subsequently extended to December 2013 for capital gains of less than 5 million yen and for dividends on listed shares of less than 1 million yen. Starting January 1, 2014, earned income from new investments of up to 1 million yen will be exempt from capital gains and dividend tax for up to 10 years. The program will be in effect until December

31, 2016, during which time taxpayers can make an investment of up to 1 million yen in stocks and stock funds each year, aggregating to a maximum of 3 million yen in total.

Under a series of special measures Japan adopted to promote venture businesses, if the founding shareholder of a qualified company sells shares in the company, a 10% capital gains tax rate will apply if the sale is made prior to public listing in an M&A transaction and, from 2008, a 10% rate applies to shares sold by the founding shareholder within three years of listing.

Bankruptcy Laws

An insolvent company in Japan can face liquidation under the Bankruptcy Act or take one of four roads to reorganization: the Civil Rehabilitation Law; the Corporate Reorganization Law; corporate reorganization under the Commercial Code; or an out-of-court creditor agreement.

Japan overhauled its bankruptcy law governing small and medium size firm bankruptcies by enacting the Civil Rehabilitation Law in 2000. The law focuses on corporate restructuring in contrast to liquidation, provides stronger protection of debtor assets prior to the start of restructuring procedures, eases requirements for initiating restructuring procedures, simplifies and rationalizes procedures for the examination and determination of liabilities, and improves procedures for approval of rehabilitation plans. Japan's Corporate Reorganization Law, generally used by large companies, was similarly revised in 2003. Amendments made corporate reorganization for large companies more cost-efficient, speedy, flexible and available at an earlier stage. By removing many institutional barriers to the restructuring process, the new bankruptcy regime accelerated the corporate restructuring process in Japan.

Previously, most corporate bankruptcies in Japan were handled through out-of-court creditor agreements because court procedures were lengthy and costly. Since bankruptcy trustees had limited powers to oversee restructuring, most judicial bankruptcies ended in liquidation, often at distressed prices. Out-of-court settlements in Japan tend to save time and expense, but can sometimes lack transparency and fairness. In practice, because 100 percent creditor consensus is required for out-of-court settlements and the court can sanction a reorganization plan with only a majority of creditors' approval, the last stage of an out-of-court workout is often a request for a judicial seal of approval.

Credit Markets

Domestic and foreign investors have free access to a variety of credit instruments at market rates. Most foreign firms obtain short-term credit from Japanese commercial banks or one of the many foreign banks operating in Japan. Medium-term loans are available from commercial banks or from trust banks and life insurance companies. Large foreign firms tend to use foreign sources for long-term financial needs.

COMPETITION FROM STATE OWNED ENTERPRISES

Japan has privatized most former state-owned enterprises. The privatization of the financial companies of the Japan Post group, including Japan Post Bank and Japan Post Insurance, however, remains incomplete. In April 2012, the Diet passed legislation to

amend the Postal Privatization Laws that were first enacted under Prime Minister Koizumi in 2005. Among other things the revised legislation (1) changes the group's organizational structure from a five company structure to a four company structure by requiring the mail delivery company and the postal network company to merge; (2) removes the deadline to fully privatize Japan Post Insurance and Japan Post Bank; (3) mandates that Japan Post group provide insurance and banking services universally in an integrated manner, which will raise costs to the Japan Post system and discourage the selling of private sector products through the Japan Post's post office network; and (4) substantially eases new product expansion, particularly after 50 percent of the postal financial entity's shares are sold.

Also, the Japan Post Company, which was established on October 1, 2012 through merger of the postal operating entities, should provide private companies access to its network comparable to that given to Japan Post entities, and select and distribute financial products of private providers through its network transparently and without discrimination. In addition, Japan should implement measures to prevent cross-subsidization among the Japan Post businesses and related entities, such as ensuring the Japan Post companies' strict compliance with the Insurance Business Law's "arm's length" rule and requiring adequate financial disclosures to demonstrate that cross-subsidization is in fact not occurring.

The U.S. Government has continued to raise concerns about the preferential treatment that Japan Post entities receive compared to private sector competitors and the impact of these advantages on the ability of private companies to compete on a level playing field.

In addition, U.S. private equity firms can still face challenges when seeking to make significant investment in "strategic industries" deemed important to Japan's national interests. Private equity buyout deals in Japan during 2012 totaled only USD 3.5 billion, which is 4% of the value in the United States. Japan does not have a sovereign wealth fund (SWF).

CORPORATE SOCIAL RESPONSIBILITY

Awareness of corporate social responsibility among both producers and consumers in Japan is high and growing, and foreign and local enterprises generally follow accepted CSR principles. Business organizations also actively promote CSR.

POLITICAL VIOLENCE

Political violence is rare in Japan. Acts of political violence involving U.S. business interests are virtually unknown.

CORRUPTION

Japan's penal code covers crimes of official corruption. An individual convicted under these statutes is, depending on the nature of the crime, subject to prison sentences up to three years and possible fines up to 2.5 million yen (for the offering party), or prison sentences up to seven years and mandatory confiscation of the monetary equivalent of the bribe (for the recipient). With respect to corporate officers who accept bribes, Japanese law also provides for company directors to be subject to fines and/or imprisonment, and some judgments have been rendered against company directors.

Although the direct exchange of cash for favors from government officials in Japan is extremely rare, the web of close relationships between Japanese companies, politicians, government organizations, and universities has been said to foster an inwardly-cooperative business climate that is conducive to the awarding of contracts, positions, etc. within a tight circle of local players. This phenomenon manifests itself most frequently and most seriously in Japan through the rigging of bids on government public works projects.

Japanese authorities have acknowledged the problem of bid-rigging and have taken steps to address it. Building on the longstanding laws on bribery of public officials and misuse of public funds, the 2006 amendments to the 2003 Bid-Rigging Prevention Act, now called the Act on Elimination and Prevention of Involvement in Bid-Rigging, aimed specifically to eliminate official collusion in bid rigging. The law authorizes the Japan Fair Trade Commission (JFTC) to demand central and local government commissioning agencies take corrective measures to prevent continued complicity of officials in bid-rigging activities, and to report such measures to the JFTC. The Act also contains provisions concerning disciplinary action against officials participating in bid rigging and compensation for overcharges when the officials caused damage to the government due to willful or grave negligence. The act prescribes possible penalties of imprisonment for up to five years and fines of up to 2.5 million yen. Nevertheless, questions remain as to whether the Act's disciplinary provisions are strong enough to ensure officials involved in illegal bid-rigging are held accountable.

Complicating efforts to combat bid rigging is the phenomenon known as amakudari, whereby government officials retire into top positions in Japanese companies, frequently in industries that they once regulated. Amakudari employees are particularly common in the financial, construction, transportation, and pharmaceutical industries, among Japan's most heavily regulated industries. The 2007 revised National Public Service Act aimed at limiting involvement of individual ministries in finding post-retirement employment for its officials and more transparent administrative procedures may somewhat ameliorate the situation. In view of strong DPJ opposition to amakudari when they were an opposition party, there were popular expectations that the DPJ-led government would move to eliminate amakudari after assuming power in 2009. However, successive DPJ governments did not make the issue a priority, and amakudari practices persist.

Japan has ratified the OECD Anti-Bribery Convention, which bans bribing foreign government officials. The OECD has identified deficiencies in Japan's implementing legislation, some of which the Japanese Government has taken steps to rectify. In 2004, Japan amended its Unfair Competition Prevention Law to extend national jurisdiction to cover the crime of bribery and in 2006 made changes to the Corporation Tax Law and the Income Tax Law expressly to deny the tax deductibility of bribes to foreign public officials.

Corruption, including bribery, raises the costs and risks of doing business. Corruption has a corrosive impact on both market opportunities overseas for U.S. companies and the broader business climate. It also deters international investment, stifles economic growth and development, distorts prices, and undermines the rule of law.

It is important for U.S. companies, irrespective of their size, to assess the business climate in the relevant market in which they will be operating or investing, and to have an effective compliance program or measures to prevent and detect corruption, including foreign bribery. U.S. individuals and firms operating or investing in foreign markets should take the time to become familiar with the relevant anticorruption laws of both the foreign country and the United States in order to properly comply with them, and where appropriate, they should seek the advice of legal counsel.

The U.S. Government seeks to level the global playing field for U.S. businesses by encouraging other countries to take steps to criminalize their own companies' acts of corruption, including bribery of foreign public officials, by requiring them to uphold their obligations under relevant international conventions. A U. S. firm that believes a competitor is seeking to use bribery of a foreign public official to secure a contract should bring this to the attention of appropriate U.S. agencies, as noted below.

U.S. Foreign Corrupt Practices Act: In 1977, the United States enacted the Foreign Corrupt Practices Act (FCPA), which makes it unlawful for a U.S. person, and certain foreign issuers of securities, to make a corrupt payment to foreign public officials for the purpose of obtaining or retaining business for or with, or directing business to, any person. The FCPA also applies to foreign firms and persons who take any act in furtherance of such a corrupt payment while in the United States. For more detailed information on the FCPA, see the FCPA Lay-Person's Guide at: http://www.justice.gov/criminal/fraud/

Other Instruments: It is U.S. Government policy to promote good governance, including host country implementation and enforcement of anti-corruption laws and policies pursuant to their obligations under international agreements. Since enactment of the FCPA, the United States has been instrumental to the expansion of the international framework to fight corruption. Several significant components of this framework are the OECD Convention on Combating Bribery of Foreign Public Officials in International Business Transactions (OECD Anti-bribery Convention), the United Nations Convention against Corruption (UN Convention), the Inter-American Convention against Corruption (OAS Convention), the Council of Europe Criminal and Civil Law Conventions, and a growing list of U.S. free trade agreements. This country is party to [add instrument to which this country is party], but generally all countries prohibit the bribery and solicitation of their public officials.

OECD Anti-bribery Convention: The OECD Anti-bribery Convention entered into force in February 1999. As of March 2009, there are 38 parties to the Convention including the United States (see http://www.oecd.org/dataoecd/59/13/40272933.pdf). Major exporters China, India, and Russia are not parties, although the U.S. Government strongly endorses their eventual accession to the Convention. The Convention obligates the Parties to criminalize bribery of foreign public officials in the conduct of international business. The United States meets its international obligations under the OECD Anti-bribery Convention through the U.S. FCPA.

UN Convention: The UN Anticorruption Convention entered into force on December 14, 2005, and there are 158 parties to it as of November 2011 (see

http://www.unodc.org/unodc/en/treaties/CAC/signatories.html). The UN Convention is the first global comprehensive international anticorruption agreement. The UN Convention requires countries to establish criminal and other offences to cover a wide range of acts of corruption. The UN Convention goes beyond previous anticorruption instruments, covering a broad range of issues ranging from basic forms of corruption such as bribery and solicitation, embezzlement, trading in influence to the concealment and laundering of the proceeds of corruption. The Convention contains transnational business bribery provisions that are functionally similar to those in the OECD Anti-bribery Convention and contains provisions on private sector auditing and books and records requirements. Other provisions address matters such as prevention, international cooperation, and asset recovery.

OAS Convention: In 1996, the Member States of the Organization of American States (OAS) adopted the first international anticorruption legal instrument, the Inter-American Convention against Corruption (OAS Convention), which entered into force in March 1997. The OAS Convention, among other things, establishes a set of preventive measures against corruption provides for the criminalization of certain acts of corruption, including transnational bribery and illicit enrichment, and contains a series of provisions to strengthen the cooperation between its States Parties in areas such as mutual legal assistance and technical cooperation. As of December 2009, the OAS Convention has 34 parties (see http://www.oas.org/juridico/english/Sigs/b-58.html) [Insert information as to whether your country is a party to the OAS Convention.]

Council of Europe Criminal Law and Civil Law Conventions: Many European countries are parties to either the Council of Europe (CoE) Criminal Law Convention on Corruption, the Civil Law Convention, or both. The Criminal Law Convention requires criminalization of a wide range of national and transnational conduct, including bribery, money-laundering, and account offenses. It also incorporates provisions on liability of legal persons and witness protection. The Civil Law Convention includes provisions on compensation for damage relating to corrupt acts, whistleblower protection, and validity of contracts, inter alia. The Group of States against Corruption (GRECO) was established in 1999 by the CoE to monitor compliance with these and related anti-corruption standards. Currently, GRECO comprises 49 member States (48 European countries and the United States). As of December 2011, the Criminal Law Convention has 43 parties and the Civil Law Convention has 34 (see www.coe.int/greco.)

Free Trade Agreements: While it is U.S. Government policy to include anticorruption provisions in free trade agreements (FTAs) that it negotiates with its trading partners, the anticorruption provisions have evolved over time. The most recent FTAs negotiated now require trading partners to criminalize "active bribery" of public officials (offering bribes to any public official must be made a criminal offense, both domestically and trans-nationally) as well as domestic "passive bribery" (solicitation of a bribe by a domestic official). All U.S. FTAs may be found at the U.S. Trade Representative Website: http://www.ustr.gov/trade-agreements/free-trade-agreements .

Local Laws: U.S. firms should familiarize themselves with local anticorruption laws, and, where appropriate, seek legal counsel. While the U.S. Department of Commerce cannot provide legal advice on local laws, the Department's U.S. and Foreign Commercial Service can provide assistance with navigating the host country's legal system and obtaining a list of local legal counsel.

Assistance for U.S. Businesses: The U.S. Department of Commerce offers several services to aid U.S. businesses seeking to address business-related corruption issues. For example, the U.S. and Foreign Commercial Service can provide services that may assist U.S. companies in conducting their due diligence as part of the company's overarching compliance program when choosing business partners or agents overseas. The U.S. Foreign and Commercial Service can be reached directly through its offices in every major U.S. and foreign city, or through its Website at www.trade.gov/cs .

The Departments of Commerce and State provide worldwide support for qualified U.S. companies bidding on foreign government contracts through the Commerce Department's Advocacy Center and State's Office of Commercial and Business Affairs. Problems, including alleged corruption by foreign governments or competitors, encountered by U.S. companies in seeking such foreign business opportunities can be brought to the attention of appropriate U.S. government officials, including local embassy personnel and through the Department of Commerce Trade Compliance Center "Report A Trade Barrier" Website at tcc.export.gov/Report_a_Barrier/index.asp .

Guidance on the U.S. FCPA: The Department of Justice's (DOJ) FCPA Opinion Procedure enables U.S. firms and individuals to request a statement of the Justice Department's present enforcement intentions under the anti-bribery provisions of the FCPA regarding any proposed business conduct. The details of the opinion procedure are available on DOJ's Fraud Section Website at www.justice.gov/criminal/fraud/fcpa . Although the Department of Commerce has no enforcement role with respect to the FCPA, it supplies general guidance to U.S. exporters who have questions about the FCPA and about international developments concerning the FCPA. For further information, see the Office of the Chief Counsel for International Counsel, U.S. Department of Commerce, Website, at http://www.ogc.doc.gov/trans_anti_bribery.html . More general information on the FCPA is available at the Websites listed below.

Exporters and investors should be aware that generally all countries prohibit the bribery of their public officials, and prohibit their officials from soliciting bribes under domestic laws. Most countries are required to criminalize such bribery and other acts of corruption by virtue of being parties to various international conventions discussed above.

ANTI-CORRUPTION RESOURCES

Some useful resources for individuals and companies regarding combating corruption in global markets include the following:

- Information about the U.S. Foreign Corrupt Practices Act (FCPA), including a "Lay-Person's Guide to the FCPA" is available at the U.S. Department of Justice's Website at: http://www.justice.gov/criminal/fraud/fcpa .

- Information about the OECD Anti-bribery Convention including links to national implementing legislation and country monitoring reports is available at: http://www.oecd.org/department/0,3355,en_2649_34859_1_1_1_1_1,00.html . See also new Anti-bribery Recommendation and Good Practice Guidance Annex for companies: http://www.oecd.org/dataoecd/11/40/44176910.pdf .

• General information about anticorruption initiatives, such as the OECD Convention and the FCPA, including translations of the statute into several languages, is available at the Department of Commerce Office of the Chief Counsel for International Commerce Website: http://www.ogc.doc.gov/trans_anti_bribery.html .

• Transparency International (TI) publishes an annual Corruption Perceptions Index (CPI). The CPI measures the perceived level of public-sector corruption in 180 countries and territories around the world. The CPI is available at: http://www.transparency.org/policy_research/surveys_indices/cpi/2009 . TI also publishes an annual *Global Corruption Report* which provides a systematic evaluation of the state of corruption around the world. It includes an in-depth analysis of a focal theme, a series of country reports that document major corruption related events and developments from all continents and an overview of the latest research findings on anti-corruption diagnostics and tools. See http://www.transparency.org/publications/gcr.

• The World Bank Institute publishes Worldwide Governance Indicators (WGI). These indicators assess six dimensions of governance in 213 countries, including Voice and Accountability, Political Stability and Absence of Violence, Government Effectiveness, Regulatory Quality, Rule of Law and Control of Corruption. See http:// info.worldbank.org/governance/wgi/index.asp . The World Bank Business Environment and Enterprise Performance Surveys may also be of interest and are available at: http://data.worldbank.org/data-catalog/BEEPS .

• The World Economic Forum publishes the *Global Enabling Trade Report*, which presents the rankings of the Enabling Trade Index, and includes an assessment of the transparency of border administration (focused on bribe payments and corruption) and a separate segment on corruption and the regulatory environment. See http://www.weforum.org/s?s=global+enabling+trade+report .

• Additional country information related to corruption can be found in the U.S. State Department's annual *Human Rights Report* available at http://www.state.gov/j/drl/rls/hrrpt/ .

• Global Integrity, a nonprofit organization, publishes its annual *Global Integrity Report*, which provides indicators for 106 countries with respect to governance and anti-corruption. The report highlights the strengths and weaknesses of national level anti-corruption systems. The report is available at: http://www.globalintegrity.org/report .

BILATERAL INVESTMENT AGREEMENTS

The 1952 U.S.-Japan Treaty of Friendship, Commerce, and Navigation gives national treatment and most favored nation treatment to U.S. investments in Japan. As of December 2012, Japan has concluded or signed bilateral investment treaties (BITs) with sixteen trading partners, including Egypt, Sri Lanka, China, Hong Kong SAR, Turkey, Pakistan, Bangladesh, Russia, Mongolia, Vietnam, the Republic of Korea, Cambodia, Laos, Uzbekistan, Peru, Colombia, Papua New Guinea, Kuwait, and Iraq, as well as a trilateral agreement with China and the Republic of Korea. The Japanese Government is currently negotiating bilateral BITs with the Kingdom of Saudi Arabia, Kazakhstan, Angola, and Uruguay. The government is also preparing to negotiate BITs with other countries possessing abundant natural resources, including Qatar, Algeria and the Ukraine.

Japan has economic partnership agreements (an EPA is analogous to a free trade agreement) containing investment chapters in force with Singapore, Mexico, Malaysia, Chile, Thailand, Indonesia, Brunei, the Philippines, Vietnam, Switzerland, India and Peru, as well as a multilateral EPA with all ten members of the Association of Southeast Asian Nations (ASEAN). It is negotiating bilateral EPAs with Australia, the Gulf Cooperation Council states, the Republic of Korea, Colombia and Mongolia, and has agreed to open official negotiations on an FTA with the European Union and a trilateral EPA with China and the Republic of Korea.

OPIC AND OTHER INVESTMENT INSURANCE PROGRAMS

U.S. OPIC insurance and finance programs are not available in Japan. Japan is a member of the Multilateral Investment Guarantee Agency (MIGA). Japan's capital subscription to the organization is the second largest, after the United States.

LABOR

Changing demographic patterns, macroeconomic trends, and regulatory reforms are gradually affecting traditional Japanese employment practices. Throughout most of the post-war period, these practices – most notably in the nation's large, internationally competitive firms – rested on three pillars: lifetime employment, seniority-based wages, and enterprise unions. Today, all three are undergoing rapid transformation, but mobility among firms of skilled and white-collar labor, at both the mid-level and executive level, remains low. Demographic pressures – fewer young workers due to the long-term trends of a declining birth rate and a rapidly aging labor force, and the subsequent structural changes in the Japanese economy – are forcing many firms to sharply reduce lifetime employment guarantees and seniority-based wages in favor of merit-based pay scales and limited-term contracts.

Labor Unions

Although labor unions play a role in the annual determination of wage scales throughout the economy, that role has been shrinking. The FY2012 Ministry of Health, Labor and Welfare (MHLW) "White Paper on Labor Economy" estimated that union membership as of June 30, 2011 had fallen by 93,000 from the previous year to 9.96 million people. This figure has been in constant decline since it peaked at 12.70 million in 1994. The number of "non-regular" workers who are union members has increased in recent years as a result of strengthened organizing efforts by some labor unions, although it is still substantially smaller than that of regular workers. With the LDP regaining power in December 2012, labor unions have expressed some concerns over the prospect of more conservative labor policies, as DPJ-led governments had been seen as more sympathetic to union issues than previous LDP administrations.

Employment Pattems and Labor Force Composition

While investors should be aware of Japan's high wage structure, growth in average wages in recent years has been slow, a situation that largely reflects the state of the economy and the increased use of "non-regular" employees. According to the MHLW White Paper, total cash salary, after rising in 2005-2006, fell steadily from 2007-2009, increased by 0.6% in 2010, and fell again by 0.2% in 2011. While Japan has accepted highly skilled foreign labor, Japanese firms have depended overwhelmingly on the local labor market to supply workers. As of the end of 2010, the number of registered foreign nationals fell 2.4% from the prior year to 2.13 million persons (or 1.67% of Japan's population of 128 million). The number of foreign nationals newly entering Japan for the purpose of employment also dropped in 2010 to 52,503, a decrease of 8% from the prior year, according to the Ministry of Justice "White Paper on Immigration Control 2011."

Traditionally, Japanese workers were classified as either "regular" or "other/non-regular" employees. This system, to a considerable degree, remains in place. Companies recruit "regular" employees directly from schools or universities and provide an employment contract with no fixed duration. In contrast, firms hire "non-regular" employees, mainly on fixed duration contracts. Since the mid-1990s, companies have increasingly used part-time workers, temporary contract workers and dispatch workers to fill short-term labor requirements and to save labor costs. In recent years, re-hiring of employees on non-regular status after retirement is on the rise.

According to the FY2012 "White Paper on Children and Youths" by the Cabinet Office, 32.3% of employees aged 15-24, 26.8% of employees aged 25-29, 25.6% of employees aged 30-34 and 28.1% of employees aged 35-44 were "non-regular" workers in FY2011. There remains deep concern among Japanese government policy makers that the number of younger workers in "non-regular" status remains stubbornly high and that the ability of such workers to find permanent employment will decline as they get older. These "non-regular" employees bore the brunt of corporate adjustment to the worldwide recession that began in September 2008, with companies reducing their recruitment of new college graduates into the work force. According to the MHLW "White Paper on Labor Economy," the ratio of non-regular employees in 2011 increased slightly from the previous year to 35.1%. The White Paper points out that although there are many who choose to work as "non-regular workers" to suit their own purposes, such as flexible working hours, statistics show that in 2010; approximately 22.5% of all non-regular workers were in such status because they were unable to land "regular" jobs. These trends coincide with a persistent decline in labor force participation by young people (age 15 to 34). According to MHLW, the number of Japanese aged 15-34 participating in the labor force fell to 17.43 million in 2011, and has accounted for less than 30% of the total labor force since 2008.

Government Measures to Increase Workforce Participation

In the face of population decline and a rapidly aging society, the Japanese Government has pursued measures to increase participation and retention of older workers in the labor force. A revision to the "Employment Stability Law for the Elderly" passed the Diet in August 2012, and requires companies to introduce employment systems allowing employees reaching retirement age (generally set at 60) to continue working until 65, if they desire. The revised law will enter into force in April 2013. The Government is also pursuing work-life-balance measures for families, such as by increasing the number of day care facilities and encouraging companies to make it easier for their employees to take childcare leave, in order to boost women's participation in the workforce. The long-term effectiveness of these measures remains to be seen.

Dispatch Work

In response to public criticism after many manufacturers terminated contracts with staffing (dispatching) companies following the global financial crisis of 2008, the Bill to Partially Revise the Labor Dispatch Law was submitted to the Diet in early 2010. This bill was intended to drastically limit dispatch work and prohibit dispatch to factories. Nevertheless, the bill did not pass in 2010 or 2011, due to the political opposition claiming that the law's revision would have adverse effects on corporate earnings and domestic employment. The DPJ compromised with the opposition and accepted a major modification to the bill which would allow dispatch to factories, and this modified version finally passed the Diet in April 2012. The new law, which bans dispatch contracts of 30 days or less except in certain narrow circumstances, went into force on October 1, 2012.

Pensions

Japan's legislature passed the Pension Security Enhancement Act in August 2011, which became effective January 1, 2012. Provisions of the Act will allow employees to contribute to an employer-sponsored defined contribution (DC) plan for the first time. Previously, only employers could contribute to a DC plan on behalf of employees. Under the new rules, employee contributions cannot exceed employer contributions. The limit on combined employer and employee contributions to a DC plan will remain the same: 51,000 yen per month if the employer sponsors only one occupational DC plan for employees or 25,500 yen if the employer also sponsors a defined benefit (DB) plan. Both employer and employee contributions receive preferential tax treatment. The Act also extends DC coverage to workers from age 60 or younger to age 65 and below.

There are two types of DC plans in Japan: employer-sponsored plans for employees, and individual plans available to the self-employed and to workers of employers who do not sponsor a pension plan. Contributions receive favorable tax treatment. In the case of employer-sponsored plans, contributions are recorded as an expense by the company and are 100% tax deductible for the participant; for individual plans, the entire contribution is tax deductible for the participant up to the contribution limit, currently 816,000 yen annually. Voluntary private pension plans in Japan (including DC and employer-sponsored defined-benefit (DB) plans) supplement the country's two-tiered public pension system, which comprises a flat-rate plan for all residents under the national pension program and an earnings-related plan under the employees' pension insurance program.

FOREIGN-TRADE ZONES/FREE PORTS

Japan no longer has free-trade zones or free ports. Customs authorities allow the bonding of warehousing and processing facilities adjacent to ports on a case-by-case basis.

FOREIGN DIRECT INVESTMENT STATISTICS

Between 1998 and December 2011, Japan's stock of FDI increased from 3.0 trillion yen to 17.5 trillion yen. In the same period investment inflows were generally strong, although net outflow has been observed for the last two years. All data in the tables below are current as of December 2012. Negative figures indicate net outflow.

Table 1a: Net FDI Inflows (Unit: billion dollars; balance-of-payment basis)

JFY 2002	JFY 2003	JFY 2004	JFY 2005	CY 2006
9.09	6.24	7.81	3.22	-6.78
CY 2007	CY 2008	CY2009	CY2010	CY2011
22.18	24.55	11.84	-1.36	-1.70

Table 1b: Ratio of Inward to Outward FDI (balance-of-payment basis)

JFY 2002	JFY 2003	JFY 2004	JFY 2005	CY 2006
1 : 3.5	1 : 4.6	1 : 4.0	1 : 14.1	n/a
CY 2007	CY 2008	CY2009	CY2010	CY2011
1 : 3.3	1 : 5.3	1 : 6.3	n/a	n/a

1. Figures were first calculated in nominal Japanese yen and converted into U.S. dollars using Bank of Japan average annual exchange rates.

Source: http://www.jetro.go.jp/en/reports/statistics/data/country2_e_cy11.xls
http://www.jetro.go.jp/en/reports/statistics/data/country1_e_cy11.xls

Table 2: Foreign Direct Investment in Japan, by country (Unit: million dollars; net and flow; balance-of-payment basis)

	CY2007	CY2008	CY2009	CY2010	CY2011	
North America	12,709	12,005	1,712	3,014	-3,120	
	U.S.A.	13,270	11,792	1,831	2,961	-3,197
	Canada	-561	213	-119	53	76
Asia	1,605	3,381	1,093	3,123	1,384	
	China	15	37	-137	314	109
	Hong Kong	47	257	-81	698	125
	Taiwan	36	66	57	21	111
	Korea	221	279	255	274	197
Singapore	1,282	2,716	756	1,575	782	
Thailand	1	6	24	9	-1	
India	3	1	14	4	9	
W. Europe	4,785	4,861	8,210	198	1,203	
	Germany	-813	1,185	389	2,205	18
U.K.	540	-1,289	5,629	4,817	1,792	
France	504	177	371	1,128	3,438	
Netherlands	-390	2,692	2,584	-7,733	3	
Belgium	148	-2,040	14	-479	-556	
Luxembourg	484	477	543	381	-406	
Switzerland	1,162	1,873	-990	51	69	
E. Europe, Russia	1	5	1	6	0	

L. America	2,831	4,020	690	-7,724	-1,388	
	Mexico	0	0	0	-7,321	-248
Brazil	0	0	-8	2	1	
Cayman Is.	1,480	3,592	965	616	-1,294	
Oceania	215	258	50	-17	90	
Middle East	3	-2	23	0	142	
Africa	33	21	61	36	-13	
TOTAL	22,181	24,550	11,839	-1,359	-1,702	

Source: http://www.jetro.go.jp/en/reports/statistics/data/country2_e_cy11.xls

Table 3: Japan's FDI inward stock by country/region (Unit: million dollars)

	end of 2007	end of 2008	end of 2009	end of 2010	end of 2011	
North America	45,947	75,680	76,184	73,900	72,863	
	U.S.	44,795	74,344	75,003	72,497	70,908
Canada	1,152	1,336	1,181	1,403	1,955	
Asia	9,390	16,769	17,336	23,279	26,671	
	China	125	225	197	399	560
Hong Kong	2,301	3,203	1,444	4,044	2,225	
Taiwan	1,534	1,892	2,656	2,255	4,584	
Korea	694	1,235	1,999	1,933	2,402	
Singapore	4,620	10,047	10,632	13,901	16,031	
Thailand	44	61	79	100	111	
India	13	18	32	40	52	
W. Europe	62,341	86,915	83,883	92,126	101,841	
	Germany	3,811	6,592	7,166	10,009	9,651
U.K.	5,962	6,750	7,318	9,386	15,894	
France	12,776	16,233	15,208	19,193	20,505	
Netherlands	26,025	36,510	36,034	36,890	39,936	
Belgium	1,947	1,362	934	94	165	
Luxembourg	2,267	4,000	4,262	4,842	4,228	
Switzerland	3,942	7,150	4,913	5,271	6,171	
E. Europe, Russia	46	63	63	77	104	
L. America	15,227	23,576	20,990	23,593	22,699	
	Mexico	5	6	6	261	20
Brazil	32	40	32	38	41	
Cayman Is.	10,469	17,363	16,965	18,784	18,463	
Oceania	779	1,075	1,095	1,245	1,406	
Middle East	20	29	51	59	208	
Africa	99	275	342	387	376	
TOTAL	133,888	204,433	199,991	214,722	226,224	

Source: http://www.jetro.go.jp/en/reports/statistics/data/11fdistocken02.xls

Table 4: FDI in Japan, by industry (Unit: million dollars) (balance of payment basis)

	CY2007	CY2008	CY2009	CY2010	CY2011	
Manufacturing (total)	1,381	2,261	3,420	1,766	2,406	
	General machinery	-22	721	115	1,089	70
Electric machinery	-391	642	1,705	-281	1,132	

Trans. equipment	331	-55	469	3,359	252	
Precision machines	20	113	94	291	-251	
Chemicals and pharmaceuticals	-1,010 663	245	307	-2,859	774	
Iron, non-ferrous metals Glass & ceramics	230	124	287	233	521	
Rubber & leather	35	4 -66	6	5	6	
Petroleum	935	300	-19	-144	-83	
Textiles	109	-3	-8	-95	124	
Food	365	-86 -138	421	220	282	
212	-90					
Non-manuf. (total)	20,800	22,289	8,349	-3,125	-4,108	
	Farming & forestry	41	1	-5	9	-5
Fish/ marine products.	-33	-	1	0	-1	
Mining	0	0	-1	64	1	
Finance/ Insurance	17,661	19,823	5,205	-1,503	-3,702	
Wholesale & retail	1,660	1,160	1,057	-229	1,588	
Services	295	473	1,343	875	794	
Real estate	1,413	581	-71	216	-239	
Communication	-633	-1,028	619	-3,244	-2,748	
Transportation	-288	43	-90	197	-259	
Construction	19	-60	16	-1	-67	
TOTAL	22,181	24,550	11,839	-1,359	-1,702	

Source: http://www.jetro.go.jp/en/reports/statistics/data/industry2_e_1009.xls

Table 5: Japanese Direct Investment Overseas, by country (Unit: million dollars; net and flow; balance-of-payment basis)

	CY2007	CY2008	CY2009	CY2010	CY2011	
North America	17,385	46,046	10,889	9,016	15,166	
	U.S.A.	15,672	44,674	10,660	9,193	14,730
Canada	1,713	1,372	229	-177	436	
Asia	19,388	23,348	20,636	22,131	39,492	
	China	6,218	6,496	6,899	7,252	12,649
Hong Kong	1,131	1,301	1,610	2,085	1,509	
Taiwan	1,373	1,082	339	-113	862	
R. Korea	1,302	2,369	1,077	1,085	2,439	
Singapore	2,233	1,089	2,881	3,845	4,492	
Thailand	2,608	2,016	1,632	2,248	7,133	
Indonesia	1,030	731	483	490	3,611	
Malaysia	325	591	616	7,058	1,411 116	
Philippines	1,045	705	809	514	1,019	
India	1,506	5,551	3,664	2,864 551	2,326	
Western Europe	20,456	22,418	17,073	14,450 1,161	39,213	
	Germany	880	3,905 1,703	2,089	-321	2,165
U.K.	3,026	6,744	2,126	4,624	14,125	
France	479					
Netherlands.	12,440	6,514	6,698	3,288	5,346	
Sweden	254	570	160	-623	-95	
Spain	10	210	162	38	124	
Latin America	9,482	29,623	17,393	5,346	11,287	
	Mexico	501	315	211	688	264
Brazil	1,244	5,371	3,753	4,316	8,290	

Cayman Isles	5,838	22,550	12,903	-1,848	223	
Oceania	4,204	6,060	7,629	6,407	8,767	
	Australia	4,140	5,232	7,136	6,371	8,149
Middle East	958	1,138	575	-348	716	
	UAE	60	194	139	-498	207
Saudi Arabia	746	892	378	117	104	
Africa	1,101	1,518	-301	-372	464	
	South Africa	82	648	143	104	459
TOTAL	73,483	130,801	74,650	57,223	115,732	

Source: http://www.jetro.go.jp/en/reports/statistics/data/country1_e_cy11.xls

Table 6: Japanese Direct Investment Overseas, by industry (Unit: million dollars, net and flow; balance of payment basis)

	CY2007	CY2008	CY2009	CY2010	CY2011	
Manufacturing (total)	39,515	45,268	32,934	17,803	57,952	
	Chemicals and Pharmaceuticals	3,744	11,647	7,407	7,902	19,618
Food	12,776	3,601	8,954	2,017	8,149	
Iron, non-ferrous & metals	2,202	3,152	3,738	3,873	5,017	
General Mach.	2,642	3,726	4,411	4,385	5,655	
Electric machinery	4,691	5,675	2,505	1,361	7,334	
Transportation equipment	8,671	10,924	566	-3,582	4,132	
Precision machinery	1,293	953	609	51	2,791	
Rubber and leather	835	771	445	634	715	
Lumber & pulp	745	734	1,207	1,068	1,268	
Textiles	371	716	477	377	672	
Petroleum	-280	652	-51	-837	216	
Glass & ceramics	837	1,417	2,042	377	1,325	
Non-manuf. (total)	33,968	85,533	41,717	39,420	577,780	
	Finance/Insurance	19,458	52,243	15,463	11,397	19,111
Wholesale & retail	4,792	13,319	8,418	1,946	12,407	
Real estate	162	162	463	765	2,447	
Services	1,406	2,721	1,263	1,596	4,022	
Transportation	2,133	2,283	2,894	2,294	1,606	
Mining	4,053	10,518	6,482	9,061	16,477	
Construction	490	389	499	302	436	
Farming/ forestry	93	59	10	145	250	
Fisheries	64	119	36	47	-7	
Communications	-331	1,675	3,870	9,899	-1,799	
TOTAL	73,483	130,801	74,650	57,223	115,732	

Source: http://www.jetro.go.jp/en/reports/statistics/data/industry1_e_1009.xls

Table 7: FDI Inflow Relative to GDP (balance-of-payment basis)

	CY2007	CY2008	CY2009	CY2010	CY2011
(a) GDP/Nom	513.0	501.2	471.1	481.1	468.2
(trillion yen)					

(b) FDI Inflow	2.65	2.52	1.12	-0.11	-0.14
(trillion yen)					
b/a (pct)	0.52	0.50	0.24	n/a	n/a

WEB RESOURCES

For the promotion of foreign direct investment (FDI) in Japan:

Japan External Trade Organization (JETRO) http://www.jetro.go.jp/investjapan

For additional FDI statistics: http://www.jetro.go.jp/en/stats/statistics
http://www.jetro.go.jp/en/invest/success_stories https://twitter.com/BuyUSAJapan

TRADE AND PROJECT FINANCING

METHODS OF PAYMENT

There are a number of methods used to settle payment in Japan: cash in advance, letter of credit used in conjunction with a documentary draft (time or sight), promissory note, documentary collection or draft, open account and consignment sales. As with U.S. domestic transactions, a major factor in determining the method of payment is the degree of trust in the buyer's ability and willingness to pay.

Because of the protection it offers to the U.S. exporter and the Japanese importer, an irrevocable letter of credit (L/C) payable at sight is commonly used for settlement of international transactions. As large Japanese general trading companies often serve as intermediaries to small and medium-sized companies, L/Cs are often issued in their name rather than in the name of the end user of the product. With the trading company taking on the risk of the transaction, the U.S. firm is protected from the possible bankruptcy of the smaller company.

Another payment option is the use of documentary collection or open account with international credit insurance that, unlike the letter of credit, allows the importer's line of credit to remain open. At the same time, this option protects the exporter if the buyer goes bankrupt or cannot pay. International credit insurance can be obtained from the Export-Import Bank of the United States or private insurers.

A payment method widely used in Japan but sometimes unfamiliar to U.S. companies is the promissory note (yakusoku tegata). Promissory notes are IOUs with a promise to pay at a later date, typically 90 to 120 days. Banks will often provide short-term financing through discounting and rollover of notes. Factoring and other forms of receivables financing (whether with or without recourse) are not common in Japan, and more conservative businesspeople find such arrangements a violation of the "relationship" between buyer and seller. It should be noted that, domestically, it is not uncommon for the buyer to request, and be granted an extension of the term of the tegata if there are cash-flow problems.

BANKING SYSTEM

While financial system deregulation and international competitive pressure has drastically changed the face of Japanese banking (the consolidation of 19 major banks into three mega banks), the connection between corporate finance and banking institutions and non-financial corporations remains much tighter in Japan than in the United States; and extends far beyond simple lender/borrower relationships. Much corporate banking business is rooted in either business groups with interlocking shareholding (keiretsu) or in regional relationships. Japanese banks are frequently shareholders in companies that conduct banking business with them.

This unique relationship between a company and its bank has been long-standing; until recently, a Japanese company rarely changed its primary lender, although it would occasionally "shop around" for better credit arrangements. Even when credit is loose, companies sometimes borrow in excess of their need in order to maintain good relations with their bank and to ensure that funds will be available in leaner years. Banks are often large shareholders in publicly traded corporations (although banks are in the process of reducing their total equity holdings), have close relationships with both local governments and national regulatory agencies, and often play a coordinating role among their clients. It remains safe to say that the Japanese commercial bank system is much more relationship-oriented than the transaction-based U.S. system.

Japanese banks were able to avoid the direct impact from the global financial crisis due to their limited exposure to structured securities. Japanese authorities took macroeconomic and financial policy steps to sustain the economy and support the functioning of financial markets. Similarly, the direct impact of the March 2011 earthquake and tsunami on major banks was relatively minor. There were no major disruptions to the payments and settlement system, and the Bank of Japan injected substantial liquidity so that banks could meet funding needs, as well as manage demand for cash withdrawals from depositors. In general, the major banks now are well-capitalized and have healthy balance sheets, but suffer from low interest rate margins and weak demand for lending.

While large corporations with suitable credit ratings (especially export-oriented firms) can rely on corporate bond issues rather than banks for financing, bank lending continues to be the primary financing method for small and medium sized companies and for many larger companies as well.

Japanese banks offer regular and time deposits and checking accounts for businesses. Checks are negotiable instruments that are in effect payable to the bearer (rather than to the order of the payee, as in the United States). This limits the usefulness of checks, and in fact, most payments are made by electronic bank transfer (which cost a few hundred yen on average), or by sending cash through the postal system. The banks (and now investment/securities firms) historically waged an uphill battle against the postal savings system for consumer deposits, but now that the postal savings bank must pay taxes and deposit insurance, in addition to losing its implicit government guarantee, competition for deposits has intensified.

Personal checking accounts are almost unknown in Japan. Most individuals use electronic bank transfers to settle accounts. Cash settlement is also very common and the Post Office has a mechanism for payment by "cash envelope" which is widely used in direct marketing and other applications. Many Japanese banks operate 24-hour cash machines (as do some credit card companies). Bank and other credit cards are easy to obtain and are widely accepted. Some bank credit cards offer revolving credit, but in most cases balances are paid in full monthly via automatic debiting from bank accounts.

The relationship among trading company, end user and exporter is an important feature of the financing environment in Japan. The Japanese general trading company (sogo shosha) is an integrated, comprehensive organization that embraces a range of functions including marketing and distribution, financing and shipping and the gathering of commercial information. It performs functions that in the United States would be carried out by import/export companies, freight forwarders, banks, law firms, accounting firms and business consultants. Thus, U.S. firms dealing with trading companies should familiarize themselves with the financing capabilities of such firms.

OPENING A BANK ACCOUNT

All financial institutions in Japan are subject to Japanese law concerning the prevention of money laundering and are required to confirm that entities and individuals are legally registered or have resident status in Japan. Generally, non-resident U.S. business entities or citizens cannot open a bank account with a financial institution in Japan.

Japanese law requires an applicant who wishes to open a bank account to present a set of documents that will enable a financial institution to confirm identify. For a U.S. business entity with a business establishment in Japan, such as a sales office, branch, or subsidiary, such documents will include (1) a certificate, certified copy, or certified abstract of their Japanese business registration, (2) a certificate showing corporate seal registration, and /or (3) other official documents as the financial institution may require.

A U.S. citizen who is a lawful resident in Japan is required to present (1) a certificate of alien registration, (2) valid visa, and (3) other official documents, as required by the bank, such as a certificate of registration of one's personal seal ("*inkan*"). For a non-resident U.S. citizen, such as a short-time visitor, there may be bank transactions that one may be able to initiate without having a deposit account. These may include currency exchange or limited funds transfer.

FOREIGN-EXCHANGE CONTROLS

Foreign exchange regulations have little impact on normal business transactions.

U.S. BANKS AND LOCAL CORRESPONDENT BANKS

In addition to U.S. banks with branches in Japan, many other U.S. banks have correspondent relationships with Japanese banks, which themselves have many branches and subsidiaries in the United States.

Leading Commercial Banks in Japan:
Bank of Tokyo-Mitsubishi UFJ
2-7-1 Marunouchi, Chiyoda-ku, Tokyo 100-8388
Tel: +81/3/3240-1111; fax: 3240-4764
http://www.bk.mufg.jp/global/index.html

Mizuho Corporate Bank
1-3-3 Marunouchi, Chiyoda-ku, Tokyo 100-8210
Tel: +81/3/3214-1111
http://www.mizuhocbk.co.jp/english

Sumitomo Mitsui Banking Corporation
1-1-2 Yurakucho, Chiyoda-ku, Tokyo 100-0006
Tel: +81/3/5512-3411; fax: 5512-4429
http://www.smbc.co.jp/global/index.html

Aozora Bank
3-1, Kudan-minami 1-chome, Chiyoda-ku, Tokyo 102-8660
Tel: +81-3-3263-1111
http://www.aozorabank.co.jp/english/

Resona Bank
2-1 Bingomachi 2-chome, Chuo-ku, Osaka 540-8610
Tel: +81/6/6271-1221; fax: 6268-1337
http://www.resona-gr.co.jp/holdings/english/index.html

Shinsei Bank

Nihonbashi Muromachi Nomura Building 4-3, Nihonbashi-muromachi 2-chome, Chuo-ku, Tokyo 103-8303
Tel: +81/3-6880-7000 http://www.shinseibank.com/english/

Citibank

Citigroup Center, 3-14 Higashi-Shinagawa 2-chome, Shinagawa-ku, Tokyo 140-8639
Tel: +81-45-330-2871
http://www.citibank.co.jp

PROJECT FINANCING

While some large U.S. companies in Japan enjoy strong relationships with the larger Japanese "city banks," most medium and small-sized U.S. firms report that it is difficult to secure the specific type of trade financing services needed for importing and distribution. In Japan, credit evaluation is heavily asset-based, and real estate is still favored as collateral despite the collapse of "bubble" era valuations. Moreover, a firm's ability to borrow may also be based on its personal relationships and rapport with bank officials rather than on typical U.S. standards of credit-worthiness. Some smaller firms report that they have been forced to secure needed financing from offshore sources. For U.S. companies with operations in Japan, teaming up with Japanese partners in a joint venture has been effective as a way to receive more favorable treatment from Japanese banks.

While most U.S. banks operating in Japan do engage in lending to subsidiaries of U.S. companies (especially their home market clients), many of them focus on higher value-added lines of business than conventional credit products. When a Japanese bank extends credit to a foreign-owned company in Japan, it generally evaluates the financial status of both the borrower and its parent company. Even in cases where the Japanese subsidiary is financially strong, the parent company is often requested to guarantee the obligation (although a "Letter of Awareness" may be accepted in lieu of a guarantee).

TYPES OF EXPORT FINANCING AND INSURANCE

The Government of Japan's programs to promote imports and foreign investment in Japan include tax incentives, loan guarantees, low-cost loans to Japanese and foreign investors for import infrastructure through the Development Bank of Japan (DBJ) and other loan programs. Underscoring the Government's emphasis on import promotion, the Ministry of Economy, Trade and Industry (METI) and the Japan External Trade Organization (JETRO) have established import divisions.

Four major public financing corporations, the Japan Bank for International Cooperation (JBIC), the Development Bank of Japan (DBJ), the Japan Finance Corporation for Small Business and Nippon Export and Investment Insurance (NEXI, formerly known as EID/MITI) offer low-interest loans to encourage imports to and investment in Japan.

The Japan Bank for International Cooperation (JBIC) is a governmental institution that encourages exports, secures access to energy resources, promotes direct overseas investments and improves Japan's external imbalances through financial assistance to the trade and investment activities of Japanese companies. It was created in October 1999 as a result of a merger of the Export-Import Bank of Japan (JEXIM) and the Overseas Economic Cooperation Fund (OECF). The financial facilities offered by JBIC include export loans, import loans, overseas investment loans and untied loans.

JBIC's import credit program for manufactured goods aims to provide support for the import of manufactured goods from developed countries to Japan. Five-year secured or guaranteed loans with up to 70 percent loan-to-value, and credit lines at preferential interest rates are available to importers, distributors and retailers incorporated in Japan who plan to increase their imports of manufactured goods (excluding food products) 10 percent or more over the previous year. Direct 70 percent loan-to-value long-term loans are also available to foreign exporters for the purchase of manufactured goods to be exported to Japan under deferred-payment terms, as well as to foreign manufacturers and intermediary financial institutions for investment in production facilities and equipment to be used to produce goods for the Japanese market.

The Development Bank of Japan (DBJ) offers loans designed to increase imports into Japan. These loans are available to Japanese companies with at least 33 percent foreign capital or registered branches in Japan of non-Japanese companies for 40 to 50 percent of project costs for the expansion of business operations in Japan.

The Japan Finance Corporation for Small Business expanded their programs to facilitate import sales. The programs aim to provide support to small-scale retailers, wholesalers and importers in Japan for investments to increase imports to Japan.

In addition, a program between U.S. Export-Import Bank (EXIM Bank) and Japan's Nippon Export and Investment Insurance (NEXI, formerly known as EID/MITI) provides for co-financing insurance for U.S. exports to developing countries. NEXI also provides advance payment insurance for U.S. exports to Japan. Also on October 2012, U.S. EXIM Bank and JBIC signed a co-financing agreement to facilitate export transactions involving U.S. and Japanese companies, by providing "one-stop-shop" export finance services to buyers in third countries purchasing both U.S. and Japanese goods and services. The two nations' export credit agencies provide a one-stop-shop financing

package, creating administrative efficiencies for foreign buyers. For additional details on these and other cooperative financing programs, U.S. companies should contact U.S. EXIM Bank.

No insurance for U.S. exporters is available from the Japanese Government.

OTHER FINANCING

Japan has been a member of the Multilateral Investment Guarantee Agency (MIGA) since it was established in 1988. In addition to the investment loan programs from Japanese Government-affiliated lenders described above, prefectures and municipalities offer various incentives, including construction, land acquisition and labor hiring subsidies, special depreciation of business assets, tax deferments for replacement of specific assets, exemption from special land-owning taxes assessed by municipalities and prefectural and municipal real estate acquisition, enterprise and municipal property tax reductions. In addition, most prefectures offer loan programs to encourage companies to establish local operations.

Japan's venture capital specialist funds are estimated to be only half the size of those in the United States. Traditionally the top Japanese venture capital firms have acted more like quasi-banks. Also, Financial Services Agency guidance to brokers to set tough standards for companies seeking to go public results in even the best companies taking up to a decade to get a listing on the over-the-counter stock market. Japan's electronic OTC market was established in October 2010 by integrating Hercules, JASDAQ and NEO platforms.

Types of Projects Receiving Financing Support:

JBIC also provides loan guarantees to private financial institutions, short-term loans designed to finance the external transactions of the governments of developing nations (bridge loans), and equity participation in the overseas projects of Japanese companies.

JBIC's international financial operations focus on projects in developing countries where local financial institutions cannot provide financing on their own. As JBIC's mandate is the support of internationalization for Japanese companies, its loans can be distinguished from Overseas Economic Cooperation operations, which target the economic development of developing countries.

Regional Development Support: The Japan Regional Development Corporation (JRDC), a government-affiliated organization which, in cooperation with local governments, promotes regional development outside of major metropolitan areas, and the Regional Economy Vitalization Corporation of Japan (REVIC) both provide support for certain types of regional projects within Japan.

Overseas Investment Loans and Overseas Project Loans: These loans are typically granted via JBIC and extended to Japanese corporations for overseas investment activities and overseas projects. Overseas investment loans can also be made to overseas joint ventures involving Japanese capital and to foreign governments for capital investments or loans to joint ventures involving Japanese capital.

Un-Tied Loans: Extended to foreign governments, foreign governmental institutions, foreign financial institutions (including multilateral development banks), and foreign

corporations for high-priority projects and economic restructuring programs in developing countries. These loans are not tied to the procurement of goods and services from Japan but are restricted to the specific purposes designated for each loan. These loans are managed by JBIC.

WEB RESOURCES

U.S. Export-Import Bank (EXIMB): http://www.exim.gov

Country Limitation Schedule: http://www.exim.gov/tools/countrylimitationschedule/index.cfm

U.S. EXIMB and JBIC "one-stop-shop" export finance services
http://www.exim.gov/newsandevents/releases/2012/Ex-Im-Bank-Japan-Bank-for-International-Cooperation-Sign-Co-financing-Agreement.cfm

Overseas Private Investment Corporation (OPIC): http://www.opic.gov

U.S. Trade and Development Agency: http://www.tda.gov/

U.S. SBA's Office of International Trade: http://www.sba.gov/oit/

USDA Commodity Credit Corporation:
http://www.fsa.usda.gov/FSA/webapp?area=about&subject=landing&topic=sao-cc

U.S. Agency for International Development (USAID): http://www.usaid.gov

The Multilateral Investment Guarantee Agency (MIGA): http://www.miga.org/

Japan External Trade Organization (JETRO) http://www.jetro.go.jp/

Japan Finance Corporation: http://www.jfc.go.jp/n/english/index.html

Japan Financial Services Agency: http://www.fsa.go.jp/en/index.html

Japan Bank for International Cooperation (JBIC) http://www.jbic.go.jp/en/

Development Bank of Japan (DBJ) http://www.dbj.jp/en/index.html

Ministry of Economy, Trade and Industry (METI) http://www.meti.go.jp/english/index.html

Nippon Export and Investment Insurance (NEXI) http://www.nexi.go.jp/en/

Regional Economy Vitalization Corporation of Japan (REVIC) http://www.revic.co.jp/index.html (Japanese only) https://twitter.com/BuyUSAJapan

BUSINESS TRAVEL

BUSINESS CUSTOMS

An understanding of Japanese business and social practices is useful, if not required, in establishing and maintaining successful business relationships in Japan. Perceived indifference to local business practices may be interpreted as a lack of commitment on the part of the exporter, and may lead to misunderstandings and lost business opportunities. One should not assume that because meetings and correspondence are carried out in English that Western social and business norms apply.

Japanese society is complex, structured, hierarchical and group-oriented. It places strong emphasis on maintaining harmony and avoiding direct confrontation. Japanese social and cultural norms tend to be group oriented rather than focused on the individual. In building relationships (which often precede a first-time sale or an agreement) one should emphasize trust, confidence, loyalty and commitment for the long term.

Group decision-making is important in Japan and has been generally described as a "bottom up" exercise rather than "top down." Family businesses founded since WWII and smaller second-tier firms are often exceptions to this rule. However, even in the large family firms, where decisions are made at the top, the process is usually managed so that company members have a sense of participation. This type of group decision-making requires time. Recognizing that it takes a longer time to cultivate business relationships in Japan than in the United States, U.S. business executives should not expect to make a deal in just a few days. Consistent follow-up is vital. Likewise, U.S. business people should recognize the importance of working with the staff level of their Japanese counterparts and not exclusively with the executive level.

Gift giving is expected on many business occasions in Japan. Regional U.S. gifts or company-logo gifts are appropriate. Quality is important, but the gift does not have to be expensive – it is the sentiment and relationship implied by the gift rather than its intrinsic value that is significant. Therefore, packaging of the gift is as important as the gift itself and should be done professionally. In Japan, sets of four are considered unlucky (the number four is pronounced the same as the word for death). Gifts that can be shared among a group are appropriate.

Business travelers to Japan should make sure to bring a large supply of business cards (with their title) when they come to Japan; printing bilingual cards is a nice touch. Business cards are exchanged to formalize the introduction process and establish the status of the parties relative to each other. Japanese bow when greeting each other but will expect to shake hands with foreign executives. A slight bow in acknowledgment of a Japanese bow is appreciated. Japanese executives deal on a last (family) name basis in business relationships, and initial business and social contacts are characterized by politeness and formality.

Business travelers visiting a Japanese firm for the first time should be accompanied by an interpreter or bilingual assistant. Many Japanese executives and decision-makers do not speak English, although they may be able to greet visitors in English and read English product literature relevant to their business or industry expertise. Although English is a required subject in Japan's secondary school curriculum, generally speaking, Japanese business people's English listening and speaking skills tend to be weaker than their reading and writing skills. Thus, the Japanese side in a business meeting generally expects visitors to bring an interpreter if they are serious about doing business. Although the cost for hiring an interpreter can be very high ($400 to $900 per day depending on the level), bringing an interpreter shows that a visiting firm is serious in its commitment to the Japanese market.

The first visit to a Japanese firm generally serves as a courtesy call to introduce U.S. executives and their company, and also allows the U.S. side to begin to evaluate a target company and its executives as potential business partners. A request to meet only with English speaking staff can mean missing the opportunity to become acquainted with higher-ranking executives.

A written contract, even if less detailed than a contract between two U.S. companies, is essential to meet legal, tax, customs and accounting requirements in Japan. Contractual commitments are perceived as representing long-term relationships so the terms and conditions, for example whether to grant exclusive rights, should be considered carefully.

Japan's travel infrastructure is on a par with that of the United States. A wide range of business travel and tourist services are available. For additional information on traveling to Japan, contact the Japan National Tourist Organization (JNTO) in New York at tel: (212) 757-5640; fax: (212) 307-6754, or visit JNTO's website at http://www.jnto.go.jp

U.S. business travelers to Japan seeking appointments with U.S. Embassy Tokyo officials should contact the Commercial Section in advance. The Commercial Section can be reached by fax at +81/3/3224-5064 or by e-mail to tokyo.office.box@trade.gov

TRAVEL ADVISORY

Japan has long been noted for its low crime and safe streets. Crimes against U.S. citizens in Japan are rare. Crime is at levels well below the U.S. national average. Violent crime is extremely rare, but does exist. Incidents of pick pocketing of foreigners in crowded shopping areas, on trains and at airports have been a sporadic concern. Some U.S. citizens believe that Japanese police procedures appear to be less sensitive and responsive to a victim's concerns than would be the case in the United States, particularly in cases involving domestic violence and sexual assault. Few victim's assistance resources or battered person's shelters exist in major urban areas, and are generally unavailable in rural areas.

To access the most up-to-date travel and safety information, please refer to the State Department's "Consular Information Sheet" for Japan at: http://travel.state.gov/travel/cis_pa_tw/cis/cis_1148.html

U.S. citizens can also obtain up-to-date safety and security information by calling 1-888-407-4747 toll-free within the U.S. and Canada, or by calling a regular toll line, 1-202-501-4444, from other countries. These numbers are available from 8:00 a.m. to 8:00 p.m. Eastern Standard Time, Monday through Friday (except U.S. federal holidays).

VISA REQUIREMENTS

A valid U.S. passport is necessary to enter and travel in Japan. By Japanese law, non-residents are required to carry their passports (or their Alien Registration Card if staying longer than 90 days) at all times.

A visa is not required for short-term business visits (up to 90 days). It is not required to have a round-trip ticket, although it is recommended. A work or investor visa may take up to two months to obtain. Immunization and health certificates are not required. Foreigners remaining in Japan longer than 90 days must obtain an Alien Registration Card, available free of charge from the municipal office of the city or ward of residence in Japan.

Upon arrival, going through both immigration and customs checks are essentially a formality for U.S. business travelers as long as passport and air ticket are in order. All foreign nationals entering Japan, with the exemption of certain categories listed below, are required to provide fingerprint scans and be photographed at the port of entry. This requirement does not replace any existing visa or passport requirements. Foreign nationals exempt from this new requirement include special permanent residents, persons under 16 years of age, holders of diplomatic or official visas, and persons invited by the head of a national administrative organization.

U.S. travelers on official business must have a diplomatic or official visa specifying the nature of travel as "As Diplomat," "As Official," or "In Transit" to be exempt from biometric collection. All other visa holders, including those with diplomatic and official visas stating "As Temporary Visitor," are subject to this requirement. SOFA personnel are exempt from the new biometrics entry requirements under SOFA Article 9 (2).

Passengers are advised to exchange some U.S. dollars for yen before leaving the airport.

U.S. Companies that require travel of foreign businesspersons to the United States should be advised that security evaluations are handled via an interagency process. Visa applicants should go to the following links.

State Department Visa Website: http://travel.state.gov/visa/

The web address for the Consular Section of the U.S. Embassy in Tokyo is:

http://japan.usembassy.gov/e/tvisa-main.html

TELECOMMUNICATIONS

Japan has excellent telecommunications systems. Fiber optic and broadband services are available throughout the country. The 3G segment of the market now comprises 95 percent of the total mobile market in Japan. According to a survey by the Ministry of Internal Affairs and Communications, the broadband service availability rate surpassed 99 percent of total households in Japan with over 30 million broadband lines in place, making it the third largest broadband country in the world after the U.S. and China. Public

WiFi hotspots can be found in increasing numbers at airports, cafes and fast food restaurants. The following web site identifies wireless hotspots around the world: http://www.hotspot-locations.com/

Public phones, some of which accept only pre-paid cards, are still common but disappearing as nearly all communication goes mobile. To call the United States and Canada from Japan, one must dial 0101 before the ten-digit U.S. telephone number.

Almost all Japanese own at least one mobile telephone or smartphone and use them constantly for e-mailing and downloading information from the Internet in addition to making telephone calls. There are a number of mobile phone networks and providers in Japan, but the Japanese mobile phone system is still not generally compatible with those of other countries, so your existing phone may not work in Japan. To determine if a particular phone is usable in Japan, please contact your service provider prior to visiting Japan. Mobile phones that work in Japan are available for rent at most major airports.

Cell phone rental services at Tokyo's Narita Airport can be found at: http://www.narita-airport.jp/en/guide/service/list/svc_19.html

Cell phone rental services at Tokyo's Haneda International Airport can be found at: http://www.haneda-airport.jp/inter/en/premises/service/internet.html#mobilePhone

Cell phone rental services at Osaka's Kansai International Airport can be found at: http://www.kansai-airport.or.jp/en/service/rental/rental_list.html

TRANSPORTATION

Japan has a system of modern highways and roads linking all parts of country. However, traffic conditions on expressways and in cities are often very congested. Most major intercity highways operate on a toll basis, and tolls can be extremely expensive, making passenger train travel very competitive, especially for international visitors.

Japan boasts the world's densest and most modern passenger railroad system, with fast, frequent services to all parts of the country. Japan's famous *shinkansen* high-speed rail lines link Tokyo with Japan's major business centers. All of Japan's large cities have highly developed subway and commuter train service. Taxi service is widely available.

LANGUAGE

The national language of Japan is Japanese (*nihongo*) and is spoken and understood all over the country. English is a required subject in Japanese high schools, and it is by far the most widely known foreign language in Japan. International business correspondence and negotiations in Japan are almost always conducted in English. This being said, however, most Japanese, including business executives, have a limited understanding and command of spoken English, although there are of course exceptions. Japanese business executives often read English much better than they can speak it or understand it when spoken. It is advisable, therefore, to be accompanied by a competent professional interpreter to all business meetings, especially an initial contact where you might be unsure of your counterparts' mastery of English.

Overseas visitors interested in the Japanese language can visit the following web sites:

"Japanese for the Western Brain" http://kimallen.sheepdogdesign.net/Japanese/index.html

Jim Breen's Japanese Page http://www.csse.monash.edu.au/~jwb/japanese.html

HEALTH

Aside from the area in the immediate vicinity of the Fukushima Daiichi Nuclear Power plant, crippled by the disaster in 2011, Japan poses no medical health risks to the business traveler. While medical care in Japan is good, English-speaking physicians and medical facilities that cater to U.S. citizens' expectations are expensive and not very widespread. Japan has a national health insurance system, which is only available to non-citizens with long-term visas for Japan. National health insurance does not pay for medical evacuation or medical care outside of Japan. Medical caregivers in Japan require payment in full at the time of treatment or concrete proof of ability to pay before treating those who are not covered by the national health insurance plan. Most major credit cards are accepted.

For additional information, please refer to the State Department's "Japan – Country Specific Information" website at http://travel.state.gov/travel/cis_pa_tw/cis/cis_1148.html

LOCAL TIME, BUSINESS HOURS, AND HOLIDAYS

Local Time: Japan is 14 hours ahead of U.S. Eastern Standard Time (EST) and 13 hours ahead of Eastern Daylight Time (EDT) from April to October. Consequently, 8:00 a.m. EST in New York City corresponds to 10:00 p.m. the same day in Tokyo. 8:00 p.m. EST in New York City corresponds to 10:00 a.m. *the next day* in Tokyo. Japan is one of the few major industrialized countries that does not observe some form of daylight saving time.

Business Hours: The typical Japanese workweek is Monday through Friday, 9:00 a.m. to 5:30 p.m., although many Japanese office workers put in long hours of overtime. Flex

work hours have become popular at some large companies. Interestingly, the overwhelming majority of Japanese take their lunch break promptly at 12:00 noon and return to the office at 1:00 p.m. sharp.

Holidays: When a national holiday falls on a Sunday, the following Monday is observed. In addition, many Japanese companies and government offices traditionally close during the New Year's holiday season (December 29-January 3), "Golden Week" (April 29-May 5) and the traditional "O-Bon" Festival (August 13-15).

In 2013, Japan will observe the following official national holidays:

New Year's Day, January 1 (Tuesday)

Adult's Day, January 14 (Monday)

National Foundation Day, February 11 (Monday)

Vernal Equinox Day, March 20 (Wednesday)

Showa Day, April 29 (Monday)

Constitution Memorial Day, May 3 (Friday)

Greenery Day, May 4 (Saturday)

Children's Day, May 5 (Sunday, observed on Monday, May 6)

Marine Day, July 15 (Monday)

Respect for the Aged Day, September 16 (Monday)

Autumnal Equinox Day, September 23 (Monday)

Health & Sports Day, October 14 (Monday)

National Culture Day, November 3 (Sunday, observed on Monday, November 4)

Labor Thanksgiving Day, November 23 (Saturday)

Emperor's Birthday December 23 (Monday)

TEMPORARY ENTRY OF MATERIALS AND PERSONAL BELONGINGS (

There is no restriction for temporary entry of laptop computers and software for personal use. Regarding materials for exhibits, Japan is a member of the International Convention to Facilitate the Importation of Commercial Samples and Advertising Materials under the ATA *carnet* System (http://www.atacarnet.com). Use of a *carnet* allows goods such as commercial and exhibition samples, professional equipment, musical instruments and television cameras to be carried or sent temporarily into a foreign country without paying duties or posting bonds. These goods cannot be sold. A *carnet* should be arranged for in advance by contacting a local office of the United States Council for International Business or its helpline at (800) ATA-2900.

WEB RESOURCES

Doing business in Japan:
U.S. Commercial Service Japan:
http://export.gov/japan/doingbusinessinjapan/index.asp

Consular information & official travel advisories for Japan:
U.S. Department of State:
http://travel.state.gov/travel/cis_pa_tw/cis/cis_1148.html

U.S. visas:
U.S. Department of State:
http://travel.state.gov/visa/visa_1750.html
U.S. Embassy Tokyo Consular Section:
http://japan.usembassy.gov/e/tvisa-main.html
Japanese customs, etiquette, and culture:
http://www.japan-guide.com
http://www.thejapanfaq.com

Japanese language:
"Japanese for the Western Brain"
http://kimallen.sheepdogdesign.net/Japanese/index.html
Jim Breen's Japanese Page
http://www.csse.monash.edu.au/~jwb/japanese.html
Business infrastructure:
Japan National Tourist Organization (JNTO):
http://www.jnto.go.jp

Health:
U.S. Department of State; Japan – Country Specific Information:
http://travel.state.gov/travel/cis_pa_tw/cis/cis_1148.html
Temporary entry of materials under the *carnet* system:
http://www.atacarnet.com
https://twitter.com/BuyUSAJapan

IMPORTANT CONTACTS

U.S. EMBASSY TRADE PERSONNEL

Commercial Service Tokyo
Andrew Wylegala, Minister-Counselor for Commercial Affairs
U.S. Embassy Tokyo, 1-10-5 Akasaka, Minato-ku, Tokyo 107-8420
Tel: +81/3/3224-5060; fax: 32244235
Web: http://export.gov/japan/
E-mail: Office.Tokyo@trade.gov

Greg Loose, Counselor for Commercial Affairs
Aaron Held, Commercial Attaché (Operations Unit)
Kevin Chambers, Commercial Attaché (Consumer Goods Unit)
Greg Briscoe, Commercial Attaché (Major Projects Unit)
Stephen Anderson, Commercial Attaché (Healthcare, Fisheries and Tourism Unit)
Greg Taevs, Commercial Attaché (Advanced Technologies Unit)
Foreign Agricultural Service (Department of Agriculture)
David Miller, Minister-Counselor for Agricultural Affairs
Elizabeth Autry, Senior Agricultural Attaché
Benjamin Petlock, Agricultural Attaché
Jennifer Clever, Agricultural Attaché
U.S. Embassy Tokyo, 1-10-5, Akasaka, Minato-ku, Tokyo 107-8420
(U.S. Address: Unit 9800, Box 475, DPO AP 96303-0475)
Tel: +81/3/3224-5105; fax: 3589-0793
Web: www.usdajapan.org/
E-mail: agtokyo@fas.usda.gov

Agricultural Trade Office (Tokyo) (Department of Agriculture)
Steve Shnitzler, Director
U.S. Embassy Tokyo, 1-10-5, Akasaka, Minato-ku, Tokyo 107-8420
(U.S. Address: Unit 9800, Box 591, DPO AP 96303-0591)
Tel: +81/3/ 3224-5115; fax: 3582-6429
Web: www.us-ato.jp/
E-mail: atotokyo@fas.usda.gov

Economic Section (Department of State)
Jessica Webster, Minister-Counselor for Economic and Science Affairs
U.S. Embassy Tokyo, 1-10-5 Akasaka, Minato-ku, Tokyo 107-8420
Tel: +81/3/3224-5020; fax: 3224-5019
Energy Section (Department of Energy)
Jeffrey Miller, Energy Attaché
U.S. Embassy Tokyo, 1-10-5 Akasaka, Minato-ku, Tokyo 107-8420
Tel: +81/3/3224-5444; fax: 3224-5769
Treasury Section (Department of the Treasury)
Christiopher Winship, Financial Attaché
U.S. Embassy Tokyo, 1-10-5 Akasaka, Minato-ku, Tokyo 107-8420
Tel: +81/3/3224-5486; fax: 3224-5490
TRADE PERSONNEL AT U.S. CONSULATES AROUND JAPAN
Commercial Service Osaka-Kobe
John Fleming, Principal Commercial Consul
U.S. Consulate General Osaka, 2-11-5 Nishitenma, Kita-ku, Osaka 530-8543
Tel: +81/6/6315-5953; fax: 6315-5963
E-mail: Office.Osaka-Kobe@trade.gov

Agricultural Trade Office (Osaka) (Department of Agriculture)
Chika Motomura, Ag. Marketing Specialist
American Consulate General Osaka, 2-11-5 Nishitenma, Kita-ku, Osaka 530-8543
(U.S. Address: Unit 45004, Box 239, APO AP 96337-5004)
Tel: +81/6/6315-5904; fax: 6315-5906
Web: www.usdajapan.org/
E-mail: atoosaka@fas.usda.gov

Consulate Nagoya
Harry Sullivan, Principal Officer

Tamiki Mizuno, Economic/Commercial Specialist
U.S. Consulate Nagoya, Nagoya International Center Building, 6F
47-1 Nagono 1-chome, Nakamura-ku, Nagoya 450-0001
Tel: +81/52/581-4501; fax: 581-3190
E-mail: MizunoTX@state.gov

Consulate General Sapporo
John Ries, Consul General
Yumi Baba, Economic/Commercial Assistant
U.S. Consulate General Sapporo, Nishi 28, Kita 1, Chuo-ku; Sapporo 064-0821
Tel: +81/11/641-1115; fax: 643-1283
E-mail: BabaYX@state.gov

Consulate Fukuoka
Jason R. Cubas, Principle Officer
Daniel Callahan, Political/Economic Officer
American Consulate Fukuoka, 2-5-26 Ohori, Chuo-ku, Fukuoka 810-0052
Tel: +81/92/751-9331; fax: +81/92/713-9222
E-mail: CallahanDC@state.gov

Consulate General Naha (Okinawa)
Alfred Magleby, Consul General
Matthew O'Connor, Political and Economic Officer
Akinori Hayashi, Econ/Commercial Specialist
American Consulate General Naha, 2-1-1 Toyama, Urasoe City
Okinawa 901-2101
Tel: +81/98/876-4211; fax: 876-4243
E-mail: HayashiAX@state.gov

CHAMBERS OF COMMERCE/TRADE ASSOCIATIONS

American Chamber of Commerce in Japan (ACCJ)
Sam Kidder, Executive Director
Masonic 39 MT Bldg. 10F; 2-4-5 Azabudai, Minato-ku; Tokyo 106-0041
Tel: +81/3/3433-5381; fax: 3433-8454
Web: http://www.accj.or.jp

American Chamber of Commerce in Japan (ACCJ) Kansai Chapter
Keizo Yamada, Director Chapter Office - Kansai
Dojima Park Bldg. 5F, 1-1-8 Dojimahama, Kita-ku, Osaka 530-0004
Tel: +81/6/6345-9880; fax: 6345-9890
Web: http://www.accj.or.jp/en/chapters/kansai/the-kansai-chapter

American Chamber of Commerce in Japan (ACCJ) Chūbu Chapter
Noriko Kato, Chūbu Operations Manager
Marunouchi Fukao Bldg. 5F; 2-11-24 Marunouchi, Naka-ku, Nagoya 460-0002
Tel: +81/52/229-1525; fax: 222-8272
Web: http://www.accj.or.jp/en/chapters/chubu/the-chubu-chapter

Japan Business Federation (Nippon Keidanren)
International Economic Affairs Bureau
1-3-2 Otemachi, Chiyoda-ku, Tokyo 100-8188
Tel: +81/3/6741-0171; fax: 6741-0301
Web: http://www.keidanren.or.jp/en

Japan Association of Corporate Executives (Keizai Doyukai)
Nihon Kogyo Club Bldg. Annex 5F, 1-4-6 Marunouchi, Chiyoda-ku, Tokyo 100-0005
Tel: +81/3/3284-0220; fax: 3212-3774
Web: http://www.doyukai.or.jp/en

Japan Foreign Trade Council, Inc.

International Affairs and Research Group
World Trade Center Bldg. 6F, 2-4-1 Hamamatsu-cho, Minato-ku, Tokyo 105-6106
Tel: +81-3-3435-5972/5964; fax: +81/3/3435-5979
Web: http://www.jftc.or.jp/english/home_e.htm

Japan-U.S. Business Council
Keidanren Kaikan, 1-3-2 Otemachi, Chiyoda-ku, Tokyo 100-0004
Tel: +81/3/6741-0401; fax: 6741-0402
Web: http://www.jubc.gr.jp/eng/index.html

Japan Chamber of Commerce and Industry
International Division
Tosho Bldg., 3-2-2 Marunouchi, Chiyoda-ku, Tokyo 100-0005
Tel: +81/3/3283-7601; fax: 3216-6497
Web: http://www.jcci.or.jp/home-e.html

Tokyo Chamber of Commerce and Industry
International Division
Tosho Bldg., 3-2-2 Marunouchi, Chiyoda-ku, Tokyo 100-0005
Tel: +81/3/3283-7523; fax: 3216-6497
Web: http://www.tokyo-cci.or.jp/english/

Osaka Chamber of Commerce and Industry
International Division
2-8 Honmachi-bashi, Chuo-ku, Osaka 540-0029
Tel: +81/6/6944-6400; fax: 6944-6293
Web: http://www.osaka.cci.or.jp/e

Kansai Economic Federation (Kankeiren)
International Affairs Department
Nakanoshima Center Bldg. 30F, 6-2-27, Nakanoshima, Kita-ku, Osaka 530-6691
Tel: +81/6/6441-0104; fax: 6441-0443
Web: http://www.kankeiren.or.jp/English

Kansai Association of Corporate Executives (Kansai Keizai Doyukai)
Executive & Administrative Dept./Planning & Research Dept.
Nakanoshima Center Bldg. 28F, 6-2-27, Nakanoshima, Kita-ku, Osaka 530-6691
Tel: +81/6/6441-1031; fax: 6441-1030
Web: http://www.kansaidoyukai.or.jp

Nagoya Chamber of Commerce & Industry (NCCI)
International Group
2-10-19 Sakae, Naka-ku, Nagoya 460-8422
Tel: +81/52/223-6742; fax: 232-5751
Web: http://www.nagoya-cci.or.jp/eng

Kyushu Economic Federation (Kyukeiren)
Tenjin Central Place 6F, 1-10-24 Tenjin, Chuo-ku, Fukuoka 810-0001
Tel: +81/92/761-4261; fax: 724-2102
Web: http://www.kyukeiren.or.jp/english/index.html

Fukuoka Chamber of Commerce and Industry
International Center
9-28 Hakata Ekimae 2-chome, Hakata-ku, Fukuoka 812-8505
Tel: +81/92/441-1117; fax: 441-1600
Web: http://www.fukunet.or.jp/english/index.html

Fukuoka Foreign Trade Association
Fukuoka Chamber of Commerce and Industry Bldg., 7F
Hakata Ekimae 2-9-28, Hakata-ku, Fukuoka 812-8505
Tel: +81/92/452-0707; fax: 452-0700

Web: http://www.fukuoka-fta.or.jp

AGRICULTURAL TRADE ASSOCIATIONS

Japan Chain Stores Association
Toranomon NN Bldg., 11F., 1-21-17 Toranomon, Minato-ku, Tokyo 105-0001
Tel: +81/3/5251-4600; fax: 5251-4601
Web: www.jcsa.gr.jp/

All Nippon Kashi Association
6-9-5 Shimbashi, Minato-ku, Tokyo 105-0004
Tel: +81/3/3431-3115; fax: 3432-1660
Email: anka-0@nifty.com

Japan Convenience Foods Industry Association
Kimura Bldg. 3F, 5-5-5 Asakusabashi, Taito-ku, Tokyo 111-0053
Tel: +81/3/3865-0811; fax: 3865-0815
Email: daihyo@sokuseki-kyokai.com
Web: http://www.instantramen.or.jp/

Japan Dairy Industry Association
Nyugyo Kaikan 4F, 1-14-19 Kudan Kita, Chiyoda-ku, Tokyo 102-0073
Tel: +81/3/3261-9161; fax: 3261-9175
Web: http://www.nyukyou.jp/

Japan Dehydrated Vegetable Association
1-9-12 Irifune, Chuo-ku, Tokyo 104-0042
Tel: +81/3/5117-2661; fax: 3552-2820
Email: kaz@primero.jp
Japan Food Service Association
Hamamatsucho Central Bldg. 9F.10F
1-29-6, Hamamatsucho, Minato-ku, Tokyo 105-0013
Tel: +81/3/5403-1060; fax: 5403-1070
Email: info-jf@jfnet.or.jp
Web: http://www.jfnet.or.jp

Japan Frozen Food Association
Kowa Nitto Bldg. 4F, 3-17-9 Tsukiji, Chuo-ku, Tokyo 104-0045
Tel: +81/3/3541-3003; fax: 3541-3012
Email: info@reishokukyo.or.jp
Web: www.reishokukyo.or.jp/

Japan Fruit Juice Association
Zenkoku Tobacco Bldg., 3F., 1-10-1 Shibadaimon, Minato-ku, Tokyo 105-0012
Tel: +81/3/3435-0731; fax: 3435-0737
Email: kaju-kyo@cello.ocn.ne.jp
Web: www.kaju-kyo.ecnet.jp/

Japan Health Food & Nutrition Food Association
2-7-27 Ichigaya Sadohara-cho, Shinjuku-ku, Tokyo 162-0842
Tel: +81/3/3268-3134; fax: 3268-3136
Email: jhnfa@jhnfa.org
Web: www.jhnfa.org/

Japan Nut Association
Kohinata Bldg #203, 2-18-10 Shinkawa, Chuo-ku, Tokyo 104-0033
Tel: n/a fax: 81/3/6662-6528
Email: jna@jt5.so-net.ne.jp
Web: http://www.jna-nut.com/

Japan Self-Service Association

Sakurai Bldg. 4F, 3-19-8 Uchi-kanda, Chiyoda-ku, Tokyo 101-0047
Tel: +81/3/3255/4825; fax: 3255-4826
Email: selkyo@jssa.or.jp

Japan Restaurant Association
BM Kabutocho Bldg., 11-7 Nihonbashi Kabutocho, Chuo-ku, Tokyo 103-0026
Tel: +81/3/5651-5601; fax: 5651-5602
Japan Wine and Spirits Importers' Association
Daiichi Tentoku Bldg., 1-13-5 Toranomon, Minato-ku, Tokyo 105-0001
Tel: +81/3/3503-6505/6506; fax: 3503-6504
Web: www.youshu-yunyu.org/english/index.html

JAPANESE GOVERNMENT AGENCIES

Ministry of Economy, Trade and Industry (METI)
Trade & Investment Facilitation Division
1-3-1 Kasumigaseki, Chiyoda-ku, Tokyo 100-8901
Tel: +81/3/3501-1662; fax: 3501-2082
Web: http://www.meti.go.jp/english/index.html

Japan External Trade Organization (JETRO)
Invest Japan Dept.
Ark Mori Bldg., 6F, 1-12-32, Akasaka, Minato-ku, Tokyo107-6006
Tel: +81/3/3582-5511
Web: http://www.jetro.go.jp

JETRO "Invest Japan" Business Support Center
Ark Mori Bldg., 7F, 1-12-32, Akasaka, Minato-ku, Tokyo107-6006
Tel: +81/3/3582-4686; fax: 3584-6024
Web: http://www.jetro.go.jp/en/invest/ibsc/

Manufactured Imports and Investment Promotion Organization (MIPRO)
World Import Mart Bldg 6F, 3-1-3 Higashi-Ikebukuro, Toshima-ku, Tokyo 170-8630
Tel: +81/3/3988-2791; fax: 3988-1629
Web: http://www.mipro.or.jp/english/
For further contact information of Japanese government agencies and quasi-governmental organizations, please contact Commercial Service Japan offices.

U.S. FEDERAL GOVERNMENT

U.S.A. Trade Information Center
Ronald Reagan Building and International Trade Center 1300 Pennsylvania Avenue, N.W., Washington, D.C. 20004
Tel: 1-800-USA-TRAD(E); fax: 202-482-3433
Email: tic@ita.doc.gov
Web: http://www.export.gov/exportbasics/eg_main_017483.asp

U.S. Department of Commerce
Assistant Secretary for Trade Promotion and
Director General of the U.S. and Foreign Commercial Service
International Trade Administration
1401 Constitution Avenue, N.W., Washington, DC 20230
Web: http://trade.gov/

U.S. Department of Commerce, Market Access and Compliance Country Desk
Office of Japan and Korea
Keith Roth, Director
International Trade Administration
Room 2320, 14th Street and Constitution Avenue, N.W., Washington, DC 20230
Tel: 202-482-2515; fax: 202-482-0469
Email: Keith.Roth@trade.gov

Web: http://www.mac.doc.gov/japan-korea/

U.S. Department of Agriculture
Foreign Agricultural Service
1400 Independence Ave., S.W., Washington, DC 20250
Email: info@fas.usda.gov
Web: http://www.fas.usda.gov

U.S. Department of State
Commercial and Business Affairs Office
2201 C Street, N.W., Room 2318, Washington, DC 20520
Tel: 202-647-1625; fax: 202-647-3953
Email: BusinessOutreachweb@state.gov
Web: http://www.state.gov/business

Export-Import Bank of the United States (Ex-Im Bank)
811 Vermont Avenue, N.W., Washington, DC 20571
Tel: (202) 565-3946 (EXIM) or (800) 565-3946 (EXIM)
Email: info@exim.gov
Web: http://www.exim.gov

Overseas Private Investment Corporation (OPIC)
1100 New York Avenue, N.W., Washington, D.C. 20527
Tel: 202-336-8400; fax: 202-336-7949
Email: info@opic.gov
Web: http://www.opic.gov
https://twitter.com/BuyUSAJapan

JAPAN INDUSTRY: STRATEGIC PROFILES[3]

AUTOMOTIVE TELEMATICS AND ITS

Automotive Telematics and ITS
Japanese automotive manufacturers are featuring more telematics systems in their vehicles to keep them globally competitive. Wireless voice and data communications and GPS (Global Positioning System) location capabilities provide drivers with location-specific information, security and functionality-enhancing services that increase driver convenience, safety and efficiency of the transportation system.

Market
The Mitsubishi Research Institute estimated the Japanese telematics market to be 460 billion yen in 2001 and projects a growth to 945 billion yen in 2010. Because Japan is much smaller geographically than the United States, vehicle density is much higher here at 500 vehicles per square mile compared to 58 in the United States. Greater vehicle density has intensified traffic congestion and the potential for collisions. Such conditions increase the opportunities for telematics related businesses to help make driving more convenient and safer.

State of the Industry

- **Significant governmental support**
  - 1996 Comprehensive Plan for Intelligent Transport Systems (ITS): led to nationwide coverage for inexpensive real-time traffic information service and non-stop collection of road tolls by 2003
  - e-Japan Strategy: sought to make Japan "the world's most advanced IT nation" by 2006; achieved what Cisco Systems calls "the most advanced network infrastructure in the world."
  - u-Japan Program: seeks to realize a "ubiquitous network society by 2010"
- **Advanced network infrastructure**
  - KDDI, one of Japan's leading information and communications companies, provides a robust and widespread network. For 2007, the company plans to construct an Ultra 3G network that converges all fixed and mobile service networks to create a ubiquitous network.
  - NTT DoCoMo, another leading telecom company, provides the Okutto-Keitai service, which achieves seamless and continuous reception of navigation information.
- **Advanced Safety Vehicles (ASVs)**
  - Feature intelligent assistance functions, e.g., danger notifications, tire-pressure alerts, and lane-departure warnings
  - All of Japan's leading car manufacturers (Toyota, Honda, Mitsubishi, Nissan and Mazda) have introduced ASVs
- **Leading navigation systems**
  - Come in 50% of new cars and are featured in one out of every three cars on the road
  - Have achieved double-digit growth for the past eight consecutive years
  - Ministry of Construction has supported the Japan Digital Road Map Association (JDRMA) in creating a comprehensive and standardized digital road map, availability of which is often a major constraint in other navigation markets
  - Features in addition to mapping and emergency support services: real-time traffic information, route suggestions, music (even karaoke), games, e-commerce, and other internet facilitated applications

Applicable technologies, parts and businesses
The main areas of ITS and areas of opportunity for telematics companies are shown in Figure 1 below.

[3] For additional information on specific Jpan industries, please contact Global Investment and Business Center, USA at IBPUSA@comcast.net

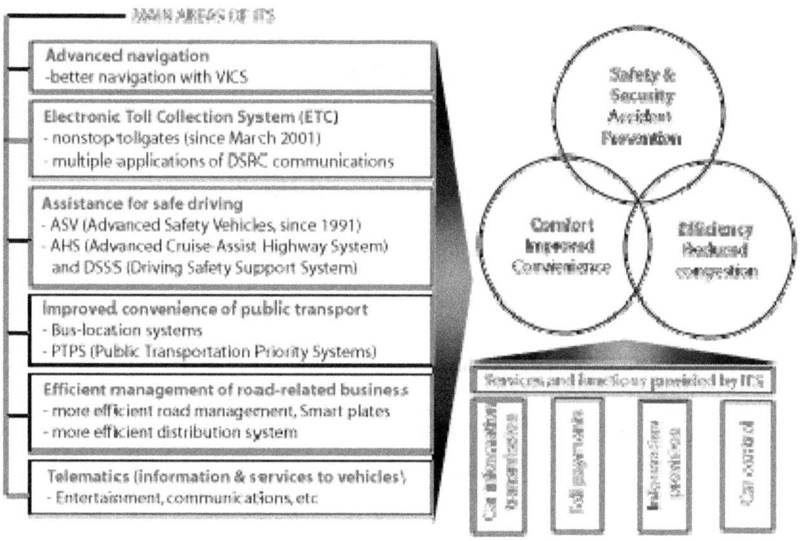

The expansion of telematics systems increases the amount of computers and mobile communication technology used in vehicles and along roads, creating a growth of opportunities for a large number of fields (See Figure 2 below).

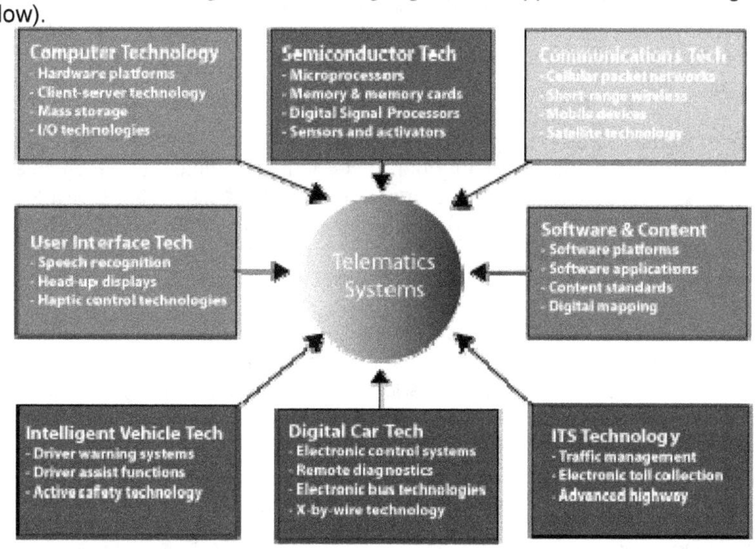

Successful American companies

- **Atheros Communications Inc. – Sunnyvale, CA**
  - Supplies Super AG wireless chipsets to the Japanese telematics service provider Mobilecast Telematics Inc.
  - Together, the companies are also developing VoIP technology and two-way information distribution/communications systems
- **Nuance – Menlo Park, CA**
  - Supplies its speech software to Toyota to speech-enable the carmaker's G-Book telematics system
- **Wind River Systems Inc. – Alameda, CA**
  - Provided VxWorks real-time operating system and TORNADO integrated development environment for CARWINGS, the infotainment and telematics system manufactured by Japan's Xanavi and featured in Nissan automobiles
- **Cellport Systems – Boulder, CO**

- Formed a joint venture with Japan's Omron Corporation under which Cellport transferred its CP3000, a voice activated two-part universal hands-free system, its manufacturing processes and sourcing in order that Omron could produce a Japanese version of the system

BIOTECHNOLOGY

JETRO is pleased to continue it's support of the biotechnology industry through participation at BIO 2006 from April 9-12, where over 55 exhibitors from Japan will come to showcase their technologies and meet with potential partners.

Past JETRO Biotechnology-related events include:

- Japan's Business Environment for Bio-Related Deal-Making
- Connecting Wisconsin Biotech with Japan

The market for the overall biotechnology industry in 2002 expanded by 7.5 percent from 2001 to ¥1,433 billion. Of the total, the biomedical market accounted for ¥818.7 billion, 7.3 percent larger than the previous year. This biomedical market breaks down into biotech pharmaceuticals worth ¥539.24 billion, and biomedical treatment and drugs-related products and services worth ¥279.45 billion. The market has been growing for the past four years (1998 to 2002) at an average annual rate of 6.7 percent. Main products of biotech pharmaceuticals are those produced by utilizing transgenic technology, cell fusion technology and cell culture technology.

Technologies in genome-based drug development, cell therapy and regenerative medicine are now in the basic research-and-development stage at major pharmaceutical companies, universities and public research institutions, with very few of them being produced on a commercial basis. Of the biotech pharmaceuticals produced in 2002, the highest proceeds of ¥120 billion came from erythropoietin, followed by monoclonal antibody in-vitro diagnostic agents (¥65 billion) and human growth hormone (¥60 billion). Showing particularly strong growth are antibody drugs, with sales growing from ¥900 million in 2001 to ¥13 billion in 2002.

Meanwhile, the actual businesses of the biomedical support market are gradually being developed into venture businesses. In the research support fields such as equipment and reagents, analysis systems like the DNA sequencer, bioinformatics, and various consigned services, in addition to the conventional liquid chromatography, have formed stable markets.

GROWTH OPPORTUNITIES

Genome-Based Drug Development

Facing intensifying competition for new drug development, many domestic pharmaceutical companies are forming alliances and tie-ups with foreign bio venture firms to make their development efforts more efficient and also spread their cost burdens and risks, while stepping up their own research and development setup. This is because in today's new drug development it is becoming even more necessary to obtain technologies and information for such development by new approaches different from conventional development methods, and it is becoming more difficult to cope only with one company's technologies and researchers.

Cell Therapy

Of the major companies involved in this field, Kirin Brewery Co. introduced technologies from Dendreon Corp., and Takara Bio Inc. from Nexell Therapeutics, both of the United States, to develop cell therapy equipment. Successful venture firms in this field include Lymphotec Inc. and Medinet Co.

Regenerative Medicine

Of the large- and medium-size companies, Terumo Corp. (in a tie-up with Diacrin, Inc. of the U.S.) and Kyowa Hakko Kogyo Co. (research being conducted on the technology of mesenchymal stem cell utilization with Keio University's School of Medicine) are active in the market.

CONSUMER ELECTRONICS

American companies involved in the consumer electronics industry will find in Japan the essential elements for business success. Japanese consumers tend to adopt new technologies earlier than those in other countries and serve as a 'proof-of-concept' market. As a result, many new products and applications are introduced in Japan first before being launched in markets around the rest of the world. Japan's strong background in semiconductors, miniaturization and product design serves as a solid foundation for developing and manufacturing high-end consumer electronics.

But American companies expanding operations into Japan do not have to begin alone: global powerhouses like Fujitsu, Toshiba and Sony are partnering with U.S. companies to jointly develop products and technologies. And not only do the U.S. companies benefit from the development and manufacturing expertise of these Japanese firms, they can also utilize the worldwide reach of these multinational firms.

Market size and outlook

Japan's Ministry of Internal Affairs and Communications (MIC) surveyed the consumer electronics market for 2004 to have been 2.7 trillion yen and estimated it to grow to 11 trillion yen by 2010, more than four times the value of 2004. When including the cellular telephone market (and including network platforms and appliances), the market size is estimated to be 20 trillion yen (See figure 1).

The MIC defines the consumer electronics market to include the following areas:

- **Service content market**
  - Content, such as entertainment information on movies, drama, etc.
  - Services, such as distance learning (tele-education), security services, etc.
- **Appliance market**
  - Digital information consumer electronics, such as TV, washing machine, PC, modems, etc.
  - Network platform market*
- **Networks, including ADSL, cable Internet, fiber-optic cables, etc.**
  - Platforms, such as ones for billing and authentication

* The MIC includes the network platform market in the consumer electronics industry due to the expected convergence of communication and entertainment electronics.

Figure 1: Projected Growth, Consumer Electronics Market, 2004-2010

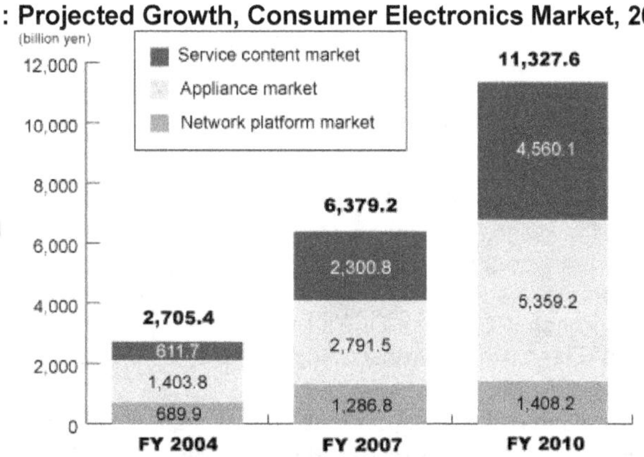

Source: Ministry of Internal Affairs and Communications

State of the industry

The Japanese consumer electronics industry anticipates the convergence of communication and entertainment electronics. By networking consumer electronics, companies seek to provide advanced services to help consumers achieve more convenience in their daily activities, particularly in the home market.

Consumer electronics are expected to make their way into home security systems helping to monitor fires or break-ins and report them to nearby fire departments or police stations. Telediagnostic systems are being developed in which a person's diagnostic information monitored by various devices in the home (e.g. thermometer, scale) is sent to their doctor or healthcare center. Consumers could also control appliances in home from their cell phone or personal digital assistant (PDA). Upon departing the home, a person can turn off all consumer electronics while turning on the security system. On the way home from work, one can start a bath or begin warming up the house.

One control system in development that focuses on entertainment consumer electronics is the E PC, which is a computer that looks like a VCR and sits as a part of entertainment consoles to serve as a control center for stereos, TVs and other equipment. Louis Burns, vice president of the desktop platforms group at Intel, told CNET, "The whole industry is turning about. You will start to see the content industry target the E PC." In Japan, Intel is working with a company to create a library of about 1,000 movies available for pay-per-view at home.

The realization of such a convergence of communication and entertainment electronics is facilitated by the following:

- **Significant governmental support**
  - e-Japan Strategy: sought to make Japan "the world's most advanced IT nation" by 2006; achieved what Cisco Systems in a press release called "the most advanced network infrastructure in the world."
  - u-Japan Program: seeks to realize a "ubiquitous network society by 2010."
- **Advanced network infrastructure**
  - KDDI, one of Japan's leading information and communications companies, provides a robust and widespread network. For 2007, the company plans to construct an Ultra 3G network that converges all fixed and mobile service networks to create a ubiquitous network.
  - NTT DoCoMo, another leading telecom company, provides the Okutto-Keitai service, which achieves seamless and continuous reception of navigation information wherein a driver can take with them on their mobile phone directions to a store from the navigation device inside their vehicle.
- **Faster technology adoption speed**
  - Approximately 90 percent of cell phones in Japan have cameras, while the figure for other major markets is 20 percent.
  - About 80 percent of desktops have embedded TV tuners, a concept that has only begun to be seen in other parts of the world.
  - T Navi, a product allowing consumers to surf the Web or shop on a TV, is gaining popularity as a revitalized version of the TV-web programs that failed to catch on in the past decade.

A major challenge manufacturers are working on is overcoming obstacles in connecting consumer electronics of different types and fields from different manufacturers. Companies able to facilitate compatibility between products and technologies stand to find significant opportunities.

Successful American companies in Japan

- **On2 Technologies Inc. – New York, NY**
  - Partnered with Saver Corporation, the market leader for transcoding technology for mobile phones in Japan, to develop the industry's first online Flash 8 video transcoding service for mobile phone users
  - Saver Corporation will license On2's Flix Engine technology for integration into its mini-it EM family of Flash 8 video transcoding servers
- **GeoVector Corporation – San Francisco, CA**
  - Established a subsidiary (kabushiki kaisha) to work closely with Japanese partners KDDI, Mapion and NEC Magnus to exploit a large base of mobile phones with the necessary embedded hardware and location specific information required to provide its 3-D "click on the real world®" search engine applications
- **NVIDIA Corporation – Santa Clara, CA**
  - Supplies graphics processors, platform processors, and wireless media processors used in a variety of consumer electronics like PCs, servers, mobile phones and used in developing and deploying PC games

- Works with world leading Japanese OEMs Fujitsu Siemens, Mitsubishi, Sony and Toshiba

ENVIRONMENTAL SERVICES & EQUIPMENT

The development of the Japanese economy has up to now been anchored in a "mass production, mass consumption and mass disposal-based society." Approximately 400 million tons of industrial waste is generated each year, putting a severe strain on final waste treatment facilities. As global environmental problems grow more acute, Japan is undergoing a concerted effort to shift toward a "recycling-based society" which promises to rapidly expand the scale and breadth of the environmental business market.

According to a study conducted in 2000 by the Ministry of the Environment, eco-business is projected to grow from a 24.7 trillion yen market in 1997 to a 40.1 trillion yen market by 2010. Moreover, since the study did not take into account several future growth areas such as fuel cells, the Ministry expects to further revise upward its projected market size numbers in the near future.

The large volume of environment-related patents in Japan attests to the strength of the nation's environmental technology base. The enactment of pro-environment legislation has further stimulated research and development in the environmental technology field. Japan's world class environment technological strength is therefore expected to spawn tremendous growth of the environmental business sector.

FOOD SERVICE INDUSTRY

The Japanese food service industry market in 2001 totaled 32 trillion yen (including take-out and prepared food items). Ever since the first foreign food service chain made a historic debut in 1970, with a no-nonsense commitment to the Japanese market, restaurant chains operated by foreign interests have held significant places in the Japanese food service industry. More recent arrivals, spearheaded by Starbucks Coffee, and followed by KEAWJAI and other Asian establishments, have opened shop in quick succession and have demonstrated strong performance.

In cases of foreign participation in the Japanese market, according to the study conducted under the three subject areas indicated above, it has become clear that success comes through a good understanding of the Japanese market, delegation of power to local partners, and the building of cooperative relationships based upon proper and necessary education. If any one of these points is neglected, the well-established status of revered chains back home, as has happened with Dunkin' Donuts and Burger King, may not help in terms of business expansion efforts in the Japanese market. More modest chains, such as Kua 'Aina, are successfully multiplying their stores in Japan, coming as they do armed with unique store design concepts and an adequate grasp of the characteristics of the Japanese market.

It is predicted, nonetheless, that in the years ahead the Japanese food service market will have an increasing number of chain operations. At the same time, Japanese menu preferences are diversifying at a rapid pace, resulting in an environment more receptive to the offerings of foreign food services. Furthermore, the Japanese are eating out more and more. Thus, real opportunities appear for foreign food services of diverse categories from around the globe to advance into the Japanese market, taking advantage of prevailing favorable conditions.

Fast Food

The Japanese food service industry has been driven by family restaurants, bistros and fast food restaurants. Among the first to arrive on the Japanese fast food scene in the early 1970s were Kentucky Fried Chicken Japan, McDonald's, Mister Donut, and Dunkin' Donuts, Lotteria and Mos Burger. Baskin Robbins31 Ice Cream (foreign) started in 1974 along with several other domestic and overseas companies, which opened their first locations and then expanded operations in rapid succession.

Cafes/Coffeehouses

In the 1990s, a variety of shop types such as Internet cafés, manga cafés and dining cafés came into being in response to consumer demand. At the same time, other shop types represented by Café Croissant operated by Family Restaurant chain Royal and McDonald's, serving espresso, are adding fuel to the competitive fire with their determination to engage in thisarena.

Casual Dining
In August 1999, in a news-making event, T.G.I. Friday's, which had already developed more than 570 restaurants worldwide, opened its first branch in Shibuya, Tokyo, with the promise of rekindling the market's vitality. Watami Food Service, which was then posting an earnings increase at a phenomenal 2-digit rate on a sustained basis as the most growth-oriented company in the food service market, formed a joint venture with Carlson Restaurants Worldwide (USA) to establish T.G.I. Friday's Japan to launch a solidly structured business. Then in April 2002, Outback Steakhouse, reportedly yielding the highest rate of profit in the United States, established Outback Steakhouse Japan in a venture with WDI, which had launched a number of foreign food service chain shops.

IT SERVICES & SOFTWARE

In 2001, the Japanese made a commitment to making Japan the most sophisticated IT nation in the world. The goal was to ensure that, within five years, at least 30 million households would have high speed Internet access, and that 10 million households would have ultra high speed Internet access. Thanks to Japan's culture of rapid technology adoption, these goals were achieved in September, 2003, three years ahead of schedule. Having achieved the goals laid out in the e-Japan project, e-Japan phase II has been initiated, and promises significant opportunities for IT services and software providers.

The United States is the dominant importer of software to Japan. In fiscal 2000, the last year which data is available for, United States companies accounted for 89.4% of all software imports into Japan. This includes a 96.5% share of OS/server imports, and a 91.2% share of custom software imports. Japanese customers clearly show a strong preference to work with American software providers.

Phase II of e-Japan mandates effective use of IT in seven fields: medical services, food, lifestyle, small- and medium-size enterprise financing, and public services. The plan includes the construction of a ubiquitous network and more stringent security measures for the foundation of a new IT society.

MEDICAL EQUIPMENT

The world market for medical equipment was roughly $169 billion dollars in 2000. The Japanese market was second in size only to the U.S., and accounted for roughly 15% of the world market. According to the Annual Report on the Survey of Pharmaceutical Industry Production compiled by the Health Policy Bureau of the Ministry of Health, Labour and Welfare, the total market for medical devices in Japan was 1,960 billion yen. (production: 1,520 billion yen, export: 400 billion yen, import: 840 billion yen).

Growth Products for Foreign Firms

Cardiac Pacemakers
For cardiac pacemakers, the import rate is almost 100% and, and there are a number of entrants in the market. Medtronic Japan continues to hold its place as the market leader.

Artificial Joints
The import rate for artificial joints is about 80% and the market is dominated by three manufacturers (Zimmer, Stryker Japan and DePuy Japan1). The market is increasing in size with the aging of the Japanese population and the according increase in cases.

Coronary Stents
For coronary stents, the top four manufacturers (Guidant, Medtronic Japan, Johnson & Johnson and Boston Scientific) account for more than 95% of the total market, and the import rate is extremely high. Coronary stents are a device used after percutaneous transluminal coronaryangioplasty (PTCA) to reduce acute coronary stoppage and re-stricture. The number of PTCA operations being performed is rising each year, and accordingly the market for coronary stents is expanding each year.

MICROELECTRONICS

Today, the electronic equipment market in Japan is hotter than ever. Among the market R&D sector, which develops and experiments with advanced technologies and new products, and the specific products sector, stay in Japan . Currently, exports account for more than 50% of the total sales of Japanese semiconductor manufacturers.

Now, having established overseas sales and production bases, Japanese electronic equipment makers purchase semiconductors not only from Japanese manufacturers but also increasingly from overseas manufacturers. At the same time, Japanese semiconductor manufacturers that produce all processes began to outsource some of their production processes, having been exposed to the global trend towards specialization in manufacturing semiconductors. They also started to create spin-off subsidiaries aiming to increase profits by reducing costs.

There are already some internationally prominent semiconductor manufacturers in Japan , and competition in product development and pricing is fierce. However, the needs of the Japanese electronic equipment makers who use semiconductors are concentrated on high value-added products. It is difficult for Japanese semiconductor manufacturers to cope with these products, because of their technology.

As a result, demands for overseas semiconductors are increasing in these product areas.
-Semiconductors used for mass-produced electronic equipment, which can be manufactured at low cost and supplied steadily (discretes, analog ICs, DRAM, SRAM, micro controllers, ASSPs etc. for PCs and peripheral devices, TVs, VCRs and audio equipment);

-Custom semiconductors for specific applications (ASSPs, ASICs/system LSIs, MPUs/MCUs, AS memory, discretes, etc. for newly-developed electronic equipment such as next generation cellular phones, digital TVs, set-top boxes, game units, routers, etc.)

Among latter products suggestions to users for the development of high value-added products, joint product development with users, and technical support are all sought after in the Japanese market. Semiconductors that include features which other manufacturers' products lack, and that have design data, have a particularly good chance of success.

Market Growth Segments

IC/LSI

In Japan, the IC/LSI market used to be composed mainly of products destined for household appliances such as AV equipment, but demand for information and communications equipment such as PCs and cellular phones began to increase in the late 1990s, resulting in a jump in the share of MOS devices which process digital signals. They accounted for 82.2% of the market in 2000. It is expected that a market for network-related equipment for household use and digital household appliances will emerge, and thus the share of analog ICs in the market will increase slightly.

Discretes

In Japan, the need for analog functions used in consumer electronic equipment has been high and the market for discretes is relatively large. In particular, power transistors for power supplies,motors and communications-related equipment account for a large share of the market. While small signal transistors and diodes take a large share in volume base, power transistors for which the unit price is relatively high have a large share in volume base.

RETAIL

Market

Valued at over 110 trillion yen in 2003, Japan's retail market is the second largest in the world with sales second only to those of the United States when compared to the world's five largest retail markets.

Below is the retail market broken down by classification and then by sales value for each business classification. The data comes from the most recent Census of Commerce (2002) from the Ministry of Economy Trade and Industry (METI), which produces the report every three years. The 2005 report will be released soon.

KEY SECTORS

Sales in three key sectors stand out: high-end specialty, home furnishings and non-store retail. Many retailers in these sectors have come to Japan not only to take advantage of the high per capital sales but also to develop products influenced by the high standards of local consumers. Products are developed with these high standards and later prove to be successful when sold in other parts of the world.

- **High-end Specialty**

  Japan possesses one of the top markets for luxury items in the world. Japanese consumers purchase 40 percent of the world's luxury goods every year. In addition, a 2002 survey found the following percentages of Tokyo women in their 20s to own an item from these high-end retailers:

  - 94% own a Louis Vuitton product
  - 92% own Gucci
  - 58% own Prada
  - 52% own Chanel
  - 44% own Christian Dior

  Foreign high-end retailers also conduct R&D activities in Japan to refine their products to meet Japanese consumer standards. These standards then serve as a benchmark for worldwide success of their products. Richard Collasse, president of Chanel K.K., noted, "Looking at our efforts in innovation, we established our own R&D unit in Japan, since this country unquestionably has the most advanced technology in cosmetics. We made this investment because we concluded that we needed to develop products for not only Japan but also the global market."

- **Home Furnishing**

  Japan's home furnishings sector has experienced considerable expansion over the past decade, growing to 3.92 trillion yen in sales and 3,860 stores in 2003. A prominent trend seen of home furnishing centers is a move beyond the conventional retail practice of selling independent products to packaging many of them by offering household solutions and coordinated furnishings.
  Non-Store Retail

  As more shoppers look to the convenience of being able to shop from their computers and phones outside of regular store hours, the non-store retail sector has been growing
  The top four media—catalog, direct mail, Internet and TV—make up 75% of sales, of which TV shopping and Internet sales have shown particularly outstanding growth.

  - **TV shopping**
    - During FY 2004, the 10 leading TV shopping companies sold a total of 164 billion yen worth of merchandise—a 25% increase from the previous year.
    - Sales for FY 2005 are forecasted to amount to more than 200 billion yen.
  - **Internet**
    - Member firms of the Japan Direct Marketing Association reported that their Internet sales doubled in FY 2002 to about 150 billion yen.
    - 67.8 million Japanese had Internet connectivity via their mobile phones as of December 2003, allowing them to make payments at convenience stores to mobile telephony-based Internet merchants and further fueling Internet sales.

Successful Foreign Companies

- **Coach Japan**

  Established: 2001
  Country: United States
  Business: imported handbags and accessories
  FY2005 sales: 39.6 billion yen

  - Japan sales constitute more than 20% of Coach's global revenues
  - Japan is Coach's second largest market after the United States
  - Fastest growing brand and holds the No. 2 position in market share in the imported handbag and accessories sector
  - Double-digit year-on-year growth rates
  - Aims to double Japan sales in next four years to 80 billion yen
- **Ikea Japan K.K.**

  Established: 2002
  Country: Sweden
  Business: home furnishings

  - During initial phase, plans to open
    - Four to six stores in Tokyo metropolitan area (first two to open in 2006)
    - Four to six stores in Kansai region
  - Acquired land on Port Island; store opening planned for 2009
  - Tommy Kullberg, president of Ikea Japan: "If Ikea can win the confidence of Japanese consumers, we can sell our products anywhere in the world."
- **Lands' End Japan**
  Established: 1993
  Country: United States
  Business: catalog and online retailer, classic American casual wear
  - Online shopping launched in 1999
  - 2005 revenue grew 11% over same period in 2004
  - Internet sales grew to reach more than 20% of company's total 2005 revenue
  - Expects sales to grow with new shopping features:
    - Lands' End Live – allows shoppers to chat with a live representative while shopping
    - Shop With A Friend – connects shoppers anywhere to "go shopping together"

ROBOTICS

Early Adoption = Business Opportunities
Japan's eagerness to embrace new technology has led to huge opportunities in the robotics industry. Consistently strong demand from highly-competitive manufacturing companies means Japan's robotics market, valued at $7 billion, is among the largest in the world. This strength has translated into leadership in the burgeoning social welfare robotics field, which is expected to fuel explosive growth to the robotics industry as a whole. The Japanese robotics market is projected to grow to $30 billion by 2010, and to $80 billion by 2025, opening up market and partnering opportunities for American companies.

Industrial Robotics
Japan's robotics market is currently dominated by industrial applications with 99% of the robots shipped in 2003 used in manufacturing. Roughly 350,000 industrial robots are currently in operation in Japan—more than three times as many in any other country in the world. Demand for industrial robots has been strong since the 1980's and, after peaking during the IT Bubble, has grown each year since 2001. Recent manufacturing advances in other Asian countries have also fueled greater demand for exports.

Consumer Robotics
Much of the projected growth in the robotics industry will be driven by the emergence of robots as

commercially viable consumer products. Rather than being limited to manufacturing applications, the next generation of robotics will play a number of roles in everyday life. Commercially available entertainment robots such as Honda's Asimo and Sony's Aibo have attracted media attention worldwide, but future robots will have more varied and practical functions.

- **Welfare**
  - Robots currently in development will be able to monitor a patient's health from home and communicate vital information directly to physicians.
- **Therapy**
  - Care facilities in Japan are already introducing robots as therapeutic aids to reduce stress levels in the elderly. For more information, please see JETRO's RoboNexus page. Robotics are also finding applications in physical therapy environments, such as injury rehabilitation.
- **Cleaning and Sanitation**
  - Robots capable of following maps and avoiding obstacles are being used to clean both public areas and private residences.
- **Entertainment**
  - In addition to Asimo and Aibo, other entertainment robots, such as the ones on display at the Aichi Exposition, are drawing media attention.

JETRO Support
JETRO is committed to supporting American robotics companies partner with Japanese companies and enter the Japanese market. JETRO actively participates in robotics-related events, including sponsorship in the RoboBusiness and RoboNexus Conferences. In July 2005, JETRO offered American companies a unique opportunity to get inside the Japanese robotics industry with the Robotics Mission. For a detailed wrap up of the Robotics Mission, please see JETRO's August/September Midwest Newsletter (pdf, 348kb).
Opportunities for American Companies
Opportunities for American companies existing in numerous fields in Japan include:

- distributing Japanese entertainment robots to U.S. retailers
- collaborating on joint robotics development in the areas of search & rescue robots and social welfare robots
- combining U.S. artificial intelligence (AI) technology with Japanese mechanics to develop better robots
- collaborating with Japanese robotics companies on developing business models to commercialize robots for the U.S. market
- joining robotics research with Japanese universities and companies

TELECOMMUNICATIONS

Long known as a hotbed of technical innovation, Japan has also emerged as the most connected country in the world. Japan's cellular phone and broadband markets are among the most advanced in the world; and Japan also leads the way in emerging telecommunications technologies such as Fiber Optics, 3G, and ubiquitous networking. Japan's leadership in these sectors presents significant opportunities for both technology and content providers.

Broadband
Broadband subscription has grown exponentially since it's introduction in 1999. The total number of broadband users in Japan stood at 14.95 million at the end of Fiscal 2003, which ended March 31, 2004. Broadband has overtaken dial-up as the top way to access the Internet in Japan, with ADSL being the most popular service. One reason for the popularity of broadband is it's cost-effectiveness: in Japan, 100 Kbps costs only $0.09, making Japan the most inexpensive place in the world to utilize broadband services. This fast-paced integration of broadband services has also put Japan in a position as the leading innovator in the data communications world. Fiber to the home (FTTH) services are catching on in Japan faster than anywhere else in the world. As of the end of Fiscal 2003, 1.15 subscribers were using fiber optic services. Fiber optic services continue to proliferate, and services offering up to 1Gbps (1,000 Mbps) are now

available.

Mobile
Japan has traditionally been a world leader in wireless services. 89.5% of the Japanese population subscribes to mobile phone services, the highest penetration rate in the world. This widespread usage of cellular phones has paved the way for high-speed adoption of new technologies, such as mobile internet access, 3G, and ubiquitous networking.
Mobile data services have been available through cellular phone providers since the launch of Docomo's I-Mode in 1999. As of September, 2003, the total number of mobile Internet users in Japan stood at nearly 70 million. This high-speed adoption of mobile technologies has led to other innovations, such as cellular phone cameras, being debuted in Japan.

3rd Generation (3G) mobile phone services also debuted in Japan before anywhere else. The first 3G service was FOMA, introduced by Docomo in 2001. Competitors au and Vodafone have since started 3G services, and the total number of subscribers is now nearly 20 million. 3G users enjoy access to wireless broadband, mobile video conferencing, and Java-based applications, all on the go.

IMPORTANT BUSINESS AND TRADE CONTACTS

BUSINESS ORGANIZATIONS

Chubu Economic Federation

Shadan Hojin, Chubu Keizai Rengokai (Chukeiren) 日本語表記

CATEGORY	Industry/Economy:Business Organizations
TYPE	Incorporated association
ADDRESS	Nagoya Sakae bldg.10F, 5-1 Buhei-cho, Higashi-ku Nagoya-shi, Aichi 461-0008
PHONE	+81-52-962-8091
FAX	+81-52-962-8090
E-MAIL	kamimura@chukeiren.or.jp
HOMEPAGE	http://www.chukeiren.or.jp/english/index2.html
REMARKS	

Fukuoka Chamber of Commerce and Industry

Fukuoka Shoko Kaigisho 日本語表記

CATEGORY	Industry/Economy:Business Organizations
TYPE	Others
ADDRESS	2-9-28 Hakata-ekimae, Hakata-ku Fukuoka-shi, Fukuoka 812-8505
PHONE	+81-92-441-1111
FAX	+81-92-474-3200
E-MAIL	fksomu@fukunet.or.jp
HOMEPAGE	http://www.fukunet.or.jp/ (Japanese only)
REMARKS	

Japan Business Federation

Shadan Hojin, Nihon Keizai Dantai Rengokai (Nihon Keidanren) 日本語表記

CATEGORY	Industry/Economy:Business Organizations
TYPE	Incorporated association
ADDRESS	Keidanren Kaikan bldg., 1-9-4 Ote-machi, Chiyoda-ku, Tokyo 100-8188
PHONE	+81-3-5204-1614
FAX	+81-3-5255-6233
E-MAIL	webmaster@keidanren.or.jp
HOMEPAGE	http://www.keidanren.or.jp/index.html
REMARKS	

Japan Junior Chamber Inc.

Shadan Hojin, Nihon Seinen Kaigisho 日本語表記

CATEGORY	Industry/Economy:Business Organizations
TYPE	Incorporated association
ADDRESS	2-14-3 Hirakawa-cho, Chiyoda-ku, Tokyo 102-0093
PHONE	+81-3-3234-5601
FAX	+81-3-3265-2409
E-MAIL	
HOMEPAGE	http://www.jaycee.or.jp/
REMARKS	

Kansai Association of Corporate Executives

Shadan Hojin, Kansai Keizai Doyukai 日本語表記

CATEGORY	Industry/Economy:Business Organizations
TYPE	Incorporated association
ADDRESS	Nakanoshima Center bldg. 28F, 6-2-27 Nakanoshima, Kita-ku Osaka-shi, Osaka 530-6691
PHONE	+81-6-6441-1031
FAX	+81-6-6441-1030
E-MAIL	kdoyukai@mbc.sphere.ne.jp

HOMEPAGE http://www.kdoyukai.on.arena.ne.jp/ (Japanese only)
REMARKS

Kansai Economic Federation, KEF

Shadan Hojin, Kansai Keizai Rengokai (Kankeiren)
CATEGORY Industry/Economy:Business Organizations
TYPE Incorporated association
ADDRESS Nakanoshima Center bldg. 30F, 6-2-27 Nakanoshima, Kita-ku, Osaka-shi, Osaka 530-6691
PHONE +81-6-6441-0101
FAX +81-6-6443-5347
E-MAIL webmaster@kankeiren.or.jp
HOMEPAGE http://www.kankeiren.or.jp/index.htm
REMARKS

Keizai Doyukai Japan Association of Corporate Executives

Shadan Hojin, Keizai Doyukai
CATEGORY Industry/Economy:Business Organizations
TYPE Incorporated association
ADDRESS Palace bldg. 8F, 1-1-1Marunouchi, Chiyoda-ku, Tokyo 100-0005
PHONE +81-3-3211-1271
FAX +81-3-3213-2946
E-MAIL contact@doyukai.or.jp
HOMEPAGE http://www.doyukai.or.jp/E_index.htm
REMARKS

National Federation of Small Business Associations, NFSBA

Zenkoku Chusho Kigyo Dantai Chuokai (Zenkoku Chuokai)
CATEGORY Industry/Economy:Business Organizations
TYPE Others
ADDRESS 1-26-19 Shinkawa chuo-ku, Tokyo
PHONE
FAX
E-MAIL nfsba@mail.chuokai.or.jp
HOMEPAGE http://www.chuokai.or.jp/english/index.html
REMARKS

Osaka Chamber of Commerce and Industry, OCCI

Osaka Shoko Kaigisho (Daisho)
CATEGORY Industry/Economy:Business Organizations
TYPE Others
ADDRESS 2-8 Honmachibashi, Chuo-ku Osaka-shi, Osaka 540-0029
PHONE +81-6-6944-6400
FAX +81-6-6944-6293
E-MAIL intl@osaka.cci.or.jp
HOMEPAGE http://www.osaka.cci.or.jp/e/
REMARKS

Sapporo Chamber of Commerce and Industry, SCCI

Sapporo Shoko Kaigisho
CATEGORY Industry/Economy:Business Organizations
TYPE Others
ADDRESS c/o Hokkaido Keizai Center, Kita-1, Nishi-2, Chuo-ku Sapporo-shi, Hokkaido 060-8610
PHONE +81-11-231-1122(ex.500-503 International section)
FAX +81-11-222-1078
E-MAIL kokusai@sapporo-cci.or.jp
HOMEPAGE http://www.sapporo-cci.or.jp

REMARKS

Sendai Chamber of Commerce and Industry

Sendai Shoko Kaigisho 日本語表記

CATEGORY	Industry/Economy:Business Organizations
TYPE	Others
ADDRESS	2-16-12 Hon-cho, Aoba-ku Sendai-shi, Miyagi 980-8414
PHONE	+81-22-265-8181
FAX	+81-22-217-1551
E-MAIL	soumu@sendaicci.or.jp
HOMEPAGE	http://www.sendaicci.or.jp/(Japanese only)
REMARKS	

The Hiroshima Chamber of Commerce and Industry

Hiroshima Shoko Kaigisho 日本語表記

CATEGORY	Industry/Economy:Business Organizations
TYPE	Others
ADDRESS	5-44 Moto-machi, Naka-ku Hiroshima-shi, Hiroshima 730-8510
PHONE	+81-82-222-6651
FAX	+81-82-222-6664
E-MAIL	hiroshima@hiroshimacci.or.jp
HOMEPAGE	http://www.hiroshima-cdas.or.jp/hiroshimacci/index.html (Japanese only)
REMARKS	

The Japan Chamber of Commerce and Industry, JCCI

Nihon Shoko Kaigisho (Nissho) 日本語表記

CATEGORY	Industry/Economy:Business Organizations
TYPE	Others
ADDRESS	3-2-2 Marunouchi, Chiyoda-ku, Tokyo 100-0005
PHONE	+81-3-3283-7823
FAX	+81-3-3211-4859
E-MAIL	info@jcci.or.jp
HOMEPAGE	http://www.jcci.or.jp/home-e.html
REMARKS	

The Kobe Chamber of Commerce and Industry, KCCI

Kobe Shoko Kaigisho (Shinsho) 日本語表記

CATEGORY	Industry/Economy:Business Organizations
TYPE	Others
ADDRESS	6-1 Minatojima-Naka-machi, Chuo-ku Kobe-shi, Hyogo 650-8543
PHONE	+81-78-303-5801
FAX	+81-78-303-2312
E-MAIL	info@kcci.hyogo-iic.ne.jp
HOMEPAGE	http://www.kcci.hyogo-iic.ne.jp
REMARKS	

The Kyoto Chamber of Commerce and Industry

Kyoto Shoko Kaigisho 日本語表記

CATEGORY	Industry/Economy:Business Organizations
TYPE	Others
ADDRESS	Karasuma-dori Ebisugawa-agaru, Nakagyo-ku Kyoto-city, Kyoto 604-0862
PHONE	+81-75-212-6400
FAX	+81-75-255-0428
E-MAIL	kyoto@kyo.or.jp
HOMEPAGE	http://www.kyo.or.jp/kyoto/ (Japanese only)
REMARKS	

The Nagoya Chamber of Commerce and Industry, NCCI

Nagoya Shoko Kaigisho (Meisho)

CATEGORY	Industry/Economy:Business Organizations
TYPE	Others
ADDRESS	2-10-19 Sakae, Naka-ku Nagoya-shi, Aichi 460-8422
PHONE	+81-52-223-5611
FAX	+81-52-231-6768
E-MAIL	info@nagoya-cci.or.jp
HOMEPAGE	http://www.nagoya-cci.or.jp/eng/top.html
REMARKS	

The Tokyo Chamber of Commerce and Industry, TCCI

Tokyo Shoko Kaigisho (Tosho)

CATEGORY	Industry/Economy:Business Organizations
TYPE	Others
ADDRESS	3-2-2 Marunouchi, Chiyoda-ku, Tokyo 100-0005
PHONE	+81-3-3283-7500
FAX	+81-3-3284-1208
E-MAIL	webmaster@tokyo-cci.or.jp
HOMEPAGE	http://www.tokyo-cci.or.jp/english/index.htm
REMARKS	

The Yokohama Chamber of Commerce and Industry, YCCI

Yokohama Shoko Kaigisho (Yokosho)

CATEGORY	Industry/Economy:Business Organizations
TYPE	Others
ADDRESS	Sangyo Boeki Center bldg. 8F, 2 Yamashita-cho, Naka-ku, Yokohama-shi, Kanagawa 231-8524
PHONE	+81-45-671-7400
FAX	+81-45-671-7410
E-MAIL	info@yokohama-cci.or.jp
HOMEPAGE	http://www.yokohama-cci.or.jp (Japanese only)

ORGANIZATIONS BY INDUSTRY

AGRICULTURE, FORESTRY, AND FISHERIES

Central Union of Agricultural Cooperatives

Zenkoku Nogyo Kyodo Kumiai Chuokai (JA Zenchu)

CATEGORY	Industry/Economy:Organizations by Industry:Agriculture, Forestry, and Fisheries
TYPE	Others
ADDRESS	JA bldg., 1-8-3 Ote-machi, Chiyoda-ku, Tokyo 100-0004
PHONE	+81-3-3245-7500
FAX	+81-3-5255-7356
E-MAIL	somukikaku.s@zenchu-ja.or.jp
HOMEPAGE	http://www.e-zenchu-ja.org/
REMARKS	

Japan Fisheries Association

Shadan Hojin, Dai-Nippon Suisankai (Dai-Sui)

CATEGORY	Industry/Economy:Organizations by Industry:Agriculture, Forestry, and Fisheries
TYPE	Incorporated association
ADDRESS	1-9-13 Akasaka, Minato-ku, Tokyo 107-0052
PHONE	+81-3-3585-6681
FAX	+81-3-3582-2337
E-MAIL	japan@suisankai.or.jp

HOMEPAGE http://www.suisankai.or.jp/index_e.html
REMARKS

Japan Forestry Association

Shadan Hojin, Nihon Ringyo Kyokai (Ringyo Kyokai)
CATEGORY Industry/Economy:Organizations by Industry:Agriculture, Forestry, and Fisheries
TYPE Incorporated association
ADDRESS Sankaido bldg. 7F, 1-9-13 Akasaka, Minato-ku, Tokyo 107-0052
PHONE +81-3-3586-8430
FAX +81-3-3586-8434
E-MAIL
HOMEPAGE
REMARKS

Japan Livestock Industry Association, JLIA

Shadan Hojin, Chuo Chikusankai (Chuchiku)
CATEGORY Industry/Economy:Organizations by Industry:Agriculture, Forestry, and Fisheries
TYPE Incorporated association
ADDRESS Toranomon 17-Mori bldg., 1-26-5 Toranomon, Minato-ku, Tokyo 105-0001
PHONE +81-3-3581-6677
FAX +81-3-5511-8205
E-MAIL jlia@jlia.lin.go.jp
HOMEPAGE http://jlia.lin.go.jp/ (Japanese only)
REMARKS

National Federation of Agricultural Cooperative Associations

ZEN-NOH
CATEGORY Industry/Economy:Organizations by Industry:Agriculture, Forestry, and Fisheries
TYPE Others
ADDRESS JA bldg., 1-8-3 Ote-machi, Chiyoda-ku, Tokyo 100-0004
PHONE +81-3-3245-7111
FAX +81-3-3245-7442
E-MAIL webmaster@zk.zennoh.or.jp
HOMEPAGE http://www.zennoh.or.jp

NATURAL RESOURCES AND ENERGY

Japan Atomic Energy Relations Organization, JAERO

Zaidan Hojin, Nihon Genshiryoku Bunka Shinko Zaidan
CATEGORY Industry/Economy:Organizations by Industry:Natural Resources and Energy
TYPE Incorporated foundation
ADDRESS Toshin bldg., 1-1-13 Shinbashi, Minato-ku, Tokyo 105-0004
PHONE +81-3-3504-1381
FAX +81-3-3580-8188
E-MAIL
HOMEPAGE http://www.jaero.or.jp/ (Japanese only)
REMARKS

Japan Atomic Industrial Forum, Inc., JAIF

Shadan Hojin, Nihon Genshiryoku Sangyo Kaigi
CATEGORY Industry/Economy:Organizations by Industry:Natural Resources and Energy
TYPE Incorporated association
ADDRESS Toshin bldg., 1-1-13 Shinbashi, Minato-ku, Tokyo 105-8605
PHONE +81-3-3508-2411
FAX +81-3-3508-2094
E-MAIL information@jaif.or.jp
HOMEPAGE http://www.jaif.or.jp/english/index.html

REMARKS

Japan Electric Power Information Center, Inc., JEPIC

Shadan Hojin, Kaigai Denryoku Chosakai 日本語表記

CATEGORY Industry/Economy:Organizations by Industry:Natural Resources and Energy
TYPE Incorporated association
ADDRESS Shibaura Shimizu bldg. 5F, 4-15-33 Shibaura, Minato-ku, Tokyo 108-0023
PHONE +81-3-4511-3210
FAX +81-3-4511-3249
E-MAIL
HOMEPAGE http://www.jepic.or.jp/english/index.html
REMARKS

National Petroleum Dealers Association, NPDA

Shadan Hojin, Zenkoku Sekiyu Kyokai (Sekiyu Kyokai) 日本語表記

CATEGORY Industry/Economy:Organizations by Industry:Natural Resources and Energy
TYPE Incorporated association
ADDRESS 2-17-8 Nagata-cho, Chiyoda-ku, Tokyo 100-0014
PHONE +81-3-5251-2201
FAX +81-3-5251-0590
E-MAIL
HOMEPAGE http://www.sekiyu.or.jp/ (Japanese only)
REMARKS

The Japan Gas Association, JGA

Shadan Hojin, Nihon Gas Kyokai (Gas Kyokai) 日本語表記

CATEGORY Industry/Economy:Organizations by Industry:Natural Resources and Energy
TYPE Incorporated association
ADDRESS 1-15-12 Toranomon, Minato-ku, Tokyo 105-0001
PHONE +81-3-3502-0111
FAX +81-3-3593-1311
E-MAIL jgaintl@gas.or.jp
HOMEPAGE http://www.gas.or.jp/indexe.html

CONSTRUCTION

Association of Water and Sewage Works Consultants Japan

Shadan Hojin, Zenkoku Joge Suido Consultant Kyokai (Suicon-Kyo) 日本語表記

CATEGORY Industry/Economy:Organizations by Industry:Construction
TYPE Incorporated association
ADDRESS Heiwado bldg. Bekkan, 1-8-7 Higashi-Azabu, Minato-ku, Tokyo 106-0044
PHONE +81-3-3584-0919
FAX +81-3-3584-2639
E-MAIL info@suikon.or.jp
HOMEPAGE http://www.suikon.or.jp/ (Japanese only)
REMARKS

Building Contractors Society, BCS

Shadan Hojin, Kenchikugyo Kyokai (Kenchiku-Kyo) 日本語表記

CATEGORY Industry/Economy:Organizations by Industry:Construction
TYPE Incorporated association
ADDRESS Tokyo Kensetsu Kaikan bldg8F., 2-5-1 Hacchobori, Chuo-ku, Tokyo 104-0032
PHONE +81-3-3551-1118
FAX +81-3-3555-2463
E-MAIL koho@bcs.or.jp
HOMEPAGE http://www.bcs.or.jp (Japanese only)
REMARKS

Infrastructure Development Institute-Japan, IDI

Shadan Hojin, Kokusai Kensetsu Gijutsu Kyokai (Koku-Ken-Kyo) 日本語表記
CATEGORY Industry/Economy:Organizations by Industry:Construction
TYPE Incorporated association
ADDRESS New-Kojimachi bldg., 5-3-23 Koji-machi, Chiyoda-ku, Tokyo 102-0083
PHONE +81-3-3263-7812
FAX +81-3-3230-4030
E-MAIL info@idi.or.jp
HOMEPAGE http://www.idi.or.jp/contentse.htm
REMARKS

Japan Civil Engineering Contractors' Association, Inc.

Shadan Hojin, Nihon Doboku Kogyo Kyokai (Do-Ko-Kyo) 日本語表記
CATEGORY Industry/Economy:Organizations by Industry:Construction
TYPE Incorporated association
ADDRESS Tokyo Kensetsu Kaikan bldg. 6F, 2-5-1 Hacchobori, Chuo-ku, Tokyo 104-0032
PHONE +81-3-3552-3201
FAX +81-3-3552-3206
E-MAIL webmaster@dokokyo.or.jp
HOMEPAGE http://www.dokokyo.or.jp/ (Japanese only)
REMARKS

Japan Federation of Construction Contractors, JFCC

Shadan Hojin, Nihon Kensetsugyo Dantai Rengokai 日本語表記
CATEGORY Industry/Economy:Organizations by Industry:Construction
TYPE Incorporated association
ADDRESS Tokyo Kensetsu Kaikan bldg. 6F, 2-5-1 Hacchobori, Chuo-ku, Tokyo 104-0032
PHONE +81-3-3553-0701
FAX +81-3-3552-2360
E-MAIL ifcc@mx1.alpha-web.ne.jp
HOMEPAGE http://nikkenren.com/ (Japanese only)
REMARKS

Japan Housing Association

Shadan Hojin, Nihon Jutaku Kyokai 日本語表記
CATEGORY Industry/Economy:Organizations by Industry:Construction
TYPE Incorporated association
ADDRESS Kojimachi Kyodo bldg., 3-2 Kojimachi, Chiyoda-ku, Tokyo 102-0083
PHONE +81-3-3265-8201
FAX +81-3-3265-8230
E-MAIL jha@ma.neweb.ne.jp
HOMEPAGE http://www1.neweb.ne.jp/wa/jha/
REMARKS

Japan Interior Industry Association, JIIA

Shadan Hojin, Interior Sangyo Kyokai 日本語表記
CATEGORY Industry/Economy:Organizations by Industry:Construction
TYPE Incorporated association
ADDRESS Kurihashi bldg., 3-13-5 Shinjuku, Shinjuku-ku, Tokyo 160-0022
PHONE +81-3-5379-8600
FAX +81-3-5379-8605
E-MAIL exam@interior.or.jp
HOMEPAGE http://www.interior.or.jp (Japanese only)
REMARKS

Japan Landscape Contractors Association, Inc.

Shadan Hojin, Nihon Zoen Kensetsugyo Kyokai (Nichi-Zo-Kyo) 日本語表記

CATEGORY Industry/Economy:Organizations by Industry:Construction
TYPE Incorporated association
ADDRESS Kojimachi Nakata bldg., 5-3 Koji-machi, Chiyoda-ku, Tokyo 102-0083
PHONE +81-3-3263-3039
FAX +81-3-3263-3856
E-MAIL zouen@mb.infoweb.ne.jp
HOMEPAGE http://www.jalc.or.jp/english/english.html
REMARKS

Japan Ocean Development Construction Association, JODCA

Shadan Hojin, Nihon Kaiyo Kaihatsu Kensetsu Kyokai (Kaiyo-Kyo) 日本語表記

CATEGORY Industry/Economy:Organizations by Industry:Construction
TYPE Incorporated association
ADDRESS Tokyo Kensetsu Kaikan bldg-nai., 2-5-1 Hacchobori, Chuo-ku, Tokyo 104-0032
PHONE +81-3-3553-4095
FAX +81-3-3553-4338
E-MAIL kaiyokyo@mx2.alpha-web.ne.jp
HOMEPAGE http://www.kaiyokyo.or.jp(Japanese only)
REMARKS

Japan Prefabricated Construction Suppliers and Manufacturers Association, JPA

Shadan Hojin, Prefab Kenchiku Kyokai (Pre-Kyo) 日本語表記

CATEGORY Industry/Economy:Organizations by Industry:Construction
TYPE Incorporated association
ADDRESS Tokyo Club bldg 2F., 3-2-6 Kasumigaseki, Chiyoda-ku, Tokyo 100-0013
PHONE +81-3-3502-9451
FAX +81-3-3502-9455
E-MAIL info@purekyo.or.jp
HOMEPAGE http://www.purekyo.or.jp/ (Japanese only)
REMARKS

Japan Railway Contractors' Association, Inc.

Shadan Hojin, Nihon Tetsudo Kensetsugyo Kyokai (Tetsu-Ken-Kyo) 日本語表記

CATEGORY Industry/Economy:Organizations by Industry:Construction
TYPE Incorporated association
ADDRESS Tokyo Kensetsu Kaikan., 2-5-1 Hacchobori, Chuo-ku, Tokyo 104-0032
PHONE +81-3-3551-2494
FAX +81-3-3551-4954
E-MAIL info@tekkenkyo.or.jp
HOMEPAGE http://www.tekkenkyo.or.jp(Japanese only)
REMARKS

National Federation of Construction Conductors

Shadan Hojin, Zenkoku Kensetsu Sangyo Dantai Rengokai (Zenkoku-Ken-San-Ren) 日本語表記

CATEGORY Industry/Economy:Organizations by Industry:Construction
TYPE Incorporated association
ADDRESS Toranomon 4-chome Mori bldg.-2gokan 6F, 4-2-12 Toranomon, Minato-ku, Tokyo 105-0001
PHONE +81-3-5473-1596
FAX +81-3-5473-8352
E-MAIL info@kensanren.or.jp
HOMEPAGE http://www.kensanren.or.jp (Japanese only)
REMARKS

National General Contractors Association of Japan, Inc

Shadan Hojin, Zenkoku Kensetsugyo Kyokai (Zen-Ken) 日本語表記

CATEGORY Industry/Economy:Organizations by Industry:Construction
TYPE Incorporated association
ADDRESS Tokyo Kensetsu Kaikan bldg., 2-5-1 Hacchobori, Chuo-ku, Tokyo 104-0032
PHONE +81-3-3551-9396
FAX +81-3-3555-3218
E-MAIL g1@zenken-net.or.jp
HOMEPAGE http://www.zenken-net.or.jp/(Japanese only)
REMARKS

The Japan Road Contractors Association, JRCA

Shadan Hojin, Nihon Doro Kensetsugyo Kyokai (Do-Ken-Kyo)
CATEGORY Industry/Economy:Organizations by Industry:Construction
TYPE Incorporated association
ADDRESS 5-1, Hatchobori 2-chome, Chuo-ku, Tokyo, 104-0032
PHONE +81-3-3537-3056
FAX +81-3-3537-3058
E-MAIL jrca@dohkenkyo.or.jp
HOMEPAGE http://www.dohkenkyo.or.jp/ (Japanese only)
REMARKS

The Overseas Construction Association of Japan, Inc., OCAJI

Shadan Hojin, Kaigai Kensetsu Kyokai (Kai-Ken-Kyo)
CATEGORY Industry/Economy:Organizations by Industry:Construction
TYPE Incorporated association
ADDRESS Nichibei bldg7F., 2-24-2 Hacchobori, Chuo-ku, Tokyo 104-0032
PHONE +81-3-3553-1631
FAX +81-3-3551-0148
E-MAIL info@ocaji.or.jp
HOMEPAGE http://www.ocaji.or.jp/english/activ_e.html

FOOD

All Nippon Kashi Association, ANKA

Zen-nihon Kashi Kyokai
CATEGORY Industry/Economy:Organizations by Industry:Food
TYPE Others
ADDRESS 6-9-5 Shinbashi, Minato-ku, Tokyo 105-0004
PHONE +81-3-3431-3115
FAX +81-3-3432-1660
E-MAIL anka@nifty.com

Brewers Association of Japan

Beer Shuzo kumiai
CATEGORY Industry/Economy:Organizations by Industry:Food
TYPE Incorporated association
ADDRESS 2-8-18 Kyobashi, Chuo-ku, Tokyo 104-0031
PHONE +81-3-3561-8386
FAX +81-3-3561-8380
E-MAIL info@brewers.or.jp
HOMEPAGE http://www.brewers.or.jp/english/index.html
REMARKS

Japan Dairy Industry Association

Shadan Hojin, Nihon Nyugyo Kyokai
CATEGORY Industry/Economy:Organizations by Industry:Food
TYPE Incorporated association

ADDRESS Nyugyo Kaikan bldg., 1-14-19 Kudan-Kita, Chiyoda-ku, Tokyo 102-0073
PHONE +81-3-3261-9161
FAX +81-3-3261-9175
E-MAIL
HOMEPAGE http://www.jdia.or.jp/ (Japanese only)
REMARKS

Japan Meat Processors Association

Shadan Hojin, Nihon Shokuniku Kako Kyokai
CATEGORY Industry/Economy:Organizations by Industry:Food
TYPE Incorporated association
ADDRESS Ham Sausage Kaikan, 1-5-6 Ebisu, Shibuya-ku, Tokyo 150-0013
PHONE +81-3-3444-1211
FAX +81-3-3441-8273
E-MAIL hamukumi@group.lin.go.jp
HOMEPAGE http://group.lin.go.jp/hamukumi/ (Japanese only)
REMARKS

Japan Oilseed Processors Association

Shadan Hojin, Nihon Shokubutsuyu Kyokai (Nichiyukyo)
CATEGORY Industry/Economy:Organizations by Industry:Food
TYPE Incorporated association
ADDRESS Yushi Kogyo Kaikan, 3-13-11 Nihonbashi, Chuo-ku, Tokyo 103-0027
PHONE +81-3-3271-2705
FAX +81-3-3271-2707
E-MAIL jopa@oil.or.jp
HOMEPAGE http://www.oil.or.jp/ (Japanese only)
REMARKS

Japan Sake Brewers Association

Nihon Shuzo Kumiai Chuokai
CATEGORY Industry/Economy:Organizations by Industry:Food
TYPE Others
ADDRESS Nihon Shuzo Kaikan, 1-1-21 Nishi-Shinbashi, Minato-ku, Tokyo 105-0003
PHONE +81-3-3501-0101
FAX +81-3-3501-6018
E-MAIL info@brewers.or.jp
HOMEPAGE http://www.japansake.or.jp/sake/english/index.html
REMARKS

The Brewing Society of Japan

Zaidan Hojin, Nihon Jozo Kyokai
CATEGORY Industry/Economy:Organizations by Industry:Food
TYPE Incorporated foundation
ADDRESS 2-6-30 Takinogawa, Kita-ku, Tokyo 114-0023
PHONE +81-3-3910-3853
FAX +81-3-3910-3748
E-MAIL
HOMEPAGE http://www.jozo.or.jp(Japanese only)
REMARKS

The Japan Soft Drinks Association

Shadan Hojin, Zenkoku Seiryo Inryo Kogyokai (Zen-Sei-In)
CATEGORY Industry/Economy:Organizations by Industry:Food
TYPE Incorporated association
ADDRESS CM bldg. 3F, 3-3-3 Muromachi, Nihonbashi, Chuo-ku, Tokyo 103-0022
PHONE +81-3-3270-7300

FAX +81-3-3270-7306
E-MAIL info@j-sda.or.jp
HOMEPAGE http://www.j-sda.or.jp/f-eng.htm
REMARKS

The Japan Soy-sauce Brewers' Association

Nihon Shoyu Kyokai
CATEGORY Industry/Economy:Organizations by Industry:Food
TYPE Others
ADDRESS Shoyu Kaikan bldg., 3-11 Nihonbashi Koami-cho, Chuo-ku, Tokyo 103-0016
PHONE +81-3-3666-3286
FAX +81-3-3667-2216
E-MAIL jssba@blue.ocn.ne.jp
HOMEPAGE http://www.soysauce.or.jp (Japanese only)

PAPER AND TEXTILES

Japan Apparel Industry Council

Shadan Hojin, Nihon Apparel Sangyo Kyokai (Appa-San-Kyo)
CATEGORY Industry/Economy:Organizations by Industry:Paper and Textiles
TYPE Incorporated association
ADDRESS TFT bldg. East Wing 9F, 3-1 Ariake, Koto-ku, Tokyo 135-8071
PHONE +81-3-5530-5481
FAX +81-3-5530-5482
E-MAIL jaic_office@jaic.or.jp
HOMEPAGE http://www.jaic.or.jp/english/index_e.html
REMARKS

Japan Chemical Fibers Association, JCFA

Nihon Kagaku Sen'i Kyokai (Kasen-Kyokai)
CATEGORY Industry/Economy:Organizations by Industry:Paper and Textiles
TYPE Others
ADDRESS Sen'i Kaikan bldg., 3-1-11 Nihonbashi Hon-cho, Chuo-ku, Tokyo 103-0023
PHONE +81-3-3241-2311
FAX +81-3-3246-0823
E-MAIL
HOMEPAGE http://www.fcc.co.jp/JCFA/
REMARKS

Japan Linen, Ramie & Jute Spinners' Association

Nihon Asa Boseki Kyokai
CATEGORY Industry/Economy:Organizations by Industry:Paper and Textiles
TYPE Others
ADDRESS Magyo Kaikan, 1-1-10 Nihonbashi Ningyo-cho, Chuo-ku, Tokyo 103-0013
PHONE +81-3-3668-4641
FAX +81-3-3668-4642
E-MAIL jp-asabo@ah.wakwak.com
HOMEPAGE http://www.asabo.com/index_en.htm
REMARKS

Japan Silk Association Inc., JSA

Shadan Hojin, Nihon Kengyo Kyokai
CATEGORY Industry/Economy:Organizations by Industry:Paper and Textiles
TYPE Incorporated association
ADDRESS 1-9-4 Yurakucho, Chiyoda-ku, Tokyo 100-0006
PHONE +81-3-3214-1691
FAX +81-3-3214-1700
E-MAIL jsasilk@sepia.ocn.ne.jp

HOMEPAGE http://www.silk-center.or.jp/ (Japanese only)
REMARKS

The Japan Cotton Traders' Association

Shadan Hojin, Nihon Menka Kyokai 日本語表記
CATEGORY Industry/Economy:Organizations by Industry:Paper and Textiles
TYPE Incorporated association
ADDRESS 1-8-2 Utsubo-Hon-machi, Nishi-ku Osaka-shi, Osaka 550-0004
PHONE +81-6-6445-8839
FAX +81-6-6445-8893
E-MAIL menkyo@jcta.co.jp
HOMEPAGE http://www.jcta.co.jp (Japanese only)

STEEL AND METALS

Japan Mining Industry Association

Nihon Kogyo Kyokai 日本語表記
CATEGORY Industry/Economy:Organizations by Industry:Steel and Metals
TYPE Others
ADDRESS Shuwa Dai-3 Toranomon bldg., 1-21-8 Toranomon, Minato-ku, Tokyo 105-0001
PHONE +81-3-3502-7451
FAX +81-3-3591-9841
E-MAIL
HOMEPAGE
REMARKS

The Japan Iron and Steel Federation, JISF

Shadan Hojin, Nihon Tekko Renmei (Tetsu-Ren) 日本語表記
CATEGORY Industry/Economy:Organizations by Industry:Steel and Metals
TYPE Incorporated association
ADDRESS Keidanren Kaikan bldg., 1-9-4 Ote-machi, Chiyoda-ku, Tokyo 100-0004
PHONE +81-3-3279-3612
FAX +81-3-3245-0144
E-MAIL tetsuren@jisf.or.jp
HOMEPAGE http://www.jisf.or.jp/ (Japanese only)

ELECTRICITY AND MACHINERY

Bicycle Association(Japan)

Shadan Hojin, Nihon Jitensha Kyokai 日本語表記
CATEGORY Industry/Economy:Organizations by Industry:Electricity and Machinery
TYPE Incorporated association
ADDRESS 8-25 Karakiyo-cho, Tennoji-ku, Osaka-shi, Osaka 543-0018
PHONE +81-6-6762-7373
FAX +81-6-6762-4102
E-MAIL
HOMEPAGE
REMARKS

Database Promotion Center, Japan, DPC

Zaidan Hojin, Detabesu Shinko senta 日本語表記
CATEGORY Industry/Economy:Organizations by Industry:Electricity and Machinery
TYPE Incorporated foundation
ADDRESS Shinbashi-Towa bldg. 5F, 2-13-8 Shinbashi, Minato-ku, Tokyo 105-0004
PHONE +81-3-3508-2430
FAX +81-3-3508-2440
E-MAIL pubs@dpc.or.jp

HOMEPAGE http://www.dpc.or.jp/english/index.html
REMARKS

Japan Association of Defense Industry, JADI

Shadan Hojin, Nihon Boei Sobi Kogyokai (Sobi KogyoKai)
CATEGORY Industry/Economy:Organizations by Industry:Electricity and Machinery
TYPE Incorporated association
ADDRESS 2-21-3 Akasaka, Minato-ku, Tokyo 107-0052
PHONE +81-3-3584-6755
FAX +81-3-3584-7363
E-MAIL
HOMEPAGE
REMARKS

Japan Automobile Manufacturers Association Inc., JAMA

Shadan Hojin, Nihon Jidosha Kogyokai (Ji-Ko-Kai)
CATEGORY Industry/Economy:Organizations by Industry:Electricity and Machinery
TYPE Incorporated association
ADDRESS Otemachi bldg. 2nd fl, 1-6-1 Otemachi, Chiyoda-ku, Tokyo 100-0004
PHONE +81-3-5219-6660 (International Dept.)
FAX +81-3-3287-2073
E-MAIL
HOMEPAGE http://www.jama.or.jp/eng/
REMARKS

Camera & Imaging Products Association

Camera Eizokiki Kogyokai
CATEGORY Industry/Economy:Organizations by Industry:Electricity and Machinery
TYPE Others
ADDRESS JCII bldg., 25 Ichiban-cho, Chiyoda-ku, Tokyo 102-0082
PHONE +81-3-5276-3891
FAX +81-3-5276-3893
E-MAIL
HOMEPAGE http://www.cipa.jp/english/index.html
REMARKS

Japan Electronic and Information Technology Industries Association

Shadan Hojin Denshi Joho Gijutu Sangyo Kyokai
CATEGORY Industry/Economy:Organizations by Industry:Electricity and Machinery
TYPE Incorporated association
ADDRESS 3rd Floor, Mitsui Sumitomo Kaijo Bldg. Annex, 11, Kanda Surugadai 3-chome, Chiyoda-ku, Tokyo 101-0062
PHONE +81-3-3518-6424
FAX +81-3-3295-8723
E-MAIL webmaster@jeita.or.jp
HOMEPAGE http://www.jeita.or.jp/english/index.htm
REMARKS

Japan Industries Association of Radiological Systems, JIRA

Shadan Hojin, Nihon Gazo Iryo System Kogyokai
CATEGORY Industry/Economy:Organizations by Industry:Electricity and Machinery
TYPE Incorporated association
ADDRESS Yushima KC bldg., 2-18-12 Yushima, Bunkyo-ku, Tokyo 113-0034
PHONE +81-3-3816-3450
FAX +81-3-3818-8920
E-MAIL jira@jira-net.or.jp
HOMEPAGE http://www.jira-net.or.jp/e/

REMARKS

Japan Machine Tool Builders' Association, JMTBA

Shadan Hojin, Nihon Kosaku Kikai Kogyokai (Nikko-Kai)

CATEGORY Industry/Economy:Organizations by Industry:Electricity and Machinery
TYPE Incorporated association
ADDRESS Kikai Shinko Kaikan bldg.104, 3-5-8 Shiba Koen, Minato-ku, Tokyo 105-0011
PHONE +81-3-3434-3961
FAX +81-3-3434-3763
E-MAIL
HOMEPAGE http://www.jmtba.or.jp
REMARKS

Japan Optical Industry Association, JOIA

Nihon Kogaku Kogyo Kyokai (Nikko-Kyo)

CATEGORY Industry/Economy:Organizations by Industry:Electricity and Machinery
TYPE Others
ADDRESS Kikai Shinko Kaikan bldg. 204, 3-5-8 Shiba Koen, Minato-ku, Tokyo 105-0011
PHONE +81-3-3431-7073
FAX +81-3-3431-7073
E-MAIL joia@01.246.ne.jp
HOMEPAGE
REMARKS

Japanese Standards Association, JSA

Zaidan Hojin, Nihon Kikaku Kyokai

CATEGORY Industry/Economy:Organizations by Industry:Electricity and Machinery
TYPE Incorporated foundation
ADDRESS 4-1-24 Akasaka, Minato-ku, Tokyo 107-8440
PHONE +81-3-3583-8005
FAX +81-3-3586-2014
E-MAIL webmaster@jsa.or.jp
HOMEPAGE http://www.jsa.or.jp/
REMARKS

The Federation of Electric Power Companies, FEPC

Denki Jigyo Rengokai (Den-Ji-Ren)

CATEGORY Industry/Economy:Organizations by Industry:Electricity and Machinery
TYPE Others
ADDRESS Keidanren Kaikan, bldg., 1-9-4 Ote-machi, Chiyoda-ku, Tokyo 100-8118
PHONE +81-3-3279-2180
FAX +81-3-3241-1517
E-MAIL webadmin@fepc.or.jp
HOMEPAGE http://www.fepc.or.jp/index_e.html
REMARKS

The Japan Electric Association, JEA

Shadan Hojin, Nihon Denki Kyokai

CATEGORY Industry/Economy:Organizations by Industry:Electricity and Machinery
TYPE Incorporated association
ADDRESS Yurakucho Denki bldg.-Kitakan, 1-7-1 Yuraku-cho, Chiyoda-ku, Tokyo 100-0006
PHONE +81-3-3216-0551
FAX +81-3-3214-6005
E-MAIL
HOMEPAGE http://www.denki.or.jp/ (Japanese only)
REMARKS

The Japan Machinery Federation, JMF

Shadan Hojin, Nihon Kikai Kogyo Rengokai (Nichi-Ki-Ren) 日本語表記

CATEGORY Industry/Economy:Organizations by Industry:Electricity and Machinery
TYPE Incorporated association
ADDRESS Kikai Shinko Kaikan bldg.104, 3-5-8 Shiba Koen, Minato-ku, Tokyo 105-0011
PHONE +81-3-3434-5381
FAX +81-3-3434-2666
E-MAIL jmfsomu@blue.ocn.ne.jp
HOMEPAGE http://www.jmf.or.jp/english/top.html
REMARKS

The Shipbuilders' Association of Japan, SAJ

Shadan Hojin, Nihon Zosen Kogyokai 日本語表記

CATEGORY Industry/Economy:Organizations by Industry:Electricity and Machinery
TYPE Incorporated association
ADDRESS Kaiyo Senpaku bldg., 1-15-16 Toranomon, Minato-ku, Tokyo 105-0001
PHONE +81-3-3502-2010
FAX +81-3-3502-2816
E-MAIL
HOMEPAGE http://www.sajn.or.jp/index_e.htm
REMARKS

The Society of Japanese Aerospace Companies, SJAC

Shadan Hojin, Nihon Koku Uchu Kogyokai 日本語表記

CATEGORY Industry/Economy:Organizations by Industry:Electricity and Machinery
TYPE Incorporated association
ADDRESS Toshin Tameike bldg., 1-1-14 Akasaka, Minato-ku, Tokyo 107-0052
PHONE +81-3-3585-0511
FAX +81-3-3585-0541

CHEMICALS

Japan Chemical Industry Association, JCIA

Shadan Hojin, Nihon Kagaku Kogyo Kyokai (Nikka-Kyo) 日本語表記

CATEGORY Industry/Economy:Organizations by Industry:Chemicals
TYPE Incorporated association
ADDRESS Kazan bldg., 3-2-4 Kasumigaseki, Chiyoda-ku, Tokyo 100-0013
PHONE +81-3-3580-0751
FAX +81-3-3580-0970
E-MAIL chemical@jcia-net.or.jp
HOMEPAGE http://www.nikkakyo.org/English/index.php3
REMARKS

Japan Cosmetic Industry Association

Nihon Keshohin Kogyo Rengokai (Sho-Ko-Ren) 日本語表記

CATEGORY Industry/Economy:Organizations by Industry:Chemicals
TYPE Others
ADDRESS Hatsumei Kaikan 4F, 2-9-14 Toranomon, Minato-ku, Tokyo 105-0001
PHONE +81-3-3502-0576
FAX +81-3-3502-0829
E-MAIL info@jcia.org
HOMEPAGE http://www.jcia.org (Japanese only)
REMARKS

Japan Thermosetting Plastics Industry Association, JTPIA

Gosei Jushi Kogyo Kyokai (Go-Ju-Kyo) 日本語表記

CATEGORY Industry/Economy:Organizations by Industry:Chemicals
TYPE Others
ADDRESS Tokyo Club bldg 2F., 3-2-6 Kasumigaseki, Chiyoda-ku, Tokyo 100-0013
PHONE +81-3-3580-0881
FAX +81-3-3580-0832
E-MAIL
HOMEPAGE
REMARKS

The Federation of Pharmaceutical Manufacturers' Associations of Japan, FPMAJ

Nihon Seiyaku Dantai Rengokai (Nichi-Yaku-Ren) 日本語表記
CATEGORY Industry/Economy:Organizations by Industry:Chemicals
TYPE Others
ADDRESS Tokyo Yakugyo Kaikan bldg., 2-1-5 Nihonbashi Hon-cho, Chuo-ku, Tokyo 103-0023
PHONE +81-3-3270-0581
FAX +81-3-3241-2090
E-MAIL
HOMEPAGE
REMARKS

The Japan Plastics Industry Federation, JPIF

Nihon Plastic Kogyo Renmei (Pla-Ko-Ren) 日本語表記
CATEGORY Industry/Economy:Organizations by Industry:Chemicals
TYPE Others
ADDRESS c/o Kaseihin Kaikan, 5-18-17 Roppongi, Minato-ku, Tokyo 106-0032
PHONE +81-3-3586-9761
FAX +81-3-3586-9760
E-MAIL jpifsohm@mb.infoweb.ne.jp
HOMEPAGE http://www.jpif.gr.jp (Japanese only)
REMARKS

The Society of Rubber Industry, Japan, SRIJ

Shadan Hojin, Nihon Gomu Kyokai (Gomu) 日本語表記
CATEGORY Industry/Economy:Organizations by Industry:Chemicals
TYPE Incorporated association
ADDRESS Tobu bldg., 1-5-26 Moto-Akasaka, Minato-ku, Tokyo 107-0051
PHONE +81-3-3401-2957
FAX +81-3-3401-4143
E-MAIL srij@srij.or.jp
HOMEPAGE http://www.srij.or.jp/ (Japanese only)

TRANSPORTATION

Bicycle Association(Japan)

Shadan Hojin, Nihon Jitensha Kyokai 日本語表記
CATEGORY Industry/Economy:Organizations by Industry:Transportation
TYPE Incorporated association
ADDRESS 8-25 Karakiyo-cho, Tennoji-ku, Osaka-shi, Osaka 543-0018
PHONE +81-6-6762-7373
FAX +81-6-6762-4102
E-MAIL
HOMEPAGE
REMARKS

Japan Automobile Manufacturers Association Inc., JAMA

Shadan Hojin, Nihon Jidosha Kogyokai (Ji-Ko-Kai) 日本語表記
CATEGORY Industry/Economy:Organizations by Industry:Transportation

TYPE Incorporated association
ADDRESS Otemachi bldg. 2nd fl, 1-6-1 Otemachi, Chiyoda-ku, Tokyo 100-0004
PHONE +81-3-5219-6660 (International Dept.)
FAX +81-3-3287-2073
E-MAIL
HOMEPAGE http://www.jama.or.jp/eng/
REMARKS

Japan Railway Contractors' Association, Inc.

Shadan Hojin, Nihon Tetsudo Kensetsugyo Kyokai (Tetsu-Ken-Kyo)
CATEGORY Industry/Economy:Organizations by Industry:Transportation
TYPE Incorporated association
ADDRESS Tokyo Kensetsu Kaikan., 2-5-1 Hacchobori, Chuo-ku, Tokyo 104-0032
PHONE +81-3-3551-2494
FAX +81-3-3551-4954
E-MAIL info@tekkenkyo.or.jp
HOMEPAGE http://www.tekkenkyo.or.jp(Japanese only)
REMARKS

Nihon Bus Association, NBA

Shadan Hojin, Nihon Bus Kyokai (Nichi-Bus-Kyo)
CATEGORY Industry/Economy:Organizations by Industry:Transportation
TYPE Incorporated association
ADDRESS Shin-Kokusai bldg., 3-4-1 Marunouchi, Chiyoda-ku, Tokyo 100-0005
PHONE +81-3-3216-4011
FAX +81-3-3216-4016
E-MAIL info@bus.or.jp
HOMEPAGE http://www.bus.or.jp (Japanese only)
REMARKS

The Japan Road Contractors Association, JRCA

Shadan Hojin, Nihon Doro Kensetsugyo Kyokai (Do-Ken-Kyo)
CATEGORY Industry/Economy:Organizations by Industry:Transportation
TYPE Incorporated association
ADDRESS 5-1, Hatchobori 2-chome, Chuo-ku, Tokyo, 104-0032
PHONE +81-3-3537-3056
FAX +81-3-3537-3058
E-MAIL jrca@dohkenkyo.or.jp
HOMEPAGE http://www.dohkenkyo.or.jp/ (Japanese only)
REMARKS

The Shipbuilders' Association of Japan, SAJ

Shadan Hojin, Nihon Zosen Kogyokai
CATEGORY Industry/Economy:Organizations by Industry:Transportation
TYPE Incorporated association
ADDRESS Kaiyo Senpaku bldg., 1-15-16 Toranomon, Minato-ku, Tokyo 105-0001
PHONE +81-3-3502-2010
FAX +81-3-3502-2816

COMMUNICATIONS

Database Promotion Center, Japan, DPC

Zaidan Hojin, Detabesu Shinko senta
CATEGORY Industry/Economy:Organizations by Industry:Communications
TYPE Incorporated foundation
ADDRESS Shinbashi-Towa bldg. 5F, 2-13-8 Shinbashi, Minato-ku, Tokyo 105-0004
PHONE +81-3-3508-2430

FAX +81-3-3508-2440
E-MAIL pubs@dpc.or.jp
HOMEPAGE http://www.dpc.or.jp/english/index.html
REMARKS

Japan Mobile Telecommunication-systems Association, JAMTA

Zaidan Hojin, Nihon Ido Tsushin System Kyokai 日本語表記
CATEGORY Industry/Economy:Organizations by Industry:Communications
TYPE Incorporated foundation
ADDRESS 3-20-1 Minami-Azabu, Minato-ku, Tokyo 106-8573
PHONE +81-3-3280-8575
FAX +81-3-3440-3803
E-MAIL
HOMEPAGE http://www.jamta.or.jp/whatse/index.html
REMARKS

Radio Engineering and Electronics Association, REEA

Zaidan Hojin, Denpa Gijutsu Kyokai 日本語表記
CATEGORY Industry/Economy:Organizations by Industry:Communications
TYPE Incorporated foundation
ADDRESS Nagata-choTBR bldg.- 208, 2-10-2 Nagata-cho, Chiyoda-ku, Tokyo 100-0014
PHONE +81-3-3519-7611
FAX +81-3-3519-7610
E-MAIL
HOMEPAGE http://www.reea.or.jp (Japanese only)
REMARKS

Telecommunications Carriers Association, TCA

Shadan Hojin, Denki Tsushin Jigyosha Kyokai 日本語表記
CATEGORY Industry/Economy:Organizations by Industry:Communications
TYPE Incorporated association
ADDRESS Tokyo Sakurada bldg.4F, 1-1-3 Nishi-Shinbashi, Minato-ku, Tokyo 105-0003
PHONE +81-3-3502-0991
FAX +81-3-3502-0992
E-MAIL enq@tca.or.jp
HOMEPAGE http://www.tca.or.jp/index-e.html
REMARKS

The Telecommunications Association, TTA

Shadan Hojin, Denki Tsushin Kyokai 日本語表記
CATEGORY Industry/Economy:Organizations by Industry:Communications
TYPE Incorporated association
ADDRESS Tokyo Opera City Tower bldg.32F, 3-20-2 Nishi-Shinjuku, Shinjuku-ku, Tokyo 163-1455
PHONE +81-3-5353-0190
FAX +81-3-5353-0191
E-MAIL eigyo@tta.or.jp
HOMEPAGE http://www.tta.or.jp (Japanese only)

TRADE AND COMMERCE

Japan Chain Stores Association, JCSA

Nihon Chain Store Kyokai 日本語表記
CATEGORY Industry/Economy:Organizations by Industry:Trade and Commerce
TYPE Others
ADDRESS Toranomon 40-MT bldg., 5-13-1 Toranomon, Minato-ku, Tokyo 105-0001
PHONE +81-3-3433-1290

FAX +81-3-3433-1297
E-MAIL honbu@jcsa.gr.jp
HOMEPAGE http://www.jcsa.gr.jp/ (Japanese only)
REMARKS

Japan Council of Shopping Centers, JCSC

Shadan Hojin, Nihon Shopping Center Kyokai 日本語表記
CATEGORY Industry/Economy:Organizations by Industry:Trade and Commerce
TYPE Incorporated association
ADDRESS Four Front Tower 13F, 3-12-1 Kachidoki, Chuo-ku, Tokyo 104-0054
PHONE +81-3-3536-8121
FAX +81-3-3536-8120
E-MAIL info@jcsc.or.jp
HOMEPAGE http://www.jcsc.or.jp
REMARKS

Japan Department Stores Association, JDSA

Nihon Hyakkaten Kyokai 日本語表記
CATEGORY Industry/Economy:Organizations by Industry:Trade and Commerce
TYPE Others
ADDRESS Yanagiya bldg. 7F, 2-1-10 Nihonbashi, Chuo-ku, Tokyo 103-0027
PHONE +81-3-3272-1666
FAX +81-3-3281-0381
E-MAIL
HOMEPAGE http://www.depart.or.jp/ (Japanese only)
REMARKS

National Association of Supermarkets, NAS

Shadan Hojin, Zenkoku Supermarket Kyokai 日本語表記
CATEGORY Industry/Economy:Organizations by Industry:Trade and Commerce
TYPE Incorporated association
ADDRESS Okubo Fuji bldg.-505, 2-7-1 Okubo, Shinjuku-ku, Tokyo 169-0072
PHONE +81-3-3207-3157
FAX +81-3-3207-5277
E-MAIL info@super.or.jp
HOMEPAGE http://www.super.or.jp (Japanese only)
REMARKS

Tokyo International Trade Fair Commission

Shadan Hojin, Tokyo Kokusai Mihon'ichi Kyokai 日本語表記
CATEGORY Industry/Economy:Organizations by Industry:Trade and Commerce
TYPE Incorporated association
ADDRESS 3-21-1 Ariake, Koto-ku, Tokyo 135-0063
PHONE +81-3-5530-1111
FAX +81-3-5530-1222
E-MAIL
HOMEPAGE http://www.bigsight.or.jp/english/index.html
REMARKS On 1 April 2003, the Tokyo International Trade Fair Commission will merge with the Tokyo International Trade Center (TITC) and will become known as Tokyo Big Sight Inc.

World Trade Center Tokyo, Inc.

Shadan Houjinn Sekai Boueki Center (Tokyo) 日本語表記
CATEGORY Industry/Economy:Organizations by Industry:Trade and Commerce
TYPE Incorporated association
ADDRESS World Trade Center Bldg. 37F, 2-4-1 Hamamatsu-cho, Minato-ku, Tokyo 105-6137
PHONE +81-3-3435-5651
FAX +81-3-3436-4368

E-MAIL info@wtctokyo.or.jp
HOMEPAGE http://www.wtctokyo.or.jp/english/

FINANCE, SECURITIES, AND INSURANCE

Japanese Bankers Association

Zenkoku Ginko Kyokai 日本語表記
CATEGORY Industry/Economy:Organizations by Industry:Finance, Securities, and Insurance
TYPE Others
ADDRESS 1-3-1 Marunouchi, Chiyoda-ku, Tokyo 100-0005
PHONE +81-3-3216-3761
FAX +81-3-3201-5608
E-MAIL
HOMEPAGE http://www.zenginkyo.or.jp/en/
REMARKS

Japan Securities Dealers Association, JSDA

Nihon Shokengyo Kyokai (Nissho-Kyo) 日本語表記
CATEGORY Industry/Economy:Organizations by Industry:Finance, Securities, and Insurance
TYPE Others
ADDRESS Tokyo Shoken Kaikan bldg., 1-5-8 Nihonbashi Kayaba-cho, Chuo-ku, Tokyo 103-0025
PHONE +81-3-3667-8451
FAX +81-3-3666-8009
E-MAIL
HOMEPAGE http://www.jsda.or.jp/ (Japanese only)
REMARKS

Regional Banks Association of Japan

Shadan Hojin, Zenkoku Chiho Ginko Kyokai (Chi-Gin-Kyo) 日本語表記
CATEGORY Industry/Economy:Organizations by Industry:Finance, Securities, and Insurance
TYPE Incorporated association
ADDRESS 3-1-2 Uchi-Kanda, Chiyoda-ku, Tokyo 101-8509
PHONE +81-3-3252-5171
FAX +81-3-3254-8664
E-MAIL
HOMEPAGE http://www.chiginkyo.or.jp/ (Japanese only)
REMARKS

The Investment Trusts Association, Japan

Shadan Hojin, Toushi Shintaku Kyokai 日本語表記
CATEGORY Industry/Economy:Organizations by Industry:Finance, Securities, and Insurance
TYPE Incorporated association
ADDRESS Tokyo Shoken Torihikijo bldg.6F, 2-1 Nihonbashi Kabuto-cho, Chuo-ku, Tokyo 103-0026
PHONE +81-3-5614-8400
FAX +81-3-5614-8448
E-MAIL jita@toushin.or.jp
HOMEPAGE http://www.toushin.or.jp/ (Japanese only)
REMARKS

The Life Insurance Association of Japan, LIAJ

Shadan Hojin, Seimei Hoken Kyokai 日本語表記
CATEGORY Industry/Economy:Organizations by Industry:Finance, Securities, and Insurance
TYPE Incorporated association
ADDRESS Shin-Kokusai bldg. 3F, 3-4-1 Marunouchi, Chiyoda-ku, Tokyo 100-0005
PHONE +81-3-3286-2624
FAX +81-3-3286-2630
E-MAIL kyokai@seiho.or.jp

HOMEPAGE http://www.seiho.or.jp/english/index.html
REMARKS

The Marine and Fire Insurance Association of Japan, Inc.

Shadan Hojin, Nihon Songai Hoken Kyokai
CATEGORY Industry/Economy:Organizations by Industry:Finance, Securities, and Insurance
TYPE Incorporated association
ADDRESS Non-Life Insurance bldg., 2-9 Kanda Awaji-cho, Chiyoda-ku, Tokyo 101-8335
PHONE +81-3-3255-1437
FAX +81-3-3255-1234
E-MAIL kokusai@sonpo.or.jp
HOMEPAGE http://www.sonpo.or.jp/english/english.html
REMARKS

The Second Association of Regional Banks

Shadan Hojin, Dai-2 Chiho Ginko Kyokai
CATEGORY Industry/Economy:Organizations by Industry:Finance, Securities, and Insurance
TYPE Incorporated association
ADDRESS 5 Sanban-cho, Chiyoda-ku, Tokyo 102-8356
PHONE +81-3-3262-2181
FAX +81-3-3262-2339
E-MAIL hp-master@dainichiginkyo.or.jp
HOMEPAGE http://www.dainichiginkyo.or.jp/
REMARKS

Trust Companies Association of Japan

Shadan Hojin, Shintaku Kyokai
CATEGORY Industry/Economy:Organizations by Industry:Finance, Securities, and Insurance
TYPE Incorporated association
ADDRESS Nihon bldg. 6F, 2-6-2 Ote-machi, Chiyoda-ku, Tokyo 100-0004
PHONE +81-3-3241-7135
FAX +81-3-3241-7200
E-MAIL
HOMEPAGE http://www.shintaku-kyokai.or.jp

OTHERS

All Japan Kimono Consultant Association

Shadan Hojin, Zen-nihon Kimono Consultant Kyokai
CATEGORY Industry/Economy:Organizations by Industry:Others
TYPE Incorporated association
ADDRESS 3-20 Kanda Nishiki-cho, Chiyoda-ku, Tokyo 101-0054
PHONE +81-3-3219-3015
FAX +81-3-3219-6032
E-MAIL
HOMEPAGE
REMARKS

Japan Advertising Agencies Association, JAAA

Shadan Hojin, Nihon Koukokugyo Kyokai
CATEGORY Industry/Economy:Organizations by Industry:Others
TYPE Incorporated association
ADDRESS 4-8-12 Ginza, Chuo-ku, Tokyo 104-0061
PHONE +81-3-3562-0876
FAX +81-3-3562-0889
E-MAIL info@jaaa.ne.jp
HOMEPAGE http://www.jaaa.ne.jp/english/

REMARKS

Motion Picture Producers Association of Japan, Inc., MPAJ

Shadan Hojin, Nihon Eiga Seisakusha Renmei (Ei-Ren) 日本語表記

CATEGORY Industry/Economy:Organizations by Industry:Others
TYPE Incorporated association
ADDRESS 2-15-2 Ginza, Chuo-ku, Tokyo 104-0061
PHONE +81-3-3547-1800
FAX +81-3-3547-0909
E-MAIL eiren@mc.neweb.ne.jp
HOMEPAGE http://www.eiren.org/(Japanese only)
REMARKS

Recording Industry Association of Japan, RIAJ

Shadan Hojin, Nihon Record Kyokai 日本語表記

CATEGORY Industry/Economy:Organizations by Industry:Others
TYPE Incorporated association
ADDRESS Nittetsu Kobiki bldg., 7-16-3 Ginza, Chuo-ku, Tokyo 104-0061
PHONE +81-3-3541-4411
FAX +81-3-3541-4460
E-MAIL info@riaj.or.jp
HOMEPAGE http://www.riaj.or.jp
REMARKS

The Japan Toy Association, JTA

Shadan Hojin, Nihon Gangu Kyokai (Nichi-Gan-Kyo) 日本語表記

CATEGORY Industry/Economy:Organizations by Industry:Others
TYPE Incorporated association
ADDRESS 4-22-4 Higashi-Komagata, Sumida-ku, Tokyo 130-8611
PHONE +81-3-3829-2513
FAX +81-3-3829-2510
E-MAIL toyfair@toys.or.jp
HOMEPAGE http://www.toys.or.jp
REMARKS

The New Business Conference, NBC News

Shadan Hojin, New Business Kyogikai 日本語表記

CATEGORY Industry/Economy:Organizations by Industry:Others
TYPE Incorporated foundation
ADDRESS Inoue Akasaka bldg.3F, 1-6-8 Akasaka, Minato-ku, Tokyo 107-0052
PHONE +81-3-3584-6080
FAX +81-3-3584-6081
E-MAIL nbc@nbc-world.or.jp
HOMEPAGE http://www.nbc-world.or.jp/ (Japanese only)

LABOR UNIONS

FEDERATIONS OF LABOR UNIONS

Japanese Trade Union Confederation

Nihon Rodokumiai Sorengokai (Rengo) 日本語表記

CATEGORY Industry/Economy:Labor Unions:Federations of Labor Unions
TYPE Others
ADDRESS Sohyo Kaikan bldg., 3-2-11 Kanda Surugadai, Chiyoda-ku, Tokyo 101-0062
PHONE +81-3-5295-0550
FAX +81-3-5295-0535
E-MAIL jtuc-kokusai@sv.rengo-net.or.jp

HOMEPAGE http://www.jtuc-rengo.or.jp
REMARKS

National Confederation of Trade Unions

Zenkoku Rodokumiai Sorengo (Zenroren) 日本語表記
CATEGORY Industry/Economy:Labor Unions:Federations of Labor Unions
TYPE Others
ADDRESS Zenroren Kaikan 4F, 2-4-4 Yushima, Bunkyo-ku, Tokyo 113-8462
PHONE +81-3-5842-5611
FAX +81-3-5842-5620
E-MAIL mkato@zenroren.gr.jp
HOMEPAGE http://www.zenroren.gr.jp/
REMARKS

National Trade Union Council

Zenkoku Rodokumiai Renraku Kyogikai (Zenrokyo) 日本語表記
CATEGORY Industry/Economy:Labor Unions:Federations of Labor Unions
TYPE Others
ADDRESS Kotsu bldg., 5-15-5 Shinbashi, Minato-ku, Tokyo 105-0004
PHONE +81-3-5403-1650
FAX +81-3-5403-1653
E-MAIL
HOMEPAGE http://www.zenrokyo.org/ (Japanese only)

CONSUMER GROUPS

*Eiyo Kaizen Fukyukai Zenkokushiyukai

Shadan Hojin, Eiyo Kaizen Fukyukai Zenkokushiyukai 日本語表記
CATEGORY Industry/Economy:Consumer Groups
TYPE Incorporated association
ADDRESS 5-1-7 Jingumae, Shibuya-ku, Tokyo 150-0001
PHONE +81-3-3409-3232
FAX +81-3-3409-3235
E-MAIL fukyukai@alto.ocn.or.jp
HOMEPAGE http://www.fukyukai.jp(Japanese only)
REMARKS

*Kansai Shohisha Dantai Renraku Kondankai

Kansai Shohisha Dantai Renraku Kondankai 日本語表記
CATEGORY Industry/Economy:Consumer Groups
TYPE Others
ADDRESS 1-3-17-711 Tani-machi, Chuo-ku Osaka-shi, Osaka 540-0012
PHONE +81-6-6941-3745
FAX +81-6-6941-5699
E-MAIL
HOMEPAGE
REMARKS

*Recycle Undo Shimin no Kai

Recycle Undo Shimin no Kai 日本語表記
CATEGORY Industry/Economy:Consumer Groups
TYPE Others
ADDRESS 2-29 Daikyo-cho, Shinjuku-ku, Tokyo 160-0015
PHONE +81-3-3226-6800
FAX +81-3-5379-1510
E-MAIL info@recycler.org
HOMEPAGE http://www.recycler.org/ (Japanese only)

REMARKS

***Zenkoku Seikatsu Gakko Renraku Kyogikai**

Zenkoku Seikatsu Gakko Renraku Kyogikai (Zenkoku-Renkyo)
CATEGORY Industry/Economy:Consumer Groups
TYPE Others
ADDRESS c/o Ashita no Nihon wo Tsukuru Kai, Shisei Kaikan., 1-3 Hibiya Koen, Chiyoda-ku, Tokyo 100-0012
PHONE +81-3-3501-8001
FAX +81-3-3501-8004
E-MAIL ashita@netjoy.ne.jp
HOMEPAGE http://www.ashita.or.jp/ (Japanese only)
REMARKS

***Zenkoku-Tomo-no-Kai**

Zenkoku Tomo no Kai
CATEGORY Industry/Economy:Consumer Groups
TYPE Others
ADDRESS 2-20-11 Nishi-Ikebukuro, Toshima-ku, Tokyo 171-0021
PHONE +81-3-3971-9602(Monday,Wednesday,Thursday) +81-3-3971-9359(Tuesday,Friday)
FAX +81-3-3971-5768
E-MAIL tomonoki@sepia.ocn.ne.jp
HOMEPAGE http://www2.ocn.ne.jp/~zentomo/ (Japanese only)
REMARKS

Association of Creating Future Japan

Zaidan Hojin, Ashita no Nihon wo Tsukuru Kyokai
CATEGORY Industry/Economy:Consumer Groups
TYPE Incorporated foundation
ADDRESS c/o Shisei Kaikan bldg., 1-3 Hibiya Koen, Chiyoda-ku, Tokyo 100-0012
PHONE +81-3-3501-8001
FAX +81-3-3501-8004
E-MAIL ashita@netjoy.ne.jp
HOMEPAGE http://www.ashita.or.jp/ (Japanese only)
REMARKS

Better Home Association

Zaidan Hojin, Better Home Kyokai
CATEGORY Industry/Economy:Consumer Groups
TYPE Incorporated foundation
ADDRESS 1-15-12 Shibuya, Shibuya-ku, Tokyo 150-8363
PHONE +81-3-3407-0471
FAX +81-3-3407-0479
E-MAIL info@betterhome.or.jp
HOMEPAGE http://www.betterhome.or.jp/ (Japanese only)
REMARKS Scholarship for foreign students who are in an undergraduate or postgraduate course at universities designated by the Association. Candidates are recommended by the designated universities.

Consumers Union of Japan, CUJ

Nihon Shohisha Renmei (Nisshoren)
CATEGORY Industry/Economy:Consumer Groups
TYPE Others
ADDRESS Asaka bldg., 1-10-16 Meguro Hon-cho, Meguro-ku, Tokyo 152-0002
PHONE +81-3-3711-7766
FAX +81-3-3715-9378
E-MAIL nishoren@jca.apc.org
HOMEPAGE http://www.jca.apc.org/nishoren/ (Japanese only)

REMARKS

Consumption Science Federation

Shohi Kagaku Rengokai 日本語表記

CATEGORY Industry/Economy:Consumer Groups
TYPE Others
ADDRESS Dai-2 Showa bldg., 17-9 Sakuragaoka-machi, Shibuya-ku, Tokyo 150-0031
PHONE +81-3-3462-2601
FAX +81-3-3461-1517
E-MAIL webmaster@shokaren.gr.jp
HOMEPAGE http://www2.convention.co.jp/consumer/list_SA06.html (Japanese only)
REMARKS

Housewives' Association

Shufu Rengokai (Shufuren) 日本語表記

CATEGORY Industry/Economy:Consumer Groups
TYPE Others
ADDRESS Shufu Kaikan, 15 Rokuban-cho, Chiyoda-ku, Tokyo 102-0085
PHONE +81-3-3265-8121
FAX +81-3-3221-7864
E-MAIL shufuren@shufuren.gr.jp
HOMEPAGE http://www.shufuren.gr.jp (Japanese only)
REMARKS

Japan Consumers' Association, JCA

Zaidan Hojin, Nihon Shohisha Kyokai (Nisshokyo) 日本語表記

CATEGORY Industry/Economy:Consumer Groups
TYPE Incorporated foundation
ADDRESS Eight bldg., 4-5-9 Hacchobori, Chuo-ku, Tokyo 104-0032
PHONE +81-3-3553-8601
FAX +81-3-3553-8986
E-MAIL jca-home@po.sphere.ne.jp
HOMEPAGE http://www1.sphere.ne.jp/jca-home/ (Japanese only)
REMARKS

Japan SEINENDAN Council

Nihon Seinendan Kyogikai (Nisseikyo) 日本語表記

CATEGORY Industry/Economy:Consumer Groups
TYPE Others
ADDRESS Nihon Seinen Kan, 15 Kasumigaoka-machi, Shinjuku-ku, Tokyo 160-0013
PHONE +81-3-3475-2490
FAX +81-3-3475-0668
E-MAIL seinen@dan.or.jp
HOMEPAGE http://www.dan.or.jp/ (Japanese only)
REMARKS

Japan Specified Non-Profit Corporation to Prevent Alcohol and Drug Problems

Tokutei Hieiri Katsudo Hojin, ASK 日本語表記

CATEGORY Industry/Economy:Consumer Groups
TYPE Others
ADDRESS Soguno-21 bldg., 3-19-3 Nihonbashi Hama-cho, Chuo-ku, Tokyo 103-0007
PHONE +81-3-3249-2551
FAX +81-3-3249-2553
E-MAIL ask@t3.rim.or.jp
HOMEPAGE http://www.ask.or.jp
REMARKS

Japan Woman's Council, JWC

Nihon Fujin Kaigi (Fujin Kaigi) 日本語表記

CATEGORY	Industry/Economy:Consumer Groups
TYPE	Others
ADDRESS	Tokyo Pro. bldg.-202, 1-33-3 Hongo, Bunkyo-ku, Tokyo 113-0033
PHONE	+81-3-3816-1862
FAX	+81-3-3816-1824
E-MAIL	i.onna@tcn-catv.ne.jp
HOMEPAGE	
REMARKS	

Japanese Consumers' Co-operative Union, JCCU

Nihon Seikatsu Kyodo Kumiai Rengokai 日本語表記

CATEGORY	Industry/Economy:Consumer Groups
TYPE	Others
ADDRESS	CO-OP PLAZA, 3-29-8 Shibuya, Shibuya-ku, Tokyo 150-8913
PHONE	+81-3-5778-8111
FAX	+81-3-5778-8112
E-MAIL	pr@jccu.coop
HOMEPAGE	http://www.jccu.coop/jccu/English_here/
REMARKS	

Japanese Mother's Congress

Nihon Hahaoya Taikai Renrakukai 日本語表記

CATEGORY	Industry/Economy:Consumer Groups
TYPE	Others
ADDRESS	Zenkoku Kyoiku Bunka Kaikan bldg., 12-1 Niban-cho, Chiyoda-ku, Tokyo 102-0084
PHONE	+81-3-3230-1836
FAX	+81-3-3230-1837
E-MAIL	
HOMEPAGE	
REMARKS	

National Association of Fisheries Cooperative's Women's Groups

Zenkoku Gyokyo Fujinbu Renraku Kyogikai (Zengyofuren) 日本語表記

CATEGORY	Industry/Economy:Consumer Groups
TYPE	Others
ADDRESS	Co-op bldg., 1-1-12 Uchi-Kanda, Chiyoda-ku, Tokyo 101-8503
PHONE	+81-3-3294-9617
FAX	+81-3-3294-9602
E-MAIL	z-shiokaze@zengyoren.or.jp
HOMEPAGE	http://www3.jf-net.ne.jp/zengyofuren/ (Japanese only)
REMARKS	

National Council for Urban Development Corporation Apartments Residents' Associations

Zenkoku Kodan Jutaku Jichikai Kyogikai 日本語表記

CATEGORY	Industry/Economy:Consumer Groups
TYPE	Others
ADDRESS	Tokyo Kawara Kaikan bldg., 1-7-9 Fujimi, Chiyoda-ku, Tokyo 102-0071
PHONE	+81-3-3265-9478
FAX	+81-3-3239-1384
E-MAIL	k_inoue@mua.biglobe.ne.jp
HOMEPAGE	http://www.jichikyo.com (Japanese only)
REMARKS	

National Federation of Regional Women's Organizations

Zenkoku Chiiki Fujin Dantai Renraku Kyogikai (Zenchifuren)
CATEGORY Industry/Economy:Consumer Groups
TYPE Others
ADDRESS Zenkoku Fujin Kaikan, 1-17-7 Shibuya, Shibuya-ku, Tokyo 150-0002
PHONE +81-3-3407-4303
FAX +81-3-3407-4305
E-MAIL chifuren@theia.ocn.ne.jp
HOMEPAGE http://www.chifuren.gr.jp(Japanese only)
REMARKS

National Liaison Committee of Consumers' Organizations
Zenkoku Shohisha Dantai Renrakukai (Zenkoku-Shodanren)
CATEGORY Industry/Economy:Consumer Groups
TYPE Others
ADDRESS PlazaF 6F,15 Rokubancho Chiyoda-ku, Tokyo 102-0085
PHONE +81-3-5216-6024
FAX +81-3-5216-6036
E-MAIL webmaster@shodanren.gr.jp
HOMEPAGE http://www.shodanren.gr.jp/ (Japanese only)
REMARKS

New Japan Women's Association
Shin Nihon Fujin no Kai (Shinfujin)
CATEGORY Industry/Economy:Consumer Groups
TYPE Others
ADDRESS Reimei bldg,1-36 Kanda Jinbo-cho, Chiyoda-ku, Tokyo 101-0051
PHONE +81-3-3293-0581
FAX +81-3-3295-7156
E-MAIL njwa@mb.infoweb.ne.jp
HOMEPAGE http://www.shinfujin.gr.jp
REMARKS

Rural Women Empowerment and Life Improvement Association
Shadan Hojin, Nosangyoson Josei Seikatsu Katsudo Shien Kyokai (Josei Seikatsu Kyokai)
CATEGORY Industry/Economy:Consumer Groups
TYPE Others
ADDRESS c/o Josei Seikatsu Kyokai, 1-9-5 Roppongi, Minato-ku, Tokyo 106-0032
PHONE +81-3-3584-6160
FAX +81-3-3584-4962
E-MAIL weli@weli.or.jp
HOMEPAGE http://www.weli.or.jp/ (Japanese only)
REMARKS

The League of Women Voters of Japan
Nihon Fujin Yukensha Domei
CATEGORY Industry/Economy:Consumer Groups
TYPE Others
ADDRESS Fusen Kaikan bldg., 2-21-11 Yoyogi, Shibuya-ku, Tokyo 151-0053
PHONE +81-3-3370-2727,+81-3-3370-5650
FAX +81-3-3370-4541
E-MAIL
HOMEPAGE
REMARKS

National Council of Agricultural Cooperative Women's Associations
JA Zenkoku Jyosei Soshiki Kyogikai

CATEGORY Industry/Economy:Consumer Groups
TYPE Others
ADDRESS c/o Zenkoku Nokyo Chuokai, 1-8-3 Ote-machi, Chiyoda-ku, Tokyo 100-0004
PHONE +81-3-3245-7542
FAX +81-3-5255-7358
E-MAIL jyosei.s@zenchu-ja.or.jp
HOMEPAGE http://www.zenchu-ja.org/ja-jyosei/ (Japanese only)
REMARKS

Women's Democratic Club

Fujin Minshu Club (Fumin) 日本語表記
CATEGORY Industry/Economy:Consumer Groups
TYPE Others
ADDRESS 3-31-18 Jingumae, Shibuya-ku, Tokyo 150-0001
PHONE +81-3-3402-3244
FAX +81-3-3401-3453
E-MAIL femin@jca.apc.org
HOMEPAGE http://www.jca.apc.org/femin/ (Japanese only)

STRATEGIC GOVERNMENT AND BUSINESS CONTACTS

LOCAL GOVERNMENTS: PREFECTURES

Aichi Prefecture
Aichi-ken 日本語表記
CATEGORY Politics/Administration:Local Governments:Prefectures
TYPE
ADDRESS 3-1-2 Sannomaru, Naka-ku Nagoya-shi, Aichi 460-8501
PHONE +81-52-961-2111
FAX
E-MAIL
HOMEPAGE http://www.pref.aichi.jp/index-e.html
REMARKS

Akita Prefecture
Akita-ken 日本語表記
CATEGORY Politics/Administration:Local Governments:Prefectures
TYPE
ADDRESS 4-1-1 Sanno, Akita-shi, Akita 010-8570
PHONE +81-18-860-1111
FAX
E-MAIL koho@pref.akita.jp
HOMEPAGE http://www.pref.akita.jp/e/
REMARKS

Aomori Prefecture
Aomori-ken 日本語表記
CATEGORY Politics/Administration:Local Governments:Prefectures
TYPE
ADDRESS 1-1-1 Nagashima, Aomori-shi, Aomori 030-8570
PHONE +81-17-722-1111
FAX +81-17-734-8002
E-MAIL webmaster@pref.aomori.jp
HOMEPAGE http://www.pref.aomori.jp/home-e.html
REMARKS

Chiba Prefecture
Chiba-ken 日本語表記
CATEGORY Politics/Administration:Local Governments:Prefectures
TYPE
ADDRESS 1-1 Ichiba-cho, Chuo-ku Chiba-shi, Chiba 260-8667
PHONE +81-43-223-2249
FAX +81-43-227-3613
E-MAIL webmaster@pref.chiba.jp
HOMEPAGE http://www.pref.chiba.jp/index-e.html
REMARKS

Ehime Prefecture
Ehime-ken 日本語表記
CATEGORY Politics/Administration:Local Governments:Prefectures
TYPE
ADDRESS 4-4-2 Ichiban-cho, Matsuyama-shi, Ehime 790-8570
PHONE +81-89-941-2111
FAX +81-89-921-6363
E-MAIL admin@pref.ehime.jp

HOMEPAGE http://www.pref.ehime.jp/index-e.htm
REMARKS

Fukui Prefecture

Fukui-ken 日本語表記
CATEGORY Politics/Administration:Local Governments:Prefectures
TYPE
ADDRESS 3-17-1 Ote, Fukui-shi, Fukui 910-8580
PHONE +81-776-21-1111
FAX
E-MAIL interfukui@pref.fukui.jp
HOMEPAGE http://www.pref.fukui.jp/english/
REMARKS

Fukuoka Prefecture

Fukuoka-ken 日本語表記
CATEGORY Politics/Administration:Local Governments:Prefectures
TYPE
ADDRESS 7-7 Higashi-Koen, Hakata-ku Fukuoka-shi, Fukuoka 812-8577
PHONE +81-92-651-1111
FAX +81-92-643-3032
E-MAIL
HOMEPAGE http://www.pref.fukuoka.jp/
REMARKS

Fukushima Prefecture

Fukushima-ken 日本語表記
CATEGORY Politics/Administration:Local Governments:Prefectures
TYPE
ADDRESS 2-16 Sugitsuma-cho, Fukushima-shi, Fukusima 960-8670
PHONE +81-24-521-1111
FAX
E-MAIL public_r@mail.pref.fukushima.jp
HOMEPAGE http://www.pref.fukushima.jp/index_e.html
REMARKS

Gifu Prefecture

Gifu-ken 日本語表記
CATEGORY Politics/Administration:Local Governments:Prefectures
TYPE
ADDRESS 2-1-1 Yabuta-Minami, Gifu-shi, Gifu 500-8570
PHONE +81-58-272-1111
FAX +81-58-275-0350
E-MAIL webmaster@govt.pref.gifu.jp
HOMEPAGE http://www.pref.gifu.jp/index_e.htm
REMARKS

Gunma Prefecture

Gunma-ken 日本語表記
CATEGORY Politics/Administration:Local Governments:Prefectures
TYPE
ADDRESS 1-1-1 Ote-machi, Maebashi-shi, Gunma 371-8570
PHONE +81-27-223-1111
FAX
E-MAIL webmaster@pref.gunma.jp
HOMEPAGE http://www.pref.gunma.jp/(English, Spanish, Portugese)
REMARKS

Hiroshima Prefecture

Hiroshima-ken 日本語表記

CATEGORY Politics/Administration:Local Governments:Prefectures
TYPE
ADDRESS 10-52 Moto-machi, Naka-ku Hiroshima-shi, Hiroshima 730-8511
PHONE +81-82-228-2111
FAX +81-82-228-4429
E-MAIL soukouhou@pref.hiroshima.jp
HOMEPAGE http://www.pref.hiroshima.jp/index-e.html
REMARKS

Hokkaido

Hokkaido 日本語表記

CATEGORY Politics/Administration:Local Governments:Prefectures
TYPE
ADDRESS Kita Nishi-Sanjo, Chuo-ku Sapporo-shi, Hokkaido 060-8588
PHONE +81-11-231-4111
FAX +81-11-251-3879
E-MAIL douminnokoe@pref.hokkaido.jp
HOMEPAGE http://www.pref.hokkaido.jp/index-e.html
REMARKS

Hyogo Prefecture

Hyogo-ken 日本語表記

CATEGORY Politics/Administration:Local Governments:Prefectures
TYPE
ADDRESS 5-10-1 Shimo-Yamate-dori, Chuo-ku Kobe-shi, Hyogo 650-8567
PHONE +81-78-341-7711
FAX
E-MAIL webmaster@koho.pref.hyogo.jp
HOMEPAGE http://web.pref.hyogo.jp/english/index.html
REMARKS

Ibaraki Prefecture

Ibaraki-ken 日本語表記

CATEGORY Politics/Administration:Local Governments:Prefectures
TYPE
ADDRESS 978-6 Kasahara-cho, Mito-shi, Ibaraki-310-8555
PHONE +81-029-301-1111
FAX
E-MAIL koho@pref.ibaraki.jp
HOMEPAGE http://www.pref.ibaraki.jp/en/menu.htm
REMARKS

Ishikawa Prefecture

Ishikawa-ken 日本語表記

CATEGORY Politics/Administration:Local Governments:Prefectures
TYPE
ADDRESS 2-1-1 Hirosaka, Kanazawa-shi, Ishikawa 920-8580
PHONE +81-76-261-1111
FAX +81-76-261-4395
E-MAIL e130500b@pref.ishikawa.jp
HOMEPAGE http://www.pref.ishikawa.jp/index_e.htm
REMARKS

Iwate Prefecture

Iwate-ken 日本語表記
CATEGORY Politics/Administration:Local Governments:Prefectures
TYPE
ADDRESS 10-1 Uchimaru, Morioka-shi, Iwate 020-8570
PHONE +81-19-651-3111
FAX +81-19-651-8044
E-MAIL gyousei@sv01.office.pref.iwate.jp
HOMEPAGE http://www.pref.iwate.jp/index.html
REMARKS Includes Korean language edition of pamphlet (http://www.pref.iwate.jp/info/korean/index.html)

Kagawa Prefecture

Kagawa-ken 日本語表記
CATEGORY Politics/Administration:Local Governments:Prefectures
TYPE
ADDRESS 4-1-10 Ban-cho, Takamatsu-shi, Kagawa 760-8570
PHONE +81-87-831-1111
FAX
E-MAIL kokusai@pref.kagawa.jp
HOMEPAGE http://www.pref.kagawa.jp/kokusai/profile/mainmenu.html
REMARKS

Kagoshima Prefecture

Kagoshima-ken 日本語表記
CATEGORY Politics/Administration:Local Governments:Prefectures
TYPE
ADDRESS 10-1 Kamoikeshinmachi, Kagoshima-shi, Kagoshima 890-8577
PHONE +81-99-286-2111
FAX
E-MAIL webkanri@po.pref.kagoshima.jp
HOMEPAGE http://www.pref.kagoshima.jp/home/english/index.html
REMARKS

Kanagawa Prefectural Government

Kanagawa-ken 日本語表記
CATEGORY Politics/Administration:Local Governments:Prefectures
TYPE
ADDRESS 1 Nihon-odori, Naka-ku, Yokohama-shi, Kanagawa-ken 231-8588
PHONE +81-45-210-1111
FAX +81-45-212-2753
E-MAIL kokusai@pref.kanagawa.jp
HOMEPAGE http://www.pref.kanagawa.jp/menu/english.htm
REMARKS

Kochi Prefecture

Kochi-ken 日本語表記
CATEGORY Politics/Administration:Local Governments:Prefectures
TYPE
ADDRESS 1-2-20 Marunouchi, Kocho-shi, Kochi 780-8570
PHONE +81-88-823-1111
FAX
E-MAIL k14104@ken.pref.kochi.jp
HOMEPAGE http://www.pref.kochi.jp/english/index.htm
REMARKS

Kumamoto Prefecture

Kumamoto-ken 日本語表記

CATEGORY Politics/Administration:Local Governments:Prefectures
TYPE
ADDRESS 6-18-1 Suizenji, Kumamoto-shi, Kumamoto 862-8570
PHONE +81-96-383-1111
FAX +81-96-381-3343
E-MAIL kokusai@pref.kumamoto.jp
HOMEPAGE http://www.pref.kumamoto.jp/english/menu.html
REMARKS

Kyoto Prefecture

Kyoto-fu 日本語表記
CATEGORY Politics/Administration:Local Governments:Prefectures
TYPE
ADDRESS Yabunouchi-cho, Shin-machi-nishiiru,Shimodachiuri-dori ,Kamigyo-ku Kyoto-shi, Kyoto 602-8570
PHONE +81-75-451-8111
FAX
E-MAIL joho@mail.pref.kyoto.jp
HOMEPAGE http://www.pref.kyoto.jp/index_e.html
REMARKS

Mie Prefecture

Mie-ken 日本語表記
CATEGORY Politics/Administration:Local Governments:Prefectures
TYPE
ADDRESS 13 Komei-cho, Tsu-shi, Mie 514-8570 (Headquarters) 3F Ust-Tsu 700 Hadokoro-cho, Tsu-shi, Mie 514-0009 (International affairs office)
PHONE +81-59-222-5974
FAX +81-59-222-5984
E-MAIL kokusai@pref.mie.jp
HOMEPAGE http://www.pref.mie.jp/ENGLISH/index.htm
REMARKS

Miyagi Prefecture

Miyagi-ken 日本語表記
CATEGORY Politics/Administration:Local Governments:Prefectures
TYPE
ADDRESS 3-8-1 Hon-cho, Aoba-ku Sendai-shi, Miyagi 980-8570
PHONE +81-22-211-2111
FAX
E-MAIL webmaster@pref.miyagi.jp
HOMEPAGE http://www.pref.miyagi.jp/english/index.htm
REMARKS

Miyazaki Prefecture

Miyazaki-ken 日本語表記
CATEGORY Politics/Administration:Local Governments:Prefectures
TYPE
ADDRESS 2-10-1 Tachibana-dori-Higashi, Miyazaki-shi, Miyazaki 880-8501
PHONE +81-985-24-1111
FAX
E-MAIL wmaster@mail.pref.miyazaki.jp
HOMEPAGE http://www.pref.miyazaki.jp/
REMARKS

Nagano Prefecture

Nagano-ken 日本語表記

CATEGORY Politics/Administration:Local Governments:Prefectures
TYPE
ADDRESS 692-2 Oaza Minami-Nagano Aza Habashita, Nagano-shi, Nagano 380-8570
PHONE +81-26-232-0111
FAX
E-MAIL jouhou@pref.nagano.jp
HOMEPAGE http://www.pref.nagano.jp/english/indexe.htm
REMARKS

Nagasaki Prefecture

Nagasaki-ken 日本語表記
CATEGORY Politics/Administration:Local Governments:Prefectures
TYPE
ADDRESS 2-13 Edo-machi, Nagasaki-shi, Nagasaki 850-8570
PHONE +81-958-24-1111
FAX +81-958-24-5596
E-MAIL pref@pref.nagasaki.jp
HOMEPAGE http://www.pref.nagasaki.jp/en/index.html
REMARKS

Nara Prefecture

Nara-ken 日本語表記
CATEGORY Politics/Administration:Local Governments:Prefectures
TYPE
ADDRESS 30 Noborioji-cho ,Nara-shi, Nara 630-8501
PHONE +81-742-22-1101
FAX
E-MAIL joho@pref.nara.jp
HOMEPAGE http://www.pref.nara.jp/
REMARKS

Niigata Prefecture

Niigata-ken 日本語表記
CATEGORY Politics/Administration:Local Governments:Prefectures
TYPE
ADDRESS 4-1 Shinko-cho, Niigata-shi, Niigata 950-8570
PHONE +81-25-285-5511
FAX
E-MAIL sitemaster@pref.niigata.jp
HOMEPAGE http://www.pref.niigata.jp/en/
REMARKS

Oita Prefecture

Oita-ken 日本語表記
CATEGORY Politics/Administration:Local Governments:Prefectures
TYPE
ADDRESS 3-1-1 Ote-machi, Oita-shi, Oita 870-8501
PHONE +81-97-536-1111
FAX
E-MAIL
HOMEPAGE http://www.pref.oita.jp/
REMARKS

Okayama Prefecture

Okayama-ken 日本語表記
CATEGORY Politics/Administration:Local Governments:Prefectures
TYPE

ADDRESS 2-4-6 Uchisange, Oakayama-shi, Okayama 700-8570
PHONE +81-86-224-2111
FAX
E-MAIL joho@pref.okayama.jp
HOMEPAGE http://www.pref.okayama.jp/kikaku/kokusai/momo/e/
REMARKS

Okinawa Prefecture
Okinawa-ken 日本語表記
CATEGORY Politics/Administration:Local Governments:Prefectures
TYPE
ADDRESS 1-2-2 Izumizaki, Naha-shi, Okinawa 900-8570
PHONE +81-98-866-2333
FAX +81-98-866-2079
E-MAIL okinawa@pref.okinawa.jp
HOMEPAGE http://www.pref.okinawa.jp/index-j.html
REMARKS

Osaka Prefecture
Osaka-fu 日本語表記
CATEGORY Politics/Administration:Local Governments:Prefectures
TYPE
ADDRESS 2-1-22 Otemae, Chuo-ku Osaka-shi, Osaka 540-8570
PHONE +81-6-6941-0351
FAX
E-MAIL webmaster@sbox.pref.osaka.jp
HOMEPAGE http://www.pref.osaka.jp/en/index.html
REMARKS

Saga Prefecture
Saga-ken 日本語表記
CATEGORY Politics/Administration:Local Governments:Prefectures
TYPE
ADDRESS 1-1-59 Jonai, Saga-shi, Saga 840-8570
PHONE +81-952-24-2111
FAX +81-952-25-0753
E-MAIL
HOMEPAGE http://www.pref.saga.jp/gaikoku/fr_english.html
REMARKS

Saitama Prefecture
Saitama-ken 日本語表記
CATEGORY Politics/Administration:Local Governments:Prefectures
TYPE
ADDRESS 3-15-1 Takasago, Saitama-shi, Saitama 336-8501
PHONE +81-48-824-2111
FAX
E-MAIL
HOMEPAGE http://www.pref.saitama.jp/index_e.html
REMARKS

Shiga Prefecture
Shiga-ken 日本語表記
CATEGORY Politics/Administration:Local Governments:Prefectures
TYPE
ADDRESS 4-1-1 Kyo-machi, Otsu-shi, Shiga 520-8577
PHONE +81-77-524-1121

FAX
E-MAIL webmaster@pref.shiga.jp
HOMEPAGE http://www.pref.shiga.jp/index-e.html
REMARKS

Shimane Prefecture

Shimane-ken 日本語表記
CATEGORY Politics/Administration:Local Governments:Prefectures
TYPE
ADDRESS 1 Tono-machi, Matsue-shi, Shimane 690-8501
PHONE +81-852-22-6463
FAX +81-852-25-3856
E-MAIL kokusai@pref.shimane.jp
HOMEPAGE http://www.pref.shimane.jp/section/kokusai/foreign/
REMARKS

Shizuoka Prefecture

Shizuoka-ken 日本語表記
CATEGORY Politics/Administration:Local Governments:Prefectures
TYPE
ADDRESS 9-6 Oute-machi, Shizuoka-shi, Shizuoka 420-8601
PHONE +81-54-221-2232
FAX +81-54-221-2542
E-MAIL webmaster@pref.shizuoka.jp
HOMEPAGE http://www.pref.shizuoka.jp/kikaku/ki-20/english/index.htm
REMARKS

Tochigi Prefecture

Tochigi-ken 日本語表記
CATEGORY Politics/Administration:Local Governments:Prefectures
TYPE
ADDRESS 1-1-20 Hanawada, Utsunomiya-shi, Tochigi 320-8501
PHONE +81-28-623-2323
FAX
E-MAIL kokusai@pref.tochigi.jp
HOMEPAGE http://www.pref.tochigi.jp/kokusai/english/index.html
REMARKS

Tokushima Prefecture

Tokushima-ken 日本語表記
CATEGORY Politics/Administration:Local Governments:Prefectures
TYPE
ADDRESS 1-1 Bandai-cho, Tokushima-shi, Tokushima 770-8570
PHONE +81-88-621-2500
FAX
E-MAIL jouhounetworkka@pref.tokushima.jp
HOMEPAGE http://www1.pref.tokushima.jp
REMARKS

Tokyo Metropolitan government

Tokyo-to 日本語表記
CATEGORY Politics/Administration:Local Governments:Prefectures
TYPE
ADDRESS 2-8-1 Nishi-Shinjuku, Shinjuku-ku, Tokyo 163-8001
PHONE +81-3-5321-1111
FAX
E-MAIL system@metro.tokyo.jp

HOMEPAGE http://www.chijihonbu.metro.tokyo.jp/english/
REMARKS

Tottori Prefecture
Tottori-ken 日本語表記
CATEGORY Politics/Administration:Local Governments:Prefectures
TYPE
ADDRESS 1-220 Higashi-machi, Tottori-shi, Tottori 680-8570
PHONE +81-857-26-7111
FAX
E-MAIL kokusai@pref.tottori.jp
HOMEPAGE http://www.pref.tottori.jp/english/
REMARKS

Toyama Prefecture
Toyama-ken 日本語表記
CATEGORY Politics/Administration:Local Governments:Prefectures
TYPE
ADDRESS 1-7 Shin-Sogawa, Toyama-shi, Toyama 930-8501
PHONE +81-76-431-4111
FAX +81-76-444-3482
E-MAIL webmaster@info.pref.toyama.jp
HOMEPAGE http://www.pref.toyama.jp/master/02guide/welcome/welcome.htm
REMARKS

Wakayama Prefecture
Wakayama-ken 日本語表記
CATEGORY Politics/Administration:Local Governments:Prefectures
TYPE
ADDRESS 1-1 Komatsubara-dori, Wakayama-shi, Wakayama 640-8585
PHONE +81-73-432-4111
FAX
E-MAIL webmaster@office.wakayama.go.jp
HOMEPAGE http://www.wakayama.go.jp/
REMARKS

Yamagata Prefecture
Yamagata-ken 日本語表記
CATEGORY Politics/Administration:Local Governments:Prefectures
TYPE
ADDRESS 2-8-1 Matsunami, Yamagata-shi, Yamagata 990-8570
PHONE +81-23-630-2211
FAX
E-MAIL jouhou@hnc.pref.yamagata.jp
HOMEPAGE http://www.pref.yamagata.jp/index-e.html
REMARKS

Yamaguchi Prefecture
Yamaguchi-ken 日本語表記
CATEGORY Politics/Administration:Local Governments:Prefectures
TYPE
ADDRESS 1-1 Taki-machi, Yamaguchi-shi, Yamaguchi 753-8501
PHONE +81-83-933-2340
FAX +81-83-933-2358
E-MAIL a12900@pref.yamaguchi.jp
HOMEPAGE http://www.pref.yamaguchi.jp/gyosei/kenjoho/english.htm
REMARKS

Yamanashi Prefecture

Yamanashi-ken

CATEGORY Politics/Administration:Local Governments:Prefectures
TYPE
ADDRESS 1-6-1 Marunouchi, Kofu-shi, Yamanashi 400-8501
PHONE +81-55-237-1111
FAX
E-MAIL koucho@pref.yamanashi.jp
HOMEPAGE http://www.pref.yamanashi.jp/english/

LOCAL GOVERNMENTS: MAJOR CITIES

Adachi City

Adachi-ku

CATEGORY Politics/Administration:Local Governments:Major Cities
TYPE
ADDRESS 1-17-1 Chuo-Honcho, Adachi-ku, Tokyo 120-8510
PHONE +81-3-3880-5111
FAX
E-MAIL kouhou@city.adachi.tokyo.jp
HOMEPAGE http://www.city.adachi.tokyo.jp/
REMARKS

Amagasaki City

Amagasaki-shi

CATEGORY Politics/Administration:Local Governments:Major Cities
TYPE
ADDRESS 1-23-1 Higashi-Nanamatsu-cho, Amagasaki-shi, Hyogo 660-8501
PHONE +81-6-6489-6880
FAX +81-6-6489-6837
E-MAIL webmaster@city.amagasaki.hyogo.jp
HOMEPAGE http://www.city.amagasaki.hyogo.jp/web/contents/foreign/eng/index.htm
REMARKS

Aomori City

Aomori-shi

CATEGORY Politics/Administration:Local Governments:Major Cities
TYPE
ADDRESS 1-22-5 Chuo, Aomori-shi, Aomori 030-8555
PHONE +81-17-734-1111
FAX +81-17-734-6865
E-MAIL aocity@city.aomori.aomori.jp
HOMEPAGE http://www.city.aomori.aomori.jp/english/idxeng.html
REMARKS

Asahikawa City

Asahikawa-shi

CATEGORY Politics/Administration:Local Governments:Major Cities
TYPE
ADDRESS 9-46 Rokujo-dori, Asahikawa-shi, Hokkaido 070-8525
PHONE +81-166-26-1111
FAX +81-166-24-7833
E-MAIL ackoho@city.asahikawa.hokkaido.jp
HOMEPAGE http://www.city.asahikawa.hokkaido.jp/files/kokusaikouryu/index/index.html
REMARKS

Bunkyo City

Bunkyo-ku 日本語表記

CATEGORY Politics/Administration:Local Governments:Major Cities
TYPE
ADDRESS 1-16-21, Kasuga, Bunkyo-ku, Tokyo 112-0003
PHONE +81-3-3812-7111
FAX
E-MAIL
HOMEPAGE http://www.city.bunkyo.tokyo.jp/
REMARKS

Chiba City

Chiba-shi 日本語表記

CATEGORY Politics/Administration:Local Governments:Major Cities
TYPE
ADDRESS 1-1 Chiba-Minato, Chuo-ku Chiba-shi, Chiba 260-8722
PHONE +81-43-245-5111
FAX
E-MAIL webmaster@city.chiba.jp
HOMEPAGE http://www.city.chiba.jp/index-e.html
REMARKS

Chiyoda City

Chiyoda-ku 日本語表記

CATEGORY Politics/Administration:Local Governments:Major Cities
TYPE
ADDRESS 1-6-11 Kudan-Minami, Chiyoda-ku, Tokyo 102-8688
PHONE +81-3-3264-2111
FAX
E-MAIL chiyoda@city.chiyoda.tokyo.jp
HOMEPAGE http://www.city.chiyoda.tokyo.jp/english/e-index.html
REMARKS

Chuo City

Chuo-ku 日本語表記

CATEGORY Politics/Administration:Local Governments:Major Cities
TYPE
ADDRESS 1-1-1 Tsukiji, Chuo-ku, Tokyo 104-8404
PHONE +81-3-3543-0211
FAX
E-MAIL chuocity@magical2.egg.or.jp
HOMEPAGE http://www.city.chuo.tokyo.jp/ (Japanese only)
REMARKS

City Arakawa Tokyo of Japan

Arakawa-ku 日本語表記

CATEGORY Politics/Administration:Local Governments:Major Cities
TYPE
ADDRESS 2-2-3 Arakawa, Arakawa-ku, Tokyo 116-8501
PHONE +81-3-3802-3111
FAX +81-3-3802-6262
E-MAIL
HOMEPAGE http://www.city.arakawa.tokyo.jp/
REMARKS

City of Akita

Akita-shi 日本語表記

CATEGORY Politics/Administration:Local Governments:Major Cities
TYPE
ADDRESS 1-1-1 Sanno, Akita-shi, Akita 010-8560
PHONE +81-18-863-2222
FAX +81-18-863-7284
E-MAIL webmaster@city.akita.akita.jp
HOMEPAGE http://www.city.akita.akita.jp/en/default.htm
REMARKS

City of Setagaya
Setagaya-ku 日本語表記
CATEGORY Politics/Administration:Local Governments:Major Cities
TYPE
ADDRESS 4-21-27 Setagaya, Setagaya-ku, Tokyo 154-8504
PHONE +81-3-5432-1111
FAX
E-MAIL
HOMEPAGE http://www.city.setagaya.tokyo.jp/
REMARKS

City of Yokohama
Yokohama-shi 日本語表記
CATEGORY Politics/Administration:Local Governments:Major Cities
TYPE
ADDRESS 1-1 Minato-cho, Naka-ku, Yokohama-shi, Kanagawa 231-0017
PHONE +81-45-671-2121
FAX +81-45-663-4670
E-MAIL
HOMEPAGE http://www.city.yokohama.jp/front/welcomeE.html
REMARKS

Edogawa City
Edogawa-ku 日本語表記
CATEGORY Politics/Administration:Local Governments:Major Cities
TYPE
ADDRESS 1-4-1 Chuo, Edogawa-ku, Tokyo 132-8501
PHONE +81-3-3652-1151
FAX
E-MAIL webmaster@city.edogawa.tokyo.jp
HOMEPAGE http://www.city.edogawa.tokyo.jp/
REMARKS

Fujisawa City
Fujisawa-shi 日本語表記
CATEGORY Politics/Administration:Local Governments:Major Cities
TYPE
ADDRESS 1-1 Asahi-cho, Fujisawa-shi, Kanagawa 251-8601
PHONE +81-466-25-1111
FAX +81-466-50-0533
E-MAIL kokusai@city.fujisawa.kanagawa.jp
HOMEPAGE http://www.city.fujisawa.kanagawa.jp/introduce/english/
REMARKS

Fukui City
Fukui-shi 日本語表記
CATEGORY Politics/Administration:Local Governments:Major Cities
TYPE

ADDRESS 3-10-1 Ote, Fukui-shi, Fukui 910-8511
PHONE +81-776-20-5111
FAX +81-776-20-5733
E-MAIL wizard@city.fukui.fukui.jp
HOMEPAGE http://www.city.fukui.fukui.jp/english/index.html
REMARKS

Fukuoka City

Fukuoka-shi 日本語表記
CATEGORY Politics/Administration:Local Governments:Major Cities
TYPE
ADDRESS 1-8-1 Tenjin, Chuo-ku Fukuoka-shi, Fukuoka 810-8620
PHONE +81-92-711-4111
FAX
E-MAIL koho.MO@city.fukuoka.jp
HOMEPAGE http://www.city.fukuoka.jp/
REMARKS

Fukushima City

Fukushima-shi 日本語表記
CATEGORY Politics/Administration:Local Governments:Major Cities
TYPE
ADDRESS 3-1 Gorouchi-machi, Fukushima-shi, Fukushima 960-8601
PHONE +81-24-535-1111
FAX +81-24-535-7311
E-MAIL info@city.fukushima.fukushima.jp
HOMEPAGE http://city.fukushima.fukushima.jp/english/center-e.html
REMARKS

Fukuyama City

Fukuyama-shi 日本語表記
CATEGORY Politics/Administration:Local Governments:Major Cities
TYPE
ADDRESS 3-5 Higashi-Sakura-machi, Fukuyama-shi, Hiroshima 720-8501
PHONE +81-84-921-2111
FAX
E-MAIL fukuyama@hiroshima-cdas.or.jp
HOMEPAGE http://www.hiroshima-cdas.or.jp/fukuyama/english/index_en.html
REMARKS

Funabashi City

Funabashi-shi 日本語表記
CATEGORY Politics/Administration:Local Governments:Major Cities
TYPE
ADDRESS 2-10-25 Minato-cho, Funabashi-shi, Chiba 273-8501
PHONE +81-47-436-2111
FAX +81-47-436-2769
E-MAIL kouhou@city.funabashi.chiba.jp
HOMEPAGE http://www.city.funabashi.chiba.jp/
REMARKS

Gifu City

Gifu-shi 日本語表記
CATEGORY Politics/Administration:Local Governments:Major Cities
TYPE
ADDRESS 18 Imazawa-cho, Gifu-shi, Gifu 500-8701
PHONE +81-58-265-4141

FAX +81-58-264-8602
E-MAIL uketsuke@city.gifu.gifu.jp
HOMEPAGE http://www.city.gifu.gifu.jp/ (Japanese only)
REMARKS

Hachioji City

Hachioji-shi 日本語表記
CATEGORY Politics/Administration:Local Governments:Major Cities
TYPE
ADDRESS 3-24-1 Moto-Hongo-cho, Hachioji-shi, Tokyo 192-8501
PHONE +81-426-26-3111
FAX
E-MAIL hachioji@city.hachioji.tokyo.jp
HOMEPAGE http://www.city.hachioji.tokyo.jp/HP-english/index.html
REMARKS

Hakodate City

Hakodate-shi 日本語表記
CATEGORY Politics/Administration:Local Governments:Major Cities
TYPE
ADDRESS 4-13 Shinonome-cho, Hakodate-shi, Hokkaido 040-8666
PHONE +81-138-21-3619
FAX +81-138-23-7604
E-MAIL hkd-intl@city.hakodate.hokkaido.jp
HOMEPAGE http://www.city.hakodate.hokkaido.jp/english.htm
REMARKS

Hamamatsu City

Hamamatsu-shi 日本語表記
CATEGORY Politics/Administration:Local Governments:Major Cities
TYPE
ADDRESS 103-2 Motoshiro-cho, Hamamatsu-shi, Shizuoka 430-8652
PHONE +81-53-457-2111
FAX
E-MAIL j-center@city.hamamatsu.shizuoka.jp
HOMEPAGE http://www.city.hamamatsu.shizuoka.jp/hamaEng/index.htm
REMARKS

Higashi-Osaka City

Higashi-Osaka-shi 日本語表記
CATEGORY Politics/Administration:Local Governments:Major Cities
TYPE
ADDRESS 1-1-1 Inaba, Higashi-Osaka-shi, Osaka 578-0925
PHONE +81-729-62-1331
FAX +81-729-61-7730
E-MAIL koho@city.higashiosaka.osaka.jp
HOMEPAGE http://www.city.higashiosaka.osaka.jp/ (Japanese only)
REMARKS

Himeji City

Himeji-shi 日本語表記
CATEGORY Politics/Administration:Local Governments:Major Cities
TYPE
ADDRESS 4-1 Yasuda, Himeji-shi, Hyogo 670-8501
PHONE +81-792-21-2111
FAX
E-MAIL info@city.himeji.hyogo.jp

HOMEPAGE http://www.city.himeji.hyogo.jp/english/himeji/
REMARKS

Hirakata City
Hirakata-shi 日本語表記
CATEGORY Politics/Administration:Local Governments:Major Cities
TYPE
ADDRESS 2-1-20 Ogaito-cho, Hirakata-shi, Osaka 573-8666
PHONE +81-72-841-1221
FAX +81-72-841-3039
E-MAIL johos@city.hirakata.osaka.jp
HOMEPAGE http://www.city.hirakata.osaka.jp/freepage/gyousei/eng/
REMARKS

Hiroshima City
Hiroshima-shi 日本語表記
CATEGORY Politics/Administration:Local Governments:Major Cities
TYPE
ADDRESS 1-6-34 Kokutaiji-machi, Naka-ku, Hiroshima 730-8586
PHONE +81-82-245-2111
FAX +81-82-504-2069
E-MAIL www-admin@city.hiroshima.jp
HOMEPAGE http://www.city.hiroshima.jp/index-E.html
REMARKS

Ichikawa City
Ichikawa-shi 日本語表記
CATEGORY Politics/Administration:Local Governments:Major Cities
TYPE
ADDRESS 1-1-1 Yawata, Ichikawa-shi, Chiba 272-8501
PHONE +81-47-334-1111
FAX +81-47-336-2300
E-MAIL mailbox@city.ichikawa.chiba.jp
HOMEPAGE http://www.city.ichikawa.chiba.jp/
REMARKS

Itabashi City
Itabashi-ku 日本語表記
CATEGORY Politics/Administration:Local Governments:Major Cities
TYPE
ADDRESS 1-51 Oyamahigashi-cho, Itabashi-ku, Tokyo 173-0014
PHONE +81-3-3964-1111
FAX +81-3-3579-4212
E-MAIL iken@city.itabashi.tokyo.jp
HOMEPAGE http://www.city.itabashi.tokyo.jp/index-e.htm
REMARKS

Iwaki City
Iwaki-shi 日本語表記
CATEGORY Politics/Administration:Local Governments:Major Cities
TYPE
ADDRESS 21 Aza Umemoto, Taira Iwaki-shi, Fukushima 970-8686
PHONE +81-246-22-1111
FAX +81-246-22-3662
E-MAIL info@city.iwaki.fukushima.jp
HOMEPAGE http://www.city.iwaki.fukushima.jp/
REMARKS

Kagoshima City

Kagoshima-shi 日本語表記

CATEGORY Politics/Administration:Local Governments:Major Cities
TYPE
ADDRESS 11-1 Yamashita-cho, Kagoshima-shi, Kagoshima 892-8677
PHONE +81-99-224-1111
FAX +81-99-224-8900
E-MAIL info@city.kagoshima.kagoshima.jp
HOMEPAGE http://www.city.kagoshima.kagoshima.jp
REMARKS

Kashiwa City

Kashiwa-shi 日本語表記

CATEGORY Politics/Administration:Local Governments:Major Cities
TYPE
ADDRESS 5-10-1 Kashiwa, Kashiwa-shi, Chiba 277-8505
PHONE +81-4-7167-1111
FAX +81-4-7166-6026
E-MAIL
HOMEPAGE http://www.city.kashiwa.chiba.jp/foreign/foreign.htm
REMARKS

Katsushika Ward

Katsushika-ku 日本語表記

CATEGORY Politics/Administration:Local Governments:Major Cities
TYPE
ADDRESS 5-13-1 Tateishi, Katsushika-ku, Tokyo 124-8555
PHONE +81-3-3695-1111
FAX +81-3-3698-1502
E-MAIL
HOMEPAGE http://www.city.katsushika.tokyo.jp/ (Japanese only)
REMARKS

Kawagoe City

Kawagoe-shi 日本語表記

CATEGORY Politics/Administration:Local Governments:Major Cities
TYPE
ADDRESS 1-3-1 Moto-machi, Kawagoe-shi, Saitama 350-8601
PHONE +81-49-224-8811
FAX +81-49-225-2895
E-MAIL webmaster@city.kawagoe.saitama.jp
HOMEPAGE http://www.city.kawagoe.saitama.jp/
REMARKS

Kawaguchi City

Kawaguchi-shi 日本語表記

CATEGORY Politics/Administration:Local Governments:Major Cities
TYPE
ADDRESS 2-1-1 Aoki, Kawaguchi-shi, Saitama 332-8601
PHONE +81-48-258-1110
FAX +81-48-257-1110
E-MAIL koho@city.kawaguchi.saitama.jp
HOMEPAGE http://www.city.kawaguchi.saitama.jp/index-true.html (Japanese only)
REMARKS

Kawasaki City

Kawasaki-shi

CATEGORY	Politics/Administration:Local Governments:Major Cities
TYPE	
ADDRESS	1 Miyamoto-cho, Kawasaki-ku Kawasaki-shi, Kanagawa 210-8577
PHONE	+81-44-200-2111
FAX	+81-44-200-2417
E-MAIL	25sosa@city.kawasaki.jp
HOMEPAGE	http://www.city.kawasaki.jp/index_e.htm
REMARKS	

Kita City

Kita-ku

CATEGORY	Politics/Administration:Local Governments:Major Cities
TYPE	
ADDRESS	1-15-22, Oji-honcho, Kita-ku, Tokyo 114-8508
PHONE	+81-3-3908-1111
FAX	
E-MAIL	
HOMEPAGE	http://www.city.kita.tokyo.jp/ (Japanese only)
REMARKS	

Kitakyushu City

Kitakyushu-shi

CATEGORY	Politics/Administration:Local Governments:Major Cities
TYPE	
ADDRESS	1-1 Jonai, Kokura-Kita-ku Kitakyushu-shi, Fukuoka 803-8501
PHONE	+81-93-582-2525
FAX	
E-MAIL	webmaster@city.kitakyushu.jp
HOMEPAGE	http://www.city.kitakyushu.jp/~english/
REMARKS	

Kobe City

Kobe-shi

CATEGORY	Politics/Administration:Local Governments:Major Cities
TYPE	
ADDRESS	6-5-1 Kano-cho, Chuo-ku Kobe-shi, Hyogo 650-8570
PHONE	+81-78-331-8181
FAX	
E-MAIL	webmaster@office.city.kobe.jp
HOMEPAGE	http://www.city.kobe.jp/index-e.html
REMARKS	

Kochi City

Kochi-shi

CATEGORY	Politics/Administration:Local Governments:Major Cities
TYPE	
ADDRESS	5-1-45 Hon-machi, Kochi-shi, Kochi 780-8571
PHONE	+81-88-822-8111
FAX	+81-88-824-6930
E-MAIL	kc-050200@city.kochi.kochi.jp
HOMEPAGE	http://www.city.kochi.kochi.jp/joho/top/index.htm
REMARKS	

Kofu City

Kofu-shi

CATEGORY	Politics/Administration:Local Governments:Major Cities

TYPE

ADDRESS 1-18-1, Marunouchi Kofu-shi, Yamanashi 400-8585

PHONE +81-55-237-1161

FAX +81-55-235-1048

E-MAIL webmaster@city.kofu.yamanashi.jp

HOMEPAGE http://www.city.kofu.yamanashi.jp/english/

REMARKS

Koriyama City

Koriyama-shi 日本語表記

CATEGORY Politics/Administration:Local Governments:Major Cities

TYPE

ADDRESS 1-23-7 Asahi, Koriyama-shi, Fukushima 963-8601

PHONE +81-249-24-2491

FAX

E-MAIL shomu@city.koriyama.fukushima.jp

HOMEPAGE http://www.city.koriyama.Fukushima.jp/

REMARKS

Koto City

Koto-ku 日本語表記

CATEGORY Politics/Administration:Local Governments:Major Cities

TYPE

ADDRESS 4-11-28 Toyo, Koto-ku, Tokyo 135-8383

PHONE +81-3-3647-9111

FAX +81-3-5634-7538

E-MAIL koho@city.koto.tokyo.jp

HOMEPAGE http://www.city.koto.tokyo.jp/ (Japanese only)

REMARKS

Kumamoto City

Kumamoto-shi 日本語表記

CATEGORY Politics/Administration:Local Governments:Major Cities

TYPE

ADDRESS 1-1 Tetori-Hon-cho, Kumamoto-shi, Kumamoto 860-8601

PHONE +81-96-328-2111

FAX +81-96-324-1713

E-MAIL shiminkouryusalon@city.kumamoto.kumamoto.jp

HOMEPAGE http://www.city.kumamoto.kumamoto.jp

REMARKS

Kurashiki City

Kurashiki-shi 日本語表記

CATEGORY Politics/Administration:Local Governments:Major Cities

TYPE

ADDRESS 640 Nishi-Nakashinden, Kurashiki-shi, Okayama 710-8565

PHONE +81-86-426-3030

FAX +81-86-421-2400

E-MAIL pubinfo@city.kurashiki.okayama.jp

HOMEPAGE http://www.city.kurashiki.okayama.jp/

REMARKS

Kyoto City

Kyoto-shi 日本語表記

CATEGORY Politics/Administration:Local Governments:Major Cities

TYPE

ADDRESS Teramachi-dori Oike-agaru, Nakagyo-ku Kyoto-shi, Kyoto 604-8571

PHONE +81-75-222-3111
FAX
E-MAIL
HOMEPAGE http://www.city.kyoto.jp/index_e.html
REMARKS

Machida City
Machida-shi 日本語表記
CATEGORY Politics/Administration:Local Governments:Major Cities
TYPE
ADDRESS 1-20-23 Naka-machi, Machida-shi, Tokyo 194-8520
PHONE +81-42-722-3111
FAX
E-MAIL
HOMEPAGE http://www.city.machida.tokyo.jp/
REMARKS

Maebashi City
Maebashi-shi 日本語表記
CATEGORY Politics/Administration:Local Governments:Major Cities
TYPE
ADDRESS 2-12-1 Ote-machi, Mebashi-shi, Gunma 371-8601
PHONE +81-27-224-1111
FAX +81-27-224-3003
E-MAIL mailadm@city.maebashi.gunma.jp
HOMEPAGE http://www.city.maebashi.gunma.jp/english/index.htm
REMARKS

Matsudo City
Matsudo-shi 日本語表記
CATEGORY Politics/Administration:Local Governments:Major Cities
TYPE
ADDRESS 387-5 Nemoto, Matsudo-shi, Chiba 271-8588
PHONE +81-47-366-1111
FAX +81-47-363-3200
E-MAIL mcity@intership.ne.jp
HOMEPAGE http://www.intership.ne.jp/~mcity/english/index.htm
REMARKS

Matsue City
Matsue-shi 日本語表記
CATEGORY Politics/Administration:Local Governments:Major Cities
TYPE
ADDRESS 86 Suetsugu-cho, Matsue-shi, Shimane 690-8540
PHONE +81-852-55-5555
FAX +81-852-55-5530
E-MAIL
HOMEPAGE http://www.city.matsue.shimane.jp/
REMARKS

Matsuyama City
Matsuyama-shi 日本語表記
CATEGORY Politics/Administration:Local Governments:Major Cities
TYPE
ADDRESS 4-7-2 Nibancho, Matsuyama-shi, Ehime 790-8571
PHONE +81-899-48-6688
FAX

E-MAIL kouho@city.matsuyama.ehime.jp
HOMEPAGE http://www.city.matsuyama.ehime.jp/
REMARKS

Meguro City
Meguro-ku 日本語表記
CATEGORY Politics/Administration:Local Governments:Major Cities
TYPE
ADDRESS 2-19-15 Kamimeguro, Meguro-ku, Tokyo 153-8573
PHONE +81-3-3715-1111
FAX
E-MAIL
HOMEPAGE http://www.city.meguro.tokyo.jp/english/
REMARKS

Minato City
Minato-ku 日本語表記
CATEGORY Politics/Administration:Local Governments:Major Cities
TYPE
ADDRESS 1-5-25 Shiba Koen, Minato-ku, Tokyo 105-8511
PHONE +81-3-3578-2111
FAX +81-3-3578-2034
E-MAIL kuminkoho@city.minato.tokyo.jp
HOMEPAGE http://www.city.minato.tokyo.jp/e/index.html
REMARKS

Mito City
Mito-shi 日本語表記
CATEGORY Politics/Administration:Local Governments:Major Cities
TYPE
ADDRESS 1-4-1 Chuo, Mito-shi, Ibaraki 310-8610
PHONE +81-29-224-1111
FAX +81-29-232-9295
E-MAIL mitocity@po.net-ibaraki.ne.jp
HOMEPAGE http://www.city.mito.ibaraki.jp/english/index.htm
REMARKS

Miyazaki City
Miyazaki-shi 日本語表記
CATEGORY Politics/Administration:Local Governments:Major Cities
TYPE
ADDRESS 1-1-1 Tachibana-dori-Nishi, Miyazaki-shi, Miyazaki 880-8505
PHONE +81-985-25-2111
FAX +81-985-27-8070
E-MAIL mzkwebm@city.miyazaki.miyazaki.jp
HOMEPAGE http://www.city.miyazaki.miyazaki.jp:8084/html/english/outline/outline_e.htm
REMARKS

Morioka City
Morioka-shi 日本語表記
CATEGORY Politics/Administration:Local Governments:Major Cities
TYPE
ADDRESS 12-2 Uchimaru, Morioka-shi, Iwate 020-8530
PHONE +81-19-651-4111
FAX +81-19-622-6211
E-MAIL web@city.morioka.iwate.jp
HOMEPAGE http://www2.city.morioka.iwate.jp/e/

REMARKS

Nagano City

Nagano-shi 日本語表記

CATEGORY Politics/Administration:Local Governments:Major Cities
TYPE
ADDRESS 1613 Oaza Turuga, Midori-cho, Nagano-shi, Nagano 380-8512
PHONE +81-26-226-4911
FAX +81-26-224-5100
E-MAIL webadmi@city.nagano.nagano.jp
HOMEPAGE http://www.city.nagano.nagano.jp/english/index-e.htm
REMARKS

Nagasaki City

Nagasaki-shi 日本語表記

CATEGORY Politics/Administration:Local Governments:Major Cities
TYPE
ADDRESS 2-22 Sakura-machi, Nagasaki-shi, Nagasaki 850-8685
PHONE +81-958-25-5151
FAX
E-MAIL n_info@hkg.odn.ne.jp
HOMEPAGE http://www1.city.nagasaki.nagasaki.jp/index_e.html
REMARKS

Nagoya City

Nagoya-shi 日本語表記

CATEGORY Politics/Administration:Local Governments:Major Cities
TYPE
ADDRESS 3-1-1 Sannomaru, Naka-ku Nagoya-shi, Aichi 460-8508
PHONE +81-52-961-1111
FAX
E-MAIL
HOMEPAGE http://www.city.nagoya.jp/
REMARKS

Naha City

Naha-shi 日本語表記

CATEGORY Politics/Administration:Local Governments:Major Cities
TYPE
ADDRESS 1-1-1 Izumizaki, Naha-shi, Okinawa 900-8585
PHONE +81-98-867-0111
FAX +81-98-863-0777
E-MAIL
HOMEPAGE http://www.city.naha.okinawa.jp/kanko/nahatabi/index2.htm
REMARKS

Nakano City

Nakano-ku 日本語表記

CATEGORY Politics/Administration:Local Governments:Major Cities
TYPE
ADDRESS 4-8-1 Nakano, Nakano-ku, Tokyo 164-8501
PHONE +81-3-3389-1111
FAX +81-3-3228-5647
E-MAIL
HOMEPAGE http://www.city.nakano.tokyo.jp/
REMARKS

Nara City

Nara-shi

CATEGORY	Politics/Administration:Local Governments:Major Cities
TYPE	
ADDRESS	1-1-1 Nijo-Oji-Minami, Nara-shi, Nara 630-8580
PHONE	+81-742-34-1111
FAX	+81-742-35-4856
E-MAIL	densan@city.nara.nara.jp
HOMEPAGE	http://www.city.nara.nara.jp/english/index.htm
REMARKS	

Nerima City

Nerima-ku

CATEGORY	Politics/Administration:Local Governments:Major Cities
TYPE	
ADDRESS	6-12-1 Toyotama-Kita, Nerima-ku, Tokyo 176-8501
PHONE	+81-3-3993-1111
FAX	+81-3-3993-4106
E-MAIL	ku@city.nerima.tokyo.jp
HOMEPAGE	http://www.city.nerima.tokyo.jp/ (Japanese only)
REMARKS	

Niigata City

Niigata-shi

CATEGORY	Politics/Administration:Local Governments:Major Cities
TYPE	
ADDRESS	602-1 Gakkocho-dori Ichiban-cho, Niigata-shi, Niigata 951-8550
PHONE	+81-25-228-1000
FAX	+81-25-228-5500
E-MAIL	soumu@city.niigata.niigata.jp
HOMEPAGE	http://www.city.niigata.niigata.jp
REMARKS	

Nishinomiya City

Nishinomiya-shi

CATEGORY	Politics/Administration:Local Governments:Major Cities
TYPE	
ADDRESS	10-3 Rokutanji-cho, Nishinomiya-shi, Hyogo 662-8567
PHONE	+81-798-35-3151
FAX	
E-MAIL	
HOMEPAGE	http://www.nishi.or.jp/ (Japanese only)
REMARKS	

Oita City

Oita-shi

CATEGORY	Politics/Administration:Local Governments:Major Cities
TYPE	
ADDRESS	2-31 Niage-machi, Oita-shi, Oita 870-8504
PHONE	+81-97-534-6111
FAX	+81-97-536-1461
E-MAIL	kochokoho@city.oita.oita.jp
HOMEPAGE	http://www.city.oita.oita.jp/en/index.html
REMARKS	

Okayama City

Okayama-shi

CATEGORY Politics/Administration:Local Governments:Major Cities
TYPE
ADDRESS 1-1-1 Daiku, Okayama-shi, Okayama 700-8544
PHONE +81-86-803-1000
FAX +81-86-225-5487
E-MAIL jouhou@city.okayama.okayama.jp
HOMEPAGE http://www.city.okayama.okayama.jp/index-e.htm
REMARKS

Okazaki City
Okazaki-shi 日本語表記
CATEGORY Politics/Administration:Local Governments:Major Cities
TYPE
ADDRESS 2-9 Juo-cho, Okazaki-shi, Aichi 444-8601
PHONE +81-564-23-6495
FAX +81-564-23-6262
E-MAIL mail@city.okazaki.aichi.jp
HOMEPAGE http://www.city.okazaki.aichi.jp/kurasi/english/guide.htm
REMARKS

Osaka City
Osaka-shi 日本語表記
CATEGORY Politics/Administration:Local Governments:Major Cities
TYPE
ADDRESS 1-3-20 Nakanoshima, Kita-ku Osaka-shi, Osaka 530-8201
PHONE +81-6-6208-8181
FAX
E-MAIL
HOMEPAGE http://www.city.osaka.jp/english/index.html
REMARKS

Ota City
Ota-ku 日本語表記
CATEGORY Politics/Administration:Local Governments:Major Cities
TYPE
ADDRESS 5-13-14 Kamata, Ota-ku, Tokyo 144-8621
PHONE +81-3-5744-1111
FAX +81-3-5744-1503
E-MAIL koho@city.ota.tokyo.jp
HOMEPAGE http://www.city.ota.tokyo.jp/
REMARKS

Otsu City
Otsu-shi 日本語表記
CATEGORY Politics/Administration:Local Governments:Major Cities
TYPE
ADDRESS 3-1 Goryo-cho, Otsu-shi, Shiga 520-8575
PHONE +81-77-523-1234
FAX
E-MAIL otsu001@mx.cable-net.ne.jp
HOMEPAGE http://www.city.otsu.shiga.jp/
REMARKS

Saga City
Saga-shi 日本語表記
CATEGORY Politics/Administration:Local Governments:Major Cities
TYPE

ADDRESS 1-1 Sakae-machi, Saga-shi, Saga 840-8501
PHONE +81-952-24-3151
FAX +81-952-29-2095
E-MAIL mweb@city.saga.saga.jp
HOMEPAGE http://www.city.saga.saga.jp/en/
REMARKS

Sagamihara City
Sagamihara-shi 日本語表記
CATEGORY Politics/Administration:Local Governments:Major Cities
TYPE
ADDRESS 2-11-15 Chuo, Sagamihara-shi, Kanagawa 229-8611
PHONE +81-42-754-1111
FAX +81-42-753-9413
E-MAIL
HOMEPAGE http://www.city.sagamihara.kanagawa.jp/topold/top_e.html
REMARKS

Saitama City
Saitama-shi 日本語表記
CATEGORY Politics/Administration:Local Governments:Major Cities
TYPE
ADDRESS 6-4-4 Tokiwa, Saitama-shi, Saitama 336-8633
PHONE +81-48-829-1111
FAX
E-MAIL
HOMEPAGE http://www.city.saitama.saitama.jp/
REMARKS From 1 April 2003, the URL will change to http://www.city.saitama.jp/

Sakai City
Sakai-shi 日本語表記
CATEGORY Politics/Administration:Local Governments:Major Cities
TYPE
ADDRESS 3-1 Minami-Kawara-machi, Sakai-shi, Osaka 590-0078
PHONE +81-722-33-1101
FAX
E-MAIL info@city.sakai.osaka.jp
HOMEPAGE http://www.city.sakai.osaka.jp/index_e.html
REMARKS

Sapporo City
Sapporo-shi 日本語表記
CATEGORY Politics/Administration:Local Governments:Major Cities
TYPE
ADDRESS Kita-1, Nishi-2, Chuo-ku Sapporo-shi, Hokkaido 060-8611
PHONE +81-11-211-2111
FAX
E-MAIL sicpfcvb@poplar.ocn.ne.jp
HOMEPAGE http://www.global.city.sapporo.jp/
REMARKS

Sendai City
Sendai-shi 日本語表記
CATEGORY Politics/Administration:Local Governments:Major Cities
TYPE
ADDRESS 3-7-1 Kokubun-cho, Aoba-ku Sendai-shi, Miyagi 980-8671
PHONE +81-22-261-1111

FAX
E-MAIL www-ad@city.sendai.jp
HOMEPAGE http://www.city.sendai.jp/index-e.html
REMARKS

Shibuya City

Shibuya-ku 日本語表記
CATEGORY Politics/Administration:Local Governments:Major Cities
TYPE
ADDRESS 1-1 Udagawa-cho, Shibuya-ku, Tokyo 150-8010
PHONE +81-3-3463-1211
FAX
E-MAIL koho@city.shibuya.tokyo.jp
HOMEPAGE http://www.city.shibuya.tokyo.jp/ (Japanese only)
REMARKS

Shinagawa City

Shinagawa-ku 日本語表記
CATEGORY Politics/Administration:Local Governments:Major Cities
TYPE
ADDRESS 2-1-36 Hiromachi, Shinagawa-ku, Tokyo 140-8715
PHONE +81-3-5742-6625
FAX +81-3-3774-6356
E-MAIL
HOMEPAGE http://www.city.shinagawa.tokyo.jp
REMARKS

Shinjuku City

Shinjuku-ku 日本語表記
CATEGORY Politics/Administration:Local Governments:Major Cities
TYPE
ADDRESS 1-4-1 Kabuki-cho, Shinjuku-ku, Tokyo 160-8484
PHONE +81-3-3209-1111
FAX +81-3-3209-9947
E-MAIL kocho@city.shinjuku.tokyo.jp
HOMEPAGE http://www.city.shinjuku.tokyo.jp/ (Japanese only)
REMARKS

Shizuoka City

Shizuoka-shi 日本語表記
CATEGORY Politics/Administration:Local Governments:Major Cities
TYPE
ADDRESS 5-1 Ote-machi, Shizuoka-shi, Shizuoka 420-8602
PHONE +81-54-254-2111
FAX +81-54-221-1005
E-MAIL info@city.shizuoka.shizuoka.jp
HOMEPAGE http://www.city.shizuoka.shizuoka.jp/
REMARKS

Suginami City

Suginami-ku 日本語表記
CATEGORY Politics/Administration:Local Governments:Major Cities
TYPE
ADDRESS 1-15-1 Asagaya-Minami, Suginami-ku, Tokyo 166-8570
PHONE +81-3-3312-2111
FAX +81-3-3312-9912
E-MAIL

HOMEPAGE http://www.city.suginami.tokyo.jp/ (Japanese only)
REMARKS

Suita City
Suita-shi 日本語表記
CATEGORY Politics/Administration:Local Governments:Major Cities
TYPE
ADDRESS 1-3-40 Izumi-cho, Suita-shi, Osaka 564-8550
PHONE +81-6-6384-1231
FAX +81-6-6337-1631
E-MAIL s_koho@city.suita.osaka.jp
HOMEPAGE http://www.city.suita.osaka.jp/ (Japanese only)
REMARKS

Sumida City
Sumida-ku 日本語表記
CATEGORY Politics/Administration:Local Governments:Major Cities
TYPE
ADDRESS 1-23-20 Azumabashi, Sumida-ku, Tokyo 130-8640
PHONE +81-3-5608-1111
FAX +81-3-5608-6408
E-MAIL
HOMEPAGE http://www.city.sumida.tokyo.jp/english/index.html
REMARKS

Taito City
Taito-ku 日本語表記
CATEGORY Politics/Administration:Local Governments:Major Cities
TYPE
ADDRESS 4-5-6 Higashi-Ueno, Taito-ku, Tokyo 110-8615
PHONE +81-3-5246-1111
FAX +81-3-5246-1147
E-MAIL kokusai@city.taito.tokyo.jp
HOMEPAGE http://www.city.taito.tokyo.jp/taito-co/english/indexe.html
REMARKS

Takamatsu City
Takamatsu-shi 日本語表記
CATEGORY Politics/Administration:Local Governments:Major Cities
TYPE
ADDRESS 1-8-15 Ban-cho, Takamatsu-shi, Kagawa 760-8571
PHONE +81-87-839-2011
FAX +81-87-839-2190
E-MAIL webmaster@city.takamatsu.kagawa.jp
HOMEPAGE http://www.city.takamatsu.kagawa.jp/english/index.html
REMARKS

Takatsuki City
Takatsuki-shi 日本語表記
CATEGORY Politics/Administration:Local Governments:Major Cities
TYPE
ADDRESS 2-1 Toen-cho, Takatsuki-shi, Osaka 569-0067
PHONE +81-726-74-7111
FAX
E-MAIL
HOMEPAGE http://www.city.takatsuki.osaka.jp/ (Japanese only)
REMARKS

the City of Kanazawa

Kanazawa-shi 日本語表記

CATEGORY	Politics/Administration:Local Governments:Major Cities
TYPE	
ADDRESS	1-1-1 Hirosaka, Kanazawa Ishikawa 920-8577
PHONE	+81-76-220-2111
FAX	+81-76-261-7755
E-MAIL	webmaster@city.kanazawa.ishikawa.jp
HOMEPAGE	http://www.city.kanazawa.ishikawa.jp/
REMARKS	

Tokorozawa City

Tokorozawa-shi 日本語表記

CATEGORY	Politics/Administration:Local Governments:Major Cities
TYPE	
ADDRESS	1-1-1 Namiki, Tokorozawa-shi, Saitama 359-8501
PHONE	+81-42-998-1111
FAX	
E-MAIL	
HOMEPAGE	http://www.city.tokorozawa.saitama.jp/
REMARKS	

Tokushima City

Tokushima-shi 日本語表記

CATEGORY	Politics/Administration:Local Governments:Major Cities
TYPE	
ADDRESS	2-5 Saiwai-cho, Tokushima-shi, Tokushima 770-8571
PHONE	+81-88-621-5111
FAX	+81-88-654-2116
E-MAIL	koho@city.tokushima.tokushima.jp
HOMEPAGE	http://www.city.tokushima.tokushima.jp (Japanese only)
REMARKS	

Toshima City

Toshima-ku 日本語表記

CATEGORY	Politics/Administration:Local Governments:Major Cities
TYPE	
ADDRESS	1-18-1 Higashi-Ikebukuro, Toshima-ku, Tokyo 170-8422
PHONE	+81-3-3981-1111
FAX	
E-MAIL	kohoka@t.toshima.ne.jp
HOMEPAGE	http://www.city.toshima.tokyo.jp/
REMARKS	

Tottori City

Tottori-shi 日本語表記

CATEGORY	Politics/Administration:Local Governments:Major Cities
TYPE	
ADDRESS	116 Shotoku-cho, Tottori-shi, Tottori 680-0017
PHONE	+81-857-22-8111
FAX	+81-857-20-3040
E-MAIL	pl-tori@city.tottori.tottori.jp
HOMEPAGE	http://www.city.tottori.tottori.jp/top/e_index.htm
REMARKS	

Toyama City

Toyama-shi 日本語表記
CATEGORY Politics/Administration:Local Governments:Major Cities
TYPE
ADDRESS 7-38 Shin-Sakura-machi, Toyama-shi, Toyama 930-8510
PHONE +81-764-31-6111
FAX
E-MAIL info@city.toyama.toyama.jp
HOMEPAGE http://www.city.toyama.toyama.jp/
REMARKS

Toyohashi City
Toyohashi-shi 日本語表記
CATEGORY Politics/Administration:Local Governments:Major Cities
TYPE
ADDRESS 1 Imahashi-cho, Toyohashi-shi, Aichi 440-8501
PHONE +81-532-51-2111
FAX +81-532-56-5711
E-MAIL kohokocho@city-toyohashi.jp
HOMEPAGE http://www.city.toyohashi.aichi.jp/menu_w.html
REMARKS

Toyonaka City
Toyonaka-shi 日本語表記
CATEGORY Politics/Administration:Local Governments:Major Cities
TYPE
ADDRESS 3-1-1 Naka-Sakurazuka, Toyonaka-shi, Osaka 561-8501
PHONE +81-6-6858-2525
FAX +81-6-6854-8089
E-MAIL koe@city.toyonaka.osaka.jp
HOMEPAGE http://www.city.toyonaka.osaka.jp/
REMARKS

Toyota City
Toyota-shi 日本語表記
CATEGORY Politics/Administration:Local Governments:Major Cities
TYPE
ADDRESS 3-60 Nishi-machi, Toyota-shi, Aichi 471-8501
PHONE +81-565-31-1212
FAX +81-565-33-2221
E-MAIL
HOMEPAGE http://www.city.toyota.aichi.jp/
REMARKS

Tsu City
Tsu-shi 日本語表記
CATEGORY Politics/Administration:Local Governments:Major Cities
TYPE
ADDRESS 23-1 Nishi-Marunouchi, Tsu-shi, Mie 514-8611
PHONE +81-59-229-3144
FAX +81-59-221-1173
E-MAIL siminka@city.tsu.mie.jp
HOMEPAGE http://www.info.city.tsu.mie.jp
REMARKS

Utsunomiya City
Utsunomiya-shi 日本語表記
CATEGORY Politics/Administration:Local Governments:Major Cities

TYPE
ADDRESS 1-1-5 Asahi, Utsunomiya-shi, Tochigi 320-8540
PHONE +81-28-632-2222
FAX +81-28-639-0627
E-MAIL u0302@city.utsunomiya.tochigi.jp
HOMEPAGE http://www.city.utsunomiya.tochigi.jp/ (Japanese only)
REMARKS

Wakayama City

Wakayama-shi 日本語表記
CATEGORY Politics/Administration:Local Governments:Major Cities
TYPE
ADDRESS 23 Nanaban-cho, Wakayama-shi, Wakayama 640-8511
PHONE +81-73-432-0001
FAX +81-73-423-4625
E-MAIL koucho@city.wakayama.wakayama.jp
HOMEPAGE http://www.city.wakayama.wakayama.jp/ (Japanese only)
REMARKS

Yamagata City

Yamagata-shi 日本語表記
CATEGORY Politics/Administration:Local Governments:Major Cities
TYPE
ADDRESS 2-3-25, Hatago-machi Yamagata-shi, Yamagata 990-8540
PHONE +81-23-641-1212
FAX +81-23-624-8899
E-MAIL kouhou@city.yamagata.yamagata.jp
HOMEPAGE http://www.city.yamagata.yamagata.jp/ (Japanese only)
REMARKS

Yamaguchi City

Yamaguchi-shi 日本語表記
CATEGORY Politics/Administration:Local Governments:Major Cities
TYPE
ADDRESS 2-1 Kameyama-cho, Yamaguchi-shi, Yamaguchi 753-8650
PHONE +81-83-934-2753
FAX +81-83-934-2643
E-MAIL koho@city.yamaguchi.yamaguchi.jp
HOMEPAGE http://www.city.yamaguchi.yamaguchi.jp/english/index.html
REMARKS

Yokosuka City

Yokosuka-shi 日本語表記
CATEGORY Politics/Administration:Local Governments:Major Cities
TYPE
ADDRESS 11 Ogawa-cho, Yokosuka-shi, Kanagawa 238-8550
PHONE +81-468-22-4000
FAX +81-468-22-7795
E-MAIL am-ga@city.yokosuka.kanagawa.jp
HOMEPAGE http://www.city.yokosuka.kanagawa.jp/e/index.html

REGIONAL BEREAU OF ECONOMU, TRADE & INDUSTRY

HOKKAIDO BUREAU OF ECONOMY, TRADE AND INDUSTRY

GENERAL COORDINATION AND POLICY PLANNING DEPARTMENT

General Affairs Division

Comprehensive coordination of the Bureau's office duties and the work related to policy evaluation

011-709-2311(Ext.2503 - 2506)

hokkaido-somu@meti.go.jp

Public Relations Office

Work related to public relations and information disclosure

011-709-2311(Ext.2507 - 2508)

hokkaido-koho@meti.go.jp

Information Systems Office

Work related to the improvement and administration of information processing systems

011-709-2311(Ext.2545 - 2546)

hokkaido-system@meti.go.jp

Office for the Promotion of Structural Improvement

Work related to the promotion of economic structural reform

011-709-2311(Ext.2520 - 2522)

hokkaido-kikaku@meti.go.jp

Budget and Accounts Division

Work related to budgets, national properties and the management of commodities

011-709-2311(Ext.2510 - 2517)

hokkaido-kaikei@meti.go.jp

Policy Planning Division

Work related to planning of policies on the revitalization of the regional economy

011-709-2311(Ext.2520 - 2522)

hokkaido-kikaku@meti.go.jp

Research Division

Work related to statistical surveys on mining and industrial production trends, large-scale retail stores' sales trends, etc.

011-709-2311(Ext.2525 - 2527、2530 - 2531)

hokkaido-chosa@meti.go.jp

INDUSTRIES DEPARTMENT

Policy Division

Work related to finance, tax systems, chambers of commerce and industry and bicycle racing

011-709-2311(Ext.2552 - 2553)

hokkaido-seisaku@meti.go.jp

Super Cluster Promotion Office

Work related to encourage the formation of bio-industrial clusters(networks) and information technology clusters(networks)

011-709-2311(Ext.2552 - 2553)

"Hokkaido Super Cluster Promotion Project" (02/09/18)

Food Machines Industry Policy Office

Work related to the promotion of "food-"related industries

011-709-2311(Ext.2552 - 2553)

hokkaido-food@meti.go.jp

Bio-industries Promotion Office

Work related to the promotion of bio-industries

011-709-2311(Ext.2554 - 2555)

hokkaido-bio@meti.go.jp

Service Industry Office

Work related to service industries, tourism-related industries and industries for an aging society

011-709-2311(Ext.2558)

hokkaido-shinki@meti.go.jp

New Business Promotion Division

Work related to the creation of new business, and support of venture companies and business startup

011-709-2311(Ext.2560 - 2561)

hokkaido-shinki@meti.go.jp

Information Policy Division

Work related to the promotion of information processing industries and computerization of regions and companies

011-709-2311(Ext.2565 - 2567)

hokkaido-joho@meti.go.jp

Manufacturing Industries Division

Work related to the promotion of manufacturing industries under the jurisdiction, such as the steel industry, machine industry, and pulp and paper industry

011-709-2311(Ext.2570 - 2571)

hokkaido-seizo@meti.go.jp

Small and Medium Enterprise Division

Work related to comprehensive coordination of measures for small and medium enterprises, countermeasures for small-scale enterprises and measures to promote small and medium subcontractor enterprises

011-709-2311(Ext.2575 - 2578)

hokkaido-chusho@meti.go.jp

Industrial Technology Division

Work related to the promotion of industrial

technologies, subsidies for technology, research and development, and industrial standardization

011-709-2311(Ext.2584 - 2589)

hokkaido-gijutsu@meti.go.jp

Patent Office

Work related to the information provision and guidance regarding industrial property rights

011-709-2311(Ext.2584 - 2589)

hokkaido-tokkyo@meti.go.jp

REGIONAL DEVELOPMENT AND PROMOTION GROUP

Regional Development Division

Work related to the planning of policies regarding regional industrial promotion

011-709-2311(Ext.2591 - 2593)

hokkaido-chiiki@meti.go.jp

Regional Economy Promotion Office

Work related to the dissemination of measures among local companies, and the finding and support of regional projects

011-709-2311(Ext.2594)

hokkaido-chiiki-shitsu@meti.go.jp

Industrial Location Division

Work related to the improvement of the industrial infrastructure for industrial location and promotion of the invitation of enterprises

011-709-2311(Ext.2595 - 2597)

hokkaido-ricchi@meti.go.jp

International Affairs Division

Work related to the promotion of the internationalization of regio

011-709-2311(Ext.2605 - 2606)

hokkaido-kokusai@meti.go.jp

Distribution Industry Division

Work related to improved efficiency and optimization of physical distribution of commodities, and to department stores and large-scale retail stores

011-709-2311(Ext.2580 - 2581)

hokkaido-ryutsu@meti.go.jp

Commerce Promotion Office

Work related to the promotion of small and medium retail commerce and of revitalization of urban areas

011-709-2311(Ext.2580 - 2581)

hokkaido-shogyo@meti.go.jp

Consumer Affairs Division

Work related to securing the safety of consumer products for daily use, and improvement of transactions and commodity prices

011-709-2311(Ext.2610 - 2611)

hokkaido-shohi@meti.go.jp

Consumer Advice Office

Work related to securing the safety of consumer products for daily use, and improvement of transactions and commodity prices

011-709-1785

ENVIRONMENTAL AFFAIRS AND NATURAL RESOURCES DEPARTMENT

Environmental Affairs and Natural Resources Division

Work related to mining, quarrying and gravel collection

011-709-2311(Ext.2621 - 2623)

hokkaido-kankyoshigen@meti.go.jp

Environmental Industries Promotion Office

Work related to the promotion of environmental industries

011-709-2311(Ext.2623 - 2624)

hokkaido-kankyoshinko@meti.go.jp

Environmental Protection Administration Division

Work related to the promotion of recycling and environmental preservation

011-709-2311(Ext.2625 - 2627)

hokkaido-kankyotaisaku@meti.go.jp

Energy Policy Division

Work related to comprehensive energy measures and energy saving measures

011-709-2311(Ext.2635 - 2636)

hokkaido-energy@meti.go.jp

New and Renewable Energy Division

Work related to the promotion of development and introduction of new energies

011-709-2311(Ext.2637 - 2638)

hokkaido-new-energy@meti.go.jp

Petroleum Division

Work related to supply and demand of petroleum products and securing the quality of petroleum products

011-709-2311(Ext.2640 - 2642)

hokkaido-sekiyu@meti.go.jp

Mining Division

Work related to mining rights and implementation of mining, and studies and development of mineral resources

011-709-2311(Ext.2645 - 2649)

hokkaido-kogyo@meti.go.jp

Coal Industry Division

Work related to the implementation and structural coordination of coal mining, and supply, demand, distribution and prices of coal

011-709-2311(Ext.2655 - 2656)

hokkaido-sekitan-jigyo@meti.go.jp

Alcohol Division

Work related to manufacture, management and sales of industrial alcohol

011-709-2311(Ext.2630 - 2631)

hokkaido-alcohol@meti.go.jp

ELECTRICITY AND GAS INDUSTRY DEPARTMENT

Electricity and Gas Industry Policy Division

Work related to electricity and gas on the whole, electric utilities and the heat supply business

011-709-2311(Ext.2702 - 2704)

hokkaido-denryokugas@meti.go.jp

Office for the Public Acceptance of the Nuclear Energy

Work related to public relations of nuclear power

011-709-2311(Ext.2702 - 2704)

hokkaido-denryokugas@meti.go.jp

Electric Power Development and Planning Division

Work related to electric power development plans, supply and demand plans for electricity and the promotion of areas of electric power sources

011-709-2311(Ext.2710 - 2712)

hokkaido-kaihatsukeikaku@meti.go.jp

Electric Power Safety Division

Work related to electric facilities, electric accident prevention countermeasure and the regulation of electric appliances

011-709-2311(Ext.2720 - 2722、2730 - 2732)

hokkaido-denryokuanzen@meti.go.jp

Gas Industry Division

Work related to approval of gas-related business, gas supply plans and statistical surveys on the gas business

011-709-2311(Ext.2740 - 2741)

hokkaido-gasjigyo@meti.go.jp

Safety Division

Work related to gas facilities, gas accident prevention countermeasure and the regulation of explosives

011-709-2311(Ext.2745 - 2746)

hokkaido-hoan@meti.go.jp

KANTO BUREAU OF ECONOMY, TRADE AND INDUSTRY

HEAD OFFICE

Address :	2-11 Kamiochiai, Saitama-shi, Saitama- ken
Postal Code :	330-9715
Telephone Number :	048-

TOKYO INTERNATIONAL TRADE OFFICE

Address :	4-6-15 Yushima, Bunkyo-ku, Tokyo-to
Postal Code :	113-0034
Telephone Number :	03-5842-7071
Facsimile Number :	03-5689-7841
Access :	12 minutes walk from JR "Okachimachi" station 5 minutes walk from Subway Chiyoda Line "Yushima" station

YOKOHAMA INTERNATIONAL TRADE OFFICE

Address :	1-1 Kaigan-Dori, Naka-ku, Yokohama-shi, Kanagawa-ken
Postal Code :	231-0002
Telephone Number :	045-201-9606
Facsimile Number :	045-201-7156
Access :	15 minutes walk from JR Negishi Line "Kannai" station 15 minutes walk from Municipal Subway Line "Kannai" station

KANZAI FAZ

With the 1992 introduction of the Law on Extraordinary Measures for the Promotion of Imports and the Facilitation of Foreign Direct Investment in Japan, the government authorized 4 districts in Kansai as Foreign Access Zones, or FAZ.

Host regions offer a variety of incentives, including preferential taxation, low-interest financing and more, to encourage foreign businesses to relocate in their respective areas and resident firms to expand their imports.

Whether your objective in Japan is to enhance export capabilities or establish a corporate presence in the local market, opening the Kansai FAZ door will take you to the most effective results possible.

Situated at the center of Japan and including the three major cities of Osaka, Kobe and Kyoto, Kansai is one of Japan's major economic zones.

Kansai is open to business people from around the world.
Its huge market, which accounts for about 20 percent of the entire GDP of Japan, provides you with plenty of business opportunities.

Attractions of KANSAI

1. The Kansai market is vast, accounting for 3 percent of world GDP. Various industries are located in Kansai.

2. Kansai is home to many companies active on the world stage as well as wide variety of supporting industries.

3. Kansai has been active in promoting venture enterprise. Many types of new business have originated in Kansai.

4. Kansai has vast potential in the field of research and development.

5. Kansai has created positive international business opportunities.

6. Kansai boasts convenient access to all major cities in Japan and throughout Asia.

7.Kansai enjoys a long and rich history and its residents enjoy a high standard living.

8. Networking and Support Systems are available.

Characteristics of Osaka Prefecture FAZ

Taking advantage of the construction of Kansai International Airport (KIX) and the development of Rinku Town, which is located the shore opposite the new airport, the area centered around the two major projects, which includes parts of Izumisano and Sennan cities and Tajiri Town, was designated as the Foreign Access Zone of Osaka Prefecture. The new zone will be further improved as a focal point for global business. Osaka Prefecture FAZ is aimed at creating the most favorable conditions for markets of commercial transactions, especially imported goods and new business opportunities.

The Osaka Prefectural Government is in the process of developing Rinku Town, which is located on the shore opposite Kansai International Airport. The government hopes Rinku Town will become a global hub for people, goods and information collected through the new airport, and as a center for business in Asia-Pacific region. Rinku Town primarily consists of a commercial and business zone, which is being improved under the concept of becoming a "Pacific City". The zone is intended to become an international business area in the 21st century.

·Rinku International Logistics Co., Ltd.

2-21, Rinku Ohrai-kita, Izumisano City, Osaka 598-0048, Japan Tel:+81-724-69-5111 Fax:+81-724-69-5211

·Rinku Gate Tower Building Co., Ltd.

1,Rinku Ohrai-kita , Izumisano City , Osaka 598-8525, Japan Tel:+81-724-60-1010 Fax:+81-724-60-1002

Characteristics of Kyoto FAZ

■Gateway port on the Japan Sea in Kansai region(Regular lines to Korea, China and Russia)

Maizuru Port boasts regular container ship lines to the principal ports of Korea and China.
A transshipment service to Pusan Port (Korea) provides marine transport for various destinations throughout

the world including Southeast Asia, Europe and the Americas.
A large-capacity high-speed ferryboat line provides a domestic line between Maizuru and Otaru (Hokkaido).

◇Line to Korea (Maizuru - Pusan line :2 per week)

Shipping Routes	Company
Pusan(SAT.)-Toyama(MON.)-Kanazawa(TUE.)-Tsuruga(WED.)-Maizuru(WED)-Pusan(THU.)	(HEUNG-A)
Pusan(SAT.)-Maizuru(MON.)-Tsuruga(MON.)-Kanazawa(TUE.)-Toyama(WED.) Sakai(THU.)-Pusan(FRI.)	(KMTC)

◇Line to China (Maizuru - Dailian･Qingdao line :weekly)

Shipping Route	Company
Qingdao(WED.)-Dailian(FRI.)-Hakata(MON.)-Kokura(TUE.)-Maizuru(THU.)-Qingdao(MON.)	(CMST)

▪Highway networks connecting to Kansai region

A network of highways connecting the cities of Kyoto (95㎞ from Maizuru), Osaka (125㎞) and Kobe(120㎞) enable one to travel to the next city in just one and a half hours.

▪Prompt clearance procedures

Trade-related governmental offices including the customs house, the immigration office, and the quarantine office are concentrated in Maizuru Port to help users promptly respond to customs procedures for export and import. Swift import clearance enables users to transport imported cargoes to the Kyoto-Osaka-Kobe district in just one day.

▪Exhibition and business conventions for countries located on the Sea of Japan

Exhibitions and business conventions for importation of goods among countries located on the Sea of Japan are held to expand economic exchange and promote business opportunities for trade related enterprises of those countries.

·Maizuru 21 Inc.

8th Floor Maizuru 21 Building,1105-1 Azakita, Maizuru, Kyoto 624-0945, Japan
Tel:+81-773-77-2421 Fax:+81-773-77-2420

CHUGOKU BEREAU OF ECONOMY TRADE AND INDUSTRY

▪ Tottori Prefectural Government Industrial Location Division
1-220, Higashi-machi, Tottori 680-8570 Tel:(0857)26-7220 Fax:(0857)21-0609
[URL]http://www.toriton.or.jp/~rich/index.htm [E-mail]rich@toriton.or.jp

■ **Shimane Prefectural Government Industrial Promotion Division**
1, Tono-machi, Matsue 690-8501 Tel:(0852)22-5295 Fax:(0852)22-6080
[URL]http://www.joho-shimane.or.jp/pref/english/site_e/site.html [E-mail]rich@joho-shimane.or.jp

■ **Okayama Prefectural Government Industry Placement Division**
4-6, Uchisange 2-chome, Okayama 700-8570 Tel:(086)224-2111 Fax:(086)221-2683
[URL]http://www.optic.or.jp/index_e.html [E-mail]info@optic.or.jp

■ **Hiroshima Prefectural Government Enterprise Promotion Division**
10-52, Moto-machi, Naka-ku, Hiroshima 730-8511 Tel:(082)223-5050 Fax:(082)223-2136
[URL]http://www.pref.hiroshima.jp/shoukou/ricchi/ricchi/rit-e1.html

■ **Yamaguchi Prefectural Government Enterprise Promotion Division**
1-1, Taki-machi, Yamaguchi 753-8501 Tel:(083)933-3145 Fax:(083)933-3178
[URL]http://www.pref.yamaguchi.jp/eindex.htm

■ **The City of Hiroshima Business Placement Promotion Office**
6-34, Kokutaiji-machi 1-chome, Naka-ku, Hiroshima 730-8586 Tel:(082)504-2241 Fax:(082)504-2259
[URL]http://www.business.econ.city.hiroshima.jp/ [E-mail]world@business.econ.city.hiroshima.jp

■ **The Japan Regional Development Corporation Location Promotion Division**
8-1, Kasumigaseki 3-chome, Chiyoda-ku, Tokyo 100-0013 Tel:(03)3501-5211 Fax:(03)3581-1345
[URL]http://www5.mediagalaxy.co.jp/chiiki/search/cyugoku/cyugoku.html

■ **The Chugoku Electric Power Co.,Inc.Economic Research Center**
4-33, Komachi, Naka-ku, Hiroshima 730-8701 Tel:(082)523-6441 Fax:(082)523-6445
[URL]http://www.energia.co.jp/top/index2.html [E-mail]economic@inet.energia.co.jp

■ **Chugoku Bureau of International Trade and Industry International Affairs Division**
6-30, Kamihatchobori, Naka-ku, Hiroshima 730-8531 Tel:(082)224-5655 Fax:(082)222-3094
[E-mail]qchgix@miti.go.jp

■ **Chugoku Region Investment Promotion Conference**
6-30, Kamihatchobori, Naka-ku, Hiroshima 730-8531 Tel:(082)224-5655 Fax:(082)222-3094
[E-mail]qchgix@miti.go.jp

KUUSHI BEREAU OF ECONOMY TRADE AND INDUSTRY

The Foreign Access Zone Project aims at facilitating imports into the Japanese market, to which Japan is committed. Foreign Access Zones (FAZ) are established where import-related facilities, businesses, etc., are to be concentrated in and around certain international airports and harbors. In Kyushu, the following four areas have been officially designated as FAZ.

.	Kitakyushu FAZ	Nagasaki FAZ	Oita FAZ	Kumamoto FAZ
Area	Kitakyushu City, Fukuoka Prefecture	Omura City, Nagasaki Prefecture	Oita City and Beppu City, Oita Prefecture	Kumamoto City and Mashiki Town, Kumamoto Prefecture
Year of Designation	1992	1992	1993	1994
Hub Port/Airport	Kitakyushu Port	Nagasaki Airport	Oita Port	Kumamoto Port
Project Organization	*Kitakyushu Import Promotion Center Co., Ltd.	*Nagasaki International Air Cargo Terminal Co.Ltd.	Oita International Trade Center Co., Ltd.	Kumamoto FAZ Co., Ltd.
Outline	The designated area includes the north	Nagasaki Airport Island and the	In the Ozai public wharf district in Oita	Distribution Center in the Port of

	exit zone of Kokura Station and the harbor districts in Kitakyushu City. As the 1st-phase project, the following were established: Kitakyushu International Distribution Center (KID) in the Tachinoura area in Moji Ward (facility for distributing imported goods); Asian Pacific Import Mart (AIM) in the north exit area of Kokura Station (facility for spporting the import business).	opposite shore. As the 1st-phase project, the following were established: airline cargo handling facilities on the airport island; Nagasaki Airport International Distribution Center with the freight agency building. As the 2nd-phase project, import support facilities were established on the opposite shore.	Port, facilities to support distribution and business were established as the import base for goods from Asian countries in eastern Kyushu.	Kumamoto is scheduled to open in Spring 1999

SEMICONDUCTORS

No.	Company Name	Address	TEL	FAX
1	TOSHIBA CORPORATION SEMICONDUCTOR COMPANY, KITAKYUSHU OPERATIONS	1-10-1 Shimoitozu, Kokurakita-ku, Kitakyushu-shi, Fukuoka 803-8686	+81-93-562-1402	+81-93-562-1405
2	SAKAMOTO ELECTRIC MFG. CO., LTD.	3-27-55 Wajiro, Higashi-ku, Fukuoka-shi, Fukuoka 811-0202	+81-92-606-2731	+81-92-608-1984
3	ULVAC KYUSHU CORPORATION	Kyoei Bldg. 3-F, 2-1-13 Toko, Hakata-ku, Fukuoka-shi, Fukuoka 812-0008	+81-92-473-7191	+81-92-473-7672
4	HAYASHI CO., LTD.	2-7-22 Enokida, Hakata-ku, Fukuoka-shi, Fukuoka 812-0004	+81-92-472-7306	+81-92-472-7339
5	TOSHIBA LSI PACKAGE SOLUTIONS CORPORATION	476-1 Kamiokuma, Miyata-machi, Kurate-gun, Fukuoka 823-0005	+81-949-33-1515	+81-949-33-3950
6	TOKYO ELECTRON KYUSHU LIMITED	1375-41 Nishishin-machi, Tosu-shi, Saga 841-0074	+81-942-81-1800	+81-942-81-1755
7	SAGA ELECTRONICS CO., LTD.	950 Tateno, Mitagawa-cho, Kanzaki-gun, Saga 842-0032	+81-952-52-3181	+81-952-52-3214
8	ISAHAYA ELECTRONICS CORPORATION	6-41 Tsukuba-machi, Isahata-shi, Nagasaki 854-0065	+81-957-26-3592	+81-957-20-9810
9	OGATA INDUSTRIAL CO., LTD.	2-9-9 Kamikumamoto, Kumamoto-shi, Kumamoto 860-0079	+81-96-352-4450	+81-96-352-0807

10	MITSUBISHI ELECTRIC CORPORATION KUMAMOTO FACTORY	997 Miyoshi, Nishigoshi-machi, Kikuchi-gun, Kumamoto 861-1104	+81-96-242-5711	+81-96-242-5890
11	MITSUI ELECTRIC CO., LTD.	312-8 Toriko, Nishihara-mura, Aso-gun, Kumamoto 861-2401	+81-96-279-3353	+81-96-279-3477
12	ISHII TOOL & ENGINEERING CORPORATION	2-1-3 Higashi Omichi, Oita-shi, Oita 870-0823	+81-97-544-1001	+81-97-554-5035
13	STK TECHNOLOGY CO., LTD.	2468-10 Misa, Oita-shi, Oita 870-0108	+81-97-527-2161	+81-97-527-1438
14	TAKAKI TOOLS & MATERIALS CO., LTD.	Oita-Kogyodanchi, 3113-7 Shimogori, Oita-shi, Oita 870-0951	+81-97-569-3115	+81-97-569-1288
15	HIJI HIGH-TECH CO., LTD.	8133 Oga, Hiji-machi, Hayami-gun, Oita 879-1504	+81-977-44-6300	+81-977-72-6191
16	DENKEN CO., LTD.	97-1 Takazaki, Hasami-machi, Oita-gun, Oita 879-5513	+81-97-583-5535	+81-97-583-5580
17	MIYAZAKI OKI ELECTRIC CO., LTD.	727 Kihara, Kiyotake-cho, Miyazaki-gun, Miyazaki 889-1695	+81-985-85-5111	+81-985-84-1547
18	FUCHIGAMI MICRO CO., LTD.	3-1 Nanei, Kagoshima-shi, Kagoshima 891-0122	+81-99-269-4121	+81-99-267-8042
19	KYUSHU FUJITSU ELECTRONICS, LTD.	5950 Soeda, Iriki-cho, Satsuma-gun, Kagoshima 895-1493	+81-996-44-2111	+81-996-44-4095

AUTOMOBILE

No.	Company Name	Address	TEL	FAX
1	MORIO PRESS INDUSTRY CORPORATION	1-14-16 Hanmichibashi, Hakata-ku, Fukuoka-shi, Fukuoka 816-0097	+81-92-411-3171	+81-92-461-0722
2	MATSUMOTO INDUSTRY CO., LTD.	76-22 Hiroshoji, Unoshima, Buzen-shi, Fukuoka 828-0022	+81-979-82-1171	+81-979-82-1521
3	TOYOTA MOTOR KYUSHU, INC.	1 Hirayama, Kamiaruki, Miyata-machi, Kurate-gun, Fukuoka 823-0015	+81-949-32-5151	+81-949-34-2380
4	TOGAMIKASEI CO., LTD.	2778-1 Shimoizumi, Kuboizumi-machi, Saga-shi, Saga 849-0903	+81-952-98-2821	+81-952-98-1301
5	ARACO KYUSHU CO., LTD.	1600 Tsuru, Kanzaki-machi, Kanzaki-gun, Saga 842-0107	+81-952-52-7111	+81-952-52-7090
6	KIKUCHI FACTORY, KYUSHU INOAC CO., LTD.	2000 Akahoshi, Kikuchi-shi, Kumamoto 861-1311	+81-968-25-0121	+81-968-25-0168

7	AISIN KYUSHU CO., LTD.	500-1 Nishi, Mainohara, Jyonan-machi, Shimomashiki-gun, Kumamoto 861-4214	+81-964-28-8181	+81-964-28-8155
8	OOZUGIKEN CO., LTD.	1447-1 Obayashi, Ozu-machi, Kikuchi-gun, Kumamoto 869-1219	+81-96-293-0753	+81-96-293-5592
9	Honda Motor Co., Ltd. (Kumamoto Factory)	1500 Hirakawa, Ozu-machi, Kikuchi-gun, Kumamoto 869-1293	+81-96-293-1111	+81-96-293-8280
10	CHK SPRING INDUSTRY CO., LTD.	503 Jyuni-machi, Hita-shi, Oita 877-8501	+81-973-22-1112	+81-973-23-4190
11	CKK CORPORATION	111 Waki, Usa-shi, Oita 879-1135	+81-978-38-4701	+81-978-38-4703
12	Honda Lock Mfg. Co., Ltd.	3700 Shimonaka, Sadowara-cho, Miyazaki-gun, Miyazaki 880-0293	+81-985-73-1211	+81-985-30-1012

ENVIRONMENT

No.	Company Name	Address	TEL	FAX
1	NISHINIHON KADEN RECYCLE CORPORATION	1-62 Hibiki-machi, Wakamatsu-ku, Kitakyushu-shi, Fukuoka 808-0021	+81-93-752-2424	+81-93-752-2425
2	ENVIRONMENT TECHNOLOGY SERVICE CO., LTD.	2-4 Nakabarushin-machi, Tobata-ku, Kitakyushu-shi, Fukuoka 804-0003	+81-93-883-0150	+81-93-883-0701
3	KYUDEN SANGYO CO., INC.	2-1-82 Watanabedori, Chuo-ku, Fukuoka-shi, Fukuoka 810-0004	+81-92-781-3061	+81-92-713-0014
4	NISHINIPPON ENVIRONMENTAL ENERGY COMPANY, INCORPORATED	1-17-8 Shirogane, Chuo-ku, Fukuoka-shi, Fukuoka 810-0012	+81-92-526-0601	+81-92-526-1620
5	NISHINIPPON PLANT ENGINEERING AND CONSTRUCTION CO., LTD.	1-10-1 Takasago, Chuo-ku, Fukuoka-shi, Fukuoka 810-8540	+81-92-533-0011	+81-92-533-1756
6	INDUST. CO., LTD.	Fukuoka SRP Center Bldg. 3-F, 2-1-22 Momochihama, Sawara-ku, Fukuoka-shi, Fukuoka 814-0001	+81-92-832-1073	+81-92-831-1779
7	ASO MINING CO., LTD.	7-18 Yoshio-machi, Iizuka-shi, Fukuoka 820-0018	+81-948-23-5837	+81-948-23-1046
8	TAGAWA SANGYO CO., LTD.	1924 Yugeta, Tagawa-shi, Fukuoka 826-0041	+81-947-44-2240	+81-947-44-8484
9	KYOEI RESOURCE DEVELOPMENT, INC.	766 Kamiiwata, Ogori-shi, Fukuoka 838-0121	+81-942-72-0497	+81-942-73-3870
10	FUJIKAIHATSU CO.. LTD. KOTAKE	135-75 Gotoku. Kotake-machi.	+81-9496-2-	+81-9496-2-

	FACTORY	Kurate-gun, Fukuoka 820-1101	1115	1068
11	TSP CO., LTD.	65-7 Asada, Ukiha-machi, Ukiha-gun, Fukuoka 839-1401	+81-9437-7-3065	+81-9437-7-2225
12	MIZOTA CORPORATION	15-1 Ise-machi, Saga-shi, Saga 840-8686	+81-952-26-2551	+81-952-24-2315
13	HUIS TEN BOSCH TECHNICAL CENTER CO., LTD.	5-3 Huis Ten Bosch-machi, Sasebo-shi, Nagasaki 859-3243	+81-956-27-0170	+81-956-27-0941
14	KONGO CO., LTD.	3-8-1 Kamikumamoto, Kumamoto-shi, Kumamoto 860-8508	+81-96-355-1111	+81-96-352-0227
15	NISHIHARA CO., LTD.	29-8 Hachioji-machi, Kumamoto-shi, Kumamoto 860-0831	+81-96-378-0657	+81-96-378-0382
16	SANYO INDUSTORY & MACHINERY CORPORATION	2-7-6 Nanei, Kagoshima-shi, Kagoshima 891-0122	+81-99-268-5191	+81-99-268-1882
17	KIRISHIMA HIGHLAND BREWERY CO., LTD.	876-15 Fumoto, Mizobe-cho, Aira-gun, Kagoshima 899-6404	+81-995-58-4868	+81-995-58-3621

BIOTECHNOLOGY

No.	Company Name	Address	TEL	FAX
1	KYUSHU MEDICAL CO., LTD.	13-4 Otemachi, Kokurakita-ku, Kitakyushu-shi, Fukuoka 803-0814	+81-93-592-1262	+81-93-592-0832
2	TOTO LTD.	2-1-1 Nakashima, Kokurakita-ku, Kitakyushu-shi, Fukuoka 802-8601	+81-93-951-2111	+81-93-951-2838
3	KYURIN CORPORATION	27-25 Morishita-machi, Yahatanishi-ku, Kitakyushu-shi, Fukuoka 806-0046	+81-93-642-3911	+81-93-642-3967
4	NINE-LABO CO., LTD.	Akasaka Egashira Bldg. 3-F, 1-5-22 Akasaka, Chuo-ku, Fukuoka-shi, Fukuoka 810-0042	+81-92-713-1903	+81-92-713-1903
5	FUJITSU KYUSHU SYSTEM ENGINEERING LIMITED	Fujitsu Kyushu R&D Center, 2-2-1 Momochihama, Sawara-ku, Fukuoka-shi, Fukuoka 814-8589	+81-92-852-3100	+81-92-852-3051
6	GENENET CO., LTD.	80-42 Yotsuyama-machi, Omuta-shi, Fukuoka 836-0067	+81-944-56-1611	+81-944-56-1615
7	GNI, K.K.	Kurume Research Center Bldg. B, 2432-3 Aikawa-machi, Kurume-shi, Fukuoka 839-0861	+81-942-36-8633	+81-942-36-8655
8	GeneACT, Inc.	2432-3 Aikawa-machi, Kurume-shi, Fukuoka 839-0861	+81-942-36-8117	+81-942-36-8113
9	BIOCOM SYSTEMS, INC.	e-ZUKA TRY VALLEY Center A204.	+81-948-25-	+81-948-25-

		576-14 Kobukuro, Iizuka-shi, Fukuoka 820-0066	1746	1746
10	ASTEC CO., LTD.	136-2 Minamizato, Shime-machi, Kasuya-gun, Fukuoka 811-2207	+81-92-935-5585	+81-92-936-6613
11	MITSUBISHI PHARMA CORPORATION, PHARMACEUTICAL DEVELOPMENT LABORATORIES	955 Koiwai, Yoshitomi-machi, Chikujyo-gun, Fukuoka 871-8550	+81-979-23-9362	+81-979-24-2769
12	KYUDO CO., LTD.	883-1 Soraku, Tateishi-machi, Tosu-shi, Saga 841-0075	+81-942-82-6519	+81-942-85-3175
13	TOYO SHINYAKU CO., LTD.	1048 Umesaka, Yubi-machi, Tosu-shi, Saga 841-0002	+81-942-81-3555	+81-942-81-3554
14	YUTOKU PHARMACEUTICAL IND. CO., LTD.	2596-1 Nodomibun, Kashima-shi, Saga 849-1312	+81-954-63-1231	+81-954-63-1240
15	ARK RESOURCE CO., LTD.	383-2 Nakashima-machi, Kumamoto-shi, Kumamoto 861-5271	+81-96-329-0880	+81-96-329-0882
16	THE CHEMO-SERO-THERAPEUTIC RESEARCH INSTITUTE	1-6-1 Okubo, Kumamoto-shi, Kumamoto 860-8568	+81-96-344-1211	+81-96-345-1345
17	TRANS GENIC INC.	Kumamoto San Nissei Bldg. 4-F, 2-11 Chuo-gai, Kumamoto-shi, Kumamoto 860-0802	+81-96-212-3363	+81-96-212-3364
18	PANAPHARM LABORATORIES CO., LTD.	1285 Kurizaki-machi, Uto-shi, Kumamoto 869-0425	+81-964-23-5111	+81-964-23-5122
19	DOJINDO LABORATORIES	2025-5 Tabaru, Mashiki-machi, Kamimashiki-gun, Kumamoto 861-2202	+81-96-286-1515	+81-96-286-1525
20	EU GENE LTD.	Techno Research Park, 1155-5 Tabaru, Mashiki-machi, Kamimashiki-gun, Kumamoto 861-2202	+81-96-287-1386	+81-96-287-1387
21	ASAHI MEDICAL CO., LTD.	2111-2 Sato, Oita-shi, Oita 870-0396	+81-97-593-1570	+81-97-592-7012
22	BIOMEDICAL TECHNOLOGY HYBRID, LTD.	Kagoshima University Research and Development Center, 1-21-40 Korimoto, Kagoshima-shi, Kagoshima 890-0065	+81-99-285-8496	+81-99-285-8496
23	SHIN NIPPON BIOMEDICAL LABORATORIES, LTD.	2438 Miyanoura, Yoshida-cho, Kagoshima-gun, Kagoshima 891-1394	+81-99-246-9050	+81-99-246-9051

- Policy Division
  E-mail:oki-seisaku@meti.go.jp
- Development Planning and Promotion Division
  E-mail:oki-kishin@meti.go.jp
- Industry Division
  E-mail:oki-sangyo@meti.go.jp
- Commerce and Distribution Division
  E-mail:oki-syomu@meti.go.jp
- Small and Medium Enterprise Division
  E-mail:oki-tyusyo@meti.go.jp
- Environmental Protection and Natural Resources Division
  Email:oki-kanshi@meti.go.jp
- Public Utilities Division
  Email:oki-koeki@meti.go.jp
- Superintendent for Petroleum and Energy Affairs
  Email:oki-sekiene@meti.go.jp

PUBLIC CORPORATIONS

LAND DEVELOPMENT

Japan Green Resources Corporation,JDCD

Midori Shigen Kodan 日本語表記

CATEGORY Politics/Administration:Public Corporations:Land Development
TYPE Public corporation
ADDRESS Fukuda bldg., 3-29 Kioi-cho, Chiyoda-ku, Tokyo 102-0094
PHONE +81-3-3222-1211
FAX +81-3-3222-1455
E-MAIL XLY04761@nifty.ne.jp
HOMEPAGE http://www.green.go.jp/index2.htm (Japanese only)
REMARKS

Japan Regional Development Corporation, JRDC

Chiiki Shinko Seibi Kodan 日本語表記

CATEGORY Politics/Administration:Public Corporations:Land Development
TYPE Public corporation
ADDRESS Toranomon Mitsui bldg., 3-8-1 Kasumigaseki, Chiyoda-ku, Tokyo 100-8906
PHONE +81-3-3501-5211
FAX +81-3-3501-5257
E-MAIL koizumi-k@region.go.jp
HOMEPAGE http://www.region.go.jp/en/index_e.html
REMARKS

Japan, Water Resources Development Public Corporation (WARDEC)

Mizushigen Kaihatsu Kodan 日本語表記

CATEGORY Politics/Administration:Public Corporations:Land Development
TYPE Public corporation
ADDRESS Land Axis Tower 6F-10F, 2-40 Kamiochiai, Saitama city, 330-6008
PHONE +81-48-600-6500
FAX +81-48-600-6510
E-MAIL webmaster@water.go.jp
HOMEPAGE http://www.water.go.jp/html/index.html (Japanese only)
REMARKS

Organization of Urban Development Corporation

Toshi Kiban Seibi Kodan 日本語表記

CATEGORY Politics/Administration:Public Corporations:Land Development

TYPE Public corporation

ADDRESS 1-14-6 Kudan-Kita, Chiyoda-ku, Tokyo 102-8201

PHONE +81-3-3263-8111

FAX +81-3-3263-8177

E-MAIL

HOMEPAGE http://www.udc.go.jp/UDC200x/concept_fr_e.html

REMARKS

The Fund for the Promotion and Development of the Amami Islands

Amami-gunto Shinko Kaihatsu Kikin 日本語表記

CATEGORY Politics/Administration:Public Corporations:Land Development

TYPE Public corporation

ADDRESS 1-5 Minato-machi, Naze-shi, Kagoshima 894-0026

PHONE +81-997-52-4511

FAX +81-997-52-4514

E-MAIL kikin@bronze.ocn.ne.jp

HOMEPAGE http://www2.ocn.ne.jp/~kikin/(Japanese only)

FINANCE

Agriculture, Forestry and Fisheries Finance Corporation of Japan, AFC

Noringyogyo Kinyukoko 日本語表記

CATEGORY Politics/Administration:Public Corporations:Finance

TYPE Public corporation

ADDRESS Koko bldg., 1-9-3 Ote-machi, Chiyoda-ku Tokyo 100-0004

PHONE +81-3-3270-2261

FAX +81-3-3270-2350

E-MAIL intl@afc.go.jp

HOMEPAGE http://www.afc.go.jp/english/eng1-main.htm

REMARKS

Development Bank of Japan

Nippon Seisaku Toshi Ginko 日本語表記

CATEGORY Politics/Administration:Public Corporations:Finance

TYPE Public corporation

ADDRESS 1-9-1 Ote-machi, Chiyoda-ku, Tokyo 100-0004

PHONE +81-3-3270-3211

FAX +81-3-3271-8472

E-MAIL

HOMEPAGE http://www.dbj.go.jp/english/index.html

REMARKS

Japan Bank for International Corporation

Kokusai Kyouryoku Ginko 日本語表記

CATEGORY Politics/Administration:Public Corporations:Finance

TYPE Public corporation

ADDRESS 1-4-1 Ote-machi, Chiyoda-ku, Tokyo 100-8144

PHONE +81-3-5218-3054

FAX +81-3-5218-3955

E-MAIL
HOMEPAGE http://www.jbic.go.jp/english/index.php
REMARKS

Japan Finance Corporation for Municipal Enterprises, JFS
Koei Kigyo Kinyukoko 日本語表記
CATEGORY Politics/Administration:Public Corporations:Finance
TYPE Public corporation
ADDRESS Gardencoat bldg, New otani bekkan, 4-1 Kioi-cho, Chiyoda-ku, Tokyo 102-0094
PHONE +81-3-5210-5900
FAX +81-3-5210-5924
E-MAIL
HOMEPAGE http://www.jfm.go.jp/
REMARKS

Japan Finance Corporation for Small Business, JFS
Chusho Kigyo Kinyukoko 日本語表記
CATEGORY Politics/Administration:Public Corporations:Finance
TYPE Public corporation
ADDRESS Koko bldg., 1-9-3 Ote-machi, Chiyoda-ku, Tokyo 100-0004
PHONE +81-3-3270-0505
FAX +81-3-3279-5910
E-MAIL
HOMEPAGE http://www.jfs.go.jp/indexe.html
REMARKS

National Life Finance Corporation, NLFC
Kokumin Seikatsu Kinyukoko 日本語表記
CATEGORY Politics/Administration:Public Corporations:Finance
TYPE Public corporation
ADDRESS Koko bldg., 1-9-3 Ote-machi, Chiyoda-ku, Tokyo 100-0004
PHONE +81-3-3270-1361
FAX
E-MAIL
HOMEPAGE http://www.kokukin.go.jp/pfce/indexe.html
REMARKS

The Okinawa Development Finance Corporation, ODFC
Okinawa Shinko Kaihatsu Kinyukoko 日本語表記
CATEGORY Politics/Administration:Public Corporations:Finance
TYPE Public corporation
ADDRESS Daito bldg 9F., 3-7-1 Kasumigaseki, Chiyoda-ku, Tokyo 100-0013
PHONE +81-3-3581-3241
FAX +81-3-5511-8233
E-MAIL
HOMEPAGE http://www.okinawakouko.go.jp/ (Japanese only)
REMARKS

The Governmet Housing Loan Corporation, GHLC
Jutaku Kinyukoko 日本語表記
CATEGORY Politics/Administration:Public Corporations:Finance
TYPE Public corporation

ADDRESS 1-4-10 Koraku, Bunkyo-ku, Tokyo 112-8570
PHONE +81-3-3812-1111
FAX +81-3-5800-8181
E-MAIL
HOMEPAGE http://www.jyukou.go.jp/ (Japanese only)
REMARKS

The Shoko Chukin Bank

Shoko Kumiai Chuo Kinko 日本語表記
CATEGORY Politics/Administration:Public Corporations:Finance
TYPE Public corporation
ADDRESS 2-10-17 Yaesu, Chuo-ku, Tokyo 104-0028
PHONE +81-3-3272-6111
FAX
E-MAIL
HOMEPAGE http://www.shokochukin.go.jp/ (Japanese only)

INTERNATIONAL AFFAIRS

Japan International Cooperation Agency, JICA

Kokusai Kyoryoku Jigyodan 日本語表記
CATEGORY Politics/Administration:Public Corporations:International Affairs
TYPE Public corporation
ADDRESS Shinjuku Mainzu Tower 6F-13F., 2-1-1 Yoyogi, Shibuya-ku, Tokyo 151-8558
PHONE +81-3-5352-5311
FAX +81-3-5352-5032
E-MAIL www@jica.go.jp
HOMEPAGE http://www.jica.go.jp/english/
REMARKS

Japan National Tourist Organization, JNTO

Kokusai Kanko Shinkokai 日本語表記
CATEGORY Politics/Administration:Public Corporations:International Affairs
TYPE Public corporation
ADDRESS 2-10-1 Yuraku-cho, Chiyoda-ku, Tokyo 100-0006
PHONE +81-3-3216-1901
FAX +81-3-3214-7680
E-MAIL
HOMEPAGE http://www.jnto.go.jp/eng/
REMARKS

The Japan Foundation

Kokusai Koryu Kikin 日本語表記
CATEGORY Politics/Administration:Public Corporations:International Affairs
TYPE Public corporation
ADDRESS Ark Mori bldg 20F-21F., 1-12-32 Akasaka, Minato-ku, Tokyo 107-6021
PHONE +81-3-5562-3511
FAX +81-3-5562-3494
E-MAIL webmaster@jpf.go.jp
HOMEPAGE http://www.jpf.go.jp/index.html
REMARKS Offers fellowships for researchers in the field of sociology, Ph.D. candidates, artists, and specialists in cultural properties. Offers subsidies for Japanese language education and introduction of Japanese culture.

INDUSTRY AND ECONOMY

Agriculture and Livestock Industries Corporation, ALIC

Nochikusangyo Shinko Jigyodan

CATEGORY Politics/Administration:Public Corporations:Industry and Economy
TYPE Public corporation
ADDRESS Azabudai bldg., 2-2-1 Azabudai, Minato-ku Tokyo 106-8635
PHONE +81-3-3582-3381
FAX +81-3-3584-1246
E-MAIL alicml@lin.go.jp
HOMEPAGE http://alic.lin.go.jp (Japanese only)
REMARKS

Employment and Human Resources Development Organization of Japan

Koyo Noryoku Kaihatsu Kiko

CATEGORY Politics/Administration:Public Corporations:Industry and Economy
TYPE Public corporation
ADDRESS Nisseki Yokohama bldg., 1-1-8 Sakuragi-cho, Naka-ku, Yokohama-shi, Kanagawa 231-8333
PHONE +81-45-683-1111
FAX +81-45-683-1271
E-MAIL
HOMEPAGE http://www.ehdo.go.jp/ (Japanese only)
REMARKS

Institute of Developing Economies Japan External Trade Organization, IDE-JETRO

Nihon Boeki Shinkokai Asia Keizai Kenkyusho (Ajiken)

CATEGORY Politics/Administration:Public Corporations:Industry and Economy
TYPE Public corporation
ADDRESS 3-2-2 Wakaba, Mihama-ku, Chiba-shi, Chiba 261-8545
PHONE +81-43-299-9500
FAX +81-43-299-9724
E-MAIL info@ide.go.jp
HOMEPAGE http://www.ide.go.jp/English/index4.html
REMARKS

Japan External Trade Organization, JETRO

Nihon Boeki Shinkokai

CATEGORY Politics/Administration:Public Corporations:Industry and Economy
TYPE Public corporation
ADDRESS 2-2-5 Toranomon, Minato-ku, Tokyo 105-8466
PHONE +81-3-3582-5511
FAX +81-3-3582-0656
E-MAIL webmaster@jetro.go.jp
HOMEPAGE http://www.jetro.go.jp/top/
REMARKS JETRO is currently established as a Public corporation and from 1 October 2003 will transform into the independent administrative institution the "Japan External Trade Institution."

Japan Small and Medium Enterprise Corporation

Chusho Kigyo Sogo Jigyoudan

CATEGORY Politics/Administration:Public Corporations:Industry and Economy
TYPE Public corporation

ADDRESS (Toranomon Office)37-Toranomon Mori bldg., 3-5-1 Toranomon, Minato-ku, Tokyo 105-8453 (Otemachi Office)Shin Koko bldg., 1-8-2 Otemachi,Chiyodaku,Tokyo,100-0004
PHONE +81-3-3433-8811
FAX +81-3-5404-7655
E-MAIL gy-koho@jasmec.go.jp
HOMEPAGE http://www.jasmec.go.jp/english/index.html
REMARKS

Metal Mining Agency of Japan, MMAJ

Kinzoku Kogyo Jigyodan 日本語表記
CATEGORY Politics/Administration:Public Corporations:Industry and Economy
TYPE Public corporation
ADDRESS Tokiwa bldg., 1-24-14 Toranomon, Minato-ku, Tokyo 105-0001
PHONE +81-3-5512-1563
FAX +81-3-3503-0570
E-MAIL wwwadm@mmaj.go.jp
HOMEPAGE http://www.mmaj.go.jp/mmaj_e/home.html
REMARKS

The Japan Institute of Labour, JIL

Nihon Rodo Kenkyu Kiko 日本語表記
CATEGORY Politics/Administration:Public Corporations:Industry and Economy
TYPE Public corporation
ADDRESS Shinjuku Monorisu Bldg., 2-3-1 Nishi-Shinjuku, Shinjuku-ku, Tokyo 163-0926
PHONE +81-3-5321-3000
FAX +81-3-5321-3015
E-MAIL jil@jil.go.jp
HOMEPAGE http://www.jil.go.jp/index-e.htm

TRANSPORTATION

Corporation for Advanced Transport and Technology

Unyu Shisetsu Seibi Jigyodan 日本語表記
CATEGORY Politics/Administration:Public Corporations:Transportation
TYPE Public corporation
ADDRESS Iino bldg., 2-1-1 Uchisaiwai-cho, Chiyoda-ku, Tokyo 100-0011
PHONE +81-3-3501-2146
FAX +81-3-3580-8173
E-MAIL webmaster@catt.go.jp
HOMEPAGE http://www.catt.go.jp (Japanese only)
REMARKS

Honshu-Shikoku Bridge Authority

Honshu Shikoku Renrakukyo Kodan 日本語表記
CATEGORY Politics/Administration:Public Corporations:Transportation
TYPE Public corporation
ADDRESS Urban Ace Sannomiya bldg., 4-1-22 Onoe-dori, Chuo-ku, Kobe-city 651-0088
PHONE +81-78-291-1000
FAX +81-78-291-1363
E-MAIL
HOMEPAGE http://www.hsba.go.jp/e-index.htm
REMARKS

Japan Highway Public Corporation, JH

Nihon Doro Kodan 日本語表記

CATEGORY Politics/Administration:Public Corporations:Transportation
TYPE Public corporation
ADDRESS Shin Kasumigaseki bldg., 3-3-2 Kasumigaseki, Chiyoda-ku, Tokyo 100-8979
PHONE +81-3-3506-0111
FAX +81-3-3506-0348
E-MAIL voice ho@gw.jh.net.go.jp
HOMEPAGE http://www.jhnet.go.jp/english_new/index.html
REMARKS

Japan Railway Construction Public Corporation, JRCC

Nihon Tetsudo Kensetsu Kodan 日本語表記

CATEGORY Politics/Administration:Public Corporations:Transportation
TYPE Public corporation
ADDRESS Sanno Grand bldg., 2-14-2 Nagata-cho, Chiyoda-ku, Tokyo 100-0014
PHONE +81-3-3506-1815
FAX +81-3-3506-1890
E-MAIL
HOMEPAGE http://www.jrcc.go.jp/ (Japanese only)
REMARKS

JRCC JNR Settlement Headquarters

Nihon Tetsudo Kensetsu Kodan Kokutetsu Seisan Jigyohonbu 日本語表記

CATEGORY Politics/Administration:Public Corporations:Transportation
TYPE Public corporation
ADDRESS 2-8-6 Nishi-Shinbashi, Minato-ku, Tokyo 105-8434
PHONE +81-3-3506-2335
FAX +81-3-3506-2330
E-MAIL tochi@jnrsh.gr.jp
HOMEPAGE http://www.jnrsh.gr.jp/ (Japanese only)
REMARKS

Metropolitan Expressway Public Corporation

Shuto Kosoku Doro Kodan 日本語表記

CATEGORY Politics/Administration:Public Corporations:Transportation
TYPE Public corporation
ADDRESS Nittochi bldg., 1-4-1 Kasumigaseki, Chiyoda-ku, Tokyo 100-8930
PHONE +81-3-3502-7311
FAX +81-3-3595-3058
E-MAIL g-post@mex.go.jp
HOMEPAGE http://www.mex.go.jp/
REMARKS

New Tokyo International Airport Authority, NAA

Shin Tokyo Kokusai Kuko Kodan (Kukokodan) 日本語表記

CATEGORY Politics/Administration:Public Corporations:Transportation
TYPE Public corporation
ADDRESS 24 Aza Kamidai, Kinone, Narita-shi, Chiba 282-8601
PHONE +81-476-34-5400
FAX +81-476-30-1573

E-MAIL naa1@naa.go.jp
HOMEPAGE http://www.narita-airport.or.jp/airport_e/index.html
REMARKS

Railway Development Fund
Tetsudo Seibi Kikin 日本語表記
CATEGORY Politics/Administration:Public Corporations:Transportation
TYPE Public corporation
ADDRESS 1-6-5 Marunouchi, Chiyoda-ku, Tokyo 106-0005
PHONE +81-3-3215-9682
FAX
E-MAIL
HOMEPAGE
REMARKS

Teito Rapid Transit Authority, TRTA
Teito Kosokudo Kotsu Eidan 日本語表記
CATEGORY Politics/Administration:Public Corporations:Transportation
TYPE Public corporation
ADDRESS 3-19-6 Higashi-Ueno, Taito-ku, Tokyo 110-0015
PHONE +81-3-3837-7041
FAX +81-3-3837-7048
E-MAIL
HOMEPAGE http://www.tokyometro.go.jp/e/index.html
REMARKS

The Hanshin Expressway Public Corporation
Hanshin Kosoku Doro Kodan 日本語表記
CATEGORY Politics/Administration:Public Corporations:Transportation
TYPE Public corporation
ADDRESS Osaka Center bldg., 4-1-3 Kyutaro-machi, Chuo-ku Osaka-shi, Osaka 541-0056
PHONE +81-6-6252-8121
FAX +81-6-6251-6933
E-MAIL soumu@hepc.go.jp
HOMEPAGE http://www.hepc.go.jp/english/index.html

BROADCASTING

Japan Broadcasting Corporation, NHK
Nippon Hoso Kyokai 日本語表記
CATEGORY Politics/Administration:Public Corporations:Broadcasting
TYPE Public corporation
ADDRESS 2-2-1 Jinnan, Shibuya-ku, Tokyo 150-8001
PHONE +81-3-3465-1111
FAX +81-3-3469-8110
E-MAIL webmaster@www.nhk.or.jp
HOMEPAGE http://www.nhk.or.jp/index-e.html

NATURAL RESOURCES AND ENERGY

Japan Atomic Energy Research Institute, JAERI
Nihon Genshiryoku Kenkyusho 日本語表記
CATEGORY Politics/Administration:Public Corporations:Natural Resources and Energy

TYPE Public corporation
ADDRESS Fukoku Seimei bldg., 2-2-2 Uchisaiwai-cho, Chiyoda-ku, Tokyo 100-0011
PHONE +81-3-3592-2111
FAX +81-3-3580-6107
E-MAIL www-admin@www.jaeri.go.jp
HOMEPAGE http://www.jaeri.go.jp/english/index.cgi
REMARKS

Japan National Oil Corporation, JNOC
Sekiyu Kodan 日本語表記
CATEGORY Politics/Administration:Public Corporations:Natural Resources and Energy
TYPE Public corporation
ADDRESS Fukoku Seimei bldg., 2-2-2 Uchisaiwai-cho, Chiyoda-ku, Tokyo 100-8511
PHONE +81-3-3597-7522
FAX +81-3-3591-0172
E-MAIL webmaster@jnoc.go.jp
HOMEPAGE http://www.jnoc.go.jp/english/index.html
REMARKS

Japan Nuclear Cycle Development Institute, JNC
Kakunenryo saikuru Kaihatsu Kiko 日本語表記
CATEGORY Politics/Administration:Public Corporations:Natural Resources and Energy
TYPE Public corporation
ADDRESS 4-49 Muramatsu, Tokai-mura, Naka-gun, Ibaraki 319-1184
PHONE +81-29-282-1122
FAX +81-29-282-8049
E-MAIL www-admin@jnc.go.jp
HOMEPAGE http://www.jnc.go.jp/jncweb/
REMARKS

New Energy and Industrial Technology Development Organization, NEDO
Shin Energy Sangyo Gijutsu Sogo Kaihatsu Kiko 日本語表記
CATEGORY Politics/Administration:Public Corporations:Natural Resources and Energy
TYPE Public corporation
ADDRESS Sanshain-60 26Fto31F, 3-1-1 Higashi-Ikebukuro, Toshima-ku, Tokyo 170-6028
PHONE +81-3-3987-9310
FAX +81-3-5992-2290
E-MAIL qinf@nedo.go.jp
HOMEPAGE http://www.nedo.go.jp/english/index.html

SCIENCE AND TECHNOLOGY

Japan Science and Technology Corporation, JST
Kagaku Gijutsu Shinko Jigyodan 日本語表記
CATEGORY Politics/Administration:Public Corporations:Science and Technology
TYPE Public corporation
ADDRESS (Tokyo)Science Plaza., 5-3 Yonban-cho, Chiyoda-ku, Tokyo 102-8666
(Kawaguchi)Kawaguchi center bldg., 4-1-8 Hon-cho,Kawaguchi-shi,Saitama 332-0012
PHONE (Tokyo)+81-3-5214-8401 (Kawaguchi)+81-48-226-5601
FAX (Tokyo)+81-3-5214-8400 (Kawaguchi)+81-48-226-5651
E-MAIL www-admin@tokyo.jst.go.jp
HOMEPAGE http://www.jst.go.jp/EN/
REMARKS

National Space Development Agency of Japan, NASDA
Uchu Kaihatsu Jigyodan
CATEGORY Politics/Administration:Public Corporations:Science and Technology
TYPE Public corporation
ADDRESS World Trade Center Bldg, 2-4-1 Hamamatsu-cho, Minato-ku, Tokyo 105-8060
PHONE +81-3-3438-6000
FAX +81-3-5402-6512
E-MAIL proffice@nasda.go.jp
HOMEPAGE http://www.nasda.go.jp/index_e.html
REMARKS

The Institute of Physical and Chemical Research, RIKEN
Rikagaku Kenkyujo
CATEGORY Politics/Administration:Public Corporations:Science and Technology
TYPE Public corporation
ADDRESS 2-1 Hirosawa, Wako-shi, Saitama 351-0198
PHONE +81-48-462-1111
FAX +81-48-462-1554
E-MAIL webmaster@postman.riken.go.jp
HOMEPAGE http://www.riken.go.jp/

WELFARE

Association for Welfare of the Mentally and Physically Disabled-Persons The National Colony Nozominosono
Tokushu Hojin Shinshin Shogaisha Fukushi Kyokai Kokuritsu Colony Nozominosono
CATEGORY Politics/Administration:Public Corporations:Welfare
TYPE Public corporation
ADDRESS 2120-2 Terao-cho, Takasaki-shi, Gunma 370-0865
PHONE +81-273-25-1501
FAX +81-273-27-7628
E-MAIL nozomi@nozomi.go.jp
HOMEPAGE http://www.nozomi.go.jp (Japanese only)
REMARKS

Farmers' Pension Fund
Nogyosha Nenkin Kikin
CATEGORY Politics/Administration:Public Corporations:Welfare
TYPE Public corporation
ADDRESS Daiwa Ginko Toranomon bldg., 1-6-21 Nishi-Shinbashi, Minato-ku, Tokyo 105-8010
PHONE +81-3-3502-6696
FAX +81-3-3592-2660
E-MAIL
HOMEPAGE http://www.nounen.go.jp/(Japanese only)
REMARKS

Government Pension Investment Fund
Nenkin Shikin Unyo Kikin
CATEGORY Politics/Administration:Public Corporations:Welfare
TYPE Public corporation

ADDRESS Nittochi bldg., 1-4-1 Kasumigaseki, Chiyoda-ku, Tokyo 100-8985
PHONE +81-3-3502-2480
FAX +81-3-3502-2058
E-MAIL
HOMEPAGE http://www.gpif.go.jp/e-index.html
REMARKS

Labour Welfare Corporation
Rodo Fukushi Jigyodan
CATEGORY Politics/Administration:Public Corporations:Welfare
TYPE Public corporation
ADDRESS Solid Square Higashi-kan 18F., 580 Horikawa-cho, Saiwai-ku, Kawasaki-shi, Kanagawa 212-0013
PHONE +81-44-556-9835
FAX +81-44-556-9919
E-MAIL kouhou@mg.rofuku.go.jp
HOMEPAGE http://www.rofuku.go.jp/ (Japanese only)
REMARKS

Postal Life Insurance Welfare Corporation
Kan'i Hoken Fukushi Jigyodan
CATEGORY Politics/Administration:Public Corporations:Welfare
TYPE Public corporation
ADDRESS Shinjuku Center bldg,1-25-1 Nishishinjuku, Shinjuku-ku, Tokyo 163-0660
PHONE +81-3-5322-0410
FAX +81-3-5322-0464
E-MAIL information@kfj.go.jp
HOMEPAGE http://www.kampo.kfj.go.jp/ (Japanese only)
REMARKS

Social Insurance Medical Fee Payment Fund
Shakai Hoken Shinryo Hoshu Shiharai Kikin
CATEGORY Politics/Administration:Public Corporations:Welfare
TYPE Public corporation
ADDRESS 2-1-3 Shinbashi, Minato-ku, Tokyo 105-0004
PHONE +81-3-3591-7441
FAX +81-3-3591-6707
E-MAIL
HOMEPAGE http://www.shiharaikikin.go.jp/ (Japanese only)
REMARKS

Social Welfare and Medical Service Corporation, WAM
Shakaifukushi Iryo Jigyodan
CATEGORY Politics/Administration:Public Corporations:Welfare
TYPE Public corporation
ADDRESS Shuwa Kamiya-cho bldg., 4-3-13 Toranomon, Minato-ku, Tokyo 105-8486
PHONE +81-3-3438-0211
FAX +81-3-3438-9949
E-MAIL webmaster2@wamnet.wam.go.jp
HOMEPAGE http://www.wam.go.jp/ (Japanese only)

ENVIRONMENT

Japan Environment Corporation, JEC

Kankyo Jigyodan

CATEGORY Politics/Administration:Public Corporations:Environment
TYPE Public corporation
ADDRESS Nittochi bldg., 1-4-1 Kasumigaseki, Chiyoda-ku, Tokyo 100-0013
PHONE +81-3-5251-1017
FAX +81-3-3592-5056
E-MAIL jec@jec.go.jp
HOMEPAGE http://www.jec.go.jp/eg/index.html
REMARKS

New Energy and Industrial Technology Development Organization, NEDO

Shin Energy Sangyo Gijutsu Sogo Kaihatsu Kiko

CATEGORY Politics/Administration:Public Corporations:Environment
TYPE Public corporation
ADDRESS Sanshain-60 26Fto31F, 3-1-1 Higashi-Ikebukuro, Toshima-ku, Tokyo 170-6028
PHONE +81-3-3987-9310
FAX +81-3-5992-2290
E-MAIL qinf@nedo.go.jp
HOMEPAGE http://www.nedo.go.jp/english/index.html
REMARKS

The Pollution-Related Health Damage Compensation and Prevention Association

Kogai Kenko Higai Hosho Yobo Kyokai

CATEGORY Politics/Administration:Public Corporations:Environment
TYPE Public corporation
ADDRESS Kurosaki bldg., 4-1-4 Roppongi, Minato-ku, Tokyo 106-0032
PHONE +81-3-3586-6041
FAX +81-3-5574-8346
E-MAIL
HOMEPAGE http://www.kouken.or.jp/ (Japanese only)

ACADEMIA, EDUCATION AND CULTURE

Japan Arts Council

Nihon Geijutsu Bunka Shinkokai (Kokuritsu Gekijo)

CATEGORY Politics/Administration:Public Corporations:Academia, Education and Culture
TYPE Public corporation
ADDRESS 4-1 Hayabusa-cho, Chiyoda-ku, Tokyo 102-8656
PHONE +81-3-3265-7411
FAX +81-3-3265-7402
E-MAIL
HOMEPAGE http://www.ntj.jac.go.jp/
REMARKS

Japan Society for the Promotion of Science, JSPS

Nihon Gakujutsu Shinkokai

CATEGORY Politics/Administration:Public Corporations:Academia, Education and Culture
TYPE Public corporation
ADDRESS 6 ichiban-cho, Chiyoda-ku, Tokyo 102-8471(Ichiban-cho office)
PHONE +81-3-3263-1722(Ichiban-cho office)
FAX +81-3-3221-2470(Ichiban-cho office)
E-MAIL

HOMEPAGE http://www.jsps.go.jp/e-home.htm
REMARKS Accepts young researchers from foreign countries for positions in Japanese universities or research institutes.

National Institute for Educational Policy Research
Kokuritsu Kyoiku Seisaku Kenkyujo 日本語表記
CATEGORY Politics/Administration:Public Corporations:Academia, Education and Culture
TYPE Public corporation
ADDRESS 6-5-22 Shimo-Meguro, Meguro-ku, Tokyo 153-8681
PHONE +81-3-5721-5750
FAX
E-MAIL info@nier.go.jp
HOMEPAGE http://www.nier.go.jp/(Japanese only)
REMARKS

National Stadium and School Health Center of Japan
Nihon Taiiku Gakko Kenko Center 日本語表記
CATEGORY Politics/Administration:Public Corporations:Academia, Education and Culture
TYPE Public corporation
ADDRESS 10 Kasumigaoka-machi, Shinjuku-ku, Tokyo 160-0013
PHONE +81-3-5410-9124
FAX +81-3-5410-9135
E-MAIL
HOMEPAGE http://www.ntgk.go.jp/ (Japanese only)
REMARKS

The Japan Scholarship Foundation
Nihon Ikueikai 日本語表記
CATEGORY Politics/Administration:Public Corporations:Academia, Education and Culture
TYPE Public corporation
ADDRESS 10-7 Ichigaya Honmura-cho, Shinjuku-ku, Tokyo 162-8412(headquarter) 162-8431(Tokyo branch)
PHONE +81-3-3269-4261
FAX +81-3-3269-4556
E-MAIL info@ikuei.go.jp
HOMEPAGE http://www.ikuei.go.jp/ (Japanese only)
REMARKS

The Promotion and Mutual Aid Corporation for Private Schools of Japan
Nihon Shiritsu Gakko Shinko Kyosai Jigyodan 日本語表記
CATEGORY Politics/Administration:Public Corporations:Academia, Education and Culture
TYPE Public corporation
ADDRESS 1-10-12 Fujimi, Chiyoda-ku, Tokyo 102-8145
PHONE +81-3-3230-1321 , +81-3-3230-7818
FAX +81-3-3230-1325
E-MAIL
HOMEPAGE http://www.shigaku.go.jp/ (Japanese only)
REMARKS

The University of the Air
Tokushu Hojin Hoso Daigaku Gakuen 日本語表記
CATEGORY Politics/Administration:Public Corporations:Academia, Education and Culture
TYPE Public corporation

ADDRESS 2-11 Wakaba, Mihama-ku Chiba-shi, Chiba 261-8586
PHONE +81-43-276-5111
FAX +81-43-297-2781
E-MAIL
HOMEPAGE http://www.u-air.ac.jp/eng/index.html

MUTUAL AID

Mutual Aid Association of Private School Personnel

Shiritsu Gakko Kyoshokuin Kyosai Kumiai
CATEGORY Politics/Administration:Public Corporations:Mutual Aid
TYPE Public corporation
ADDRESS 1-7-5 Yushima, Bunkyo-ku, Tokyo 113-8577
PHONE +81-3-3813-5321
FAX +81-3-3813-5356
E-MAIL
HOMEPAGE http://www.shigaku.go.jp/ (Japanese only)
REMARKS

Mutual Aid Associations of Agriculture, Forestry and Fishery Corporation Personnel

Norin-Gyogyo Dantai Shokuin Kyosai Kumiai (Norinnenkin)
CATEGORY Politics/Administration:Public Corporations:Mutual Aid
TYPE Public corporation
ADDRESS 4-1-1 Toranomon, Minato-ku, Tokyo 105-8080
PHONE +81-3-3432-3111
FAX +81-3-3432-3750
E-MAIL
HOMEPAGE http://www.norin-nenkin.or.jp/ (Japanese only)
REMARKS

Mutual Aid Fund for Official Casualties and Retirement of Volunteer Firemen

Shobo Dan'in-tou Komu Saigai Hosho-tou Kyosai Kikin
CATEGORY Politics/Administration:Public Corporations:Mutual Aid
TYPE Public corporation
ADDRESS Nihon Shobo Kaikan., 2-9-16 Toranomon, Minato-ku, Tokyo 105-0001
PHONE +81-3-3595-0541
FAX +81-3-3581-7720
E-MAIL
HOMEPAGE
REMARKS

Organization for Worker's Retirement Allowance Mutual Aid

Kinrosha Taishokukin kyosai Kiko
CATEGORY Politics/Administration:Public Corporations:Mutual Aid
TYPE Public corporation
ADDRESS Taishokukin bldg., 1-7-6 Shiba Koen, Minato-ku, Tokyo 105-0011
PHONE +81-3-3436-0151
FAX +81-3-3437-4438
E-MAIL chutaikyo@support.email.ne.jp
HOMEPAGE http://www.taisyokukin.go.jp/ (Japanese only)

OTHERS

Japan Keirin Association

Tokusyu Hojin, Nihon Jitensha Shinkokai

CATEGORY Politics/Administration:Public Corporations:Others
TYPE Public corporation
ADDRESS 1-9-15 Akasaka, Minato-ku, Tokyo 107-8461
PHONE +81-3-3582-3311
FAX +81-3-3505-5477
E-MAIL
HOMEPAGE http://www.keirin.go.jp/ (Japanese only)
REMARKS

Japan Motorcycle Racing Organization

Nihon Kogata Jidosha Shinkokai (Nichidoshin)

CATEGORY Politics/Administration:Public Corporations:Others
TYPE Public corporation
ADDRESS TFT bldg west side 6F., 3-1 Ariake Koto-ku, Tokyo 135-0063
PHONE +81-3-3570-5511
FAX +81-3-3570-5541
E-MAIL
HOMEPAGE http://www.autorace.or.jp/
REMARKS

Japan Racing Association, JRA

Nippon Chuo Keibakai

CATEGORY Politics/Administration:Public Corporations:Others
TYPE Public corporation
ADDRESS 1-1-19 Nishi-Shinbashi, Minato-ku, Tokyo 105-0003
PHONE +81-3-3503-8221
FAX +81-3-3503-8226
E-MAIL
HOMEPAGE http://www.jair.jrao.ne.jp/index2.html
REMARKS

Japan Worker's Housing Association

Nihon Kinrosha Jutaku Kyokai (Kinjukyo)

CATEGORY Politics/Administration:Public Corporations:Others
TYPE Public corporation
ADDRESS 1-32-3 Hongo, Bunkyo-ku, Tokyo 113-0033
PHONE +81-3-3811-6261
FAX +81-3-3811-6269
E-MAIL info@kjk.go.jp
HOMEPAGE http://www.kjk.go.jp/ (Japanese only)
REMARKS

National Consumer Affairs Center of Japan, NCAC

Kokumin Seikatsu Center

CATEGORY Politics/Administration:Public Corporations:Others
TYPE Public corporation
ADDRESS 3-13-22 Takanawa, Minato-ku, Tokyo 108-8602
PHONE +81-3-3443-9061
FAX +81-3-3443-1201
E-MAIL webmaster@kokusen.go.jp
HOMEPAGE http://www.kokusen.go.jp/ncac_index_e.html

REMARKS

Northern Territories Issue Association

Tokushu Hojin Hoppo Ryodo Mondai Taisaku Kyokai 日本語表記

CATEGORY Politics/Administration:Public Corporations:Others
TYPE Public corporation
ADDRESS Jochi Kioizaka bldg., 6-26-3 Kioi-cho Chiyoda-ku, Tokyo 102-0094
PHONE +81-3-3263-7691
FAX +81-3-3263-7693
E-MAIL hok_tok@hoppou.go.jp
HOMEPAGE http://www.hoppou.go.jp/index.shtml (Japanese only)
REMARKS

The National Association of Racing, NAR

Chiho Keiba Zenkoku Kyokai 日本語表記

CATEGORY Politics/Administration:Public Corporations:Others
TYPE Public corporation
ADDRESS 2-2-1 Azabudai, Minato-ku, Tokyo 106-8639
PHONE +81-3-3583-6841
FAX +81-3-3585-0481
E-MAIL
HOMEPAGE http://www.keiba.go.jp/index.html (Japanese only)
REMARKS

The Nippon Foundation

Nippon Zaidan 日本語表記

CATEGORY Politics/Administration:Public Corporations:Others
TYPE Public corporation
ADDRESS 1-2-2 Akasaka Minato-ku Tokyo 107-8404
PHONE +81-3-6229-5111
FAX +81-3-6229-5110
E-MAIL webmaster@ps.nippon-foundation.or.jp
HOMEPAGE http://www.nippon-foundation.or.jp/eng/index.php3

JAPAN EXTERNAL TRADE ORGANIZATION CONTACTS

DOMESTIC OFFICES

Note:
-* only in Japanese
-To dial Japan from overseas, dial your international carrier number + 81 + the number, but drop the first 0.

Office	Address	Contact
Headquarters	2-5, Toranomon 2-chome, Minato-ku, Tokyo 105-8466	TEL: 03-3582-5511 FAX: 03-3587-0219
Osaka *	Bingo-machi Nomura Bldg. 4F, 2-1-8, Bingo-machi, Chuo-ku, Osaka 541-0051	TEL: 06-6203-3601 FAX: 06-6222-5675
Hokkaido	Sapporo MN Bldg. 5F, Kita 1, Nishi 3 Chuo-ku,Sapporo 060-0001	TEL: 011-261-7434 FAX: 011-221-0973
Aomori *	Meijiseimei Aomori Chuo Bldg. 7F, 1-23-5, Chuo, Aomori 030-0822	TEL: 017-734-2575 FAX: 017-773-2877
Morioka *	Nourin Kaikan Bldg. 6F, 1-3-6 Saien, Morioka 020-0024	TEL: 019-651-2359 FAX: 019-622-1695
Sendai *	Gyoshinki Bldg. 5F, 3-6-16, Honcho	TEL: 022-223-7484

	Aoba-ku, Sendai 980-0014	TEL: 022-223-7750 FAX: 022-262-6230
Akita	Taguchi Bldg. 1F, 2-1-40 San-noh, Akita 010-0951	TEL: 018-865-8062 FAX: 018-888-1771
Yamagata *	CoCo21 Bldg. 5F, 1-4-47 Nanuka-machi, Yamagata 990-0042	TEL: 023-622-8225 FAX: 023-623-1014
Fukushima *	Big Pallet Fukushima 3F, 19-8, Kitasenbo, Hidenoyama, Asaka-machi, Koriyama 963-0101	TEL: 024-947-9800 FAX: 024-947-9810
Chiba *	World Business Garden Marib East 23F, 2-6 Nakase, Mihama-ku, Chiba 261-7123	TEL: 043-271-4100 FAX: 043-271-4480
Yokohama	YCS Bldg. 3F, 5-1, Sakae-cho, Kanagawa-ku, Yokohama 221-0052	TEL: 045-451-9061 FAX: 045-451-9060
Niigata *	Ebara Niigata Bldg. 5F, 16-4 Shinko-cho, Niigata 950-0965	TEL: 025-284-6991 FAX: 025-284-7910
Toyama	Joho Bldg. 2F, 527, Takata Toyama 930-0866	TEL: 076-444-7901 FAX: 076-444-7903
Kanazawa *	Ishikawa-ken Jiba Sangyo Shinko Center Shinkan 4F, 2-20, Kuratsuki, Kanazawa 920-0223	TEL: 076-268-9601 FAX: 076-268-9603
Fukui	Fukui Chamber of Commerce & Industry Bldg. 6F, 2-8-1, Nishikida Fukui 918-8004	TEL: 0776-33-1661 FAX: 0776-33-7110
Nagano *	Nagano-ken Chusho Kigyo Shido Center Bldg. 1F, 131-10, Nakagosho-Okada Nagano 380-0936	TEL: 026-227-6080 FAX: 026-224-2771
Suwa *	Suwa Godochosha Bldg. 5F, 1-1644-10 Kamigawa, Suwa 392-0021	TEL: 0266-52-3442 FAX: 0266-57-0244
Gifu	Gifu Fureai Plaza 6F, 5-14-53, Yabutaminami, Gifu 500-8384	TEL: 058-271-4910 FAX: 058-271-4909
Shizuoka	Shimizu Marine Bldg. 5F 9-25, Hinode-cho, Shimizu, Shizuoka 424-0922	TEL: 0543-52-8643 FAX: 0543-52-2798
Nagoya	Nishiki SIS Bldg. 1F, 3-10-33, Nishiki, Naka-ku, Nagoya 460-0003	TEL: 052-211-4517 FAX: 052-202-0750
Mie	Kenmin Service Center Bldg. 2F, 1-954 Sakae-machi, Tsu 514-0004	TEL: 059-228-2647 FAX: 059-228-3185
Kobe	Kobe C.I.T. Center Bldg. 6F, 5-1-14 Hamabedori, Chuo-ku, Kobe 651-6591	TEL: 078-231-3081 FAX: 078-232-3439
Tottori *	Tottori Chamber of Commerce & Industry Bldg. 2F, 3-102, Hon-cho, Tottori 680-0031	TEL: 0857-29-6622 FAX: 0857-29-4874
Matsue	Shimane-kenritsu Sangyo Koryu Kaikan 3F, 1-2-1, Gakuen-minami, Matsue 690-0826	TEL: 0852-27-3121 FAX: 0852-22-4196
Okayama *	Okayama Chamber of Commerce & Industry Bldg. 5F, 3-1-15, Kousei-cho, Okayama 700-0985	TEL: 086-224-0853 FAX: 086-224-0854
Hiroshima	Hiroshima Chamber of Commerce & Industry Bldg. 4F, 5-44, Moto-machi Naka-ku, Hiroshima 730-0011	TEL: 082-228-2563 FAX: 082-228-2596
Yamaguchi	Kaikyo Messe Shimonoseki Kokusai	TEL: 0832-31-5022

	Boeki Bldg. 2F, 3-3-1, Buzenda-cho, Shimonoseki 750-0018	FAX: 0832-33-3506
Tokushima *	Tokushima Life Science Research Center Bldg. 3F, 209-5, Hiraishisumiyoshi Kawauchi-cho, Tokushima 771-0134	TEL: 088-665-8126 FAX: 088-665-6869
Kagawa	Takamatsu Chamber of Commerce & Industry Bldg. 5F, 2-2-2, Ban-cho, Takamatsu 760-0017	TEL: 087-851-9407 FAX: 087-822-1931
Ehime *	Item Ehime 3F, 2-1-28, Okaga, Matsuyama 791-8057	TEL: 089-952-0015 FAX: 089-952-8588
Kochi *	Kochi Chuo Dai-ichi Seimei Bldg. 6F 2-26, Sakai-machi, Kochi 780-0834	TEL: 088-823-1320 FAX: 088-823-6413
Fukuoka *	Elgala, 7F, 1-4-2, Tenjin, Chuo-ku, Fukuoka, 810-0001	TEL: 092-741-8783 FAX: 092-714-0709
Kitakyushu	AIM Bldg. 8F, 3-8-1, Asano, Kokurakita-ku, Kitakyushu 802-0001	TEL: 093-541-6577 FAX: 093-551-2685
Nagasaki	Nagasaki Shoko Kaikan Bldg. 9F, 4-1 Sakura-machi, Nagasaki 850-0031	TEL: 095-823-7704 FAX: 095-828-0037
Kumamoto *	Kumamoto-shi Sangyo Bunka Kaikan Bldg. 4F, 7-10, Hanabata-cho, Kumamoto 860-0806	TEL: 096-354-4211 FAX: 096-324-0751
Oita *	Oita International Trade Center Bldg. 3F, 6, Ozai, Oita 870-0266	TEL: 097-592-4081 FAX: 097-592-0499
Kagoshima	Kagoshima-ken Sangyo Kaikan Bldg. 6F, 9-1, Meizan-cho, Kagoshima 892-0821	TEL: 099-226-9156 FAX:099-222-8389
Okinawa *	Daido Kasai Kume Bldg. 6F, 2-2-20, Kume, Naha 900-0033	TEL: 098-868-7546 FAX: 098-862-5977

OVERSEAS OFFICES

NORTH AMERICA

U.S.A				
	JETRO ATLANTA	245 Peachtree Center Avenue, Suite 2208, Marquis One Tower, Atlanta, GA 30303, U.S.A.	TEL: FAX:	1-404-681-0600 1-404-681-0713
	JETRO CHICAGO	401 North Michigan Avenue, Suite 660, Chicago, IL 60611, U.S.A.	TEL: FAX:	1-312-832-6000 1-312-832-6066
	JETRO DENVER	1200 17th Street, Suite 1110 Denver, CO 80202, U.S.A.	TEL: FAX:	1-303-629-0404 1-303-893-9522
	JETRO HOUSTON	1221 Mckinney, One Houston Center, Suite 4141, Houston, TX 77010, U.S.A.	TEL: FAX:	1-713-759-9595 1-713-759-9210
	JETRO LOS ANGELES	777, S.Figueroa Street, Suite 4900 Los Angeles, CA 90017, U.S.A.	TEL: FAX:	1-213-624-8855 1-213-629-8127
	JETRO NEW YORK	42nd Floor, McGraw-Hill Building 1221 Avenue of the Americas, New York, NY 10020-1079, U.S.A.	TEL: FAX:	1-212-997-0400 1-212-997-0464
	JETRO SAN FRANCISCO	235 Pine Street, Suite 1700, San Francisco, CA 94104,	TEL: FAX:	1-415-392-1333 1-415-788-6927

		U.S.A.		
CANADA				
	JETRO MONTREAL	1 Place Ville-Marie, Suite 1506 Montreal, QC H3B 2B5, CANADA	TEL: FAX:	1-514-879-5617 1-514-879-5618
	JETRO TORONTO	181 University Avenue, Suite 1600 Toronto, ON M5H 3M7, CANADA	TEL: FAX:	1-416-861-0000 1-416-861-9666
	JETRO VANCOUVER	World Trade Centre 660-999 Canada Place Vancouver, BC V6C 3E1, CANADA		

CENTRAL AND SOUTH AMERICA

ARGENTINA				
	JETRO BUENOS AIRES	Avda. del Libertador 498 Piso 29, (C1001ABR) Buenos Aires, ARGENTINA	TEL: FAX:	54-11-4327-2399 54-11-4327-2708
BRASIL				
	JETRO SAO PAULO	Avenida Paulista, 854-8 Andar, Conj. 82 CEP 01310-913, Sao Paulo-SP. BRASIL	TEL: FAX:	55-11-3141-0788 55-11-3253-3351
CHILE				
	JETRO SANTIAGO	Av. Andres Bello 2777, Piso 27, Oficina 2703, Edificio de la Industria, Las Condes, Santiago, CP 6760276, CHILE	TEL: FAX:	56-2-2033406 56-2-2033140
COLOMBIA				
	JETRO BOGOTA	Carrera 16A, No. 78-65 Piso 4, Edificio Carlos Alberto, Bogota, COLOMBIA	TEL: FAX:	57-1-256-4418 57-1-611-1985
COSTA RICA				
	JETRO SAN JOSE	Oficentro Ejecutivo La Sabana, Anexo a la Torre 6, Piso 2, Sabana Sur San Jose, COSTA RICA	TEL: FAX:	506-296-7885 506-291-1364
MEXICO				
	JETRO MEXICO	Paseo de las Palmas No. 239 Piso 3, Col. Lomas de Chapultepec, C.P. 11000, Mexico, D.F. MEXICO	TEL: FAX:	52-55-5202-7900 52-55-202-8003
PANAMA				
	JETRO PANAMA	World Trade Centre, Piso 10, Calle 53, Marbella, Panama, PANAMA	TEL: FAX:	507-263-5850 507-263-2881
PERU				
	JETRO LIMA	Av. Victor Andres Belaunde 147 Edificio Real Uno Of. 702 San Isidro, Lima, PERU	TEL: FAX:	51-1-441-5175 51-1-440-0527
VENEZUELA				
	JETRO CARACAS	Centro Gerencial Mohedano Piso 4, Oficina 4-A-2, Calle Los Chaguaramos. La Castellana, Caracas, VENEZUELA	TEL: FAX:	58-212-261-4823 58-212-261-6871

EUROPE

AUSTRIA			
JETRO WIEN	Mariahilferstrasse 41-43/3. Stock, 1060 Wien OSTERREICH / AUSTRIA	TEL: FAX:	43-1-587-56-28 43-1-586-22-93
BELGIUM			
JETRO BRUXELLES	Rue d'Arlon 69-71, Boite 2, B-1040 Bruxelles, BELGIQUE	TEL: FAX:	32-2-282-0500 32-2-280-2530
CZECH			
JETRO PRAHA	Parizska 11/67,110 00 Praha 1, CZECH REPUBLIC	TEL: FAX:	420-22481-4971 420-22481-3998
DENMARK			
JETRO COPENHAGEN	Fiolstraede 17, 4th Floor, 1171 Copenhagen K, DENMARK	TEL: FAX:	45-33-63-73-83 45-33-11-01-36
FINLAND			
JETRO HELSINKI	World Trade Center Helsinki P.O.Box 800 (Aleksanterinkatu 17), 00101 Helsinki, FINLAND	TEL: FAX:	358-9-6969-4545 358-9-6969-4546
FRANCE			
JETRO LYON	20, Place Louis Pradel, 69001 Lyon, FRANCE	TEL: FAX:	33-4-72-98-07-07 33-4-72-98-07-08
JETRO PARIS	151 bis, Rue Saint-Honore, 75001 Paris, FRANCE	TEL: FAX:	33-1-42-61-27-27 33-1-42-61-19-46
GERMANY			
JETRO BERLIN	Friedrichstadt Passagen-Quartier 205, Friedrichstr. 70, 10117 Berlin BUNDESREPUBLIK DEUTSCHLAND	TEL: FAX:	49-30-2094-5560 49-30-2094-5561
JETRO DUSSELDORF	Konigsallee 58, 40212 Dusseldorf, BUNDESREPUBLIK DEUTSCHLAND	TEL: FAX:	49-211-136020 49-211-326411
JETRO FRANKFURT	Rossmarkt 17, 60311 Frankfurt, BUNDESREPUBLIK DEUTSCHLAND	TEL: FAX:	49-69-28-32-15 49-69-28-33-59
JETRO MUNCHEN	Promenadeplatz 12, 80333 Munchen, BUNDESREPUBLIK DEUTSCHLAND	TEL: FAX:	49-89-2908420 49-89-29084289
GREECE			
JETRO ATHENS	30 Anagnostopoulou Street, Kolonaki, 106 73, Athens, GREECE	TEL: FAX:	30-210-3630820 30-210-3621231
HUNGARY			
JETRO BUDAPEST	1051 Budapest, Bajcsy-Zsilinszky ut 12, HUNGARY	TEL: FAX:	36-1-266-7687 36-1-266-7688
IRELAND			
JETRO DUBLIN	2nd Floor, Statoil Building. 1, Setanta Place, Dublin 2, IRELAND	TEL: FAX:	353-1-671-4003 353-1-671-4302
ITALY			

	JETRO MILANO	Via Agnello 6/1 20121 Milano, ITALIA	TEL: FAX:	39-02-7211791 39-02-72023072
NETHERLANDS				
	JETRO AMSTERDAM	World Trade Center, Amsterdam, Tower-C 4th Floor, Strawinskylaan 447, 1077 XX Amsterdam, THE NETHERLANDS	TEL: FAX:	31-20-6765075 31-20-6647597
NORWAY				
	JETRO OSLO	Wergelandsveien 7, 0167 Oslo, NORWAY	TEL: FAX:	47-22-36-12-17 47-22-36-08-13
POLAND				
	JETRO WARSZAWA	IPC Business Center, ul. Koszykowa 54, 00-675 Warszawa, POLAND	TEL: FAX:	48-22-6308-508 48-22-6308-512
PORTUGAL				
	JETRO LISBON	Empreendimento Das Amoreiras, Av. Eng-Duarte Pacheco, Torre 2, 11 Andar, Sala 12, 1070-102 Lisboa / PORTUGAL	TEL: FAX:	351-21-387-5028 351-21-383-1818
ROMANIA				
	JETRO BUCHAREST	International Business Center Modern, 34-36 Carol I, 5th Floor Sect 2, Bucharest, ROMANIA	TEL: FAX:	40-21-250-9601 40-21-250-9600
RUSSIA				
	JETRO MOSCOW LIAISON OFFICE	121059, Moscow, Berezhkovskaja Naberezhnaja 2, Hotel and Business Center "Radisson-Slavjanskaja", South Wing, Entresol Floor, RUSSIAN FEDERATION	TEL: FAX:	7-095-941-88-66 7-095-941-88-69
SPAIN				
	JETRO MADRID	Plaza de Colon, 2, Torres de Colon, I, 7, 28046 Madrid, ESPANA	TEL: FAX:	34-91-391-2100 34-91-310-3659
SWEDEN				
	JETRO STOCKHOLM	Kungsgatan 48, 4th Floor, 11135 Stockholm, SWEDEN	TEL: FAX:	46-8-4118173 46-8-4111888
SWITZERLAND				
	JETRO GENEVE	80, rue de Lausanne, 1202 Geneve, SWITZERLAND	TEL: FAX:	41-22-732-1304 41-22-732-0772
	JETRO ZURICH	Stampfenbachstrasse 38, 8023 Zurich, SWITZERLAND	TEL: FAX:	41-1-362-2323 41-1-362-7056
U.K.				
	JETRO LONDON (Japan Trade Centre)	Leconfield House, Curzon Street, London, W1J 5HZ, U.K.	TEL: FAX:	44-20-7470-4700 44-20-7491-7570
	JAPAN SHIP CENTRE (JETRO)	Ground Floor, 9 Marshalsea Road, London, SE1 1EP, U.K.	TEL: FAX:	44-20-7403-1666 44-20-7403-1777
UZBEKISTAN				

JETRO TASHKENT	c/o International Business Center 107-B Amir Temur Street, Tashkent 700084, UZBEKISTAN	TEL: FAX:	998-71-120-5591 998-71-120-5590

ASIA

BANGLADESH			
JETRO DHAKA	Sharif Plaza 3rd Floor, 39, Kamal Ataturk Avenue, Banani, Dhaka, BANGLADESH	TEL: FAX:	880-2-8818222 880-2-8818224
CHINA			
JETRO BEIJING	7003 Chang Fu Gong Office Building, Jia-26, Jian Guo Men Wai Street, Beijing, CHINA 100022	TEL: FAX:	86-10-6513-7075 86-10-6513-7079
JETRO DALIAN	5th Floor, Senmao Building, 147 Zhongshan Road, Dalian, CHINA 116011	TEL: FAX:	86-411-3609-418 86-411-3609-498
JETRO HONG KONG	Suites 807-811, One Pacific Place, 88 Queensway, HONG KONG, CHINA	TEL: FAX:	852-2526-4067 852-2868-1455
JETRO SHANGHAI	Room 2102-2112, Shanghai International Trade Centre., 2201, Yan An Xi Road, Shanghai 200336, CHINA	TEL: FAX:	86-21-62700489 86-21-62700499
INDIA			
JETRO MUMBAI	95, Maker Chambers VI, 9th Floor, Nariman Point, Mumbai 400021, INDIA	TEL: FAX:	91-22-2202-8342 91-22-2204-8507
JETRO NEW DELHI	8th Floor, Ambadeep 14, Kasturba Gandhi Marg, New Delhi 110001, INDIA	TEL: FAX:	91-11-2331-2194 91-11-2331-3453
INDONESIA			
JETRO JAKARTA	Summitmas I, 6th Floor, Jl. Jend. Sudirman Kav. 61-62, Jakarta 12190, INDONESIA	TEL: FAX:	62-21-5200264 62-21-5200261
KOREA			
JETRO SEOUL	3rd Floor, Young Poong Bldg., 33, Sorin-dong , Chongro-ku, Seoul, REPUBLIC OF KOREA	TEL: FAX:	82-2-739-8657 82-2-739-4658
MALAYSIA			
JETRO KUALA LUMPUR	23rd Floor, Menara Tun Razak, Jalan Raja Laut, 50350 Kuala Lumpur, MALAYSIA	TEL: FAX:	60-3-26930244 60-3-26930132
MYANMAR			
JETRO YANGON	Sedona Business Suites #04-02, No.1 kaba Aye Pagona Road, Yakin Township, Yangon, UNION OF MYANMAR	TEL: FAX:	95-1-544051 95-1-544048
PAKISTAN			
JETRO KARACHI	2nd Floor, Block-B, Finance and Trade Centre (FTC), Shahrah-e-Faisal, KARACHI, PAKISTAN	TEL: FAX:	92-21-5210459 92-21-5684426
PHILIPPINES			
JETRO MANILA	44th Floor, Philamlife Tower, 8767 Paseo de Roxas, Makati City 1226, Metro Manila, PHILIPPINES	TEL: FAX:	63-2-892-4376 63-2-818-7490

SINGAPORE		
JETRO SINGAPORE	Hong Leong Building, #38-01 to 05 #37-02A 16 Raffles Quay, SINGAPORE 048581	TEL: 65-6221-8174 FAX: 65-6224-1169
SRI LANKA		
JETRO COLOMBO	4th Floor, Carson Cumberbatch Building, No.65C, Dharmapala Mawatha,Colombo 7, SRI LANKA	TEL: 94-11-2323354 FAX: 94-11-2541221
THAILAND		
JETRO BANGKOK	JETRO Building, 159 Rajadamri Rd., Bangkok 10330, THAILAND	TEL: 66-2-253-6441 FAX: 66-2-253-2020
VIETNAM		
JETRO HANOI	3rd Floor, 63 Ly Thai To, Hanoi, S.R.VIETNAM	TEL: 84-4-8250630 FAX: 84-4-8250552
JETRO HO CHI MINH	14th Floor, Sun Wah Tower 115, Nguyen Hue Street, District 1, Ho Chi Minh City, VIETNAM	TEL: 84-8-821-9363 FAX: 84-8-821-9362

OCEANIA

AUSTRALIA		
JETRO MELBOURNE	Level 21, 101 Collins Street, Melbourne, VIC 3000, AUSTRALIA	TEL: 61-3-9654-4949 FAX: 61-3-9654-2962
JETRO SYDNEY	Level 19, Gateway Building, 1 Macquarie Place, Sydney NSW 2000, AUSTRALIA	TEL: 61-2-9241-1181 FAX: 61-2-9251-7631
NEW ZEALAND		
JETRO AUCKLAND	Level 10, Westpac Trust Tower, 120 Albert Street, Auckland, NEW ZEALAND	TEL: 64-9-379-7427 FAX: 64-9-309-5046

MIDDLE EAST AND AFRICA

COTE D'IVOIRE		
JETRO ABIDJAN	F62, Immeuble le Jeceda, Bld. de la Republique, Plateau, Abidjan, COTE D'IVOIRE	TEL: 225-20-21-78-15 FAX: 225-20-22-78-16
EGYPT		
JETRO CAIRO	7th Floor, World Trade Center Cairo, 1191 Corniche El Nill, Cairo, EGYPT	TEL: 20-2-574-1111 FAX: 20-2-575-6966
IRAN		
JETRO TEHRAN	1st Floor, No.21, 17th Street, Gandhy Avenue Post Code 15178, Tehran, IRAN	TEL: 98-21-877-7357 FAX: 98-21-877-8431
ISRAEL		
JETRO TEL-AVIV	Migdaley Aviv B, 8th Floor 48 Derech Petach Tikva, Tel-Aviv 66184, ISRAEL	TEL: 972-3-688-1739 FAX: 972-3-537-9157
KENYA		

JETRO NAIROBI	International House, 4th Floor, Mama Ngina Street, Nairobi, KENYA	TEL: FAX:	254-20-226741 254-20-242456
NIGERIA			
JETRO LAGOS	Flat No.1, No.4A Kofo Abayomi Street, Victoria Island, Lagos, NIGERIA	TEL: FAX:	234-1-2613751 234-1-2618482
SAUDI ARABIA			
JETRO RIYADH	Abunayyan Building, King Abdulaziz road, Riyadh, SAUDI ARABIA	TEL: FAX:	966-1-478-4393 966-1-476-1815
SOUTH AFRICA			
JETRO JOHANNESBURG	1st Floor, Sanlam Park West, 9 Fredman Drive, Sandton 2196, REPUBLIC OF SOUTH AFRICA	TEL: FAX:	27-11-784-6084 27-11-784-8725
TANZANIA			
JETRO DAR ES SALAAM	JETRO Dar Es Salaam will be closed as of December 22,2003 -regular services are no longer available.		
TURKEY			
JETRO ISTANBUL	Buyukdere Caddesi, Maya Akar Center, B Block, Kat 14, Daire 54 Esentepe, 34394 Istanbul, TURKEY	TEL: FAX:	90-212-275-5180 90-212-288-0739
U.A.E.			
JETRO DUBAI	Room No.2401, 24th Floor, Al Moosa Tower-2, Sheikh Zayed Road, Dubai, THE UNITED ARAB EMIRATES	TEL: FAX:	971-4-3328264 971-4-3328305
ZIMBABWE			
JETRO HARARE	JETRO Harare will be closed as of December 30,2003 -regular services are no longer available.		

JETRO INVEST JAPAN BUSINESS SUPPORT CENTER (IBSC) AND

JETRO Invest Japan Business Support Center (IBSC) and Business Support Centers (BSC) offer free office space with consulting services and more!

To support foreign investment and market-entry activities in Japan, JETRO operates the IBSC in Tokyo and BSCs in Yokohama, Nagoya, Osaka, Kobe, and Fukuoka. In addition to providing free office space, the centers are staffed with advisors who provide complementary consulting services.

Invest Japan Business Support Center (Tokyo)
Akasaka Twin Tower, 2-17-22, Akasaka, Minato-ku, Tokyo 107-0052
Tel.03-5562-3131 Fax.03-5562-3100
Yokohama Business Support Center
Yokohama Creation Square, 5-1, Sakae-cho, Kanagawa-ku, Yokohama 221-0052
Tel.045-451-9071 Fax.045-451-9070
Nagoya Business Support Center
Nishiki SIS Bldg., 10-33 Nishiki 3-Chome, Naka-ku, Nagoya-shi 460-0003
Tel.052-222-4711 Fax.052-222-4750
Osaka Business Support Center
ATC Bldg., ITM-5F, 1-10, Nanko Kita 2-Chome, Suminoe-ku, Osaka 559-0034

Tel.066-614-8910 Fax.066-614-8914

Kobe Business Support Center

Kobe Fashion Mart, Japan Market Center, 9, Koyocho Naka 6-chome, Higashinada-ku, Kobe-shi 658-0032
Tel.078-857-7221 Fax.078-857-7222

Fukuoka Business Support Center

Elgala 7F, 1-4-2, Tenjin, Chuo-ku, Fukuoka-shi, 810-0001
Tel.092-735-4224 Fax.092-735-4223

JETRO IMPORTED HOUSING EXHIBITION SITES

JETRO Imported Housing Exhibitions introduce Japanese consumers to popular models of imported housing from such countries as the US, Canada, and the UK. Through these exhibitions, JETRO provides information to consumers and companies interested in house imports. Various information on imported housing and related companies is available at the information corner set up in each exhibition site.

Location

SENDAI

Kahoku TBC Sogo-Jutaku Tenjijo, 45, Hachimansaki-mae, Rifu-aza, Rifu-cho, Miyagi-gun 981-0112
TEL/FAX .022-767-9530

NAGOYA

JETRO Nagoya Imported Housing Exhibition FAMES, 73, Futakata-cho, Nishi-ku, Nagoya 452-0817
TEL.052-503-7300 FAX.052-503-7222

HIROSHIMA

RCC Jutaku-Ten Premier, 4-9-4, Kannonshinmachi, Nishi-ku, Hiroshima 733-0036
TEL.082-291-5520 FAX.082-291-5520

AREAS APPROVED FOR FAZ

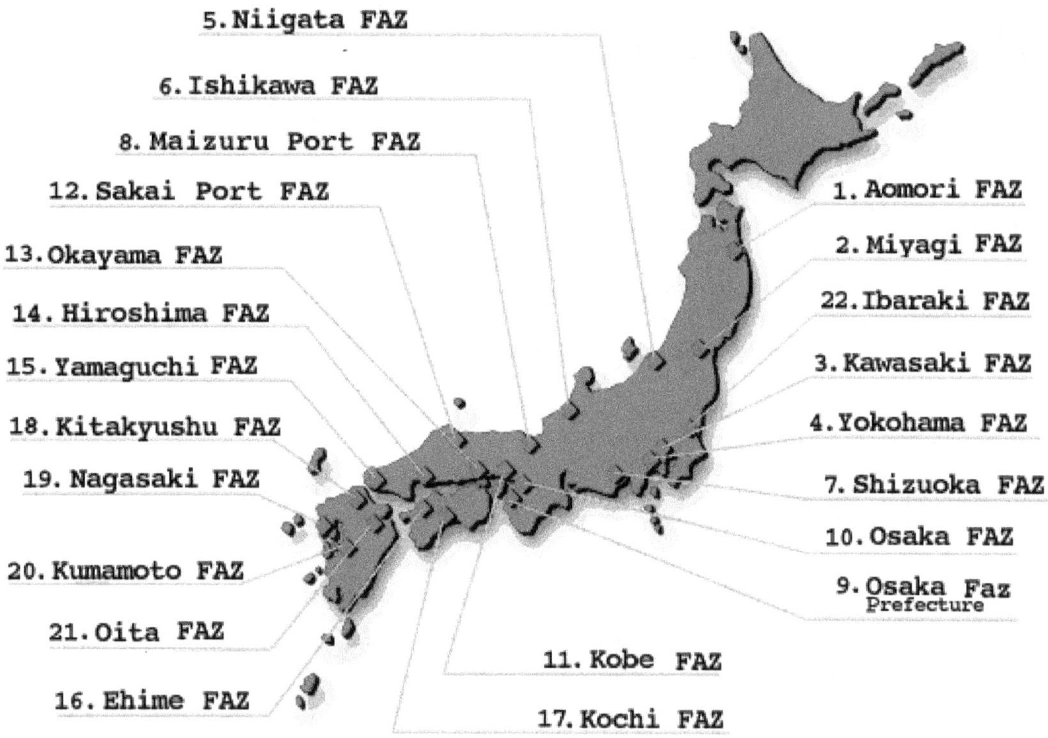

1. **Aomori Prefecture (Hachinohe Port Area)**
   Hachinohe Port Trade Center Co., Ltd.
   Hachinohe Port Trade Center 3F. 3-9,
   Toyosu, Hachinohe City, Aomori 039-1162, Japan
   TEL:+81-178-72-1505 FAX:+81-178-72-1503

2. **Miyagi Prefecture (Sendai Port / Sendai Airport Area)**
   Sendai Port Trade Promotion Center Co., Ltd.
   3rd Floor, Sendai Port International Business Support Center
   1-3, Minato3chome, Miyagino-ku, Sendai City, Miyagi 980-0014, Japan
   TEL:+81-22-265-8730 FAX:+81-22-265-8735

   Sendai Air-Cargo Terminal Co., Ltd.
   Sendai Airport, Minamihara, Shimomasuda, Natori City, Miyagi 989-2401, Japan
   TEL:+81-22-383-6201 FAX:+81-22-383-6204

3. **Kawasaki City (Kawasaki Port Area)**
   Kawasaki FAZ Inc.
   6-10, Higashiohgishima, Kawasaki-ku, Kawasaki City, Kanagawa 210-0869, Japan
   TEL:+81-44-272-2050 FAX:+81-44-272-2059

4. **Yokohama City (Yokohama Port Area)**
   Yokohama Port International Cargo Center Co., Ltd.

No.22, Daikoku-futo, Tsurumi-ku, Yokohama City,
Kanagawa 230-0054 Japan
TEL:+81-45-510-2000 FAX:+81-45-510-2019

Yokohama Import Mart Inc.
Yokohama World Porters, 3F
2-2-1 Shinko, Naka-ku, Yokohama City, Kanagawa 231-0023, Japan
TEL:81-45-222-2099 FAX:81-45-222-2095

5. **Niigata Prefecture (Niigata Port Area)**
Niigata World Trade Terminal Co., Ltd.
3228-2, Yokodoi, Toyosaka City, Niigata 950-3303, Japan
TEL:+81-25-388-1001 FAX:+81-25-388-1008

6. **Ishikawa Prefecture (Komatsu Airport Area)**
Hokuriku International Air Cargo Terminal Co., Ltd.
Ha-39, Kusano-machi, Komatsu City, Ishikawa 923-0996, Japan
TEL:+81-761-23-7025 FAX:+81-761-23-7027

7. **Shizuoka Prefecture (Shimizu Port Area)**
Shimizu Port Research & Development Co., Ltd.
1375-16, Shimizu Okitsu Seikenji-cho, Shizuoka City, Shizuoka 424-0206, Japan
TEL:+81-543-69-6666 FAX:+81-543-69-5300

8. **Kyoto Prefecture (Maizuru Port Area)**
Maizuru 21 Inc.
Maizuru 21 Bldg.3F Kita 1105-1, Azakita, Maizuru City,
Kyoto 624-0945, Japan
TEL:+81-773-77-2421 FAX:+81-773-77-2420

9. **Osaka Prefecture (Kansai International Airport Area)**
Rinku International Logistics Co., Ltd.
2-21, Rinku-Orai-Kita, Izumisano City, Osaka 598-0048, Japan
TEL:+81-724-69-5111 FAX:+81-724-69-5211

Rinku Gate Tower Bldg. Co., Ltd.
12F Rinku Gate Tower Bldg., 1, Rinku-Orai-Kita, Izumisano City,
Osaka 598-0048, Japan
TEL:+81-724-60-1010 FAX:+81-724-60-1002

10. **Osaka City (Osaka Port Area)**
ATC Corporation
2-1-10, Nanko-kita, Suminoe-ku, Osaka City,
Osaka 559-0034, Japan
TEL:+81-6-6615-5000 FAX:+81-6-6615-5020

World Trade Center Building(Osaka), Inc.
1-14-16, Nanko-kita, Suminoe-ku, Osaka City,
Osaka 559-0034, Japan
TEL:+81-6-6615-6000 FAX:+81-6-6615-6040

11. **Kobe City (Kobe Port Area)**
Kobe Air Cargo City Terminal Co., Ltd.
4-16, Koyocho-Higashi, Higashinada-ku, Kobe City,
Hyogo 658-0031, Japan
TEL:+81-78-858-1500 FAX:+81-78-858-1501

12. **Tottori Prefecture and Shimane Prefecture (Sakai Port Area)**

Sakaiminato Internatilnal Trade Center Inc.
Yume Minato Tower 2F., 255-3, Takenouchi-Danchi,
Sakaiminato City, Tottori 684-0046, Japan
TEL:+81-859-47-3900 FAX:+81-859-47-3906

13. **Okayama Prefecture (Okayama Airport Area)**
Okayama Airport Terminal Co., Ltd.
1277, Nichioji, Okayama City, Okayama 701-1131, Japan
TEL:+81-86-294-5201 FAX:+81-86-294-5242

Mizushima Port International Logistics Center Co., Ltd.
8262-1, Shinminato, Tamashima Otoshima, Kurashiki City,
Okayama 713-8103, Japan

14. **Hiroshima Prefecture (Hiroshima Airport Area)**
Hiroshima Air Cargo Terminal Co., Ltd.
67-1, Zennyuji, Hongo-cho, Toyota-gun, Hiroshima 729-0416, Japan
TEL:+81-848-60-8050 FAX:+81-848-60-8051

15. **Yamaguchi Prefecture (Shimonoseki Port Area)**
Yamaguchi International Trade & Cultural Center
Kaikyo Messe Shimonoseki
3-3-1, Buzenda-cho, Shimonoseki City, Yamaguchi 750-0018, Japan
TEL:+81-832-31-5778 FAX:+81-832-31-5787

16. **Ehime Prefecture (Matsuyama Port Area)**
Ehime Foreign Access Zone Co., Ltd.
Item Ehime,
2-1-28, Okaga, Matsuyama City, Ehime 791-8057, Japan
TEL:+81-89-951-1211 FAX:+81-89-951-2955

17. **Kochi Prefecture (Port of Kochi Zone)**
Kochi Trade Service Co., Ltd.
4700 Shinko, Niida, Kochi City, Kochi 780-0012, Japan
TEL:+81-88-847-4600 FAX:+81-88-837-3038

18. **Kitakyushu City (Kitakyushu Port Area)**
Kitakyushu Import Promotion Center Co., Ltd. (KIPRO)
8th Floor, Asia-Pacific Import Mart (AIM), 3-8-1 Asano, Kokurakita-ku, Kitakyushu City, Fukuoka 802-0001, Japan
TEL:+81-93-551-8828 FAX:+81-93-551-8826

19. **Nagasaki Prefecture (Nagasaki Airport Area)**
Nagasaki International Air Cargo Terminal Co.,Ltd.
593-8, Mishima-cho, Omura City, Nagasaki 856-0816, Japan
TEL:+81-957-54-9755 FAX:+81-957-54-9622

20. **Kumamoto Prefecture (Kumamoto Port Area)**
Kumamoto Foreign Access Zone Co., Ltd.
Sangyo Bunka Kaikan 4F., 7-10, Hanabata-cho, Kumamoto City, Kumamoto 860-0806, Japan
TEL:+81-96-354-6687 FAX:+81-96-354-6608

21. **Oita Prefecture (Oita Port Area)**
Oita International Trade Center Co.,Ltd.(OITAC)
Oita International Trade Center 4F., 6 Ozai, Oita City,
Oita 870-0266, Japan
TEL:+81-97-592-5931 FAX:+81-97-593-3338

22. **Ibaraki Prefecture(Hitachinaka Port Area)**
    Hitachinaka Urban development Co.,Ltd.
    38, Shinkou-cho, Hitachinaka City, Ibaraki 312-0005,Japan
    TEL:+81-29-264-2121 FAX:;81-29-264-2122

JETRO FAZ SUPPORT CENTERS

JETRO established the JETRO FAZ Support Center Tokyo in order to support the activities of the Foreign Access Zones by supplying information and conducting publicity campaigns. This aims to expand imports to Japan and stimulate investment in Japan from abroad.

The JETRO FAZ Support Center Tokyo collects and disseminates information relating to approved FAZs throughout Japan. The center offers advisory services to parties interested in starting a business within FAZ borders, parties seeking regional business information, and parties with the corporate desire to export to or invest in Japan.

The Tokyo Center maintains a library of printed materials on every FAZ and a wide range of other subjects of special interest to the foreign businessperson, as follows:

Regional resources: information on each area's economy, market, infrastructure, investment climate and available real estate, business directories, maps, etc.
General resources: statistics, white papers, trade/investment reference materials, laws and standards, individual product markets, dictionaries, yearbooks, JETRO reports, etc.

A wide range of electronic information can be accessed through the Tokyo Center's computer system. Sources include JETRO's extensive on-line resources and data stored on CD-ROM. Users can perform searches to obtain specific information about a variety of subjects, including FAZs, investment in Japan, importers interested in specific products, import procedures for specific products, information about individual companies, and much more.

Visitors to the Tokyo Center can also view videos produced by organizations including JETRO, FAZ third-sector companies and regional governments around Japan.

Model replicas, panel displays and brochures provide the information you'll need to find the FAZ best suited to you.

English-speaking consultants staff the Tokyo Center to answer questions about FAZs. Individual consultations can be arranged to discuss trading and investing in general, how to find and select partners, and much more.

Address: 3rd Floor, Akasaka Twin Tower, 2-17-22, Akasaka, Minato-ku, Tokyo 107-0052

Tel: +81-3-3584-6021

Fax: +81-3-3584-6024

E-mail: tokyofaz@jetro.go.jp

URL: http://www.jetro.go.jp/

Open: 9:00 a.m. - 5:00 p.m.

Closed: Saturday, Sunday, national holidays, end-of-year/New Year holidays.

Centers	Contact	Services
Sendai 	3rd Floor,Sendai Port International Business Support Center. 1-3, Minato 3-chome,Miyagino-ku,Sendai 983-0001 Tel:022-388-7740 Fax:022-388-7741	information; consulting
Kawasaki 	3rd Floor, Institute of Industry Promotion Kawasaki 66-20 Horikawa-cho, Saiwai-ku, Kawasaki City, Kanagawa 212-0013 Tel: +81-44-522-7931 Fax: +81-44-520-2030	information; consulting
Osaka 	ITM-2A, Asia Pacific Trade Center(ATC) 2-1-10 Nankokita, Suminoe-ku, Osaka City, Osaka 559-0034 Tel: +81-6-6615-5255 Fax: +81-6-6615-5256	information; consulting
Osaka Rinku 	15th Floor, Rinku Gate Tower Building 1 Rinku-Orai-Kita, Izumisano City, Osaka 598-0048 Tel: +81-724-60-1022 Fax: +81-724-60-1023	information; consulting; business matching service
Kobe 	3rd Floor, Kobe Kimec Center Building 1-chome Minatojima Minamimachi, Chuo-ku, Kobe City, Hyogo 650-0047 Tel: +81-78-304-0051 Fax: +81-78-306-5318	information; consulting

Saikaiminato 	211-2 Takeuchi-danchi, Sakaiminato City, Tottori 684-0046 Tel: +81-859-45-2203 Fax: +81-859-45-2172	information; consulting
Yamaguchi 	2nd Floor, Yamaguchi International Trade and Cultural Center 3-3-1 Buzenda-cho, Shimonoseki City, Yamaguchi 750-0018 Tel: +81-832-31-5022 Fax: +81-832-33-3506	information; consulting; fairs and other events
Ehime 	3rd Floor, Item Ehime 2-1-28 Okaga, Matsuyama City, Ehime 791-8057 Tel: +81-89-952-6055 Fax: +81-89-952-5877	information; consulting; import fairs and marketing
Kitakyushu 	8th Floor, Asia-Pacific Import Mart (AIM), 3-8-1 Asano, Kokurakita-ku, Kitakyushu City, Fukuoka, 802-0001 Tel: +81-93-541-6577 Fax: +81-93-551-2685	information; consulting; import fairs and events
Oita 	3rd Floor, Oita International Trade Center Bldg., Oaza Ozai 6, Oita City, Oita 870-0266 Tel: +81-975-24-2079 Fax: +81-975-93-3490	information; consulting

US AND COUNTRY CONTACTS RELATED TO BUSINESS

U.S. EMBASSY TRADE PERSONNEL

Commercial Service Tokyo
Alan Turley, Minister-Counselor for Commercial Affairs
U.S. Embassy, Tokyo
1-10-5 Akasaka, Minato-ku, Tokyo 107-8420
Phone: +81/3/3224-5060 Fax: +81/3/3589-4235
www.csjapan.doc.gov

American Business Information Center (ABIC)
Phone: +81/3/3224-5075 Fax: +81/3/3589-4235
(U.S. Address: Unit 45004, Box 204, APO AP 96337-5004)

Ira Kasoff, Counselor
E. Keith Kirkham, Attache, Information Technology
Rick A. de Lambert, Attache, Transport, Machinery & Safety
John E. Simmons, Attache, Medical Equipment, Healthcare & Intellectual Property Protection
Greg Briscoe, Attache
Steven Corless, Attache

U.S. Trade Center
Frank G. Carrico, Director
World Import Mart 7F
3-1-3 Higashi-Ikebukuro, Toshima-ku, Tokyo 170-8630
Phone: +81/3/3987-2441 Fax: +81/3/3987-2447
(U.S. Address: c/o American Embassy Tokyo
Unit 45004, Box 229, APO AP 96337-5004)

Commercial Service Osaka
Kenneth B. Reidbord, Principal Commercial Consul
Charles Reese, Commercial Consul
American Consulate General Osaka-Kobe
2-11-5 Nishitenma, Kita-ku, Osaka 530-8543
Phone: +81/6/315-5957 Fax: +81/6/315-5963
(U.S. Address: Unit 45004, Box 239, APO AP 96337-5004)

Commercial Service Nagoya
Gary Konop, Principal Commercial Consul
American Consulate Nagoya
3-10-33 Nishiki, Naka-ku, Nagoya 460-0003
Phone: +81/52/203-4277 Fax: +81/52/201-4612
(U.S. Address: Unit 45004, Box 280, APO AP 96337-5004)

Commercial Service Sapporo
Michael Meserve, Consul General
Peter H. Barlerin, Econ/Commercial Officer
American Consulate General Sapporo
Nishi 28, Kita 1, Chuo-ku, Sapporo 064-0821
Phone: +81/11/641-1115 Fax: +81/11/643-1283
(U.S. Address: Unit 45004, Box 276, APO AP 96337-5004)

Commercial Service Fukuoka
Scott A. Smith, Consul
American Consulate Fukuoka

2-5-26 Ohori, Chuo-ku, Fukuoka 810-0052
Phone: +81/92/751-9331 Fax: +81/92/725-3772
(U.S. Address: Unit 45004, Box 242, APO AP 96337-5004)

Naha Consulate
Robert S. Luke, Consul General
American Consulate General Naha
No.2564 Nishihara, Urasoe City, Okinawa 901-2101
Phone: +81/98/876-4211 Fax: +81/98/876-4243
(U.S. Address: PSC 556, Box 840, FPO AP 96372-0840)

Foreign Agricultural Service
Suzanne K. Hale, Minister-Counselor for Agricultural Affairs
(effective November, 2000)
Michael D. Woolsey, Senior Agricultural Attache
Casey E. Bean, Agricultural Attache
Kevin Latner, Agricultural Attache (effective August, 2000)
Terrence Barber, Senior Director, Japan ATOs (until August, 2000)
David C. Miller, Director, Agricultural Trade Office (Tokyo)
Karen B. Halliburton, Deputy Director, Agricultural Trade Office (Tokyo)
Daniel A. Martinez, Director, Agricultural Trade Office (Osaka)
U.S. Embassy, Tokyo
1-10-5 Akasaka, Minato-ku, Tokyo 107-8420
(U.S. Address: Unit 45004, Box 226, APO AP 96337-5004)
Phone: +81/3/3224-5105 Fax: +81/3/3589-0793
ATO Tokyo Phone: +81/3/3505-6050 or +81/3/3224/5115 Fax: +81/3/3582-6429
ATO Osaka Phone: +81/6/6315-5904 Fax: +81/6/6315-5906
www.atojapan.org

State Department Economic Section
Michael W. Michalak, Minister-Counselor for Economic Affairs
U.S. Embassy, Tokyo
1-10-5 Akasaka, Minato-ku, Tokyo 107-8420
(U.S. Address: Unit 45004, Box 203, APO AP 96337-5004)
Phone: +81/3/3224-5022 Fax: +81/3/3224-5010

Energy Department
Giulia Bisconti, Energy Attache
U.S. Embassy, Tokyo
1-10-5 Akasaka, Minato-ku, Tokyo 107-8420
(U.S. Address: Unit 45004, Box 219, APO AP 96337-5004)
Phone: +81/3/3224-5444 Fax: +81/3/3224-5769

Treasury Department
Robert Dohner, Financial Attache
U.S. Embassy, Tokyo
1-10-5 Akasaka, Minato-ku, Tokyo 107-8420
(U.S. Address: Unit 45004, Box 216, APO AP 96337-5004)
Phone: +81/3/3224-5486 Fax: +81/3/3224-5490

WASHINGTON-BASED U.S. GOVERNMENT JAPAN CONTACTS

U.S. Department of Commerce
Majory E. Searing, Acting Assistant Secretary and Director General of the
U.S. Foreign and Commercial Service
Robert Francis, Office Director, Japan
Office of Japan (OJ)
International Trade Administration

Room 2320, 14th Street and Constitution Avenue, N.W., Washington, DC 20230
OJ Phone: 202-482-1820 Fax: 202-482-0469

For further contact information on the U.S. Department of Commerce and U.S. based multipliers relevant for Japan, please contact the OJ.

JAPANESE TRADE ASSOCIATIONS/CHAMBERS OF COMMERCE

KEIDANREN
Masakazu Kubota, Director
International Relations Bureau
1-9-4 Ohtemachi, Chiyoda-ku, Tokyo 100-8188
Phone: +81/3/3279-1411 Fax: +81/3/5255-6255
www.keidanren.or.jp

KEIZAI DOYUKAI
Tohru Anjo, Managing Director, Research and International Development
Nihon Kogyo Club Bldg., 1-4-6 Marunouchi, Chiyoda-ku, Tokyo 100-0005
Phone: +81/3/3284-0220 Fax: +81/3/3212-3774
www.doyukai.or.jp

Japan Foreign Trade Council, Inc.
Shigetoshi Matsumoto, General Manager, International Affairs and Research Group
World Trade Center Bldg.
2-4-1 Hamamatsu-cho, Minato-ku, Tokyo 105-6106
Phone: +81/3/3435-5950 Fax: +81/3/3435-5979
www.jftc.or.jp

Japan-U.S. Business Council
Kunihiko Maeda, Executive Director
Otemachi Bldg. Suite 439, 1-6-1 Otemachi, Chiyoda-ku, Tokyo 100-0004
Phone: +81/3/3216-5823 Fax: +81/3/3284-1576

Japan Chamber of Commerce and Industry
Matsuo Shimojima, General Manager
International Div.
Tosho Bldg., 3-2-2 Marunouchi, Chiyoda-ku, Tokyo 100-0005
Phone: +81/3/3283-7607 Fax: +81/3/3216-6497
www.jcci.or.jp/home-e.html

Tokyo Chamber of Commerce & Industry
Matsuo Shimojima, General Manager
International Div.
Tosho Bldg., 3-2-2 Marunouchi, Chiyoda-ku, Tokyo 100-0005
Phone: +81/3/3283-7607 Fax: +81/3/3216-6497
www.tokyo-cci.or.jp

Osaka Chamber of Commerce and Industry
International Division
Shunji Kawamura, Director
2-8 Honmachi-bashi, Chuo-ku, Osaka 540-0029
Phone: +81/6/6944-6400 Fax: +81/6/6944-6293
http://new.osaka.cci.or.jp/e/

Kansai Economic Federation (Kankeiren)
Teruo Aoyagi, General Manager
International Affairs Department
Nakanoshima Center Bldg. 30F
6-2-27, Nakanoshima, Kita-ku, Osaka 530-6691
Phone: +81/6/6441-0104 Fax: +81/6/6441-0443
www.kankeiren.or.jp

The Kansai Committee for Economic Development
(KANSAI KEIZAI DOYUKAI)
Shuichi Kaneko, Senior Researcher
Nakanoshima Center Bldg. 28F
6-2-27, Nakanoshima, Kita-ku, Osaka 530-6691
Phone: +81/6/6441-1031 Fax: +81/6/6441-1030
http://kdoyukai.on.arena.ne.jp

Nagoya Chamber of Commerce and Industry
Takanori Kitamura, General Manager, International Division
2-10-19 Sakae, Naka-ku, Nagoya 460-8422
Phone: +81/52/223-5729 Fax: +81/52/232-5751
www.nagoya-cci.or.jp

The American Chamber of Commerce in Japan (ACCJ)
5F, Bridgestone Toranomon Bldg.
3-25-2 Toranomon, Minato-ku, Tokyo 105-0001
Phone: +81/3/3433-5381 Fax: +81/3/3436-1446
www.accj.or.jp

The American Chamber of Commerce in Japan (ACCJ) Kansai Chapter
Herbis Plaza Bldg. 6F, 2-5-25 Umeda, Kita-ku
Osaka 530-0001
Phone: +81/6/6343-7505 Fax: +81/6/6343-7506
www.accj.or.jp

AGRICULTURAL TRADE ASSOCIATIONS

Japan Chain Stores Association
Toranomon #40 Mori Bldg., 5-13-1 Toranomon
Minato-ku, Tokyo 105-0001
Phone: +81/3/3433-1290 Fax: +81/3/3433-1297

Japan Confectionery Association
JB Bldg. 7F, 6-9-5 Shinbashi
Minato-ku, Tokyo 105-0004
Phone: +81/3/3431-3115 Fax: +81/3/3432-1660

Japan Convenience Foods Industry Association
Kimura Bldg. 8th Floor, 5-5-5, Asakusabashi
Taito-ku, Tokyo 111-0053
Phone: +81/3/3865-0811 Fax: +81/3/3865-0815
E-mail: fvbf8260@mb.infoweb.ne.jp
www2.inter.co.jp/instantramen

Japan Dairy Products Association
1-14-19 Kudan Kita
Chiyoda-ku, Tokyo 102-0073

Phone: +81/3/3264-4131 Fax: +81/3/3264-4139
E-mail: jdpa@mx1.alpha-web.ne.jp

Japan Dehydrated Vegetable Association
3-4-1 Nihonbashi Kayabacho
Chuo-ku, Tokyo 103-0025
Phone: +81/3/3669-0286 Fax: +81/3/3639-2555
E-mail: primerd@mb.inforweb.ne.jp

Japan Food Service Association
1-29-6, Hamamatsucho
Minato-ku, Tokyo 105-0013
Phone: +81/3/5403-1060 Fax: +81/3/5403-1070
E-mail: jfnet@jfsa.or.jp

Japan Frozen Food Association
10-6 Nihonbashi Kobunacho
Chuo-ku, Tokyo 103-0024
Phone: +81/3/3667-6671 Fax: +81/3/3669-2117
E-mail: info@reishokukyo.or.jp
www.reishokukyo.or.jp/

Japan Fruit Juice Association
Dai 2 Toyo Bldg.,
2-1-21 Nihonbashi
Chuo-ku, Tokyo 103-0027
Phone: +81/3/3275-1031 Fax: +81/3/3275-1067

Japan Health Food & Nutrition Food Association
2-7-27 Ichigaya Sadohara-cho
Shinjuku-ku, Tokyo 162-0842
Phone: +81/3/3268-3131 Fax: +81/3/3268-3135
E-mail: jhnfa@mxl.alpha-web.ne.jp
www.health-station.com/jhnfa/

Japan Restaurant Association
Ginza 8-10 Bldg.
8-10-8 Ginza
Chuo-ku, Tokyo 104-0061
Phone: +81/3/3571-2438 Fax: +81/3/3571-7090
E-mail: jp.res.@joy.ne.jp
www.joy.ne.jp/restaurant/

Japan Wine And Spirits Importers Association
Daiichi Tentoku Bldg.
1-13-5 Toranomon
Minato-ku, Tokyo 105-0001
Phone: +81/3/3503-6505/6506 Fax: +81/3/3503-6504

MARKET RESEARCH FIRMS IN JAPAN

A.T. Kearney K.K.
ARK Mori Bldg., East 32F
1-12-32 Akasaka, Minato-ku, Tokyo 107-6032
Phone: +81/3/5561-9155 Fax: +81/3/5561-9190
www.atkearney.com

Boston Consulting Group K.K.
New Otani Garden Court, 4-1 Kioi-cho, Chiyoda-ku, Tokyo 102-0094
Phone: +81/3/5211-0300 Fax: +81/3/5211-0333
www.bcg.co.jp

Deloitte & Tohmatsu Consulting Co., Ltd.
Toranomon Kotohira Kaikan
1-2-8 Toranomon, Minato-ku, Tokyo 105-0001
Phone: +81/3/5521-5555 Fax: +81/3/5512-6271
www.dtcg.tohmatsu.co.jp

Fuji Chimera Research Institute, Inc.
F.K Bldg., 2-5 Nihonbashi Kodenma-cho, Chuo-ku, Tokyo 103-0001
Phone: +81/3/3664-5815 Fax: +81/3/3661-5134
www.fcr.co.jp

The Japan Research Institute, Ltd.
16 Ichibancho, Chiyoda-ku, Tokyo 102-0082
Phone: +81/3/3288-4700 Fax: +81/3/3288-4750
www.jri.co.jp

Nikkei Research Inc.
Park Side 1 Bldg., 2-2-7 Kanda Tsukasa-cho
Chiyoda-ku, Tokyo 101-0048
Phone: +81/3/5296-5111 Fax: +81/3/5296-5110
www.nikkei-r.co.jp

Sanwa Research Institute Corp.
Shimbashi Sanwa Toyo Bldg., 1-11-7 Shimbashi, Minato-ku, Tokyo 105-8631
Phone: +81/3/3572-9030 Fax: +81/3/3572-6230
www.sric.co.jp

Yano Research Institute Ltd.
2-46-2, Honcho, Nakano-ku, Tokyo 164-8620
Phone: +81/3/5371-6900 Fax: +81/3/5371-6967
www.yano.co.jp/eyrihome/index.htm

U.S. FEDERAL GOVERNMENT

TPCC Trade Information Center number in Washington
Tel: 1-800-USA-TRADE
tradeinfo.doc.gov/

U.S. Department of State
Office of Coordinator for Business Affairs
Tel: 202-647-1625 Fax: 202-647-3953

U.S. Department of Commerce MAC Country Desk Officer
(for market access and regulatory problems only)
Robert Francis, Office Director, Japan
Office of Japan (OJ)
International Trade Administration
Room 2320, Washington DC 20230
Tel: 202-482-1820 Fax: 202-482-0469

U.S. Department of Agriculture
Foreign Agricultural Service
AgExport Services Division
Tel: 202-690-3576

Overseas Private Investment Corporation
1100 New York Avenue, N.W., Washington, D.C. 20527
Tel: 202-336-8799 Fax: 202-408-9859
www.opic.gov

LOCAL CHAMBERS OF COMMERCE IN JAPAN

The HAKODATE Chamber Commerce and Industry http://www2.hotweb.or.jp/hakocci/

The OTARU Chamber Commerce and Industry http://www.mics.co.jp/otarucci/

The SAPPORO Chamber Commerce and Industry http://www.sapporo-cci.or.jp/

The OBIHIRO Chamber Commerce and Industry http://www.occi.or.jp

The KITAMI Chamber Commerce and Industry http://www.okhotsk.or.jp/~syokokac

The ABASHIRI Chamber Commerce and Industry http://www.ohotuku26.or.jp/organization/abacci/title.html

The NEMURO Chamber Commerce and Industry http://www.marimo.or.jp/~nemurocc/

The TAKIKAWA Chamber Commerce and Industry http://www.msknet.ne.jp/nks/takikawa/

The FUKAGAWA Chamber Commerce and Industry http://www.msknet.ne.jp/nks/fukagawa/

The SUNAGAWA Chamber Commerce and Industry http://www.msknet.ne.jp/nks/sunagawa/

The FURANO Chamber Commerce and Industry http://www.furano.or.jp/furano-cci/

The NAYORO Chamber Commerce and Industry http://www.hokkai.or.jp/nayocci/

The EBETSU Chamber Commerce and Industry http://www1.sphere.ne.jp/ebet-cci/ebetsu/

The TOMAKOMAI Chamber Commerce and Industry http://www.tomakomai.or.jp/cci/home.htm

The ENIWA Chamber Commerce and Industry http://www.annupuri.com/eniwacci/

The AOMORI Chamber Commerce and Industry http://www.acci.or.jp/

The HIROSAKI Chamber Commerce and Industry http://www.hcci.or.jp

The TOWADA Chamber Commerce and Industry http://www.hi-net.or.jp/towada/

The KUROISHI Chamber Commerce and Industry http://www.k-cci.or.jp

The GOSHOGAWARA Chamber Commerce and Industry http://www.gocci.or.jp/

The MUTSU Chamber Commerce and Industry http://www.mutsucci.or.jp/

The MORIOKA Chamber Commerce and Industry http://www.ccimorioka.or.jp

The KAMAISHI Chamber Commerce and Industry http://www.rnac.or.jp/~kcci/

The MIYAKO Chamber Commerce and Industry http://www.nnet.ne.jp/~mcci/

The HANAMAKI Chamber Commerce and Industry http://www.michinoku.ne.jp/~chamber/

The MIZUSAWA Chamber Commerce and Industry http://www.michinoku.ne.jp/~mcci

The KITAKAMI Chamber Commerce and Industry http://www.kitakami.ne.jp/~kcci/

The KUJI Chamber Commerce and Industry http://www.rnac.or.jp/~kujicci/

The SENDAI Chamber Commerce and Industry http://www.sendaicci.or.jp

The SHIOGAMA Chamber Commerce and Industry http://www.sendaicci.or.jp/shiogama

The ISHINOMAKI Chamber Commerce and Industry http://www.sendaicci.or.jp/ishinomaki

The KESENNUMA Chamber Commerce and Industry http://www.sendaicci.or.jp/kesennuma

The FURUKAWA Chamber Commerce and Industry http://www.sendaicci.or.jp/furukawa

The SHIROISHI Chamber Commerce and Industry http://www.sendaicci.or.jp/shiroishi

The AKITA Chamber Commerce and Industry http://www.bic-akita.or.jp/akitacci/index.html

The YAMAGATA Chamber Commerce and Industry http://www.yamagata-cci.or.jp

The SAKATA Chamber Commerce and Industry http://www.sakata-cci.or.jp

The TSURUOKA Chamber Commerce and Industry http://www.trcci.or.jp/

The YONEZAWA Chamber Commerce and Industry http://www.ycci.or.jp

The SHINJO Chamber Commerce and Industry http://shinjo.dewa.or.jp/shinjcci/

The TENDO Chamber Commerce and Industry http://www.jvnet.or.jp/~tendocci

The FUKUSHIMA Chamber Commerce and Industry http://www.fukushima-cci.or.jp

The KORIYAMA Chamber Commerce and Industry http://www.fusion.isp.ntt.co.jp/sasukene/kcci/

The AIZUWAKAMATSU Chamber Commerce and Industry http://www.f-open.or.jp/~fks145

The IWAKI Chamber Commerce and Industry http://www.asaka.ne.jp/~kaigisyo/

The HARAMACHI Chamber Commerce and Industry http://www.soma.or.jp/~haramati/index.html

The SOMA Chamber Commerce and Industry http://www.soma.or.jp/~somacci/index.html

The NIIGATA Chamber Commerce and Industry http://www.niigata-cci.or.jp

The SANJO Chamber Commerce and Industry http://www.sanjo-cci.or.jp

The NIITSU Chamber Commerce and Industry http://island.qqq.or.jp/hp/niitsu/

The TSUBAME Chamber Commerce and Industry http://www.tsubame-cci.or.jp/

The OJIYA Chamber Commerce and Industry http://www.nttl-net.ne.jp/occi/

The MURAKAMI Chamber Commerce and Industry http://www.mu-cci.or.jp

The TOKAMACHI Chamber Commerce and Industry http://www.tiara.or.jp/~kaigisyo/

The KAMO Chamber Commerce and Industry http://island.qqq.or.jp/hp/kamocci/

The TOYAMA Chamber Commerce and Industry http://www.ccis-toyama.or.jp/toyama/

The TAKAOKA Chamber Commerce and Industry http://www.ccis-toyama.or.jp/takaoka/

The HIMI Chamber Commerce and Industry http://www.ccis-toyama.or.jp/himi/

The SHINMINATO Chamber Commerce and Industry http://www.ccis-toyama.or.jp/scci/

The UOZU Chamber Commerce and Industry http://www.ccis-toyama.or.jp/uozu/

The KANAZAWA Chamber Commerce and Industry http://www.nsknet.or.jp/kaigisho/index.htm

The KOMATSU Chamber Commerce and Industry http://www.kissnet.or.jp/komatcci/

The NANAO Chamber Commerce and Industry http://www.noto.or.jp/nanao/cci/

The KAGA Chamber Commerce and Industry http://www.kagaworld.or.jp

The UEDA Chamber Commerce and Industry http://www.ueda.ne.jp/~ucci/

The MATSUMOTO Chamber Commerce and Industry http://www.mcci.or.jp

The IIDA Chamber Commerce and Industry http://www.iidacci.or.jp

The OKAYA Chamber Commerce and Industry http://www.online.co.jp/community/okasho/okasho.htm

The SUWA Chamber Commerce and Industry http://shinshu.online.co.jp/community/suwacci/

The SHIMOSUWA Chamber Commerce and Industry http://cci.shimosuwa.nagano.jp

The SUZAKA Chamber Commerce and Industry http://www.suzaka.or.jp

The INA Chamber Commerce and Industry http://www.valley.or.jp/~inacci/welcome.html

The SHINONOI Chamber Commerce and Industry http://www.avis.ne.jp/~shinonoi/

The SHIOJIRI Chamber Commerce and Industry http://www.shiojiri.ne.jp/~scci/

The KOMORO Chamber Commerce and Industry http://www.janis.or.jp/users/kcci/welcome.html

The NAKANO Chamber Commerce and Industry http://www.m-shinano.com/nakano/nakano.htm

The MATSUSHIRO Chamber Commerce and Industry http://www.cnet-na.ne.jp/m/mcci-yeg/SHOUKOU.HTM

The KOMAGANE Chamber Commerce and Industry http://www.avis.ne.jp/~koma-cci/

The CHINO Chamber Commerce and Industry http://www.icon.pref.nagano.jp/usr/chinocci/

The SAKU Chamber Commerce and Industry http://www.pascal.ne.jp/~sakucci/

The KOSHOKU Chamber Commerce and Industry http://www.icon.pref.nagano.jp/usr/koshoku-cci/

The MITO Chamber Commerce and Industry http://www.inetcci.or.jp/~mito/

The TSUCHIURA Chamber Commerce and Industry http://www.tcci.or.jp

The KOGA Chamber Commerce and Industry http://www.inetcci.or.jp/~koga/

The HITACHI Chamber Commerce and Industry http://www.inetcci.or.jp/~hitachi/index.html

The ISHIOKA Chamber Commerce and Industry http://www.sunshine.ne.jp/~icci/

The SHIMODATE Chamber Commerce and Industry http://www.inetcci.or.jp/~simodate/

The NAKAMINATO Chamber Commerce and Industry http://www.inetcci.or.jp/~n-minato

The KATSUTA Chamber Commerce and Industry http://www.inetcci.or.jp/~katsuta

The TOCHIGI Chamber Commerce and Industry http://www.tochigi-cci.or.jp

The UTSUNOMIYA Chamber Commerce and Industry http://www.tsinet.or.jp/utsunomiya-cci/

The ASHIKAGA Chamber Commerce and Industry http://www.takauji.or.jp/acci

The KANUMA Chamber Commerce and Industry http://www.kanumacci.org/

The OYAMA Chamber Commerce and Industry http://www.oyama-cci.or.jp/

The NIKKO AREA Chamber Commerce and Industry http://www.nikkocci.or.jp/

The OTAWARA Chamber Commerce and Industry http://www.nasu-net.or.jp/~ohcci/

The SANO Chamber Commerce and Industry http://www.dango.or.jp/sanocci/

The MOOKA Chamber Commerce and Industry http://www.moka-cci.or.jp

The TAKASAKI Chamber Commerce and Industry http://www.gunmanet.or.jp/takacci

The MAEBASHI Chamber Commerce and Industry http://www.maebashi-cci.or.jp

The KIRYU Chamber Commerce and Industry http://www.sunfield.or.jp/kcci

The TATEBAYASHI Chamber Commerce and Industry http://www.tatebayashi-cci.or.jp/

The ISEZAKI Chamber Commerce and Industry http://www.kakaa.or.jp/icci/

The OTA Chamber Commerce and Industry http://www.otacci.or.jp

The NUMATA Chamber Commerce and Industry http://www2.wind.ne.jp/tengu-cci/

The FUJIOKA Chamber Commerce and Industry http://www.fujioca.com/cci/

The KAWAGOE Chamber Commerce and Industry http://www.kawagoe.or.jp/

The KAWAGUCHI Chamber Commerce and Industry http://www.gsquare.or.jp/kcci/

The KUMAGAYA Chamber Commerce and Industry http://www.kumagaya.or.jp/ccibear/

The URAWA Chamber Commerce and Industry http://www.gsquare.or.jp/urawacci/

The OMIYA Chamber Commerce and Industry http://www.omiya-cci.or.jp

The CHICHIBU Chamber Commerce and Industry http://cci.chichibu.ne.jp/

The GYODA Chamber Commerce and Industry http://www.sakitama.or.jp/gyoda

The HONJO Chamber Commerce and Industry http://www.honjocci.or.jp

The FUKAYA Chamber Commerce and Industry http://www.fukaya-cci.or.jp

The TOKOROZAWA Chamber Commerce and Industry http://www.snw.co.jp/~cci

The WARABI Chamber Commerce and Industry http://www.saitama-j.or.jp/~wcci/

The AGEO Chamber Commerce and Industry http://www.netweb.or.jp/ageo-cci/

The SAYAMA Chamber Commerce and Industry http://www.sayama.or.jp/~cci

The SOKA Chamber Commerce and Industry http://www.sokacity.or.jp

The KASUKABE Chamber Commerce and Industry http://www.saitama-j.or.jp/~kasukabe/

The CHOSHI Chamber Commerce and Industry http://www.choshinet.or.jp/choshi/cci/

The CHIBA Chamber Commerce and Industry http://www.chiba-cci.or.jp/chiba/

The ICHIKAWA Chamber Commerce and Industry http://www.ichikawa-cci.or.jp/

The MATSUDO Chamber Commerce and Industry http://www.intership.ne.jp/matsudo-cci/

The MOBARA Chamber Commerce and Industry http://www.mobara-cci.or.jp/

The NODA Chamber Commerce and Industry http://www02.so-net.ne.jp/~nodacci/

The YACHIMATA Chamber Commerce and Industry http://www.choshinet.or.jp/~ycmt/

The TOGANE Chamber Commerce and Industry http://www.mmjp.or.jp/togane-cci/

The KASHIWA Chamber Commerce and Industry http://www.kashiwa-cci.or.jp/

The ICHIHARA Chamber Commerce and Industry http://www.bay-wave.ne.jp/~icci/

The SAKURA Chamber Commerce and Industry http://www.sakura-cci.or.jp

The YACHIYO Chamber Commerce and Industry http://island.qqq.or.jp/hp/yachiyocci/

The URAYASU Chamber Commerce and Industry http://www.urayasu-cci.or.jp/

The KIMITSU Chamber Commerce and Industry http://www.kimitsucci.or.jp

The TOKYO Chamber Commerce and Industry http://www.tokyo-cci.or.jp/

The HACHIOJI Chamber Commerce and Industry http://www.seagull.co.jp/hcci/

The OME Chamber Commerce and Industry http://www.ome.or.jp

The TACHIKAWA Chamber Commerce and Industry http://www.cydoc.co.jp/ta-cci/

The MUSASHIFUCHU Chamber Commerce and Industry http://island.qqq.or.jp/hp/m-fuchucci/

The MACHIDA Chamber Commerce and Industry http://www.machida-cci.or.jp/

The TAMA Chamber Commerce and Industry http://www.tamacci.or.jp

The YOKOHAMA Chamber Commerce and Industry http://yokohama-cci.or.jp

The YOKOSUKA Chamber Commerce and Industry http://www.miuland.com/ycci/

The KAWASAKI Chamber Commerce and Industry http://www.kawasaki-cci.or.jp

The ODAWARA Chamber Commerce and Industry http://www.shokonet.or.jp/odawara/

The HIRATSUKA Chamber Commerce and Industry http://www.shokonet.or.jp/hiratuka/

The FUJISAWA Chamber Commerce and Industry http://www.fujisawa-cci.or.jp

The CHIGASAKI Chamber Commerce and Industry http://www.chigasaki-cci.hitnet.or.jp/

The ATSUGI Chamber Commerce and Industry http://www.iris.or.jp/~atsugi/

The KAMAKURA Chamber Commerce and Industry http://www.shokonet.or.jp/kamakura/menu.html

The MIURA Chamber Commerce and Industry http://www.miuland.com/mcci/

The SAGAMIHARA Chamber Commerce and Industry http://www.ssp21.or.jp/

The KOFU Chamber Commerce and Industry http://www.kofucci.or.jp

The FUJIYOSHIDA Chamber Commerce and Industry http://www.fyoshidacci.or.jp

The SHIZUOKA Chamber Commerce and Industry http://www.shizuoka-cci.or.jp/

The HAMAMATSU Chamber Commerce and Industry http://www.hamamatsu-cci.or.jp

The NUMAZU Chamber Commerce and Industry http://www.numazu-cci.or.jp

The MISHIMA Chamber Commerce and Industry http://www.mishima-cci.or.jp/

The FUJI Chamber Commerce and Industry http://www.fuji-cci.or.jp/

The SHIMODA Chamber Commerce and Industry http://shizuoka-cci.across.or.jp/shimoda/

The ITO Chamber Commerce and Industry http://www.izu.co.jp/~itoshoko/

The FUJIEDA Chamber Commerce and Industry http://www.fujieda.or.jp/

The FUKUROI Chamber Commerce and Industry http://www.across.or.jp/fukuroi/

The GIFU Chamber Commerce and Industry http://www.gcci.or.jp

The OGAKI Chamber Commerce and Industry http://www.ginet.or.jp/ogakicci/

The TAJIMI Chamber Commerce and Industry http://www.tajimi.or.jp

The NAKATSUGAWA Chamber Commerce and Industry http://www.takenet.or.jp/ncci/

The TOKI Chamber Commerce and Industry http://www.takenet.or.jp/~tokicci/

The MIZUNAMI Chamber Commerce and Industry http://www.cci.mizunami.gifu.jp

The KAKAMIGAHARA Chamber Commerce and Industry http://www.gcs.ne.jp/ccik/

The KANI Chamber Commerce and Industry http://www.cci.kani.gifu.jp/

The NAGOYA Chamber Commerce and Industry http://www.nagoya-cci.or.jp/

The OKAZAKI Chamber Commerce and Industry http://www.gol.com/okazakicci/

The TOYOHASHI Chamber Commerce and Industry http://www.toyohashi-cci.or.jp/

The HANDA Chamber Commerce and Industry http://handa-cci.mite.ne.jp/

The SETO Chamber Commerce and Industry http://www.taikokk.com/setocci

The GAMAGORI Chamber Commerce and Industry http://www.gfnet.co.jp/~gcci/

The TOYOKAWA Chamber Commerce and Industry http://www.tsc.co.jp/~tte/

The ANJO Chamber Commerce and Industry http://www.anjo-cci.or.jp/

The NISHIO Chamber Commerce and Industry http://www.japan-net.ne.jp/~cci2213/

The TSUSHIMA Chamber Commerce and Industry http://www.synnet.or.jp/t-cci/

The KASUGAI Chamber Commerce and Industry http://www.aichinet.ne.jp/~kcci/

The TOKONAME Chamber Commerce and Industry http://www.gld.mmtr.or.jp/~cci4422d/

The KONAN Chamber Commerce and Industry http://www.ylw.mmtr.or.jp/~konancci

The KOMAKI Chamber Commerce and Industry http://www.k-net.or.jp/~cci/

The INUYAMA Chamber Commerce and Industry http://www.gld.mmtr.or.jp/~icci

The YOKKAICHI Chamber Commerce and Industry http://www.miehis.co.jp/yokkaichi-cci/

The TSU Chamber Commerce and Industry http://www.mint.or.jp/tsucci/

The ISE Chamber Commerce and Industry http://www.ise-cci.or.jp

The MATSUZAKA Chamber Commerce and Industry http://www.mctv.ne.jp/~kaigisho/

The SUZUKA Chamber Commerce and Industry http://www.scci.or.jp

The KUWANA Chamber Commerce and Industry http://www.kuwana.or.jp/chamber/

The TOBA Chamber Commerce and Industry http://www.u-net.or.jp/~tobacci/

The FUKUI Chamber Commerce and Industry http://www.fcci.or.jp/index.htm

The TSURUGA Chamber Commerce and Industry http://www.tsuruga.or.jp

The TAKEFU Chamber Commerce and Industry http://www.hokuriku.ne.jp/takefu/

The OBAMA Chamber Commerce and Industry http://www.fukui-iic.or.jp/obamacci/

The SABAE Chamber Commerce and Industry http://www.sabaecci.com/

The OTSU Chamber Commerce and Industry http://www.biwa.or.jp/~otsucci/

The NAGAHAMA Chamber Commerce and Industry http://www.biwa.or.jp/~succes/

The HIKONE Chamber Commerce and Industry http://www.hikone-cci.or.jp

The YOKAICHI Chamber Commerce and Industry http://www.bcap.co.jp/odakocci/

The KUSATSU Chamber Commerce and Industry http://www.biwa.or.jp/~kstcci/

The KYOTO Chamber Commerce and Industry http://www.kyo.or.jp/kyoto/

The MAIZURU Chamber Commerce and Industry http://www.kyo.or.jp/maizuru/

The AYABE Chamber Commerce and Industry http://www.kyo.or.jp/ayabe/

The UJI Chamber Commerce and Industry http://www.kyo.or.jp/uji/

The KAMEOKA Chamber Commerce and Industry http://www.kyo.or.jp/kameoka/

The JOYO Chamber Commerce and Industry http://www.kyo.or.jp/joyo/

The OSAKA Chamber Commerce and Industry http://www.osaka.cci.or.jp/

The SAKAI Chamber Commerce and Industry http://www.sakaicci.or.jp

The HIGASHIOSAKA Chamber Commerce and Industry http://www2.marinet.or.jp/~hcci/

The IZUMIOTSU Chamber Commerce and Industry http://www.kanku-city.or.jp/icci/

The KISHIWADA Chamber Commerce and Industry http://www.sensyu.ne.jp/kcci/kisiwadacci.htm

The IBARAKI Chamber Commerce and Industry http://www.infomart.or.jp/ibasho/

The SUITA Chamber Commerce and Industry http://www.infomart.or.jp/suitacci/

The YAO Chamber Commerce and Industry http://duonet.co.jp/YAOCCI/

The TOYONAKA Chamber Commerce and Industry http://www.ooaana.or.jp/

The MORIGUCHIKADOMA Chamber Commerce and Industry http://www.hi-ho.ne.jp/mk-cci/

The MATSUBARA Chamber Commerce and Industry http://www.matsubara-cci.or.jp

The IZUMI Chamber Commerce and Industry http://www.ins.ne.jp/~izumicci/

The KOBE Chamber Commerce and Industry http://www.kcci.hyogo-iic.ne.jp

The HIMEJI Chamber Commerce and Industry http://www.himeji-cci.or.jp/

The AKASHI Chamber Commerce and Industry http://www.apricoweb.ne.jp/company/acci/

The ITAMI Chamber Commerce and Industry http://www.itami.or.jp/icci

The AIOI Chamber Commerce and Industry http://www.net117.or.jp/~AIOICCI/

The AKO Chamber Commerce and Industry http://www.memenet.or.jp/ako-cci/

The MIKI Chamber Commerce and Industry http://www.mikicci.or.jp/

The SUMOTO Chamber Commerce and Industry http://www.awaji-is.or.jp/chamber/

The TATSUNO Chamber Commerce and Industry http://www.tatsuno.or.jp/

The ONO Chamber Commerce and Industry http://www.onocci.or.jp

The NARA Chamber Commerce and Industry http://www.nara-i.or.jp/index.html

The KASHIHARA Chamber Commerce and Industry http://www.mahoroba.or.jp/~kcci/

The WAKAYAMA Chamber Commerce and Industry http://www.wakayama-cci.or.jp/wakayama.htm

The KAINAN Chamber Commerce and Industry http://www.wakayamanet.or.jp/kainan-cci/

The TANABE Chamber Commerce and Industry http://www.aikis.or.jp/~t-cci/index.html

The TOTTORI Chamber Commerce and Industry http://www.tottori-cci.or.jp/

The SAKAIMINATO Chamber Commerce and Industry http://www.sakaiminato.com/

The MATSUE Chamber Commerce and Industry http://www.joho-shimane.or.jp/cc/matuecci/

The HAMADA Chamber Commerce and Industry http://www.joho-shimane.or.jp/cc/cci3202/

The IZUMO Chamber Commerce and Industry http://www.joho-shimane.or.jp/cc/izumocci/

The HIRATA Chamber Commerce and Industry http://www.joho-shimane.or.jp/cc/hchamber/

The MASUDA Chamber Commerce and Industry http://www.joho-shimane.or.jp/cc/masudacc/

The ODA Chamber Commerce and Industry http://www.joho-shimane.or.jp/cc/ohdacci/

The YASUKI Chamber Commerce and Industry http://www.joho-shimane.or.jp/cc/ycci/

The GOTSU Chamber Commerce and Industry http://www.joho-shimane.or.jp/cc/gotsucci/

The OKAYAMA Chamber Commerce and Industry http://www.optic.or.jp/okayama-cci/

The TSUYAMA Chamber Commerce and Industry http://www.tvt.ne.jp/~kaigisho/

The TAMANO Chamber Commerce and Industry http://www.tamano.or.jp/usr/cci/index.htm

The KOJIMA Chamber Commerce and Industry http://kjmcci.kct.ne.jp/cci/

The BIZEN Chamber Commerce and Industry http://www.optic.or.jp/bvcci/

The SOJA Chamber Commerce and Industry http://www.kibiji.ne.jp/scci/

The HIROSHIMA Chamber Commerce and Industry http://www.hiroshima-cdas.or.jp/hiroshimacci/index.html

The FUKUYAMA Chamber Commerce and Industry http://www.fukuyama.or.jp/

The MIHARA Chamber Commerce and Industry http://www.mhr-cci.or.jp/

The FUCHU Chamber Commerce and Industry http://www.fuchu.or.jp/~fuchucci/

The MIYOSHI Chamber Commerce and Industry http://www.hiroshima-cdas.or.jp/mcci/index.html

The SHOBARA Chamber Commerce and Industry http://www.hiroshima-cdas.or.jp/scci/

The TAKEHARA Chamber Commerce and Industry http://www.urban.ne.jp/home/takecci/

The INNOSHIMA Chamber Commerce and Industry http://www.fsinet.or.jp/~innosima/

The HATUKAICHI Chamber Commerce and Industry http://www.netmarketweb.com/hatsukaichicci/

The SHIMONOSEKI Chamber Commerce and Industry http://www.shimonoseki.cci.or.jp/

The UBE Chamber Commerce and Industry http://www.joho-yamaguchi.or.jp/ube-cci/

The YAMAGUCHI Chamber Commerce and Industry http://www.joho-yamaguchi.or.jp/ycci/

The HOFU Chamber Commerce and Industry http://www.joho-yamaguchi.or.jp/hcci/

The TOKUYAMA Chamber Commerce and Industry http://www.joho-yamaguchi.or.jp/tcci/

The HAGI Chamber Commerce and Industry http://www.joho-yamaguchi.or.jp/hagi-cci/

The IWAKUNI Chamber Commerce and Industry http://agicsv01.joho-yamaguchi.or.jp/icci/html/top.html

The HIKARI Chamber Commerce and Industry http://www.joho-yamaguchi.or.jp/hikarcci/

The YANAI Chamber Commerce and Industry http://www.joho-yamaguchi.or.jp/cci/

The SHINNANYO Chamber Commerce and Industry http://www.joho-yamaguchi.or.jp/scci/

The TOKUSHIMA Chamber Commerce and Industry http://www.tokushimacci.or.jp

The NARUTO Chamber Commerce and Industry http://www.narutocci.or.jp

The KOMATSUSHIMA Chamber Commerce and Industry http://www.netwave.or.jp/~komacci/

The KAMOJIMA Chamber Commerce and Industry http://www.kamojimacci.or.jp

The AWAIKEDA Chamber Commerce and Industry http://www.netwave.or.jp/~ikedacci/

The ANAN Chamber Commerce and Industry http://www.anancci.or.jp

The TAKAMATSU Chamber Commerce and Industry http://www.takacci.or.jp

The MARUGAME Chamber Commerce and Industry http://www.marugame.or.jp

The SAKAIDE Chamber Commerce and Industry http://www.sakaide.or.jp/

The KANONJI Chamber Commerce and Industry http://www.kan-cci.or.jp/

The TADOTSU Chamber Commerce and Industry http://www.netwave.or.jp/~tadotsu

The ZENTSUJI Chamber Commerce and Industry http://www.netwave.or.jp/~aaa/

The MATSUYAMA Chamber Commerce and Industry http://www.ehime-iinet.or.jp/jemcci/

The NIIHAMA Chamber Commerce and Industry http://www.ehime-iinet.or.jp/niicci/

The KAWANOE Chamber Commerce and Industry http://www.ehime-iinet.or.jp/kawa-cci/

The KOCHI Chamber Commerce and Industry http://www.joho-kochi.or.jp/kochicci/

The FUKUOKA Chamber Commerce and Industry http://www.media-line.or.jp/fcci

The KITAKYUSHU Chamber Commerce and Industry http://www.kitakyushucci.or.jp

The OMUTA Chamber Commerce and Industry http://www.omutacci.or.jp

The IIZUKA Chamber Commerce and Industry http://www.cyberbeing.com/iizuka-cci/

The NOGATA Chamber Commerce and Industry http://www.nogata-cci.or.jp/

The YAME Chamber Commerce and Industry http://www.joho-fukuoka.or.jp/kigyo/yame_cci/

The YUKUHASHI Chamber Commerce and Industry http://www.mmjp.or.jp/ycci

The CHIKUGO Chamber Commerce and Industry http://www.joho-fukuoka.or.jp/kigyo/chikugo3/

The AMAGI Chamber Commerce and Industry http://www.joho-fukuoka.or.jp/kigyo/amagicci/

The NAKAMA Chamber Commerce and Industry http://www1.sphere.ne.jp/nakama/

The SAGA Chamber Commerce and Industry http://www.infosaga.or.jp/group/saga/start.htm

The KARATSU Chamber Commerce and Industry http://www.infosaga.or.jp/group/karatu/start.htm

The IMARI Chamber Commerce and Industry http://www.infosaga.or.jp/group/imari/start.htm

The TOSU Chamber Commerce and Industry http://www.infosaga.or.jp/group/tosu/start.htm

The ARITA Chamber Commerce and Industry http://www.infosaga.or.jp/group/arita/start.htm

The OGI Chamber Commerce and Industry http://www.infosaga.or.jp/group/ogi/start.htm

The TAKEO Chamber Commerce and Industry http://www.infosaga.or.jp/group/takeo/start.htm

The KASHIMA Chamber Commerce and Industry http://www.infosaga.or.jp/group/kasima/start.htm

The NAGASAKI Chamber Commerce and Industry http://www.us1.nagasaki-noc.ne.jp/~ncci

The SHIMABARA Chamber Commerce and Industry http://www.shimabara-cci.or.jp/

The ISAHAYA Chamber Commerce and Industry http://www.isahaya-cc.ac.jp/icci/

The HOKUSHO Chamber Commerce and Industry http://www.try-net.or.jp/~h-cci/

The KUMAMOTO Chamber Commerce and Industry http://www.infonet.kmt-ics.co.jp/home1/kumcci/index.html

The HITOYOSHI Chamber Commerce and Industry http://www.hitoyoshi-cci.or.jp/

The HONDO Chamber Commerce and Industry http://www.amakusa.ne.jp/SH/hondo/

The BEPPU Chamber Commerce and Industry http://www.coara.or.jp/~beppucci/

The MIYAKONOJO Chamber Commerce and Industry http://www.miyazaki-cci.or.jp/miyakonjo/

The MIYAZAKI Chamber Commerce and Industry http://www.miyazaki-cci.or.jp/miyazaki/

The NOBEOKA Chamber Commerce and Industry http://www.miyazaki-cci.or.jp/nobeoka/

The HYUGA Chamber Commerce and Industry http://www.miyazaki-cci.or.jp/hyuga/

The TAKANABE Chamber Commerce and Industry http://www.miyazaki-cci.or.jp/takanabe/

The NICHINAN Chamber Commerce and Industry http://www.joho-fukuoka.or.jp/kigyo/amagicci/

The KOBAYASHI Chamber Commerce and Industry http://www.miyazaki-cci.or.jp/kobayashi/

The KUSHIMA Chamber Commerce and Industry http://www.miyazaki-cci.or.jp/kushima/

The SAITO Chamber Commerce and Industry http://www.miyazaki-cci.or.jp/saito/

The KAGOSHIMA Chamber Commerce and Industry http://www.kagoshima-cci.or.jp

The SENDAI Chamber Commerce and Industry http://www.satumasendai-cci.or.jp

INTERNATIONAL TRADE ADVISERS

Name	Address
Abe Kazunori	2-5-28, Yokocho, Sanjou-city, Niigata,-pref.
Ochiai Masaharu	1273-99,Aobadai,Tokorozawa-city,Saitama
Kado Motonori	3-8-4,Nishisakaidani-cho,Oharano,Nishigyoku,Kyoto
Kawano Masashi	5199-17,Oaza-Kawaminami,Kawaminami,Koyugun,Miyazaki
Kiyota Tetsuji	414-14,Shimoyori,Tasakimachi,Kumamoto,Kumamoto
Sasaki Hiroshi	28-3,Mimuro,Saitama city,Saitama prefecture
Sato Kokichi	1-25-3,Sakae-ku,Koyamadai,Yokohama
Nagano Yasuo	3-6-37 Nukui-minamicho,Koganei City Tokyo
Nishijima Shinya	1-2-8,Yamato-cho,Shimonoseki-city,Yamaguchi

Matsumura Noboru	1-10-14 Koyamadai,Sakae-ku,Yokohama,Kanagawa,Japan
Yano Eiichi	Elgala7F,4-2,1-Chome,Tenjin,Chuo-ku,Fukuoka,Japan
Yuki Umei	1-1-10,Tsuruma,Machida-city,Tokyo
Asano Osamu	1-2-7,Aoyama,Nara-city.Nara
Adachi Yoshiaki	6-23-14,Seiwadai,Kita-ku,Kobe,Hyogo
Arai Takashi	2-1013,Nishikubo-cho 1-4,Hodogaya-ku,Yokohama
Omori Hiroyuki	103,17-4 Kitazono-cho,Kawaguchi-city,Saitama
Ogita Kozo	Ota-ku,Tokyo
Kamiya Nobuhito	4-15-10,Kitahirano,Himeji-shi,Hyogo-ken
Kanri Toru	2-15-520,Saiwaicho 1-chome,Mihama-ku,Chiba
Kobayashi Kiminori	1-39-3 Nishi Toride Ibaraki 302-0025 Japan
Komiyama Takushi	6-2-19,Kitamikunigaokacho,Sakai-city,Osaka 590-0021
Sakusabe Kazuji	5-9-1-1504Isobe,Mihamaku,Chiba-city,Chiba
Sakurai Akio	2-1160-1,Sakashita-cho,Kasugai-shi,Aichi
Sato Ichiro	4-18-9,Fujiwaradai-Nakamachi,Kita-ku,Kobe,Hyogo,Japan
Shibata Masayuki	4-9-404,Shimoshinozaki,Edogawa-ku,Tokyo
Takeda Yutaka	17-101,3-9,Hiyodoridai,Kita-ku,Kobe
Takeyasu Tetsuo	1-9-11,Kawana,Fujisawa-shi,Kanagawaken
China Hiroshi	1-14-22,Maehara,Ginowan City,Okinawa
Nakazawa Yutaka	5-10-32,Minamishinagawa,Shinagawa-ku,Tokyo
Nakajima Kazuharu	102,1-864-1,Kawabemachi,Oume-shi,Tokyo
Nakamura Makoto	129-4,Honmoku-manzaka,Naka-ku,Yokohama-shi,Kanagawa
Nanasawa Isamu	1-5-17-101,Shinohara-Minamimachi,Nada-ku,Kobe-city,Hyogo
Reiko Nebashi	3-21-5, Kami-Ikebukuro, Toshima-ku,Tokyo
Nogi Katsuyuki	8-8,Mefukiyoshigaoka,Takarazuka-shi,Hyogo
Nomoto Koji	Rm.1006,3-15-2 Higashi Ikebukuro,Toshima-ku,Tokyo
Hatakkeyama Shigeo	211,Viewparkminamisendai,6-13-15,Nishinakada,Taihaku-ku,Sendai,Miyagi
Hayashi Katsuhiko	663-127 Higashi-fukai,Nagareyama.270-0101
Hidaka Isao	
Hirayama Masaru	3-33-906,2-chome Saiwaicho,Naniwa-ku,Osaka
Hoshino Tatsuo	8-5-27,Akasaka,Minato-ku,Tokyo
Hoshino Masao	World Trade Center Amsterdam, Strawinskylaan 801, 1077 xx Amsterdam, The Netherlands
Hori Minako	Tokyo
Maeda Shinsuke	761 Nagara Soja-city Okayama
Matsuzawa Hiroyuki	51-2-4-303,Kojimacho 3-chome,Chofu,Tokyo 182-0026 Japan
Matsuyama Kenji	4-8-D403,Kamishinden,Toyonaka-shi,Osaka
Takahiro Mishima	2-46-4,Eifuku,Suginami-ku,Tokyo
Yamauchi Masakazu	7-16-42-203,Negishidai,Asaka-city,Saitama Pref.

Yamaura Kaoru	237 Higashiyamada-cho,Tsuzuki-ku,Yokohama
Yamada Kozo	3-14-16 Yachiyodai-minami,Yachiyo,Chiba
Yoshida Yasuhide	7-10-102,Takasu 2-chome,Mihamaku,Chiba 261-0004 JAPAN
Kato Yukiyoshi	3-504,2-13 Shirasagi,Nakano-ku,Tokyo
Hamanaka Hidetoshi	3-31-22-305 Sekimachi-minami, Nerima-ku,Tokyo
Hideno Mitsuji	1-11-9,Azaminominami,Aoba-ku,Yokohama,Kanagawa
Yasuda Tamotsu	4-30-2,Midoriku,Chiba-city,Chiba Pref.
Watariguchi Katsuhiko	20-27
Aoki Setsuko	3-2-5-403 Azamino,Aoba-ku,Yokohama
Amamoto Yukinori	1-5-203 Takahamadai,Hiratsukashi,Kanagawa-ken
Shinichiro Iijima	1-9-9-1401,Dekimachi,Higashi-ku,Nagoya-city,Aichi
Ito Shuji	8-9-4-302, Waseda Misato-city, Saitama pref.
Inada Masaharu	1-7-3 Tanotsu Higashi-ku Fukuoka
Ohtani Yoshihiro	7-66-9,Jindaiji kitamachi,Chofu-shi,Tokyo
Kikuchi Akio	497-46,Yahagi-cho,Chuo-ku,Chiba-shi,Chiba-Pref
Kita Yuko	6-10-22,Akabane-nishi,Kita-ku,Tokyo
Sawanobori Kuniaki	1-16-7-509,Hoyacho,Nishitokyo-city,Tokyo
Shibata Hiroshi	4-3-14,Nigawacho,Nishinomiya City,Hyogo
Suzuki Akimi	16-3 Ajikidai 6-chome,Sakaemachi,Inbagun,Chibaken
Suzuki Shinji	5-14-6, Takada-nishi,Kohoku-ku,Yokohama
Takeuchi Atsushi	5-3-5 Midorigaoka Yachiyo-city Chiba Pref,Japan
Taniyama Kiyoshi	353-24,Yoshizato,Wakayama City
Nakajima Teruo	3-7-3,Kugenuma Kaigan,Fujisawa Shi,Kanagawa Ken
Hayashida Takaharu	4-108-3,Okamoto,Kasuga,Fukuoka
Higuchi Masatoshi	
Hiraki Masanori	#805,3-14,Tamatsukuri-motomachi,Tennoji-ku,Osaka
Fujii Kikuo	3-18,Higashi Tomigaoka 5-chome,Nara-city,Nara-ken
Masuda Koichi	5-112,Nishihara,Iwatsuki-city,Saitama Pref.
Mori Yukuta	1-3-11 Fujimi-cho,Iwata-shi,Shizuoka-ken,438-0083,Japan
Yasuda Katsumi Pref.	Sywahara-danchi 2-1-101, Wako Suwahara-danchi 2-1-101, Wako,Saitama
Yamanouchi Michio	24-2,Higashimine-machi,Ota-ku,Tokyo
Yoshii Tadahiko	224 Higashi-kibougaoka,Asahi-ku,Yokohama-city
Yoshida Tadashi	9-36-9,Miyama,Funabashi-shi,Chiba
Sanada Masatsugu	2-8-15,Inadashinmachi,Higashiosaka-city,Osaka
Toki Tadahisa	4-3-24,Miyamae,Suginami-ku,Tokyo
Habakari Tadashi	1-15-8,Hachimandai,Sakura,Chiba 285-0867
Fujita Toshimitsu	2-1-6,Kitahama,Wakamatsu-ku,Kitakyusyu-shi,Fukuoka
Aoki Shigeyuki	4-1-4-409 Shakujiidai,Nerima-ku,Tokyo

Akai Yoshio	3001-4,Koube-cho,Tsu,Mie
Ashida Shigeru	6-32 Yamanoue-Nishimachi,Hirakata,Osaka
Arai Masanobu	3-23-12,Katsutadai,Yachiyo City,Chiba
Iijima Minoru	4-9-30 Sakuraga-oka,Setagayaku,Tokyo
Ishimaru Makoto	7 Kumi,Takajyo Danchi,Oita
Itoh Mamoru	3-6-25,Matsugaoka,Akashi,673-0862,Japan
Ohtani Iwao	3-11-9,Yukarigaoka,Sakura-shi Chiba Japan
Ohashi Shohei	416,9-21,Wakayamacho,Nishinomiya-city,Hyogo
Katamoto Yoshikiyo	3-8-2,Tomigaoka,Nara-shi,Japan
Kamahori Takao	2695-74,Yamazaki,Noda City,Chiba,Prefecture
Kuriki Hiroshi	5-36-902,Mukogawa-cho,Takarazuka-city,Hyogo
Kobayashi Eiji	1-94,Takeishi,Hanamigawaku,Chiba City,Chiba
Kondoh Terumichi	3-25-19,Inokuchi-dai,Nishi-ku,Hiroshima
Sato Katsumi	24-10,Kitamine,Ota-ku,Tokyo
Shimizu Akira	4-4-1-501 Mita,Tama-ku,Kawasaki-shi
Suzuki Atsushi	Koh,245-2,Minaminagaicho,Nara-city,Nara
Takada Hozumi	2-4-36,Miikedai,Sakai City,Osaka
Takizawa Tomiichi	8-9-6,Nishi-Sakuragaoka,Sanyo-cho,Akaiwagun,Okayama Pref.
Tokuyama Yukikazu	3171-1,Yodoyacho,Kurayoshi City,Tottori
Tochino Hirohisa	1-16-30-511,Gakuenkita,Nara-shi,Nara
Tomikawa Naoki	Fl.1-6-3 Nihonbashi-muromachi,Chuo-ku,Tokyo
Nakai Kazumasa	1-3-30-807, Uenohigashi, Toyonaka, Osaka 560-0013
Nakagawa Yoshihiro	288-6,Chishaku-cho,Yokkaichi-shi,Mie-ken
Nakamura Yoichi	1-31-3,Daiwa-nishi,Kawanishi-City,HyogoPref.
Nagayoshi Katsumi Indonesia	MidPlaza-2,24th floor,Jl. Jendral Sudirman Kav. 10-11,Jakarta 10220
Nishiguchi Hiroyuki	3-36-9 Makituka-dai,Sakai
Kouichi Hashimoto	2-12-12-804,Honan,Suginami-ku,Tokyo
Haruna Toshinori	4B Sujatha,103,4th Street,Abhiramapuram,Chennai,600 018,India
Hirokawa Choji	Ru47-6,Hitotsuhari,Komatsu,Ishikawa
Homma Masaru	2-8-15,Midorigaoka,Hannan-shi,Osaka
Makishima Takeo	2-5-1-707,Saiwai,Ichikawa-city,Chiba
Morita Fumimaru	601,2-19-1,Befu,Jyounan-ku,Fukuoka
Yamanishi Kenichi	12-54, Karuizawa, Ikoma, Nara, Japan
Yambe Toshio	5-10-26-708,Nishikasai,Edogawa-ku,Tokyo
Yuba Toshiya	9-21-303,Kitakawahori-cho,Ten-noji-ku,Osaka
Ikezaki Motohiko city,Kanagawa	Sugatanidai Sky-heights B-302,Suenaga,Takatsu-ku,Kawasaki-
Izaki Takao	2-28-19,Shinmachi,Setagaya-ku,Tokyo

Inanaga Masuo	FE310,3-9 Tsujido Higashi Kaigan,Fujisawa
Iwata Hideaki	1-3-11-701,Maruyamadai,Wako-shi,Saitama-ken
Osakada Susumu	1-10-415,Matsunouchi-cho,Ashiya,Hyogo
Kawata Yasuhiro	4-18-6,Negishi,Taito-ku,Tokyo
Kumamoto Kazuo	6-2-6-102,Shimomeguro,Meguro-ku,Tokyo
Saino Akio	3-2-29 Jinmachi-Nishi,Higashine City
Sasaki Kouichi	126,Kurakida,Nakano,Soma-city,Fukushima
Shimada Hisao	189 Fujinokisono-machi,Toyama-shi,Toyama-ken
Shiraishi Katsuhiko	13-1,Katsuradainishi 2-chome,Sakaeku,Yokohama
Shirakawa Yasumasa	6-9-13-101,Saginomiya,Nakano-ku,Tokyo
Suzuki Yasushi city,Kanagawa	103Hikarino-machi,415-2Kawakami-cho,Totsuka-ku,Yokohama-
Isao Takagi	701,3-6-8,Komone,Itabashi-ku,Tokyo
Takahashi Shinji	25-28-607,Hinoike-cho,Nishinomiya,Hyogo
Takahara Kyoichi	3-8-5 Nanatsugidai,Shiroi,Inbagun,Chiba
Tanaka Takao	133,Azumada-cho,Toyohashi-city,Aichi,440-0066
Tnase Otomaro	117-25,Aza-Kashiki,Taromaru,Gifu-city,Gifu
Namba Kentaro	502,Towa City Corp Issha,4-183,Issha,Meito-ku,Nagoya,Aichi
Funayama Akira	2-12-3,Hachimanyama,Setagaya-ku,Tokyo
Fumuro Takashi	2-6-23,Nishitomi,Fujisawa,Kanagawa,Japan
Hojima Yoshiaki	3-57-4 Kyoden,Sakata-city,Yamagata
Mizutani Mitsunobu	3-11-603,Kami-machi,Tajimi-city,Gifu
Mizobata Kazuo	1-10-61,Uenohigashi Toyonaka Osaka
Mori Atsuyuki	1-12-26-210,Shakujidai,Nerima-ku,Tokyo
Morihana Yoji	3-11-9,Ishiodai,Kasugai-City,Aichi Pref. Japan
Yasuda Tsutomu	2-15-3kamiaso,Asao-ku,Kawasaki-shi,Kanagawa
Yamaoka Hiroaki	18-17 Nishi-tomigaoka 8-chome Nara,Nara Pref.,631-0006
Yamada Fumio	Kawaguchi Parktower 2302,No.1-7-1,Saiwai-cho,kawaguchi-shi,Saitama-ken
Yoshikawa Hideo	5-32-22,Hongohdai,Sakaeku,Yokohama,Kanagawa
Watanabe Ichiro	5-21-6,Numama,Zushi,Kanagawa
Ishizaki Itaru	8-25,Shimo-hoya 3-chome,Nishitokyo-city,Tokyo
Ohi Yoshio	1-6-5,Mikageyamate,Higashinada-ku,Kobe,Japan
Mabuchi Yaen	2-381-4,Katsushika-cho,Funabashi City,Chiba Prefecture
Watanabe Toshiyuki	2-3-20,Funado,Abiko-city,Chiba
Oshige Yasuo	6-6,Kinsei-cho,Kagoshima-city,892-0828,Japan
Kaji Katsumi	4-5-6-306,Konandai,Konan-ku,Yokohama,Kanagawa
Kitami Yoshihisa	1-25-1,Nishi-shinjuku,Shinjuku-ku,Tokyo
Sato Shigeo	2-1-1004,Higashi Sapporo 3-1,Shiroishi-ku,Sapporo

Takeuchi Kazushige	5-8-8-402,Higashigotanda,Shinagawa-ku,Tokyo 141-0022
Tanaka Shinichiro	4-2-13-203,Akasakadori,Nada-ku,Kobe-city,Hyogo
Nakazawa Massie	Osaki 5-2-1-1003,Shinagawa-ku,Tokyo
Nishihara Yasuo	1-33-26,Kokuryo-cho,Chofu City,Tokyo
Hirosawa Tsutomu	6-12-14,Minami-ikuta,Tama-ku,Kawasaki,Kanagawa
Fujimoto Osamu	8-5-11-510,Arima,Miyamae-ku,Kawasaki-shi,Kanagawa Pref.
Maekawa Kazumi	15-803 Shinmachi 1-33,Nishiku Osaka
Matsuno Shinzo	3-13-27,Horinouchi,Hachioji-city,Tokyo
Matsumoto Mitsuyasu	14738 Nagashima,Takeo-cho,Takeo-shi,Saga-ken
Moribe Tetsuo	2-2-302 Wakabadai,Asahiku,Yokohama
Morimoto Shigehiko	TachibanaShinjyuku Bldg,2-26-3,Nishi-shinjuku,Shinjuku-ku,Tokyo
Yoshikawa Taiji	5-10-1,Sagamihara,Sagamihara-shi,Kanagawa-ken
Adachi Yoichi	1-25-15,Hiyoshi-honcho,Kohoku-ku,Yokohama,Japan
Izumi Mitsuyuki	5-7-13-605,Kitaurawa,Saitama-city,Saitama
Ohnishi Hiromichi	17-5-204,Matsukazedai,Aoba-ku,Yokohama-shi,Kanagawa
Okamoto Nobukazu	3-1-3-204,Ohtsugaoka,Shonan-machi,Chiba
Kasuga Takashi	3-9-13,Yoshino,Higashi-ku,Nagoya,Aichi
Kawata Satoshi	5-4,Iihara,Kawaguchi,Saitama Pref.
Kawamata Jiro	4-4-16Kohokudai,Abiko-city,Chiba
Kawamura Shingo	311-7,Kamikashio-cho,Totsuka-ku,Yokohama,Kanagawa
Kitabatake Junichi	21-16,Katsuradai-naka,Sakae-ku,Yokohama
Kurachi Kiyokazu	1-416,Kamiasahi,Midori-ku,Nagoya-city,Aichi
Goda Kenji	2-5-9, Uwabara, Niihama-shi, Ehime-ken, Japan
Konishi Masami	4075,Miki-cho oaza Tanaka,Kita-gun,Kagawa
Sakurai Masafumi	1-47-7,Yoyogi,Shibuya-ku,Tokyo
Sakurai Mitsuo	3-23-3,Kitanodai,Hachiojishi,Tokyo
Sawada Hiroyuki	2-9-6,Shirokanedai,Minato-ku,Tokyo
Shinohara Akira	1-30-2-403 Unomori,Sagamihara-shi,Kanagawa
Tokuyama Koichiro	13-10,Nihonbashi-Odammacho,Chuo-ku,Tokyo
Nagai Isao	1-9-6,Miyama,Funabashi-city,Chiba Pref.
Tadashi Nakamura	3-5-6-304,Kandaiji Kanagawa-ku,Yokohama,Japan
Fujita Toyoaki	1-4-1,Ohtemachi,Chiyoda-ku,Tokyo
Maeda Tsuyoshi	3-21-4 Fuse Shinmachi,Kashiwa,Chiba,Japan
Maeda Misao	1-1-12,Uenosaka,Toyonaka-city,Osaka
Matsushita Yoshiko	702,7-11,Yaezaki-cho,Hiratsuka,Kanagawa
Matsuno Kohko	3-84-1,E609,Mutsukawa,Minamiku,Yokohama
Morioka Kazuhiro	5-9-11,Kitashinagawa,Shinagawa-ku,Tokyo
Yamamori Atsushi	Romage-1003,1-2-41,Owaricho,Kanazawa
Yonekawa Toshikazu	3-2-9 Iwamoto-chou,Chiyoda-ku,Tokyo

Ikeda Masaaki	550-2,Rokken-cho,Kasukabe-shi,Saitama
Ito Shin-ichi	1510 Bldg.,1-5-10 Kotobuki,Taito-ku,Tokyo
Ohno Nobuyuki	No13,4-1-20,Hibarigaoka,Nishi-Tokyo,Tokyo
Okada Tomoyasu	930-42 Ikedahonmachi,Omihachiman-shi,Shiga
Kunimitsu Katsuhiro	3-8-7-301,Nishiogi-minami,Suginami-ku,Tokyo
Sakaguchi Setsuki	8,Nakase 1-chome,Mihama-ku,Ciba-shi,Chiba
Sakuta Kenzo	40-8-202,Saganoarisugawa-cho,Ukyo-ku,Kyoto-shi,Kyoto
Takanashi Yoshinori	4-7-20,Suwa,Iwatsuki-shi,Saitama
Fukuda Kaoru	A-313,2-5-18,Daimon-cho,Higashikurume-shi,Tokyo
Matsudaira Norikuni	18-8-804 Shinsen-cho,Shibuya-ku,Tokyo
Arai Nobuyuki	18-2 Shiohama 2-chome Kohto-ku Tokyo
Ishizaki Kiyonori	2-7-7-303,Yagumo,Meguro-ku,Tokyo,Japan
Itoh Masami	Rune inage1-424,Miyanogidai1-7,Hanamigawa-ku,Chiba-city,Chiba
Inaba Hisao	5-28-2,Asakusabashi,Taito-ku,Tokyo
Uemori Yoshimi	6-8,5chome Daiwa-nishi Kawanishi-city
Ochiai Satoshi	7-36-10-403,Tsukagoshi,Warabi-si,Saitama
Kawai Tsukasa	33-13,Sakae 3-chome,Naka-ku,Nagoya
Kawaguchi Hiroyasu	Nagae 1642-452 Hayama 240-0113 Japan
Kanno Hideaki	Suntopia 2nd Bldg.Suite 203 4-3-15 Tamagawa,Setagaya-ku,Tokyo 158-0094
Kobayashi Shinichi	1-3-11-3F,Fukagawa,Kouto-ku,Tokyo
Konno Shozo	5-24 2-chome,Nagamachi,Taihaku-ku,Sendai-shi,Miyagi
Sakuta Sachio	28-30,Akazutsumi,3-chome,Setagaya-ku,Tokyo,Japan
Shibao Kiyoto	A804,2-4-11,Hisamoto,Takatsu-ku,Kawasaki-city,Kanagawa
Shimizu Masaaki	4-6-18,Harayama,Midori-ku,Saitama-city,Saitama Pref. 336-0931
Shiratsuchi Junji	A-304,3-51-1 Nohkendai Kanazawa-ku,Yokohama
Nakajima Katsuhiro	4-10-10,Chuo,Yamato-shi,Kanagawa-ken
Nishikiori Satoshi	23-36,Moegino,Aoba-ku,Yokohama-shi,Kanagawa
Hatano Tadashi	5-10-29,Midorigaoka,Hamurashi,Tokyo
Hayasaka Tatsuji	Ascent Myogadani 7F,4-6-22,Kohinata,Bunkyo-ku,Tokyo
Hiratsuka Junichi	Gakuen-Higashi-Machi 2Chome 4 D-304,Nishi-ku,Kobe
Fukuda Hiroto	4-26-8 Yayoi-cho,Nakano-ku,Tokyo
Fujita Tsuneo	2157-7,Yaida,Inamachi,Tsukuba-gun,Ibaraki
Motojima Shigeto	
Mori Teruyuki	2-14-9,Nihonbashi,Chuo-ku,Tokyo
Yamanaka Miyoko	9-3-22,Okidome,Ikaruga-cho,Ikoma-gun,Nara
Yamanokuchi Izumi	4-9-10-103,Tanashi-cho, Nishi Tokyo-city,Tokyo
Yoshinaka Toshiro	2-12-37 Kitashigigaoka,Heguri-cho,Ikoma-gun,Nara-ken
Watanabe Shoji	47,Umezu-Takase-cho,Ukyo-ku,Kyoto

Arai Shigeyoshi	2-4-11-1104,Chigasaki,Chigasaki-shi,Kanagawa
Ando Hisao	1-25 Okurayama-Hilltown,1-5Osone,Kohokuku,Yokohama-city,Kanagawa
Ikegami Akira	2-450,Maruko-dori,Nakahara-ku,Kawasaki-shi
Ishiura Junzo	1-3-704,Shinkotoni5-2,Kitaku,Sapporo,001-0905,Japan
Itoh Katsuyasu	3-49 Gonyoshi-cho Nakagawa-ku Nagoya
Ito Hitokazu	6-4-10-410 Nishiki-cho Tachikawa-shi,Tokyo
Inoue Teruaki	4-12-23,Ajinadai,Hatsukaichi-shi,Hiroshima,738-0053,JAPAN
Ueda Makoto	3-18-2 Seikadai,Seika-cho,Sorakugun,Kyoto
Okajima Nobuyuki	6-5,kachidoki,Chuo-ku,Tokyo
Okada Yukiko JAPAN	1-5-28-202,Sakuragaoka,Hodogaya-ku,Yokohama-city,Kanagawa 240-0011
Onoda Kazuo	20-1,Yoshima-kogyodanchi,Iwaki,Fukushima
Gakuhari Yokichi	7-2-10-310,Uchiya,Saitama
Kadoi Yoshitaka	169 Ijirino,Soja,Okayama
Kando Takahiko	801-119,Nakashima,Takaya-cho,Higashihiroshima
Kikuchi Shigeru	5-11-9,Yakumo Meguro-ku,Tokyo
Kimura Toru	3-5-4-301,Maruyamadai,Wako-shi,Saitama
Kusano Hidenobu	1-8-11,Shinmei Saitama-shi Saitama-ken,Japan
Kuramochi Mitsuyoshi	1764-12,Mukaihara Kami Inayoshi Chiyoda-town
Kose Shizuo	4-107-5-303,Miyahara-cho,Saitama,Saitama
Kobori Keiichiro	6-1-28,Miyamoto-dori,Chuo-ku,Kobe,Hyogo
Sakato Hidenori	11-31-104,Hikarigaoka,Higashi-ku,Hiroshima City
Shiota Yasuhiro	1468-1 Asahi-chyo, Hamada-shi, Shimane
Shigematsu Yasuhide	3-11-8 Shimohoya,Nishitokyo City,Tokyo
Shirado Shigeo	1212-27 Matsugasaki,Kashiwa City,Chiba
Shinzaki Seiji	861,Tanoue,Kurashiki-shi,Okayama
Suzuki Masayuki	22664-2,Shinohara-cho,Hamamatsu-shi,Shizuoka Pref.
Seki Heiji	1-10-1,Kandanishiki-cho,Chiyoda-ku,Tokyo
Tsunekawa Yasuo	1-9-4 Omiya,Ichinomiya-city Aichi
Terao Kunihiko	35-7,Hanegi 2-chome,Setagaya-ku,Tokyo
Nishitani Yoichi	Kikuna-haitsu 1-607,480-1 Mamedo-cho Kohoku-ku,Yokohama,Japan
Nobori Shoichiro	2-2-1,Kataseyama,Fujisawa-shi,Kanagawa
Hattori Michiko	4-16-9-406,Higashimachi,Kumamoto City,Kumamoto
Fukushima Yoshinari	1-3-3-207,Nishi Mizuhodai,Fujimi-shi,Saitama
Furuse Teruaki	#201,25-14,Chuoh4-chome,,Nakano-ku,Tokyo
Maeda Maoaki	3084-24-32-9,Kashiwabara,Sayama-shi,Saitama
Makimoto Seiji	4-29-5,Karato-dai,Kita-ku,Kobe,Hyogo
Masuda Hideo	10-18-21-505,Tokiwa,Urawa-ku,Saitama-city,Saitama
Moriuchi Shinji	572-254,Magechi,Kumagaya-city,Saitama

Yashiro,Sadao	17-3,Shimotakaido 2-chome,Suginami-ku,Tokyo
Yamaguchi Noritaka	4-6-23,Kurihara,Adachi-ku,Tokyo
Yamada Takazo	617,2-9-20,Yamada-Higashi.Suita-city,Osaka
Yamada Yutaka	Room601,kachidokibldg.1-2-6 Higurashi,Matsudo,Chiba
Ishikawa Aiko	4-2-1-525 Kamisoshigaya,Setagayaku,Tokyo
Iwasa Haruo	E-507,876-2,Kita-Akitsu,Tokorozawa,Saitama
Iwasaki Yasuo	4-16-1 Fujiwaradai Nakamachi,Kitaku,Kobe City
Okamura Ryo	5-3-7 Someino,Sakura city,Chiba
Oguchi Rikio	19-48,Yoshino,Matsumoto City,Nagano
Katsuda Hideki	13-2 Awaji 2 Chome,Higashiyodogawa-ku,Osaka
Katsuragi Akira	K-603,29 Shin-Ashiya Kami,Suita City,Osaka Pref.
Kikuchi Yuji	7-1-613 Nakayamasatsukiday Takarazuka-city Hyogo
Shiraishi Seiji	4-1-508 Honmokuhara,Naka-ku,Yokohama
Dan Michihiko	1-14 Mure 7-chome,Mitaka,Tokyo 181-0002,Japan
Hanasaki Kiyoji	1-244-1-119,Midorigaoka,Itami City,Hyogo Pref,664-0012
Hayashi Yukio	Iguchi 5-6-2,Mitakashi,Tokyo
Yanagawa Kazuo	1-30-5,Yanagihashi,Taito-ku,Tokyo
Yano Shizuo	A101,148 Naka-kibougaoka,Asahi-ku,Yokohama
Watari Akira	5-17-14,Koyanagicho,Fuchuu,Tokyo
Igarashi Masami	2-41-4-203,Daizawa,Setagaya-ku,Tokyo 155-0032
Shimoda Isao	Nagashima 2nd Bldg.408,Chuo1-57-12,Kasukabe,Saitama
Takeda Masaharu	8-5-27,Akasaka,Minatoku,Tokyo
Mitsuishi Yoshiaki	248-7, Kamiyamamori,Ekiya-cho,Fukuyama-city,Hiroshima
Miyagawa Kunio	1-7-5-9F,Sakuragicho,Saitama-city,Saitama Pref.
Amitani Akihiro	2-25-13,Sakuragaoka,Fujishiro-machi,Kitasomagun,Ibaraki
Saito Shigeru	L-403,Shin-ashiya Kami 29, Suita-city,Osaka
Tani Hiroshi	1-12-35,Nanko-kita,Suminoe-ku,Osaka
Deguchi Osamu	1040-25,Nakamozucho 6-cho,Sakai-shi,Osaka
Miyauchi Sigeki	2-16-15,Furukawa-minami,Matuyama-city,Ehime
Yoshida Harunobu	2-9-8-505,Nakagawa,Tsuzuki-ku,Yokohama
Okada Naozumi	44-7,Wakamiya,Anjo-cho,Anjo,Aichi
Kano Takeshi	6-4-15-405,Goshikiyama,Tarumi-ku,Kobe
Suo Teruo	2-8 Oppama Higashi-cho,Yokosuka,Kanagawa
Suzuki Sadao	22-14,6-chome,Sanarudai,Hamamatsu
Takagi Yoshiro	5-14-1-306,Tateishi,Katsushika-ku,Tokyo
Tanaka Toshio Japan	5F Mitsubishi Trust & Banking Bldg,3-2-1 Chuo,Chuo-ku,Chiba-city 260-0013
Hatta Hideki	7-12-205,Tsutsumi-cho,Yoshida-machi,Niigata
Masaki Rie	2-27-23,Dialand,Nagasaki-city,Nagasaki

Matsumono Hiromi	#401,4-40,Minamimotomachi,Shinjuku,Tokyo
Ando Hidenori	No.106,Fujiyamadai-415,Kasugai-city Aichi
Izuhara Hirohiko	6-21,Ichiriyama-cho Nagata-ku Kobe Hyogo
Oi Minoru	59,Naniwa-machi,Chuo-ku,Kobe 650-0035
Okochi Takeo	4-3-301 ParkTown, 3-chome Sengendai-nishi, Koshigaya City,Saitama Pref.
Okazaki Masataka	69-36,Hamanomachi,Takamatsu-city,Kagawa
Keyota Yisao	11-1402,2-chome26,Shirako,Wako-shi,Saitama Prefecture,Japan
Kobayashi Takehiro	6F,3-1-3,Higashi-ikebukuro,Toshima-ku,Tokyo
Kohigashi Kazuhiro	84-2, Koudocho, Ono-city, Hyogo
Sawada Keisuke	1-13,Gion 2 Chome,Asaminami-ku,Hiroshima City,Japan
Shiga Tadasuke	5-1,Kamei-cho,Takamatsu-shi,Kagawa
Simizu Naohisa	2-1-16 Dekijima Niigata city,Niigata Pref.
Shuto Shozo	3-1-1206,Momochihama 4-chome,Sawara-ku,Fukuoka
Suzuki Takeshi	1642-186 Nagae,Hayamacho,Miura-gun,Kanagawa-ken
Takeuchi Haruyoshi	4-9-18-707 Kitashinjuku,Shinjuku-ku,Tokyo
Nakagawa Juro	2-17-3,Izumi-Honcho,Komae-city,Tokyo
Nashiro Toru	1-22-3, Shuri-Yamakawa, Naha, Okinawa
Hashimoto Masakatsu	4-40,Yayoi-cho,Nagasaki-city,Nagasaki
Hattori Mitsuji	No.23-Midori-cho Mobara city
Fujiwara Koichi	609-1-1-1 Ohishi Higashi-machi,Nada-ku,Kobe,Japan
Maki Yoshio	11-1,Sarugaku-cho,Shibuya-ku,Tokyo
Matsuda Yasunori	4-16-14,Midori-ga-oka,Mobaracity,Chiba
Monji Takako	3-6-1,Kitakyuhoji-machi,Chuo-ku,Osaka
Yamanaka Seiichi	3-34-2-504,Akatsuka-Shinmachi,Itabashi-ku,Tokyo
Yoshida Hirohiko	13-10,Nihonbashi-Odenmacho,Chou-ku,Tokyo,Japan
Kurosawa Kiyuji	27-5,Fuji Bldg.1F,Tachimachi,Aoba-ku,Sendai-city
Takahashi Yasuharu	No.5-10-1,Hanakoganei,Kodaira-shi,Tokyo
Hamaguchi Yasuhisa	46,Muramatsu-cho,Ise-shi,Mie
Saito Tetsushi	190-19 Higashi Shizuoka City,Shizuoka
Shibata Yoji	2-6-3-1104,Komatsugawa,Edogawa-ku,Tokyo
Michihiro Ito	25-5-106,Minamioonoda,Taihaku-ku Sendai-shi Miyagi-pref.
Inoue Takahiko	2-8-6-208,Hanegi,Setagaya-ku,Tokyo
Oishi Hironobu	1-5-5 Otemachi,Chiyoda-ku,Tokyo
Okumura Haruo	79-22,Torigaoka,Totsuka-ku,Yokohama-city
Kawagita Masaaki	21-27 Iwata Tsu-chi, Mie-Pref.
Kinoshita Yoshifumi	1-2-1-1903,Takasago,Urawa-ku,Saitama-shi,Saitama
Kuboi Shigeki	2-8-2 Nihonbashi, Chu0-ku, Tokyo
Kuroda Kiyohiro	5-2,Koyodai,Hojo-city,Ehime Pref.
Kobayashi Yoshiomi	2-8-10-305,Oomachi,Kamakura-city,Kanagawa

Saito Yoshiyuki	6-13-10,Yutaka-cho,Shinagawa-ku,Tokyo
Sato Toshimitsu	3-16-1-704 Masago Mihama-ku,Chiba-city,Chiba
Shiota Miyuki	6-6,Kinsei-cho,Kagoshima-city,Kagoshima
Shirakawa miho	10-7,Teraoasahi-dori,Niigata-shi,Niigata
Sugano Yoshimi Netherlands	World Trade Center,Strawinskylaan 1025,1077 XX Amsterdam,The
Sugiyama Eiichi	2-15,Meieki5-chome,Nakamura-ku,Nagoya
Masaaki Seki	10-10-214,Fuyuki, Koutou-ku,Tokyo
Soga Shinobu	2-12-2,Matsugaoka,Tokorozawa-shi,Saitama
Takagi Kenichiro	3-28-8-428,Yaguchi,Ota-ku,Tokyo
Takano Masaru	3-2-18,Nihonbashi Muromachi,Chuo-ku,Tokyo
Takahashi Hiroyuki	3-5-45-105,Kamisugi,Aoba-ku,Sendai,Miyagi
Takeda Taishi	4-9-13 Hachobori, Chuo-ku, Tokyo
Shinji Tashiro	EDS Bldg.2-12,Shibuya 4-chome,Shibuya-ku,Tokyo 150-0002 Japan
Date Ichiji	4-1-1 Dosho-machi,Chuou-ku,Osaka City,Osaka
Hiroshi Tsuji	1-7-1-504,Sakasedai,Takarazuka-city,Hyogo
Dimizu Susumu	Fukokuseimei Buioding 10th Floor,2-2-2,Uchisaiwaicho,Chiyoda-ku,Tokyo
Tomura Kazutami	Ko-711 Higashine,Higashine-shi,Yamagata-ken
Nakashima Ikuo	15-301,5-1-13,Kidukabutodai,Souraku-gun,Kyoto
Nakamoto Ikuo	4-5,Marunouchi 1-chome,Chiyoda-ku,Tokyo
Nishigaki Hiroyuki	12-3,Ninokuchi-cho,Kashihara,Nara,Japan
Haruna Akira	24-24 Osonedai Kohoku-ku,Yokohama,Kanagawa
Hirano Masaru	6-26-3,Maehara-higashi,funabashi,chiba 274-0824
Fukasawa Toshio	776-1,Kannari,Tomioka-shi,Gunma,Japan
Fukumoto Masahide	6-6 Kinsei Cho Kagoshima-city
Fujita Yutaka	1-19-9,Yoshida,Nagano-city,Nagano
Matsukawa Motoharu	2-5-5-7,Tsutsumi-machi,Aomori-city,Aomori
Manabe Tadashi	2-2-1 Hakataekimae,Hakataku,Fukuoka city
Moritsugu Kzuhiro	1-35-405,Minami12jo,Nishi12chome,Chuo-ku,Sapporo
Yamazaki Takeomi	1703 4-jodori 9-chome,Asahikawa-city,Hokkaido
Yamashina Teruhito	1-2-26,Tsutsumicho-dori,Toyama-shi,Toyama
Yamada Keiichi	2-7,Juoukanishi-machi,Saiki-city,Oita
Yamanaka Kazuto	5-18-8,Kamiyoga,Setagaya-ku,Tokyo
Yonei Shikoh	313-3,Ishinden-cho,Tsu-City,Mie Pref.
Ryu Tokushige	Rm 106 I-BLK 418-1 Ogori Ogori-city Fukuoka
Wada Isao	2-7-2-202,Fukuzumi-cho,Gifu-shi,Gifu
Iwashimizu Hiroyuki	1-7-24,Nishionuma,Sagamihara Kanagawa
Uno Fumio	2-4-27,Shinfujita Bldg.14F,Dojima,Kita-ku,Osaka
Horikita Daisuke	4-22-31,5-jo,Kitano,Kiyota-ku,Sapporo-city,Hokkaido

Yosino Hitoshi	12-4-902,Hacchobori 4-chome,Chuo-ku,Tokyo
Arimatsu Hidetoshi	100-82 Shiromeguri Kamakura City,Kanagawa Pref.
Ando Takumi	204,3-11-11,Sekimachiminami,Nerima-ku,Tokyo
Ikeda Katsuhiko	3992-3 Kouji,Shirako-town,Chosei-gun,Chiba Prefecture
Ichiyanagi Mitsuhiro	8-3-14,Hachigasaki,Matsudo-city,Chiba
Ohtani Noriyo	3-1-3 Higashi-Ikebukuro,Toshima-ku,Tokyo
Kawaguchi Taiji	3-49-26,Asumigaoka,Midori-ku,Chiba-shi,Chiba-ken
Kawaguchi Mitsuaki	7-15-10-302,Sakuragawa,Aomori-city,Aomori
Kitabayashi Takao	2-6-25,Sanno,Akita-city,Akita
Saito Sadao	3-17-16,Motobuto,Saitama City,Saitama,Pref.
Shibayama Yukio	3-11-8 Minami-otsuka,Toshima-ku,Tokyo
Suzuki Shigeo	120-1,Inakadatemura,Toyomaki,nishimorikosi,Minamitsugaru-gun,Aomori
Takaenoki Toru	1-34-7,Miwadai,Higashi-ku,Fukuoka
Tsujimoto Yasuo	3-25-24,Iwatominami,Komae-city,Tokyo
Tsunekane Shigeya	4-43-2-207,Honcho,Funabashi,Chiba
Terada Kazuo	1-4-10,Minami-ikebukuro,Toshima-ku,Tokyo
Nagamitsu Masaaki	2-4-39 Omotecho,Okayama City 700-0822
Higuchi Toshio	3-2-1-203,Nishikubo,Musashino-shi,Tokyo
Hishida Kiyotaka	6F,3-1-3,Higashi-ikebukuro,Toshima-ku,Tokyo
Hirabayashi Atsumi	2297,Kitahotaka,Hotaka,Minamiazumi-gun,Nagano-ken
Fukaya Yoshitaka	3-32-7,Hongo,Bunkyo-ku,Tokyo
Furuse Masayuki	10-12 Shimanose-cho Sasebo Nagasaki
Maeda Takeo	24-10-2,Oomushi,Takefu,Fukui
Murohashi Giichi	2-5-11,Nishi-oi, Shinagawa-ku,Tokyo
Yachi Masahiko	6-1-1-104,Tsurumaki,Tama-city,Tokyo
Yuhi Yoshihiro	1-14-16,Asahigaoka,Kakegawa,Shizuoka
Yoda Katsuyuki	Ohkubo 1-7-22,Narashino City,Chiba PREF. JAPAN
Washiyama Shigeo	2-13-5-911 Okano Nishi-ku Yokohama Japan

SENIOR TRADE ADVISORS ABROAD

USA

Alabama
Satoshi Kakuda
Alabama Development Office
Fax : 1-334-353-1330

Arkansas
Shinichi Toyomoto
Arkansas Department of Economic Development
Fax : 1-501-324-9856
California

Shizuo Nakamura
International Business Center
Fax : 1-714-558-3905

Colorado
Takaaki Koshio
Colorado office of Economic Development and International Trade
Fax :1-303-892-3820

Florida
Katsuhiko Kobayashi
Enterprise Florida, Inc.
Fax :1-407-316-4672

Massachusetts
Toyokazu Masuda
Massachusetts Department of Economic Development
Fax : 1-617-227-3488

Michigan
Hidemi Saito
Michigan Economic Development Corporation
Fax : 1-313-256-9319

Missouri
Koichi Ando
State of Missouri
Fax : 1-314-863-7091

North Carolina
Hitoshi Suzuki
North Carolina Department of Commerce
Fax : 1-919-733-0110
Ohio
Aiichiro Morita
Ohio Department of Development
Fax : 1-614-463-1540

Oregon
Koichi Ogino
Oregon Economic & Community Development Department
Fax :1-503-222-5050

Pennsylvania
Ikuo Kato
Pennsylvania Department of Community and Economic Development
Fax : 1-717-705-5736

Tennessee
Kenji Miura
Tennessee Department of Economic and Community Development
Fax : 1-615-741-7306

Texas
Hideo Onishi
Texas Economic Development
Fax : 1-512-936-0193

Washington

Naoto Hatori
State of Washington Office of Trade and Economic Development
Fax : 1-206-256-1870
Wisconsin
Shinichiro Noda
State of Wisconsin Department of Commerce
Fax : 1-608-266-5551

Canada

Guelph
Takashi Harada
Agriculture and Agri-Food Canada
Fax : 1-519-837-9782

Vancouver
Yoshihiko Takeno
BC Advanced Systems Institutes
Fax : 1-604-689-4198

U.K.

Birmingham
Yukio Yamauchi
Birmingham Chamber of Commerce & Industry
Fax : 44-121-455-8670

London
Nobuhiko Yoshida
British Trade International
Fax : 44-20-7215-4981

France

Paris
Kazuo Sato
Centre Francais Du Commerce Exterieur
Fax : 33-1-40-73-30-68

Paris
Yoshihiro Sawada
JETRO PARIS (Direction des Relations Economiques Exterieures Bureau)
Fax : 33-1-42-61-19-46

Germany

Dusseldorf
Koichi Kawakyu
Deutsch-Japanischer Wirtschaftskreis
Fax : 49-211-4560-8511

Dresden
Shoji Isaki
Wirtschaftsfoerderung Sachsen GmbH
Fax : 49-351-2138-399

Italia

Milano
Seiji Yasukochi
Associazione Industriale Lombarda
Fax : 39-02-58304951

Spain

Madrid
Tetsuo Mizuyoshi
Instituto Espanol de Comercio Exterior
Fax : 34-91-349-0680

Austria

Wien
Shinichi Tomonari
Austrian Federal Economic Chamber
Fax :43-1-50105-255

Portugal

Lisbon

Investimentos, Comercio & Turismo de Portugal
Fax : 351-21-353-6482

Netherlands

Hague
Shigemichi Mori
Netherlands Foreign Trade Agency(EVD)
Fax :31-70-778-8252

Denmark

Copenhagen
Junichiro Izaki
Royal Danish Ministry of Foreign Affairs
Fax : 45-33-92-07-17

Austraria

Sydney
Yasushi Kowata
Austrade
Fax : 61-2-9390-2767

SUPPLEMENTS

ASSOCIATIONS IN JAPAN

IMPORTER'S ASSOCIATIONS IN JAPAN

- Japan Machine Tools Importers' Association
- Japan Electronic Products Importers Association
- Japan Iron & Steel Scrap Importers Association
- Japan Automobile Importers Association
- Japan Watch Importers' Association

EXPORTER'S ASSOCIATIONS IN JAPAN

- Japan Pearl Exporters' Association
- Japan Machinery Center for Trade and Investment
- Japan Overseas Rolling Stock Association
- Japan Cotton Waste & General Fibre Exporters Association
- Japan Iron & Steel Exporters' Association

MANUFACTURER'S ASSOCIATIONS IN JAPAN

- Japan Pharmaceutical Manufacturers Association
- The Japan Food Machinery Manufacturer's Association
- Japan Electric Measuring Instruments Manufacturers' Association
- The Association of Powder Process Industry and Engineering, Japan
- Japan Analytical Instruments Manufacturers Association
- Japan Paint Manufacturers Association
- Japanese Marine Equipment Association
- Nishijin Textile Industrial Association
- Japan Auto Accessories Manufacturers' Association
- Japan Automobile Manufacturers Association, Inc.
- The Society of Japanese Aerospace Companies
- The Association of Liquid Filtration and Purification Industry
- Nippon Electric Control Equipment Industries Association
- Japan Sake Brewers Association
- Japan Packaging Machinery Manufacturers Association
- Japan Construction Equipment Manufacturers Association
- Japan Metal Stamping Association
- The Japan Pharmaceutical Manufacturers Association
- Computer Software Association of Japan (CSAJ)
- The Shipbuilders' Association of Japan
- Japan Sewing Machinery Manufacturers Association
- Catalyst Manufacturers Association

ASSOCIATIONS BY INDUSTRY

- Japan DIY Industry Association
- Japan Adhesive Industry Association
- Japan Association of Rolling Stock Industries

- Japan Auto Parts Industries Association
- Semiconductor Equipment Association of Japan
- Japanese Association of Healthcare Information Systems Industry
- Electonic Industries Association of Japan
- Japan Bioindustry Association
- The Japan Society of Mechanical Engineers
- Japan Housing Association
- Communications and Information network Association of Japan
- Japan Information Technology Service Industry Association
- Japan Die & Mold Industry Association
- Computer Entertainment Supplier's Association
- Japan Boating Industry Association
- Japan Association of Rapid Prototyping Industry
- Japan Pharmaceutical Association
- Optoelectronic Industry and Technology Development Association
- Japanese Society for Rights of Authors, Composers and Publishers
- Japan Business Machine and Information System Industries Association
- Japan Electronics and Information Technology Industries Association
- The Recording Industry Association of Japan
- Japan Pharmaceutical Wholesalers Association
- Japan Book Publishers Association
- The Japan Newspaper Publishers & Editors Association
- Telecommunications Carriers Association
- The Japanese Bankers Association
- Japan Internet Providers Association
- The General Insurance Association of Japan
- The Life Insurance Association of Japan
- Japan Association of Travel Agents
- Japan Association of Graphic Arts Technology
- The Japanese Institute of Certified Public Accountants
- Japan Association for Financial Planners
- Japanese Nursing Association
- Japan Industrial Designers' Association
- Japan Interior Designers' Association
- The Japan Institute of Architects
- Japan Restaurant Association
- Japan Advertising Agencies Association
- Japan Magazine Advertising Association
- Japan Chemical Industry Association
- Japan Petrochemical Industry Association
- The National Association of Commercial Broadcasters in Japan
- Japan Soap and Detergent Association
- Japan Canners Association
- Japan Copper and Brass Association
- Japan Glass Bottle Association
- Japan Frozen Food Association
- Japan Scientific Feeds Association

OTHER ASSOCIATIONS

- Japan Chamber of Commerce & Industry
- Japan Foreign Trade Council, Inc.

- Tokyo Trade Center
- Keidanren
- New Media Development Association
- Foreign Correspondents' Club of Japan
- Japan Football Association
- Nihon Sumo Kyokai
- Osaka International Business Promotion Center
- Japan Trucking Association
- Japanese Standards Association
- Japan Commercial Arbitration Association
- Miso Health Promotion Committee
- Japan Marketing Research Association
- The Japan Direct Marketing Association
- Interoperability Technology Association for Information Processing, Japan
- Japan Pyrotechnics Association
- Japan Electronic Data Interchange Council

IMPORTANT FOOD INDUSTRY ASSOCIATIONS

Organization	Website	Category
American Association of Cereal Chemists	www.scisoc.org/aacc/	Food Industry Associations
British Columbia Functional Food and Nutraceutical Network	www.bcfn2.com/netlinks.html	Food Industry Associations
UK Food and Drink Federation	www.fdf.org.uk	Food Industry Associations
California Dairy Research Foundations	www.cdrf.org	Food Industry Associations
The Sugar Bureau	www.sugar-bureau.co.uk	Food Industry Associations
PROEUHEALTH	www.vtt.fi	Food Industry Associations
Food Development Centre (Health Canada)	www.gov.mb.ca	Food Industry Associations
Food Future	www.foodfuture.org.uk	Food Industry Associations
Flooz	www.Flooz.com	Online-currency startup
Food Navigator	www.foodnavigator.com	Food Industry Associations
Finish National Consumer Research	www.kuluttajatutkimuskeskus.fi	Food Industry Associations
Grocery Manufacturers of America	www.gmabrands.com	Food Industry Associations
Health Development Agency	www.HDA.nhs.uk	Food Industry Associations
Nutraceuticalsworld	www.nutraceuticalsworld.com	Food Industry Associations
Japan Functional Food Research Assn	www.jafra.qr.jp	Food Industry

		Associations
Night Time Milk	www.ahmarketing.co.uk/nighttimemilk.htm	Food Industry Associations
New Hope Natural Media	www.newhope.com	Food Industry Associations
National Institutes of Health/Office of Dietary Supplements	www.ods.nih.gov	Food Industry Associations
Medicinal Food News	www.medicinalfoodnews.com	Food Industry Associations
USprobiotics	www.usprobiotics.org	Food Industry Associations
US Potato Board	www.healthypotato.com	Food Industry Associations
AHD International, LLC	www.ahdintl.com	Food Industry Associations

MEDIA ASSOCIATIONS

NEWSPAPERS

Foreign Press Center Japan, FPC

Zaidan Hojin, Foreign Press Center 日本語表記

CATEGORY Media/Publishing:Media Associations:Newspapers
TYPE Incorporated foundation
ADDRESS Nihon Press Center bldg., 2-2-1 Uchisaiwai-cho, Chiyoda-ku, Tokyo 100-0011
PHONE +81-3-3501-3401
FAX +81-3-3501-3622
E-MAIL rr@fpcjpn.or.jp
HOMEPAGE http://www.fpcj.jp
REMARKS

Japan Audit Bureau of Circulations, JABC

Shadan Hojin, Nihon ABC Kyokai 日本語表記

CATEGORY Media/Publishing:Media Associations:Newspapers
TYPE Incorporated association
ADDRESS c/o Shisei Kaikan bldg., 1-3 Hibiya Koen, Chiyoda-ku, Tokyo 100-0012
PHONE +81-3-3501-1491
FAX +81-3-3501-1494
E-MAIL admin@jabc.or.jp
HOMEPAGE http://www.jabc.or.jp/ (Japanese only)
REMARKS

Japan Congress of Journalists, JCJ

Nihon Journalist Kaigi 日本語表記

CATEGORY Media/Publishing:Media Associations:Newspapers
TYPE Others
ADDRESS Matsumura bldg.-402, 1-4-8 Sarugaku-cho, Chiyoda-ku, Tokyo 101-0064
PHONE +81-3-3291-6475
FAX +81-3-3291-6478
E-MAIL jcj@tky.3web.ne.jp
HOMEPAGE http://www.jcj.gr.jp/e_index.html
REMARKS

Japan Local Newspaper Association, JLNA

Shadan Hojin, Nihon Chiho Shinbun Kyokai (Nichishinkyo)

CATEGORY Media/Publishing:Media Associations:Newspapers
TYPE Incorporated association
ADDRESS Onosho bldg. 601, 6 Samon-cho, Shinjuku-ku, Tokyo 160-0017
PHONE +81-3-5379-1531
FAX +81-3-5379-1533

Japan National Press Club, NPC

Shadan Hojin, Nihon Kisha Club

CATEGORY Media/Publishing:Media Associations:Newspapers
TYPE Incorporated association
ADDRESS Nihon Press Center bldg., 2-2-1 Uchisaiwai-cho, Chiyoda-ku, Tokyo 100-0011
PHONE +81-3-3503-2722
FAX +81-3-3503-7271

Nippon Press Center, Ltd.

Kabushikigaisha, Nippon Press Center

CATEGORY Media/Publishing:Media Associations:Newspapers
TYPE Private company
ADDRESS 2-2-1 Uchisaiwai-cho, Chiyoda-ku, Tokyo 100-0011
PHONE +81-3-3580-1581
FAX +81-3-3580-1585

The Foreign Correspondents' Club of Japan

Shadan Hojin, Nihon Gaikoku Tokuhain Kyokai

CATEGORY Media/Publishing:Media Associations:Newspapers
TYPE Incorporated association
ADDRESS Yurakucho Denki bldg. Kitakan 20F, 1-7-1 Yuraku-cho, Chiyoda-ku, Tokyo 100-0006
PHONE +81-3-3211-3161
FAX +81-3-3284-1688
E-MAIL info@fccj.or.jp
HOMEPAGE http://www.fccj.or.jp/

The Japan Newspaper Publishers and Editors Association, NSK

Shadan Hojin, Nihon Shinbun Kyokai (Shinbun Kyokai)

CATEGORY Media/Publishing:Media Associations:Newspapers
TYPE Incorporated association
ADDRESS Nihon Press Center bldg., 2-2-1 Uchisaiwai-cho, Chiyoda-ku, Tokyo 100-8543
PHONE +81-3-3591-4401
FAX +81-3-3591-6149
E-MAIL s_intl@pressnet.or.jp
HOMEPAGE http://www.pressnet.or.jp/

BROADCASTING

Copyright Research and Information Center, CRIC

Shadan Hojin, Chosakuken Joho Center

CATEGORY Media/Publishing:Media Associations:Broadcasting
TYPE Incorporated association
ADDRESS Tokyo Opera City Tower 11F, 3-20-2 Nishi-shinjuku, Shinjuku-ku, Tokyo 163-1411
PHONE +81-3-5353-6921
FAX +81-3-5353-6920
E-MAIL copyright@cric.or.jp
HOMEPAGE http://www.cric.or.jp/cric_e/

Japan Cable Television Association, JCTA

Shadan Hojin, Nihon Cable TV Renmei
CATEGORY Media/Publishing:Media Associations:Broadcasting
TYPE Incorporated association
ADDRESS SDI Gotanda bldg., 7-13-6 Nishi-Gotanda, Shinagawa-ku, Tokyo 141-0031
PHONE +81-3-3490-2022
FAX +81-3-3490-2575
E-MAIL renmei@catv.or.jp
HOMEPAGE http://www.catv.or.jp/english/INDEX77.htm

The National Association of Commercial Broadcasters in Japan, NAB

Shadan Hojin, Nihon Minkan Hoso Renmei (Minporen)
CATEGORY Media/Publishing:Media Associations:Broadcasting
TYPE Incorporated association
ADDRESS Bungei-Shunju bldg. Nishikan, 3-23 Kioi-cho, Chiyoda-ku, Tokyo 102-8577
PHONE +81-3-5213-7711
FAX +81-3-5213-7703
E-MAIL webmaster@nab.or.jp
HOMEPAGE http://www.nab.or.jp/htm/english/englishtop0.htm

PUBLISHING

***Shuppan Rinri Kyogikai, Shutsurinkyo**

Shuppan Rinri Kyogikai (Shutsurinkyo)
CATEGORY Media/Publishing:Media Associations:Publishing
TYPE Others
ADDRESS c/o Nihon Zasshi Kyokai, 1-7 Kanda Surugadai, Chiyoda-ku, Tokyo 101-0062
PHONE +81-3-3291-0775
FAX +81-3-3293-6239

Japan Association of Graphic Arts Technology, JAGAT

Shadan Hojin, Nihon Insatsu Gijutsu Kyokai
CATEGORY Media/Publishing:Media Associations:Publishing
TYPE Incorporated association
ADDRESS 1-29-11 Wada, Suginami-ku, Tokyo 166-8539
PHONE +81-3-3384-3111
FAX +81-3-3384-3481
E-MAIL asiaforum@jagat.or.jp
HOMEPAGE http://www.jagat.or.jp/
REMARKS

Japan Book Publishers Association

Shadan Hojin, Nihon Shoseki Shuppan Kyokai
CATEGORY Media/Publishing:Media Associations:Publishing
TYPE Incorporated association
ADDRESS 6 Fukuro-machi, Shinjuku-ku, Tokyo 162-0828
PHONE +81-3-3268-1303
FAX +81-3-3268-1196
E-MAIL rd@jbpa.or.jp
HOMEPAGE http://www.jbpa.or.jp/default-e.htm

Japan Electronic Publishing Association (JEPA)

Nihon Denshi Shuppan Kyokai
CATEGORY Media/Publishing:Media Associations:Publishing
TYPE Others
ADDRESS Tomodasanwa Bldg. 5F, 1-37, Kanda Jimbocho, Chiyoda-ku, Tokyo 101-0051
PHONE +81-3-3219-2958
FAX +81-3-3219-2940

E-MAIL wwwmaster@jepa.or.jp
HOMEPAGE http://www.jepa.or.jp (Japanese only)
REMARKS

Japan Magazine Publishers Association, JMPA

Shadan Hojin, Nihon Zasshi Kyokai (Zasshi Kyokai)
CATEGORY Media/Publishing:Media Associations:Publishing
TYPE Incorporated association
ADDRESS 1-7 Kanda Surugadai, Chiyoda-ku, Tokyo 101-0062
PHONE +81-3-3291-0775
FAX +81-3-3293-6239
E-MAIL
HOMEPAGE http://www.j-magazine.or.jp/
REMARKS

Japan Publishing Industry Foundation for Culture, JPIC

Zaidan Hojin, Shuppan Bunka Sangyo Shinko Zaidan
CATEGORY Media/Publishing:Media Associations:Publishing
TYPE Incorporated foundation
ADDRESS NE Jinbocho bldg. 3F, 3-9 Kanda Jinbo-cho, Chiyoda-ku, Tokyo 101-0051
PHONE +81-3-5211-7282
FAX +81-3-5211-7285
E-MAIL info@jpic.or.jp
HOMEPAGE http://www.jpic.or.jp/ (Japanese only)

Textbook Publishers Association of Japan

Shadan Hojin, Kyokasho Kyokai
CATEGORY Media/Publishing:Media Associations:Publishing
TYPE Incorporated association
ADDRESS 1-9-28 Sengoku, Koto-ku, Tokyo 135-0015
PHONE +81-3-5606-9781
FAX +81-3-5606-3086
E-MAIL textbook@gol.com
HOMEPAGE http://www.textbook.or.jp(Japanese only)

The Japan Copyright Council

Shadan Hojin, Nihon Chosakuken Kyogikai
CATEGORY Media/Publishing:Media Associations:Publishing
TYPE Incorporated association
ADDRESS c/o Shisei Kaikan bldg., 1-3 Hibiya Koen, Chiyoda-ku, Tokyo 100-0012
PHONE +81-3-3501-3271
FAX +81-3-3501-3289
E-MAIL
HOMEPAGE http://www.jc-right.or.jp (Japanese only)

ADVERTISING

Japan Advertising Agencies Association, JAAA

Shadan Hojin, Nihon Koukokugyo Kyokai
CATEGORY Media/Publishing:Media Associations:Advertising
TYPE Incorporated association
ADDRESS 4-8-12 Ginza, Chuo-ku, Tokyo 104-0061
PHONE +81-3-3562-0876
FAX +81-3-3562-0889
E-MAIL info@jaaa.ne.jp
HOMEPAGE http://www.jaaa.ne.jp/english/
REMARKS

Japan Advertising Council, AC Tokyo Office

Shadan Hojin, Kokyo Kokoku Kiko

CATEGORY	Media/Publishing:Media Associations:Advertising
TYPE	Incorporated association
ADDRESS	1-9-9 Tsukiji, Chuo-ku, Tokyo 104-0045
PHONE	+81-3-5551-5195
FAX	+81-3-5551-7562
E-MAIL	
HOMEPAGE	http://www.ad-c.or.jp
REMARKS	

Japan Advertising Federation, JAF

Shadan Hojin, Zen-nihon Kokoku Renmei (Zenkoren)

CATEGORY	Media/Publishing:Media Associations:Advertising
TYPE	Incorporated association
ADDRESS	Kochiwa bldg., 4-8-12 Ginza, Chuo-ku, Tokyo 104-0061
PHONE	+81-3-3562-2966
FAX	+81-3-3535-4766
E-MAIL	jaf@ad-zenkoren.org
HOMEPAGE	http://www.ad-zenkoren.org/(Japanese only)
REMARKS	

Japan Advertising Review Organization, Inc. JARO

Shadan Hojin, Nihon Kokoku Shinsa Kiko

CATEGORY	Media/Publishing:Media Associations:Advertising
TYPE	Incorporated association
ADDRESS	Dai-3 Kosan bldg., 2-16-7 Ginza, Chuo-ku, Tokyo 104-0061
PHONE	+81-3-3541-2811
FAX	+81-3-3541-2816
E-MAIL	
HOMEPAGE	http://www.jaro.or.jp/
REMARKS	

Japan Magazine Advertising Association, JMAA

Shadan Hojin, Nihon Zasshi Kokoku Kyokai (Zakkokyo)

CATEGORY	Media/Publishing:Media Associations:Advertising
TYPE	Incorporated association
ADDRESS	Nihon Zasshi Kaikan bldg., 1-7-1 Kanda Surugadai, Chiyoda-ku, Tokyo 101-0062
PHONE	+81-3-3291-6202
FAX	+81-3-3291-6240
E-MAIL	jmaa@zakko.or.jp
HOMEPAGE	http://www.zakko.or.jp/jpn/

NEWSPAPERS AND NEWS AGENCIES

GENERAL NEWSPAPERS

Asahi Shimbun

Kabushikigaisha, Asahi Shinbunsha

CATEGORY	Media/Publishing:Newspapers and News Agencies:General Newspapers
TYPE	Private company
ADDRESS	5-3-2 Tsukiji, Chuo-ku, Tokyo 104-8011
PHONE	+81-3-3545-0131
FAX	
E-MAIL	
HOMEPAGE	http://www.asahi.com/english/english.html
REMARKS	

Chunichi Shimbun Co., Ltd. Tokyo Headquarter

Chunichi Shimbun Kabushikigaisha Tokyo Honsha

CATEGORY Media/Publishing:Newspapers and News Agencies:General Newspapers
TYPE Private company
ADDRESS c/o Chunichi Shinbun Tokyo Honsha, 2-3-13 Konan, Minato-ku, Tokyo 108-8010
PHONE +81-3-3471-2211
FAX +81-3-3470-2529
E-MAIL webmaster@tokyo-np.co.jp
HOMEPAGE http://www.tokyo-np.co.jp/ (Japanese only)
REMARKS

Nihon Keizai Shimbun, Inc.

Kabushikigaisha, Nihon Keizai Shinbunsha

CATEGORY Media/Publishing:Newspapers and News Agencies:General Newspapers
TYPE Private company
ADDRESS 1-9-5 Ote-machi, Chiyoda-ku, Tokyo 100-8066
PHONE +81-3-3270-0251
FAX
E-MAIL webmaster@nikkei.co.jp
HOMEPAGE http://www.nni.nikkei.co.jp/
REMARKS

Sankei Shimbun Co., Ltd.

Kabushikigaisha, Sangyo Keizai Shinbunsha

CATEGORY Media/Publishing:Newspapers and News Agencies:General Newspapers
TYPE Private company
ADDRESS 1-7-2 Ote-machi, Chiyoda-ku, Tokyo 100-8077
PHONE +81-3-3231-7111
FAX +81-3-3271-3541
E-MAIL webmaster@sankei.co.jp
HOMEPAGE http://www.sankei.co.jp/main.html (Japanese only)
REMARKS

The Chunichi Shimbun

Kabushikigaisha, Chunichi Shinbunsha

CATEGORY Media/Publishing:Newspapers and News Agencies:General Newspapers
TYPE Private company
ADDRESS 1-6-1 Sannomaru, Naka-ku Nagoya-shi, Aichi 460-8511
PHONE +81-52-201-8811
FAX +81-52-221-1220
E-MAIL webmaster@chunichi.co.jp
HOMEPAGE http://www.chunichi.co.jp/ (Japanese only)
REMARKS

The Hokkaido Shimbun Press

Kabushikigaisha, Hokkaido Shinbunsha

CATEGORY Media/Publishing:Newspapers and News Agencies:General Newspapers
TYPE Private company
ADDRESS 3-6 Odori-Nishi, Chuo-ku Sapporo-shi, Hokkaido 060-8711
PHONE +81-11-221-2111
FAX +81-11-210-5508
E-MAIL info@hokkaido-np.co.jp
HOMEPAGE http://www.hokkaido-np.co.jp/ (Japanese only)
REMARKS

The Mainichi Newspapers

Kabushikigaisha, Mainichi Shinbunsha 日本語表記
CATEGORY Media/Publishing:Newspapers and News Agencies:General Newspapers
TYPE Private company
ADDRESS 1-1-1 Hitotsubashi, Chiyoda-ku, Tokyo 100-8051
PHONE +81-3-3212-0321
FAX +81-3-3212-3351
E-MAIL mdn@mainichi.co.jp
HOMEPAGE http://www.mainichi.co.jp/english/index.html
REMARKS

The Nishinippon Shimbun

Kabushikigaisha, Nishi-Nihon Shinbunsha 日本語表記
CATEGORY Media/Publishing:Newspapers and News Agencies:General Newspapers
TYPE Private company
ADDRESS 1-4-1 Tenjin, Chuo-ku Fukuoka-shi, Fukuoka 810-8721
PHONE +81-92-711-5555
FAX +81-92-711-5188
E-MAIL info@fukuoka-now.com
HOMEPAGE http://www.nishinippon.co.jp/e_index.html
REMARKS

The Yomiuri Shimbun (The Daily Yomiuri)

Kabushikigaisha, Yomiuri Shimbun Tokyo-honsha 日本語表記
CATEGORY Media/Publishing:Newspapers and News Agencies:General Newspapers
TYPE Private company
ADDRESS 1-7-1 Ote-machi, Chiyoda-ku, Tokyo 100-8055
PHONE +81-3-3217-8215
FAX +81-3-3217-8293
E-MAIL webmaster@yomiuri.co.jp
HOMEPAGE http://www.yomiuri.co.jp/index-e.htm

FOREIGN-LANGUAGE NEWSPAPERS

Mainichi Daily News

Mainichi Daily News 日本語表記
CATEGORY Media/Publishing:Newspapers and News Agencies:Foreign-language Newspapers
TYPE Private company
ADDRESS c/o Mainichi Shinbunsha, 1-1-1 Hitotsubashi, Chiyoda-ku, Tokyo 100-8051
PHONE +81-3-3212-0321
FAX +81-3-3211-2509
E-MAIL mdn@mainichi.co.jp
HOMEPAGE http://www.mainichi.co.jp/english/index.html
REMARKS

The Daily Yomiuri

The Daily Yomiuri 日本語表記
CATEGORY Media/Publishing:Newspapers and News Agencies:Foreign-language Newspapers
TYPE Private company
ADDRESS c/o Yomiuri Shinbunsha, 1-7-1 Ote-machi, Chiyoda-ku, Tokyo 100-8055
PHONE +81-3-3216-8866
FAX +81-3-3217-8247
E-MAIL webmaster@yomiuri.co.jp
HOMEPAGE http://www.yomiuri.co.jp/index-e.htm
REMARKS

The Japan Times, Ltd.

Kabushikigaisha, Japan Times
CATEGORY Media/Publishing:Newspapers and News Agencies:Foreign-language Newspapers
TYPE Private company
ADDRESS 4-5-4 Shibaura, Minato-ku, Tokyo 108-8071
PHONE +81-3-3453-5312
FAX +81-3-3452-0659
E-MAIL
HOMEPAGE http://www.japantimes.co.jp/
REMARKS

The Nikkei Weekly

The Nikkei Weekly
CATEGORY Media/Publishing:Newspapers and News Agencies:Foreign-language Newspapers
TYPE Private company
ADDRESS c/o Nihon Keizai Shinbunsha, 1-9-5 Ote-machi, Chiyoda-ku, Tokyo 100-0086
PHONE +81-3-3270-0251
FAX +81-3-5255-2629
E-MAIL webmaster@nikkei.co.jp
HOMEPAGE http://www.nni.nikkei.co.jp/FR/SERV/TNW/subscript.html
REMARKS

Tokyo News Service

Tokyo News Tsushinsha
CATEGORY Media/Publishing:Newspapers and News Agencies:Foreign-language Newspapers
TYPE Private company
ADDRESS Tukiji Hamarikyu bldg., 5-3-3 Tsukiji, Chuo-ku, Tokyo 104-8004
PHONE +81-3-3542-6511
FAX +81-3-3545-3628
E-MAIL editorial.a@tokyonews.co.jp
HOMEPAGE http://www.tokyonews.co.jp/ (Japanese only)

NEWS AGENCIES

Jiji Press, Ltd.

Kabushikigaisha, Jiji Tsushinsha
CATEGORY Media/Publishing:Newspapers and News Agencies:News Agencies
TYPE Private company
ADDRESS Shisei Kaikan bldg., 1-3 Hibiya Koen, Chiyoda-ku, Tokyo 100-8568
PHONE +81-3-3591-1111
FAX +81-3-3508-1298
E-MAIL webmaster@jiji.com
HOMEPAGE http://www.jiji.com/ (Japanese only)
REMARKS

Kyodo News, Kyodo

Shadan Hojin, Kyodo Tsushinsha (Kyodo)
CATEGORY Media/Publishing:Newspapers and News Agencies:News Agencies
TYPE Incorporated association
ADDRESS 2-2-5 Toranomon, Minato-ku, Tokyo 105-8474
PHONE +81-3-5573-8000
FAX
E-MAIL
HOMEPAGE http://home.kyodo.co.jp/

FOREIGN NEWSPAPER OFFICES IN JAPAN

China Daily News

Chuka Nippo 日本語表記
CATEGORY Media/Publishing:Newspapers and News Agencies:Foreign Newspaper Offices in Japan
TYPE Private company
ADDRESS 5-18-12 Mita, Minato-ku, Tokyo 108-0073
PHONE +81-3-3446-1526
FAX +81-3-3446-1527
E-MAIL
HOMEPAGE
REMARKS

China Times

Chugoku Jiho 日本語表記
CATEGORY Media/Publishing:Newspapers and News Agencies:Foreign Newspaper Offices in Japan
TYPE Private company
ADDRESS Monaku Shinnakano bldg 701, 4-44-12 Honcho, Nakano-ku, Tokyo 164-0012
PHONE +81-3-5385-5366
FAX +81-3-5385-5376
E-MAIL
HOMEPAGE http://news.chinatimes.com/
REMARKS

Dong a Ilbo

Toa Nippo 日本語表記
CATEGORY Media/Publishing:Newspapers and News Agencies:Foreign Newspaper Offices in Japan
TYPE Private company
ADDRESS Asahi Shinbun Shinkan 9F, 5-3-2 Tsukiji, Chuo-ku, Tokyo 104-8011
PHONE +81-3-3248-1251
FAX +81-3-3248-1254
E-MAIL newsroom@donga.com
HOMEPAGE http://english.donga.com/
REMARKS

Financial Times (Japan)

Financial Times 日本語表記
CATEGORY Media/Publishing:Newspapers and News Agencies:Foreign Newspaper Offices in Japan
TYPE Private company
ADDRESS Yamato Seimei bldg. 21F, 1-1-7 Uchisaiwai-cho, Chiyoda-ku, Tokyo 100-0004
PHONE +81-3-3581-3900
FAX +81-3-3581-0366
E-MAIL
HOMEPAGE http://www.ft.com, http://www.ftjapan.co.jp
REMARKS

Frankfurter Allgemeine Zeitung

Frankfurter Allgemeine Zeitung 日本語表記
CATEGORY Media/Publishing:Newspapers and News Agencies:Foreign Newspaper Offices in Japan
TYPE Private company
ADDRESS 4-36-18 Soshigaya, Setagaya-ku, Tokyo 157-0072
PHONE +81-3-3483-8686
FAX +81-3-3483-8682
E-MAIL
HOMEPAGE http://www.faz.com
REMARKS

International Herald Tribune/The Asahi Shinbun

Herald Asahi 日本語表記

CATEGORY Media/Publishing:Newspapers and News Agencies:Foreign Newspaper Offices in Japan
TYPE Private company
ADDRESS c/o Asahi Shinbunsha Tokyo Honsha, 5-3-2 Tsukiji , Chuo-ku, Tokyo 104-8011
PHONE +81-3-5540-7641
FAX +81-3-3542-6172
E-MAIL aen@mx.asahi-np.co.jp
HOMEPAGE http://www.iht.com/frontpage.htm
REMARKS

Le Monde

Le Monde 日本語表記
CATEGORY Media/Publishing:Newspapers and News Agencies:Foreign Newspaper Offices in Japan
TYPE Private company
ADDRESS 6-12-18 Shirogane, Minato-ku, Tokyo 108-0072
PHONE +81-3-3446-6062
FAX +81-3-3446-6098
E-MAIL pons@lemonde.fr
HOMEPAGE http://www.lemonde.fr/ (French only)
REMARKS

Los Angeles Times

Los Angeles Times 日本語表記
CATEGORY Media/Publishing:Newspapers and News Agencies:Foreign Newspaper Offices in Japan
TYPE Private company
ADDRESS Yomiuri bldg. 8F, 1-7-1 Ote-machi, Chiyoda-ku, Tokyo 100-0004
PHONE +81-3-3246-1888
FAX +81-3-3270-2949
E-MAIL latimes-tokyo@pop02.odn.ne.jp
HOMEPAGE http://www.latimes.com/
REMARKS

Peoples Daily

Jinmin Nippo 日本語表記
CATEGORY Media/Publishing:Newspapers and News Agencies:Foreign Newspaper Offices in Japan
TYPE National
ADDRESS 1-2-17 Mita, Meguro-ku, Tokyo 153-0062
PHONE +81-3-5791-4097
FAX
E-MAIL info@peopledaily.co.jp
HOMEPAGE http://j.people.ne.jp/home.html
REMARKS

The Chosun Ilbo

Chosen Nippo Nihon Shisha 日本語表記
CATEGORY Media/Publishing:Newspapers and News Agencies:Foreign Newspaper Offices in Japan
TYPE Private company
ADDRESS Togin bldg, 822, 1-4-2 Marunouchi, Chiyoda-ku, Tokyo 100-0005
PHONE +81-3-3216-2711
FAX +81-3-3214-1080
E-MAIL webmaster@chosun.com
HOMEPAGE http://www.chosun.com
REMARKS

The Hankook Ilbo

Kankoku Nippo 日本語表記

CATEGORY Media/Publishing:Newspapers and News Agencies:Foreign Newspaper Offices in Japan
TYPE Private company
ADDRESS Yomiuri bldg 8F, 1-7-1 Otemachi, Chiyoda-ku, Tokyo 100-8055
PHONE +81-3-3270-8371
FAX
E-MAIL hkilbo@interlink.or.jp
HOMEPAGE http://www.hankooki.com/
REMARKS

The New York Times

New York Times 日本語表記
CATEGORY Media/Publishing:Newspapers and News Agencies:Foreign Newspaper Offices in Japan
TYPE Private company
ADDRESS Asahi Shinbunsha bldg 9fl, 5-3-2 Tsukiji, Chuo-ku, Tokyo 104-8011
PHONE +81-3-3545-0950
FAX +81-3-3545-1301
E-MAIL
HOMEPAGE http://www.nytimes.com/
REMARKS

The Straits Times

The Straits Times 日本語表記
CATEGORY Media/Publishing:Newspapers and News Agencies:Foreign Newspaper Offices in Japan
TYPE Private company
ADDRESS 5A, 6-6-28 Akasaka, Minato-ku, Tokyo 107-0052
PHONE +81-3-3582-6259
FAX +81-3-3589-5480
E-MAIL spho@flamenco.plala.or.jp
HOMEPAGE http://straitstimes.asia1.com.sg/
REMARKS

The Times

The Times 日本語表記
CATEGORY Media/Publishing:Newspapers and News Agencies:Foreign Newspaper Offices in Japan
TYPE Private company
ADDRESS c/o Asahi Shinbunsha, 5-3-2 Tsukiji, Chuo-ku, Tokyo 104-0045
PHONE +81-3-3545-0714
FAX +81-3-5565-3105
E-MAIL
HOMEPAGE http://www.the-times.co.uk/
REMARKS

Wall Street Journal

Wall Street Journal 日本語表記
CATEGORY Media/Publishing:Newspapers and News Agencies:Foreign Newspaper Offices in Japan
TYPE Private company
ADDRESS Nikkei bldg. 11F, 1-9-5 Ote-machi, Chiyoda-ku, Tokyo 100-8066
PHONE +81-3-3241-1671
FAX +81-3-3246-1098
E-MAIL
HOMEPAGE http://www.wsj.com
REMARKS

Washington Post

Washington Post 日本語表記
CATEGORY Media/Publishing:Newspapers and News Agencies:Foreign Newspaper Offices in Japan

TYPE Private company
ADDRESS Avex bldg. 3fl., 3-1-30 Minami-Aoyama, Minato-ku, Tokyo 107-8586
PHONE +81-3-5411-6031
FAX +81-3-5411-6050
E-MAIL
HOMEPAGE http://www.washingtonpost.com/

FOREIGN NEWS AGENCIES IN JAPAN

*Shinkasha Tsushin, Tokyo Shisha

Shinkasha Tsushin, Tokyo Shisha 日本語表記
CATEGORY Media/Publishing:Newspapers and News Agencies:Foreign News Agencies in Japan
TYPE National
ADDRESS 3-35-23 Ebisu, Shibuya-ku, Tokyo 150-0013
PHONE +81-3-3441-3766
FAX +81-3-3446-3995
E-MAIL
HOMEPAGE
REMARKS

Agence France-presse

AFP, Agence France-presse 日本語表記
CATEGORY Media/Publishing:Newspapers and News Agencies:Foreign News Agencies in Japan
TYPE Private company
ADDRESS c/o Asahi Shinbunsha, 5-3-2 Tsukiji, Chuo-ku, Tokyo 104-0045
PHONE +81-3-3545-3061
FAX +81-3-3546-2594
E-MAIL afptyo.desk@afp.com
HOMEPAGE http://www.afp.com/english/home/
REMARKS

ITAR-TASS

ITAR-TASS, Russian News Agency 日本語表記
CATEGORY Media/Publishing:Newspapers and News Agencies:Foreign News Agencies in Japan
TYPE National
ADDRESS 1-5-1 Hon-cho, Shibuya-ku, Tokyo 151-0071
PHONE +81-3-3377-0380
FAX +81-3-3378-0606
E-MAIL sm@itar-tass.com
HOMEPAGE http://www.itar-tass.com
REMARKS

Reuters Japan Ltd.

Reuter Japan Kabushiki Gaisha 日本語表記
CATEGORY Media/Publishing:Newspapers and News Agencies:Foreign News Agencies in Japan
TYPE Private company
ADDRESS Shuwa Kamiyacho bldg. 3F, 4-3-13 Toranomon, Minato-ku, Tokyo 105-0001
PHONE +81-3-3432-4141
FAX
E-MAIL
HOMEPAGE http://www.reuters.com/
REMARKS

The Associated Press

AP, Associated Press 日本語表記
CATEGORY Media/Publishing:Newspapers and News Agencies:Foreign News Agencies in Japan
TYPE Private company
ADDRESS c/o Asahi Shinbunsha, 5-3-2 Tsukiji, Chuo-ku, Tokyo 104-0045

PHONE +81-3-3545-5901
FAX +81-3-3545-0895
E-MAIL
HOMEPAGE http://www.ap.org/
REMARKS

United Press International

UPI, United Press International
CATEGORY Media/Publishing:Newspapers and News Agencies:Foreign News Agencies in Japan
TYPE Private company
ADDRESS 1-24-15 Ebisu, Shibuya-ku, Tokyo 150-0013
PHONE +81-3-3586-2370
FAX +81-3-5421-1339
E-MAIL webmaster@upi.com
HOMEPAGE http://www.upi.com/
REMARKS

Yonhap News Agency

Rengo News
CATEGORY Media/Publishing:Newspapers and News Agencies:Foreign News Agencies in Japan
TYPE Private company
ADDRESS Kyodo Tsushin Kaikan bldg 9fl, 2-2-5 Toranomon, Minato-ku, Tokyo 105-0001
PHONE +81-3-3584-4681
FAX +81-3-3584-4021
E-MAIL
HOMEPAGE http://www.yonhapnews.co.kr

BROADCAST STATIONS

TV STATIONS (TERRESTRIAL)

Asahi National Broadcasting Co., Ltd.

Zenkoku Asahi Hoso, Kabushikigaisha (Televi Asahi)
CATEGORY Media/Publishing:Broadcast Stations:TV stations (terrestrial)
TYPE Private company
ADDRESS 1-1-1 Roppongi, Minato-ku, Tokyo 106-8001
PHONE +81-3-3587-5111
FAX +81-3-3505-3535
E-MAIL
HOMEPAGE http://www.tv-asahi.co.jp/anb/kokusai/
REMARKS

Fuji Television Network, Inc.

Kabushikigaisha, Fuji Television, CX-TV
CATEGORY Media/Publishing:Broadcast Stations:TV stations (terrestrial)
TYPE Private company
ADDRESS 2-4-8 Daiba, Minato-ku, Tokyo 137-8088
PHONE +81-3-5500-8888
FAX +81-3-5500-8007
E-MAIL
HOMEPAGE http://www.fujitv.co.jp
REMARKS

Japan Broadcasting Corporation, NHK

Nippon Hoso Kyokai
CATEGORY Media/Publishing:Broadcast Stations:TV stations (terrestrial)

TYPE Public corporation
ADDRESS 2-2-1 Jinnan, Shibuya-ku, Tokyo 150-8001
PHONE +81-3-3465-1111
FAX +81-3-3469-8110
E-MAIL webmaster@www.nhk.or.jp
HOMEPAGE http://www.nhk.or.jp/index-e.html
REMARKS

Nippon Television Network Corp.

Nihon Televi Hosomo, Kabushikigaisha, NTV
CATEGORY Media/Publishing:Broadcast Stations:TV stations (terrestrial)
TYPE Private company
ADDRESS 14 Niban-cho, Chiyoda-ku, Tokyo 102-8004
PHONE +81-3-5275-1111
FAX
E-MAIL
HOMEPAGE http://www.ntv.co.jp/
REMARKS

Television Tokyo Channel 12, Ltd.

Kabushikigaisha, Televi Tokyo
CATEGORY Media/Publishing:Broadcast Stations:TV stations (terrestrial)
TYPE Private company
ADDRESS 4-3-12 Toranomon, Minato-ku, Tokyo 105-8012
PHONE +81-3-3432-1212
FAX +81-3-3432-0814
E-MAIL webmaster@tv-tokyo.co.jp
HOMEPAGE http://www.tv-tokyo.co.jp/ (Japanese only)
REMARKS

Tokyo Broadcasting System Inc.

Kabushikigaisha, Tokyo Hoso, TBS
CATEGORY Media/Publishing:Broadcast Stations:TV stations (terrestrial)
TYPE Private company
ADDRESS 5-3-6 Akasaka, Minato-ku, Tokyo 107-8066
PHONE +81-3-3746-1111
FAX
E-MAIL
HOMEPAGE http://www.tbs.co.jp/index.html

SATELLITE BROADCASTING AND CATV STATIONS

Cable Television Tokyo, td.

Kabushikigaisha, Cable Television Tokyo, CTT
CATEGORY Media/Publishing:Broadcast Stations:Satellite Broadcasting and CATV Stations
TYPE Private company
ADDRESS Shiba Koen Studio 2F, 4-4-7 Shiba Koen, Minato-ku, Tokyo 105-0011
PHONE +81-3-3432-0022
FAX +81-3-3432-8855
E-MAIL info@rosenet.ne.jp
HOMEPAGE http://www.cabletv.co.jp/ (Japanese only)
REMARKS

Japan Cable Television, Ltd., JCTV

Kabushikigaisha, Nihon Cable Television, JCTV
CATEGORY Media/Publishing:Broadcast Stations:Satellite Broadcasting and CATV Stations
TYPE Private company

ADDRESS Colombus 7F, 1-3-10 Jingumae, Shibuya-ku, Tokyo 150-0001
PHONE +81-3-3405-3191
FAX +81-3-3405-5454
E-MAIL webmaster@jctv.co.jp
HOMEPAGE http://www.jctv.co.jp/ (Japanese only)
REMARKS

Satellite News Corporation

Kabushikigaisha, Satellite News, BBC World
CATEGORY Media/Publishing:Broadcast Stations:Satellite Broadcasting and CATV Stations
TYPE Private company
ADDRESS JBP Obaru bldg., 5-52-2 Jingumae, Shibuya-ku, Tokyo 150-0001
PHONE +81-3-3406-9777
FAX +81-3-3406-9782
E-MAIL sncuser@snctv.co.jp
HOMEPAGE http://www.bbcworld-japan.com (Japanese only)
REMARKS

Star Channel Inc.

Kabushikigaisha, Star Channel
CATEGORY Media/Publishing:Broadcast Stations:Satellite Broadcasting and CATV Stations
TYPE Private company
ADDRESS 1-11-9 Azabudai, Minato-ku, Tokyo 106-8645
PHONE +81-3-5563-6777
FAX +81-3-5563-6799
E-MAIL
HOMEPAGE http://www.star-ch.co.jp/pc/star
REMARKS

WOWOW, Inc.

Kabushikigaisha Wowow
CATEGORY Media/Publishing:Broadcast Stations:Satellite Broadcasting and CATV Stations
TYPE Private company
ADDRESS 1-5-8, Moto Akasaka, Minato-ku, Tokyo 107-8080
PHONE +81-3-5414-8111
FAX +81-3-5414-8100
E-MAIL wowow@post.email.ne.jp
HOMEPAGE http://www.wowow.co.jp/ (Japanese only)

RADIO STATIONS (SHORT WAVE)

Nihon Short-Wave Broadcasting Co., Ltd. NSB

Kabushikigaisha, Nihon Tanpa Hoso, (Radio Tanpa)
CATEGORY Media/Publishing:Broadcast Stations:Radio Stations (short wave)
TYPE Private company
ADDRESS 1-9-15 Akasaka, Minato-ku, Tokyo 107-8373
PHONE +81-3-3583-8151
FAX +81-3-3583-9062
E-MAIL
HOMEPAGE http://www.tampa.co.jp/ (Japanese only)

FOREIGN BROADCASTERS' OFFICES IN JAPAN

American Broadcasting Company

ABC News
CATEGORY Media/Publishing:Broadcast Stations:Foreign Broadcasters' Offices in Japan
TYPE Private company

ADDRESS Dai-1 Kyodo bldg., 41-1 Udagawa-cho, Shibuya-ku, Tokyo 150-0042
PHONE +81-3-3496-5301
FAX +81-3-3496-7620
E-MAIL
HOMEPAGE http://abc.go.com/
REMARKS

ARD German TV Network

ARD Doitsu Televi 日本語表記
CATEGORY Media/Publishing:Broadcast Stations:Foreign Broadcasters' Offices in Japan
TYPE
ADDRESS 2-4-10 Shoto, Shibuya-ku, Tokyo 150-0046
PHONE +81-3-3465-2222
FAX +81-3-3485-4459
E-MAIL ardtvjpn@tkc.att.ne.jp
HOMEPAGE
REMARKS Public broadcasting

Australian Broadcasting Corporation

Australia Hoso Kyokai 日本語表記
CATEGORY Media/Publishing:Broadcast Stations:Foreign Broadcasters' Offices in Japan
TYPE
ADDRESS c/o NHK Hoso Center, 2-2-1 Jinnan, Shibuya-ku, Tokyo 150-8001
PHONE +81-3-3469-8089
FAX +81-3-3468-8445
E-MAIL abctok@gol.com
HOMEPAGE http://www.abc.net.au/
REMARKS Public broadcasting

British Broadcasting Corporation

Eikoku Hoso Kyokai 日本語表記
CATEGORY Media/Publishing:Broadcast Stations:Foreign Broadcasters' Offices in Japan
TYPE
ADDRESS NTV Yonbancho Bekkan 4fl, 5-6 Yonban-cho, Chiyoda-ku, Tokyo 102-0081
PHONE +81-3-3288-0011
FAX +81-3-3288-0010
E-MAIL
HOMEPAGE http://www.bbc.co.uk/
REMARKS Public broadcasting

CBS

CBS News 日本語表記
CATEGORY Media/Publishing:Broadcast Stations:Foreign Broadcasters' Offices in Japan
TYPE Private company
ADDRESS TBS Hoso Center, 5-3-6 Akasaka, Minato-ku, Tokyo 107-0052
PHONE +81-3-3587-1861
FAX +81-3-3584-7429
E-MAIL
HOMEPAGE
REMARKS

China Radio International

Chugoku Kokusai Hosokyoku 日本語表記
CATEGORY Media/Publishing:Broadcast Stations:Foreign Broadcasters' Offices in Japan
TYPE National

ADDRESS Gakugei Daigaku Parkside 304, 3-19-16 Nozawa, Setagaya-ku, Tokyo 154-0003
PHONE +81-3-5481-6217
FAX +81-3-5481-6219
E-MAIL
HOMEPAGE
REMARKS

German Television Network

Doitsu Televi Kyokai 日本語表記
CATEGORY Media/Publishing:Broadcast Stations:Foreign Broadcasters' Offices in Japan
TYPE
ADDRESS c/o TBS Hoso Center 13F, 5-3-6 Akasaka, Minato-ku, Tokyo 107-0052
PHONE +81-3-3586-8188
FAX +81-3-3586-8199
E-MAIL
HOMEPAGE http://www.zdf.de/ (German only)
REMARKS Public broadcasting

Korean Broadcasting System, KBS Japan

Kankoku Hoso Kosha 日本語表記
CATEGORY Media/Publishing:Broadcast Stations:Foreign Broadcasters' Offices in Japan
TYPE
ADDRESS c/o NHK Higashikan-710C, 2-2-1 Jinnan, Shibuya-ku, Tokyo 150-0041
PHONE +81-3-3485-5100
FAX +81-3-3485-6529
E-MAIL
HOMEPAGE http://www.kbs.co.kr/aboutkbs/e_index.html
REMARKS Public broadcasting

Korean MBC TV and Radio Corporation

Kankoku Bunka Hoso Tokyo Shisha 日本語表記
CATEGORY Media/Publishing:Broadcast Stations:Foreign Broadcasters' Offices in Japan
TYPE Private company
ADDRESS Fuji TV Media Tower 18fl, 2-4-8 Daiba, Minato-ku, Tokyo 135-0091
PHONE +81-3-5500-5871
FAX +81-3-5500-5875
E-MAIL mbcsysop@mbc.co.kr
HOMEPAGE http://www.imbc.com/ (Korean only)
REMARKS

NBC News

NBC News 日本語表記
CATEGORY Media/Publishing:Broadcast Stations:Foreign Broadcasters' Offices in Japan
TYPE Private company
ADDRESS NTV Yonbancho Bekkan 4fl, 5-6 Yonban-cho, Chiyoda-ku, Tokyo 102-0081
PHONE +81-3-3265-5881
FAX +81-3-3238-9934
E-MAIL ayamamot@nbc.com
HOMEPAGE http://www.msnbc.com
REMARKS

Seoul Broadcasting System

Kankoku Seoul Hoso 日本語表記
CATEGORY Media/Publishing:Broadcast Stations:Foreign Broadcasters' Offices in Japan
TYPE Private company
ADDRESS c/o NTV Yonbancho Bekkan 4fl, 5-6 Yonban-cho, Chiyoda-ku, Tokyo 102-0081

PHONE +81-3-5275-4800
FAX +81-3-5275-4097
E-MAIL webmaster@sbswebvision.com
HOMEPAGE http://www.sbs.co.kr/ (Korean only)
REMARKS

Swedish TV

Sweden Televi 日本語表記
CATEGORY Media/Publishing:Broadcast Stations:Foreign Broadcasters' Offices in Japan
TYPE
ADDRESS c/o NHK Hoso Center-710G, 2-2-1 Jinnan, Shibuya-ku, Tokyo 150-0041
PHONE +81-3-3485-1569
FAX +81-3-3468-6559
E-MAIL
HOMEPAGE
REMARKS Public broadcasting

BASIC TITLES FOR JAPAN

IMPORTANT!
All publications are updated annually!
Please contact IBP, Inc. at ibpusa3@gmail.com for the latest ISBNs and additional information

Title
Japan A "Spy" Guide - Strategic Information and Developments
Japan A Spy" Guide"
Japan Agricultural and Fishery Products Import Regulations Handbook
Japan Agriculture, Forestry, Fisheries, Mining, Electricity, Water, Gas & Construction
Japan Air Force Handbook
Japan Air Force Handbook
Japan Army Weapon Systems Handbook
Japan Army Weapon Systems Handbook
Japan Army Weapon Systems Handbook
Japan Army, National Security and Defense Policy Handbook
Japan Army, National Security and Defense Policy Handbook
Japan Aviation and Aerospace Industry and Programs Handbook
Japan Aviation and Aerospace Industry Handbook
Japan Banking & Financial Market Handbook
Japan Business and Investment Opportunities Yearbook
Japan Business and Investment Opportunities Yearbook
Japan Business and Investment Opportunities Yearbook Volume 1 Strategic Information and Opportunities
Japan Business and Investment Opportunities Yearbook Volume 2 Leading Export-Import, Business, Investment Opportunities and Projects
Japan Business Intelligence Report - Practical Information, Opportunities, Contacts
Japan Business Intelligence Report - Practical Information, Opportunities, Contacts
Japan Business Law Handbook - Strategic Information and Basic Laws
Japan Business Law Handbook - Strategic Information and Basic Laws
Japan Business Law Handbook - Strategic Information and Basic Laws
Japan Business Law Handbook - Strategic Information and Basic Laws
Japan Clothing & Textile Industry Handbook
Japan Clothing & Textile Industry Handbook
Japan Company Laws and Regulations Handbook
Japan Constitution and Citizenship Laws Handbook - Strategic Information and Basic Laws

Title
Japan Consumer Products Import Regulations Handbook
Japan Country Study Guide - Strategic Information and Developments
Japan Country Study Guide - Strategic Information and Developments
Japan Country Study Guide - Strategic Information and Developments Volume 1 Strategic Information and Developments
Japan Customs, Trade Regulations and Procedures Handbook
Japan Customs, Trade Regulations and Procedures Handbook
Japan Diplomatic Handbook - Strategic Information and Developments
Japan Diplomatic Handbook - Strategic Information and Developments
Japan Ecology & Nature Protection Handbook
Japan Ecology & Nature Protection Handbook
Japan Ecology & Nature Protection Laws and Regulation Handbook
Japan Economic & Development Strategy Handbook
Japan Economic & Development Strategy Handbook
Japan Education System and Policy Handbook
Japan Emission Trading Laws, Regulations and Programs Handbook
Japan Energy Conservation Laws and Regulations Handbook
Japan Energy Efficiency Laws, Regulations and Equipment Standards Handbook
Japan Energy Policy, Laws and Regulation Handbook
Japan Energy Sector Handbook
Japan Energy Sector Handbook
Japan Environment Market Report
Japan Export-Import and Trade Regulations and Procedures Handbook
Japan Export-Import Procedures for Foreign Companies Handbook
Japan Export-Import Trade and Business Directory
Japan Export-Import Trade and Business Directory
Japan Foreign Policy and Government Guide
Japan Foreign Policy and Government Guide
Japan Government and Business Contacts Handbook
Japan Government and Business Contacts Handbook
Japan Government Procurement Policy Handbook
Japan Government t Procurement Policy Handbook
Japan Government t Procurement Policy Handbook
Japan Healthcare Sector Organization, Management and Payment Systems Handbook - Strategic Information, Programs and Regulations
Japan Immigration Laws and Regulations Handbook - Strategic Information and Basic Laws
Japan Industrial and Business Directory
Japan Industrial and Business Directory
Japan Industrial Products Import Regulations Handbook
Japan Insolvency (Bankruptcy) Laws and Regulations Handbook - Strategic Information and Basic Laws
Japan Intelligence & Security Activities & Operations Handbook
Japan Intelligence & Security Activities & Operations Handbook
Japan Intelligence, Security Activities & Operations Handbook
Japan Intelligence, Security Activities & Operations Handbook
Japan Internet and E-Commerce Investment and Business Guide - Strategic and Practical Information: Regulations and Opportunities
Japan Internet and E-Commerce Investment and Business Guide - Strategic and Practical Information: Regulations and Opportunities
Japan Investment and Business Guide - Strategic and Practical Information

Title
Japan Investment and Business Guide - Strategic and Practical Information
Japan Investment and Business Guide - Strategic and Practical Information
Japan Investment and Business Guide - Strategic and Practical Information
Japan Investment and Business Guide Volume 2 Business, Investment Opportunities and Incentives
Japan Investment and Trade Laws and Regulations Handbook
Japan Justice System and National Police Handbook
Japan Justice System and National Police Handbook
Japan Labor Laws and Regulations Handbook - Strategic Information and Basic Laws
Japan Land Ownership and Agriculture Laws Handbook
Japan Major Policy Programs Reports Yearbook Vol.4, 2006
Japan Major Policy Programs Reports Yearbook Vol.4, 2006
Japan Major Policy Programs Reports Yearbook Vol.4, 2006
Japan Major Policy Programs Reports Yearbook Vol.5, 2007
Japan Major Policy Programs Reports Yearbook Vol.5, 2007
Japan Major Policy Programs Reports Yearbook Vol.5, 2007
Japan Medical & Pharmaceutical Industry Handbook
Japan Medical & Pharmaceutical Industry Handbook
Japan Mineral & Mining Sector Investment and Business Guide - Strategic and Practical Information
Japan Mineral & Mining Sector Investment and Business Guide - Strategic and Practical Information
Japan Mining Laws and Regulations Handbook
Japan National Defense Program Handbook
Japan National Defense Program Handbook
Japan National Defense Program Handbook
Japan New International Technology Development Strategy Handbook
Japan New International Technology Development Strategy Handbook
Japan New International Technology Development Strategy Handbook
Japan Prime Minister Handbook
Japan Prime Minister Handbook
Japan Recent Economic and Political Developments Yearbook
Japan Recent Economic and Political Developments Yearbook
Japan Recent Economic and Political Developments Yearbook
Japan Research & Development Policy Handbook
Japan Space Agency and Programs Handbook
Japan Space Programs and Exploration Handbook
Japan Special Economic Zones Handbook
Japan Special Economic Zones Handbook
Japan Special Economic Zones Handbook
Japan Specifications and Standards for Foods, Food Additives, etc. Under The Food Sanitation Law
Japan Starting Business (Incorporating) in....Guide
Japan Tax Guide
Japan Taxation Laws and Regulations Handbook
Japan Telecom Industry Business Opportunities Handbook
Japan Telecom Laws and Regulations Handbook
Japan Telecommunication Industry Business Opportunities Handbook
Japan Transportation Policy and Regulations Handbook
Japan: How to Invest, Start and Run Profitable Business in Japan Guide - Practical Information, Opportunities, Contacts

Belize Customs, Export-Import Regulations, Incentives and Procedures Handbook - Strategic, Practical Information, Regulations
Benin Customs, Export-Import Regulations, Incentives and Procedures Handbook - Strategic, Practical Information, Regulations
Bermuda Customs, Export-Import Regulations, Incentives and Procedures Handbook - Strategic, Practical Information, Regulations
Bhutan Customs, Export-Import Regulations, Incentives and Procedures Handbook - Strategic, Practical Information, Regulations
Bolivia Customs, Export-Import Regulations, Incentives and Procedures Handbook - Strategic, Practical Information, Regulations
Bosnia and Herzegovina Customs, Export-Import Regulations, Incentives and Procedures Handbook - Strategic, Practical Information, Regulations
Botswana Customs, Export-Import Regulations, Incentives and Procedures Handbook - Strategic, Practical Information, Regulations
Brazil Customs, Export-Import Regulations, Incentives and Procedures Handbook - Strategic, Practical Information, Regulations
Brunei Customs, Export-Import Regulations, Incentives and Procedures Handbook - Strategic, Practical Information, Regulations
Bulgaria Customs, Export-Import Regulations, Incentives and Procedures Handbook - Strategic, Practical Information, Regulations
Burkina Faso Customs, Export-Import Regulations, Incentives and Procedures Handbook - Strategic, Practical Information, Regulations
Burundi Customs, Export-Import Regulations, Incentives and Procedures Handbook - Strategic, Practical Information, Regulations
Cambodia Customs, Export-Import Regulations, Incentives and Procedures Handbook - Strategic, Practical Information, Regulations
Cameroon Customs, Export-Import Regulations, Incentives and Procedures Handbook - Strategic, Practical Information, Regulations
Canada Customs, Export-Import Regulations, Incentives and Procedures Handbook - Strategic, Practical Information, Regulations
Cape Verde Customs, Export-Import Regulations, Incentives and Procedures Handbook - Strategic, Practical Information, Regulations
Cayman Islands Customs, Export-Import Regulations, Incentives and Procedures Handbook - Strategic, Practical Information, Regulations
Central African Republic Customs, Export-Import Regulations, Incentives and Procedures Handbook - Strategic, Practical Information, Regulations
Chad Customs, Export-Import Regulations, Incentives and Procedures Handbook - Strategic, Practical Information, Regulations
Chile Customs, Export-Import Regulations, Incentives and Procedures Handbook - Strategic, Practical Information, Regulations
China Customs, Export-Import Regulations, Incentives and Procedures Handbook - Strategic, Practical Information, Regulations
Colombia Customs, Export-Import Regulations, Incentives and Procedures Handbook - Strategic, Practical Information, Regulations
Comoros Customs, Export-Import Regulations, Incentives and Procedures Handbook - Strategic, Practical Information, Regulations
Congo Customs, Export-Import Regulations, Incentives and Procedures Handbook - Strategic, Practical Information, Regulations
Congo, Democratic Republic Customs, Export-Import Regulations, Incentives and Procedures Handbook - Strategic, Practical Information, Regulations
Cook Islands Customs, Export-Import Regulations, Incentives and Procedures Handbook - Strategic, Practical Information, Regulations
Costa Rica Customs, Export-Import Regulations, Incentives and Procedures Handbook - Strategic, Practical Information, Regulations
Cote d'Ivoire Customs, Export-Import Regulations, Incentives and Procedures Handbook - Strategic, Practical Information, Regulations
Croatia Customs, Export-Import Regulations, Incentives and Procedures Handbook - Strategic, Practical Information, Regulations
Cuba Customs, Export-Import Regulations, Incentives and Procedures Handbook - Strategic, Practical Information, Regulations
Cyprus Customs, Export-Import Regulations, Incentives and Procedures Handbook - Strategic, Practical Information,

Regulations
Czech Republic Customs, Export-Import Regulations, Incentives and Procedures Handbook - Strategic, Practical Information, Regulations
Denmark Customs, Export-Import Regulations, Incentives and Procedures Handbook - Strategic, Practical Information, Regulations
Djibouti Customs, Export-Import Regulations, Incentives and Procedures Handbook - Strategic, Practical Information, Regulations
Dominica Customs, Export-Import Regulations, Incentives and Procedures Handbook - Strategic, Practical Information, Regulations
Dominican Republic Customs, Export-Import Regulations, Incentives and Procedures Handbook - Strategic, Practical Information, Regulations
Ecuador Customs, Export-Import Regulations, Incentives and Procedures Handbook - Strategic, Practical Information, Regulations
Egypt Customs, Export-Import Regulations, Incentives and Procedures Handbook - Strategic, Practical Information, Regulations
El Salvador Customs, Export-Import Regulations, Incentives and Procedures Handbook - Strategic, Practical Information, Regulations
Equatorial Guinea Customs, Export-Import Regulations, Incentives and Procedures Handbook - Strategic, Practical Information, Regulations
Eritrea Customs, Export-Import Regulations, Incentives and Procedures Handbook - Strategic, Practical Information, Regulations
Estonia Customs, Export-Import Regulations, Incentives and Procedures Handbook - Strategic, Practical Information, Regulations
Ethiopia Customs, Export-Import Regulations, Incentives and Procedures Handbook - Strategic, Practical Information, Regulations
Fiji Customs, Export-Import Regulations, Incentives and Procedures Handbook - Strategic, Practical Information, Regulations
Finland Customs, Export-Import Regulations, Incentives and Procedures Handbook - Strategic, Practical Information, Regulations
France Customs, Export-Import Regulations, Incentives and Procedures Handbook - Strategic, Practical Information, Regulations
Gabon Customs, Export-Import Regulations, Incentives and Procedures Handbook - Strategic, Practical Information, Regulations
Gambia Customs, Export-Import Regulations, Incentives and Procedures Handbook - Strategic, Practical Information, Regulations
Georgia Republic Customs, Export-Import Regulations, Incentives and Procedures Handbook - Strategic, Practical Information, Regulations
Germany Customs, Export-Import Regulations, Incentives and Procedures Handbook - Strategic, Practical Information, Regulations
Ghana Customs, Export-Import Regulations, Incentives and Procedures Handbook - Strategic, Practical Information, Regulations
Gibraltar Customs, Export-Import Regulations, Incentives and Procedures Handbook - Strategic, Practical Information, Regulations
Greece Customs, Export-Import Regulations, Incentives and Procedures Handbook - Strategic, Practical Information, Regulations
Greenland Customs, Export-Import Regulations, Incentives and Procedures Handbook - Strategic, Practical Information, Regulations
Grenada Customs, Export-Import Regulations, Incentives and Procedures Handbook - Strategic, Practical Information, Regulations
Guatemala Customs, Export-Import Regulations, Incentives and Procedures Handbook - Strategic, Practical Information, Regulations
Guernsey Customs, Export-Import Regulations, Incentives and Procedures Handbook - Strategic, Practical Information, Regulations
Guinea Customs, Export-Import Regulations, Incentives and Procedures Handbook - Strategic, Practical Information, Regulations
Guinea-Bissau Customs, Export-Import Regulations, Incentives and Procedures Handbook - Strategic, Practical Information, Regulations
Guyana Customs, Export-Import Regulations, Incentives and Procedures Handbook - Strategic, Practical Information, Regulations
Haiti Customs, Export-Import Regulations, Incentives and Procedures Handbook - Strategic, Practical Information, Regulations

Honduras Customs, Export-Import Regulations, Incentives and Procedures Handbook - Strategic, Practical Information, Regulations
Hungary Customs, Export-Import Regulations, Incentives and Procedures Handbook - Strategic, Practical Information, Regulations
Iceland Customs, Export-Import Regulations, Incentives and Procedures Handbook - Strategic, Practical Information, Regulations
India Customs, Export-Import Regulations, Incentives and Procedures Handbook - Strategic, Practical Information, Regulations
Indonesia Customs, Export-Import Regulations, Incentives and Procedures Handbook - Strategic, Practical Information, Regulations
Iran Customs, Export-Import Regulations, Incentives and Procedures Handbook - Strategic, Practical Information, Regulations
Iraq Customs, Export-Import Regulations, Incentives and Procedures Handbook - Strategic, Practical Information, Regulations
Ireland Customs, Export-Import Regulations, Incentives and Procedures Handbook - Strategic, Practical Information, Regulations
Isle of Man Customs, Export-Import Regulations, Incentives and Procedures Handbook - Strategic, Practical Information, Regulations
Israel Customs, Export-Import Regulations, Incentives and Procedures Handbook - Strategic, Practical Information, Regulations
Italy Customs, Export-Import Regulations, Incentives and Procedures Handbook - Strategic, Practical Information, Regulations
Jamaica Customs, Export-Import Regulations, Incentives and Procedures Handbook - Strategic, Practical Information, Regulations
Japan Customs, Export-Import Regulations, Incentives and Procedures Handbook - Strategic, Practical Information, Regulations
Jordan Customs, Export-Import Regulations, Incentives and Procedures Handbook - Strategic, Practical Information, Regulations
Kazakhstan Customs, Export-Import Regulations, Incentives and Procedures Handbook - Strategic, Practical Information, Regulations
Kenya Customs, Export-Import Regulations, Incentives and Procedures Handbook - Strategic, Practical Information, Regulations
Kiribati Customs, Export-Import Regulations, Incentives and Procedures Handbook - Strategic, Practical Information, Regulations
Korea, North Customs, Export-Import Regulations, Incentives and Procedures Handbook - Strategic, Practical Information, Regulations
Korea, South Customs, Export-Import Regulations, Incentives and Procedures Handbook - Strategic, Practical Information, Regulations
Kosovo Customs, Export-Import Regulations, Incentives and Procedures Handbook - Strategic, Practical Information, Regulations
Kuwait Customs, Export-Import Regulations, Incentives and Procedures Handbook - Strategic, Practical Information, Regulations
Kyrgyzstan Customs, Export-Import Regulations, Incentives and Procedures Handbook - Strategic, Practical Information, Regulations
Laos Customs, Export-Import Regulations, Incentives and Procedures Handbook - Strategic, Practical Information, Regulations
Latvia Customs, Export-Import Regulations, Incentives and Procedures Handbook - Strategic, Practical Information, Regulations
Lebanon Customs, Export-Import Regulations, Incentives and Procedures Handbook - Strategic, Practical Information, Regulations
Lesotho Customs, Export-Import Regulations, Incentives and Procedures Handbook - Strategic, Practical Information, Regulations
Liberia Customs, Export-Import Regulations, Incentives and Procedures Handbook - Strategic, Practical Information, Regulations
Libya Customs, Export-Import Regulations, Incentives and Procedures Handbook - Strategic, Practical Information, Regulations
Lithuania Customs, Export-Import Regulations, Incentives and Procedures Handbook - Strategic, Practical Information, Regulations
Macao Customs, Export-Import Regulations, Incentives and Procedures Handbook - Strategic, Practical Information, Regulations
Macedonia Customs, Export-Import Regulations, Incentives and Procedures Handbook - Strategic, Practical Information,

Regulations
Madagascar Customs, Export-Import Regulations, Incentives and Procedures Handbook - Strategic, Practical Information, Regulations
Madeira Customs, Export-Import Regulations, Incentives and Procedures Handbook - Strategic, Practical Information, Regulations
Malawi Customs, Export-Import Regulations, Incentives and Procedures Handbook - Strategic, Practical Information, Regulations
Malaysia Customs, Export-Import Regulations, Incentives and Procedures Handbook - Strategic, Practical Information, Regulations
Maldives Customs, Export-Import Regulations, Incentives and Procedures Handbook - Strategic, Practical Information, Regulations
Mali Customs, Export-Import Regulations, Incentives and Procedures Handbook - Strategic, Practical Information, Regulations
Malta Customs, Export-Import Regulations, Incentives and Procedures Handbook - Strategic, Practical Information, Regulations
Marshall Islands Customs, Export-Import Regulations, Incentives and Procedures Handbook - Strategic, Practical Information, Regulations
Mauritania Customs, Export-Import Regulations, Incentives and Procedures Handbook - Strategic, Practical Information, Regulations
Mauritius Customs, Export-Import Regulations, Incentives and Procedures Handbook - Strategic, Practical Information, Regulations
Mexico Customs, Export-Import Regulations, Incentives and Procedures Handbook - Strategic, Practical Information, Regulations
Micronesia Customs, Export-Import Regulations, Incentives and Procedures Handbook - Strategic, Practical Information, Regulations
Moldova Customs, Export-Import Regulations, Incentives and Procedures Handbook - Strategic, Practical Information, Regulations
Monaco Customs, Export-Import Regulations, Incentives and Procedures Handbook - Strategic, Practical Information, Regulations
Mongolia Customs, Export-Import Regulations, Incentives and Procedures Handbook - Strategic, Practical Information, Regulations
Morocco Customs, Export-Import Regulations, Incentives and Procedures Handbook - Strategic, Practical Information, Regulations
Mozambique Customs, Export-Import Regulations, Incentives and Procedures Handbook - Strategic, Practical Information, Regulations
Myanmar Customs, Export-Import Regulations, Incentives and Procedures Handbook - Strategic, Practical Information, Regulations
Namibia Customs, Export-Import Regulations, Incentives and Procedures Handbook - Strategic, Practical Information, Regulations
Nauru Customs, Export-Import Regulations, Incentives and Procedures Handbook - Strategic, Practical Information, Regulations
Nepal Customs, Export-Import Regulations, Incentives and Procedures Handbook - Strategic, Practical Information, Regulations
Netherlands Customs, Export-Import Regulations, Incentives and Procedures Handbook - Strategic, Practical Information, Regulations
New Caledonia Customs, Export-Import Regulations, Incentives and Procedures Handbook - Strategic, Practical Information, Regulations
New Zealand Customs, Export-Import Regulations, Incentives and Procedures Handbook - Strategic, Practical Information, Regulations
Nicaragua Customs, Export-Import Regulations, Incentives and Procedures Handbook - Strategic, Practical Information, Regulations
Niger Customs, Export-Import Regulations, Incentives and Procedures Handbook - Strategic, Practical Information, Regulations
Nigeria Customs, Export-Import Regulations, Incentives and Procedures Handbook - Strategic, Practical Information, Regulations
Northern Mariana Islands Customs, Export-Import Regulations, Incentives and Procedures Handbook - Strategic, Practical Information, Regulations
Norway Customs, Export-Import Regulations, Incentives and Procedures Handbook - Strategic, Practical Information, Regulations
Oman Customs, Export-Import Regulations, Incentives and Procedures Handbook - Strategic, Practical Information, Regulations

Pakistan Customs, Export-Import Regulations, Incentives and Procedures Handbook - Strategic, Practical Information, Regulations
Palau Customs, Export-Import Regulations, Incentives and Procedures Handbook - Strategic, Practical Information, Regulations
Palestine Customs, Export-Import Regulations, Incentives and Procedures Handbook - Strategic, Practical Information, Regulations
Panama Customs, Export-Import Regulations, Incentives and Procedures Handbook - Strategic, Practical Information, Regulations
Papua New Guinea Customs, Export-Import Regulations, Incentives and Procedures Handbook - Strategic, Practical Information, Regulations
Paraguay Customs, Export-Import Regulations, Incentives and Procedures Handbook - Strategic, Practical Information, Regulations
Peru Customs, Export-Import Regulations, Incentives and Procedures Handbook - Strategic, Practical Information, Regulations
Philippines Customs, Export-Import Regulations, Incentives and Procedures Handbook - Strategic, Practical Information, Regulations
Pitcairn Islands Customs, Export-Import Regulations, Incentives and Procedures Handbook - Strategic, Practical Information, Regulations
Poland Customs, Export-Import Regulations, Incentives and Procedures Handbook - Strategic, Practical Information, Regulations
Polynesia French Customs, Export-Import Regulations, Incentives and Procedures Handbook - Strategic, Practical Information, Regulations
Portugal Customs, Export-Import Regulations, Incentives and Procedures Handbook - Strategic, Practical Information, Regulations
Qatar Customs, Export-Import Regulations, Incentives and Procedures Handbook - Strategic, Practical Information, Regulations
Romania Customs, Export-Import Regulations, Incentives and Procedures Handbook - Strategic, Practical Information, Regulations
Russia Customs, Export-Import Regulations, Incentives and Procedures Handbook - Strategic, Practical Information, Regulations
Rwanda Customs, Export-Import Regulations, Incentives and Procedures Handbook - Strategic, Practical Information, Regulations
Saint Kitts and Nevis Customs, Export-Import Regulations, Incentives and Procedures Handbook - Strategic, Practical Information, Regulations
Saint Lucia Customs, Export-Import Regulations, Incentives and Procedures Handbook - Strategic, Practical Information, Regulations
Saint Vincent and The Grenadines Customs, Export-Import Regulations, Incentives and Procedures Handbook - Strategic, Practical Information, Regulations
Samoa (American) Customs, Export-Import Regulations, Incentives and Procedures Handbook - Strategic, Practical Information, Regulations
Samoa (Western) Customs, Export-Import Regulations, Incentives and Procedures Handbook - Strategic, Practical Information, Regulations
San Marino Customs, Export-Import Regulations, Incentives and Procedures Handbook - Strategic, Practical Information, Regulations
Sao Tome and Principe Customs, Export-Import Regulations, Incentives and Procedures Handbook - Strategic, Practical Information, Regulations
Saudi Arabia Customs, Export-Import Regulations, Incentives and Procedures Handbook - Strategic, Practical Information, Regulations
Scotland Customs, Export-Import Regulations, Incentives and Procedures Handbook - Strategic, Practical Information, Regulations
Senegal Customs, Export-Import Regulations, Incentives and Procedures Handbook - Strategic, Practical Information, Regulations
Serbia Customs, Export-Import Regulations, Incentives and Procedures Handbook - Strategic, Practical Information, Regulations
Seychelles Customs, Export-Import Regulations, Incentives and Procedures Handbook - Strategic, Practical Information, Regulations
Sierra Leone Customs, Export-Import Regulations, Incentives and Procedures Handbook - Strategic, Practical Information, Regulations
Singapore Customs, Export-Import Regulations, Incentives and Procedures Handbook - Strategic, Practical Information, Regulations
Slovakia Customs, Export-Import Regulations, Incentives and Procedures Handbook - Strategic, Practical Information,

Regulations
Slovenia Customs, Export-Import Regulations, Incentives and Procedures Handbook - Strategic, Practical Information, Regulations
Solomon Islands Customs, Export-Import Regulations, Incentives and Procedures Handbook - Strategic, Practical Information, Regulations
Somalia Customs, Export-Import Regulations, Incentives and Procedures Handbook - Strategic, Practical Information, Regulations
South Africa Customs, Export-Import Regulations, Incentives and Procedures Handbook - Strategic, Practical Information, Regulations
Spain Customs, Export-Import Regulations, Incentives and Procedures Handbook - Strategic, Practical Information, Regulations
Sri Lanka Customs, Export-Import Regulations, Incentives and Procedures Handbook - Strategic, Practical Information, Regulations
St. Helena Customs, Export-Import Regulations, Incentives and Procedures Handbook - Strategic, Practical Information, Regulations
St. Pierre & Miquelon Customs, Export-Import Regulations, Incentives and Procedures Handbook - Strategic, Practical Information, Regulations
Sudan Customs, Export-Import Regulations, Incentives and Procedures Handbook - Strategic, Practical Information, Regulations
Sudan South Customs, Export-Import Regulations, Incentives and Procedures Handbook - Strategic, Practical Information, Regulations
Suriname Customs, Export-Import Regulations, Incentives and Procedures Handbook - Strategic, Practical Information, Regulations
Swaziland Customs, Export-Import Regulations, Incentives and Procedures Handbook - Strategic, Practical Information, Regulations
Sweden Customs, Export-Import Regulations, Incentives and Procedures Handbook - Strategic, Practical Information, Regulations
Switzerland Customs, Export-Import Regulations, Incentives and Procedures Handbook - Strategic, Practical Information, Regulations
Syria Customs, Export-Import Regulations, Incentives and Procedures Handbook - Strategic, Practical Information, Regulations
Taiwan Customs, Export-Import Regulations, Incentives and Procedures Handbook - Strategic, Practical Information, Regulations
Tajikistan Customs, Export-Import Regulations, Incentives and Procedures Handbook - Strategic, Practical Information, Regulations
Tanzania Customs, Export-Import Regulations, Incentives and Procedures Handbook - Strategic, Practical Information, Regulations
Thailand Customs, Export-Import Regulations, Incentives and Procedures Handbook - Strategic, Practical Information, Regulations
Togo Customs, Export-Import Regulations, Incentives and Procedures Handbook - Strategic, Practical Information, Regulations
Tonga Customs, Export-Import Regulations, Incentives and Procedures Handbook - Strategic, Practical Information, Regulations
Trinidad and Tobago Customs, Export-Import Regulations, Incentives and Procedures Handbook - Strategic, Practical Information, Regulations
Tunisia Customs, Export-Import Regulations, Incentives and Procedures Handbook - Strategic, Practical Information, Regulations
Turkey Customs, Export-Import Regulations, Incentives and Procedures Handbook - Strategic, Practical Information, Regulations
Turkmenistan Customs, Export-Import Regulations, Incentives and Procedures Handbook - Strategic, Practical Information, Regulations
Turks & Caicos Customs, Export-Import Regulations, Incentives and Procedures Handbook - Strategic, Practical Information, Regulations
Tuvalu Customs, Export-Import Regulations, Incentives and Procedures Handbook - Strategic, Practical Information, Regulations
Uganda Customs, Export-Import Regulations, Incentives and Procedures Handbook - Strategic, Practical Information, Regulations
Ukraine Customs, Export-Import Regulations, Incentives and Procedures Handbook - Strategic, Practical Information, Regulations
United Arab Emirates Customs, Export-Import Regulations, Incentives and Procedures Handbook - Strategic, Practical Information, Regulations

United Kingdom Customs, Export-Import Regulations, Incentives and Procedures Handbook - Strategic, Practical Information, Regulations
United States Customs, Export-Import Regulations, Incentives and Procedures Handbook - Strategic, Practical Information, Regulations
Uruguay Customs, Export-Import Regulations, Incentives and Procedures Handbook - Strategic, Practical Information, Regulations
Uzbekistan Customs, Export-Import Regulations, Incentives and Procedures Handbook - Strategic, Practical Information, Regulations
Vanuatu Customs, Export-Import Regulations, Incentives and Procedures Handbook - Strategic, Practical Information, Regulations
Vatican City Customs, Export-Import Regulations, Incentives and Procedures Handbook - Strategic, Practical Information, Regulations
Venezuela Customs, Export-Import Regulations, Incentives and Procedures Handbook - Strategic, Practical Information, Regulations
Vietnam Customs, Export-Import Regulations, Incentives and Procedures Handbook - Strategic, Practical Information, Regulations
Virgin Islands, British Customs, Export-Import Regulations, Incentives and Procedures Handbook - Strategic, Practical Information, Regulations
Wake Atoll Customs, Export-Import Regulations, Incentives and Procedures Handbook - Strategic, Practical Information, Regulations
Yemen Customs, Export-Import Regulations, Incentives and Procedures Handbook - Strategic, Practical Information, Regulations
Zambia Customs, Export-Import Regulations, Incentives and Procedures Handbook - Strategic, Practical Information, Regulations
Zimbabwe Customs, Export-Import Regulations, Incentives and Procedures Handbook - Strategic, Practical Information, Regulations

www.ingramcontent.com/pod-product-compliance
Lightning Source LLC
LaVergne TN
LVHW080031210926
848481LV00011B/3152